ABOUT THE AUTHOR

Rania Abouzeid has spent more than fifteen years reporting on the Middle East, and has written for *The New Yorker*, the *Guardian* and *TIME* magazine among others. A former New America fellow, she has won several international prizes for her work including the Frontline Club Print Award, the Michael Kelly Award and George Polk Award. Rania grew up in Australia and now lives in Beirut, Lebanon.

PRAISE FOR *NO TURNING BACK*

unparalleled account of the Syrian uprising, drawing on six years of
nersive reporting."
The New Yorker

stunning take on Syria's tragedy by the veteran Middle East reporter
nia Abouzeid... Abouzeid's writing is clear, her analysis sharp, her sym-
hy deep as she answers this key question of our age." *The Spectator*

iis is journalism at its very best: brave; personal; written with aching
uty." Lyse Doucet, BBC's Chief International Correspondent

i here is no better way to refocus on Syria than to read Rania Abouzeid's
book…an extraordinary book that deserves to be read widely."
Financial Times

"Offers page after page of extraordinary reporting and many flashes of
exquisitely descriptive prose." *New York Times Book Reviews*

"After *No Turning Back*, you won't
Syria wit
dying) tl

000002195504

NO TURNING BACK

Life, Loss, and Hope
in Wartime Syria

RANIA ABOUZEID

A Oneworld Book

First published in Great Britain and Australia by Oneworld Publications, 2018
This mass market paperback edition published 2019

ISBN 978-1-78607-515-4
eISBN 978-1-78607-418-8

Printed and bound in Great Britain by Clays Ltd, Elcograf S.p.A.

Oneworld Publications
10 Bloomsbury Street
London WC1B 3SR
England

Stay up to date with the latest books,
special offers, and exclusive content from
Oneworld with our newsletter

Sign up on our website
oneworld-publications.com

MIX
Paper from
responsible sources
FSC® C018072

FOR MY PARENTS, MY SISTERS, MY FAMILY

I carried your love and support in my heart every time I crossed the mountains,
while on my shoulders I bore the guilt of taking you with me

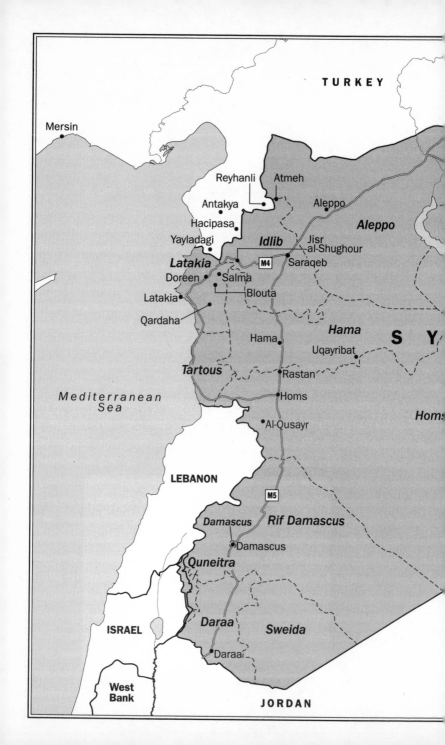

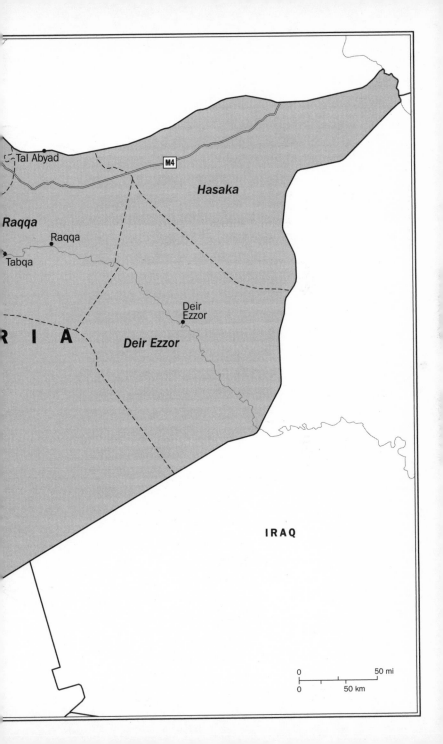

CONTENTS

This is a book of firsthand reporting, investigated over six years and countless trips inside Syria, Turkey, Jordan, Lebanon, Washington, and several European towns and cities. It tells but a sliver of the Syrian tragedy, how a country unraveled one person at a time.

Syria has ceased to exist as a unified state except in memories and on maps. In its place are many Syrias. The war there has become a conflict where the dead are not merely nameless, reduced to figures. They are not even numbers. In mid-2013, the United Nations abandoned trying to count Syria's casualties due to the difficulty of verifying information, although estimates put the death toll at well over 500,000 people. Half of Syria's population of twenty-three million is now displaced. No life is inconsequential. Each is a thread in a communal tapestry, holding the larger intact.

In the summer of 2011, I was blacklisted by the Syrian regime, but not as a journalist. Instead, I was branded a spy for several foreign states, placed on the wanted lists of three of the four main intelligence directorates in Damascus, and banned from entering the country. This forced me to focus on the rebel side by illegally trekking across the Turkish border into northern Syria, although I still managed a few trips to government-held areas. I state this only by way of introduction. This book is not another reporter's war journal. I went to Syria to see, to investigate, to listen—not to talk over people who can speak for themselves. They are not voiceless. It is not my story. It is theirs.

I did my own fixing, translating, transcribing, logistics, security, research and fact-checking. Any errors are hence mine alone. There are no composite characters, although some names have been changed to protect identities. Some of the people in these pages are now dead, others have disappeared or are in exile, and some are still inside a country that no longer resembles one. Everything I recount is true to the best of my knowledge.

These things happened.

These things continue to happen.

Some of these things should never happen again.

A portion of my earnings from this book will be donated to Inara, an apolitical nonsectarian charity that "provides life-altering medical care for children from conflict areas who have catastrophic injuries or illnesses and are unable to access treatment due to war." Founded by CNN correspondent Arwa Damon, Inara is a 501c3 registered charity in the state of New York, and operates across the Middle East. (www.inara.org)

I have employed the Arabic use of *kunyas*, nicknames that start with Abu or Um ("father of" or "mother of"), which are commonly used even if a person is childless. They are informal, respectful manners of greeting and also serve as noms de guerre.

IN RASTAN

Suleiman Tlass Farzat. The wealthy manager of an insurance office in Hama, who became a civilian activist in his hometown of Rastan.

Samer Tlass. Suleiman's cousin, a lawyer.

Maamoun. A mobile-phone repairman-turned-civilian activist.

Merhi Merhi. A civilian activist.

Mohammad Darwish. A student who sparked Rastan's first protests and often led chants.

First Lieutenant Abdel-Razzak Tlass. One of the earliest defectors, a member of the Khalid bin Walid Battalion and later a leader of the Farouq Battalions in Homs. Suleiman's relative.

NON–FREE SYRIAN ARMY ISLAMISTS

Mohammad (from Jisr al-Shughour). Grew up in Latakia. A former prisoner in Damascus's Palestine Branch and a member of Jabhat al-Nusra.

Abu Ammar. Mohammad's childhood neighbor.

Abu Othman. An Islamic legal scholar (or *Shari'iy*) from Aleppo. Mohammad's onetime cellmate in Palestine Branch and a prisoner in Sednaya.

Abu Mohammad al-Jolani. The leader of Jabhat al-Nusra, an Islamic State of Iraq (ISI) offshoot established in Syria in summer 2011 and Al-Qaeda's Syria branch.

Abu Maria al-Qahtani. An Iraqi who served as Jabhat al-Nusra's lead *Shari'iy*. Jolani's deputy.

Saleh. A former Sednaya Prison detainee from eastern Syria. Part of Nusra's inner circle.

Abu Loqman. Saleh's former cellmate in Sednaya Prison and, later, ISIS's emir in Raqqa.

Abu Bakr al-Baghdadi. The Iraqi leader of the Islamic State of Iraq and, later, ISIS. Self-proclaimed caliph.

Abu Mohammad al-Adnani. A Syrian, and Jabhat al-Nusra's chief *amni* (security agent) before he was appointed the ISIS spokesman.

Firas al-Absi. A non–Al-Qaeda militant stationed at Syria's Bab al-Hawa border with Turkey.

THE FREE SYRIAN ARMY

Abu Azzam (Mohammad Daher). A fourth-year Arabic-literature university student in Homs. From Tabqa, eastern Syria, he became a commander in the Farouq Battalions.

Bandar. A university student from eastern Syria, Abu Azzam's sometime roommate in Homs.

Bassem. Bandar's brother and Abu Azzam's colleague in the Farouq Battalions.

Abu Hashem (Hamza Shemali). A realtor-turned-Farouq foreign liaison who later headed the Hazm Movement.

Abu Sayyeh (Osama Juneid). A lawyer-turned-Farouq military commander.

Sheikh Amjad Bitar. A cleric from Homs and key Farouq financier.

Bilal Attar and **Abulhassan Abazeed**. The founders of the Shaam News Network (SNN) and, later, senior members of the Farouq Battalions.

Okab Sakr. A Lebanese politician and member of Saad Hariri's Future Movement political party.

General Salim Idris. The head of the FSA's Supreme Military Council.

IN SARAQEB

Ruha. A nine-year-old girl (in 2011).

Maysaara (Ruha's father) and **Manal** (Ruha's mother).

Alaa, Mohammad, Tala, Ibrahim. Ruha's siblings.

Zahida. Ruha's grandmother.

Mariam. Ruha's aunt.

Mohammad. Ruha's uncle, married to her Aunt Noora.

IN LATAKIA

Talal, an Alawite from Blouta, Latakia Province, living in Damascus.

Lojayn, 13 (in 2013), **Hanin** (10), **Jawa** (8). Talal's daughters.

Dr. Rami Habib. A physician operating a field clinic in the town of Salma.

Revolution is an intimate, multipart act. First, you silence the policeman in your head, then you face the policemen in the streets. In early 2011, the Middle East was electrified by an indigenous democratic fervor, not the cynical imported kind that exploited the slogans of democracy to cloak military coups and foreign interventions. Ordinary men and women unlearned fear. Their demands, powerful in their simplicity, ricocheted from Tunisia to Egypt, Libya, Bahrain, and Yemen: *Dignity! Freedom! Bread!* They didn't call it a "spring." This was a new revolutionary pan-Arabism, born of shared humiliation and frustration, spread by the tools of social media and satellite television. In Syria, it began timidly, with small public gatherings in solidarity with protesters elsewhere—such as the one on February 23, 2011, in front of the Libyan Embassy in Damascus, and the detention in the southern city of Daraa of a group of teenagers accused of writing antiregime graffiti on school walls.

Protests were banned in Syria under an emergency law in place since 1963—as long as the ruling Baath Party. News of the vigil on February 23 spread through word of mouth and Facebook, the social platform recently unblocked by the government (to better monitor calls for dissent, many suspected). The plainclothes, not-so-secret, police, or *mukhabarat*, arrived more than forty minutes before the scheduled 5 p.m. start, followed by black-clad policemen carrying Kalashnikovs. Antiriot police, in olive-green uniforms and black helmets, transparent face shields at the ready, blocked both ends of the narrow, tree-lined street housing the Libyan Embassy. They wielded worn truncheons, the stumpy ends flayed of the black skin that still covered their handles. There'd been a small, peaceful vigil in the same place the night before, but this night would be different.

EGYPT'S HOSNI MUBARAK had resigned two weeks earlier. Tunisia's Zine el Abidine Ben Ali had fled in mid-January, and Libyan opposition fighters had just seized control of chunks of the east of their country. In Damascus, President Bashar al-Assad gloated over the fall of his much older counterparts. This was the fate of leaders who didn't listen to their people, he said. Syria was different, he added, largely because of its foreign policy—because Assad's rhetorical hostility to Israel and the hegemony of the United States, his support for Palestinians and the militant groups Hamas and the Lebanese Hizballah, were in line with perceived popular Syrian sentiment.

Assad was forty-five, his carefully crafted image that of the everyman. He was the husband who casually dined in Damascene restaurants with his glamorous wife, Asma. The father who strolled through a *souq* with his children. The reformer who introduced the Internet to the general public in 2000, the same year he ascended to power after the death of his father and predecessor, Hafez al-Assad. Bashar al-Assad was the young leader with plans for change, hamstrung by his father's old guard and regional crises. He just needed time! Or so the popular narrative went. In a region where power is measured in generations, by 2011 Bashar had "only" been president for eleven years. And he had proven his resilience. He'd outlasted American neoconservative threats of regime change. He'd overcome global isolation after the 2005 murder of former Lebanese premier Rafik Hariri (widely blamed on Damascus and its Lebanese ally, Hizballah). He mitigated the effects of US sanctions and the Iraq War next door, while strengthening Syria's longstanding ties to Iran. Like his father, Bashar al-Assad knew how to play the waiting game of Middle East politics. He waited until his enemies, foreign and local, were voted out of office, died or were killed, or realized they needed him. All he had to do was survive and wait.

Facebook calls in the first week of February for "days of rage" against the Syrian regime had fizzled. A self-immolation in late January, imitating the Tunisian produce vendor Mohammad Bouazizi, who ignited the Tunisian uprising, did nothing but harm the Syrian man involved. Syria *was* different. One of the most pivotal states in the Middle East, Iran's lynchpin in its "axis of resistance" linking Syria to Hizballah and Hamas, would not yield easily—but it would bend a little, as it did on February 17, 2011.

On that day, the son of a store owner in Hariqa, near Damascus's Souq al-Hamidiyeh, was insulted and beaten by traffic police. Nothing unusual, but then, in defiance of the state of emergency, a crowd of thousands massed, their chants of "The people will not be humiliated!" and "Thieves! Thieves!" bringing the interior minister to the scene. The minister, caught in the throng, stood on the ledge of his car door, promised an investigation, and wagged his finger at the crowd: "Shame on you! This is a demonstration!"

"No! No! It's not a demonstration!" those nearest to him replied. "We all love the president!"

Perhaps that's why Damascus, the "beating heart of Arabism," decided not to allow a sizable display of pan-Arab solidarity outside the Libyan Embassy on February 23, less than a week later. Its people, after all, might get used to protesting.

THE MINUTES RUSHED past 5:30 p.m. Few things in Damascus started on time, and the vigil outside the Libyan Embassy was no different. Dusk fell, extinguishing the muted warmth of a shy winter sun. Uniformed men outnumbered the crowd of two hundred or so (double the night before) congregated in a nearby park. Unable to get any closer to the embassy, they chanted where they stood. "Ambassador resign!" "You are a traitor, not one of us!"

The crowd inched forward. It was dark now. "Okay, you've made your point," an officer told them. "If you don't mind, retreat and go back to where you were."

"If you don't mind, we want to walk," said a woman in the front line.

The crowd sensed an opportunity, picked up a new chant, crept closer. "Peacefully!" somebody shouted. "To the embassy!" came the reply.

The security forces' response was swift, like a pirouette in combat boots. The antiriot police lowered their face shields and surged forward as Kalashnikov-wielding police officers retreated in tandem. Truncheons shattered the mass of bodies. Shrill cries. Fists and black boots pummeled backs and legs. *Mukhabarat* agents shoved men into a minibus. A twenty-eight-year-old university student clung to the metal bars of a fence as blows thrashed his slight frame. "Leave me alone! Why can't you just talk to me?" he pleaded. The protester was ripped from the fence and tossed into the minibus. The vehicle was moving now, with fourteen detainees, all men. "You traitors! You animals! You want to demonstrate?" the security men onboard shouted as they beat the protesters. "You dogs, you sons of bitches!"

The wheels stopped at a *mukhabarat* branch. Syria's *mukhabarat* were divided into four main intelligence agencies: Military Intelligence, Political Security, State Security (also known as General Security), and (the most feared) Air Force Intelligence. The agencies were headquartered in Damascus and divided into dozens of branches and subbranches extending throughout the country, each with its own detention and interrogation facilities. They operated independently, with little low-level coordination, in a tangled surveillance matrix known as the *jihaz il amnee*, or security apparatus, its many tentacles spying on the population and each other.

The fourteen men were directed to plastic chairs, expecting further beatings. Instead, they were offered water and the use of the bathroom before being addressed by an officer who didn't introduce himself. "We are all the sons of this country, we don't doubt your nationalism or your love for your country, but we would prefer that this episode not be repeated," the officer said. Some of the men, perhaps emboldened by the civil reception, asked why they'd been called traitors and beaten. "Ignorance," the officer said. "Some people are smart and aware, and others are not. Perhaps you came across some of those who are not. We also support the Libyan people," he added, "but if demonstrations were useful, we'd all take part in them, but they're not."

The fourteen men were released hours later. Some, like the twenty-eight-year-old, had never been detained before. The young man had gone to the Libyan Embassy, like many others that evening, to test the boundaries of what the Syrian state would tolerate. He went because he wanted freedom of the press and a law to allow political parties other than the Baath. He went because he didn't think it right that his personal ambitions— a job and a home—seemed unattainable. He left the *mukhabarat* branch that night emboldened. He would protest again, he said, until something in Syria changed: "It's a conscious decision that I have taken. I don't know where it will lead me, but there is no turning back."

At the same time, in the southern city of Daraa, bordering Jordan, some two dozen young men and teenagers had been rounded up by security forces, blamed for scribbling graffiti on school walls that said LET THE REGIME FALL, and IT'S YOUR TURN, DOCTOR, referring to Assad's training as an ophthalmologist. The "Daraa children," as they were dubbed in the media, weren't children, and many had nothing to do with the writing on the walls, but tales of their harsh treatment in custody (real and embellished) sparked protests for their release, demonstrations that ignited the Syrian revolution in mid-March and christened Daraa as its birthplace. Protesters shed the pretense of pan-Arab solidarity and called for reform (but not regime change) in Syria. The state's initial tepid response of violence and lectures reverted to its more familiar violence, but Syria had already changed. The great wall of fear had cracked, the silence was shattered. The confrontation was existential—for all sides—from its inception. There was no turning back.

2011

SULEIMAN
MARCH 15, 2011. HOMS, SYRIA.

Suleiman Tlass Farzat was on a date. It was early evening, an unfashionable hour, and the café in Homs was almost empty. Arabic pop music melded into the hum of conversation floating from the few occupied tables. Swirls of smoke danced to the gurgling of *narghilehs*, infusing the café with the sweet smell of fruit-flavored tobacco. Outside, elsewhere, a revolution was stirring, but Suleiman was still unaware of that. A television, playing quietly in the corner, was not far from his table. He wasn't paying attention to it.

Suleiman was a son of money. Well read. Elegant. A man who wore labels effortlessly, and not for show. Warm olive skin and a permanent five o'clock shadow. All eyelashes and a sweet dimpled grin, a smile that made you involuntarily smile back. He carried himself with a confidence born of privilege but had the manners not to flaunt it. At twenty-six, he had much of what young men hope for—pretty girls on his arm, money in his pocket, the keys to a brand-new metallic-blue Volkswagen GTI (its beige headrests still covered in plastic), and a family name that opened doors with the regime.

Suleiman was from the same clan as Major General Mustafa Tlass, one of former President Hafez al-Assad's most trusted loyalists. Mustafa and Hafez met at the Homs Military Academy in the 1950s, and their decades-long friendship continued through the November 1970 coup that brought Hafez al-Assad to power. Tlass was Syria's longest-serving defense minister, a post he held for thirty-two years until he retired in 2004. He was a Sunni in the highest echelons of the security state that Hafez built and stacked with his Alawite coreligionists. Tlass was not merely elite, he was so elite that he was part of the small committee that ushered in Bashar al-Assad's pre-anointed succession after the death of his father, Hafez, in June 2000.

The rise of Mustafa Tlass also meant the rise of his hometown, Rastan, where Suleiman lived. Rastan was shaped like an inverted droplet, its northern part tucked into a bulge where the winding Orontes River was dammed. Powerful, rich families like Suleiman's lived in stone-faced villas within view of the dam in lower Rastan. Poorer ones were confined to upper Rastan's drab low-rise concrete. The town's fifty thousand people sat in the middle of a line between Homs and Hama, about twenty kilometers from each city, along the asphalt aorta locals called the international highway but maps listed as the M5. It linked Syria's two most populous provinces—the capital, Damascus, and the northern commercial heart, Aleppo.

Defense Minister Tlass turned Rastan into a town of military sons, its men swelling the officer corps. All a potential recruit from Rastan had to do was approach the defense minister or his aides to be fast-tracked into a military college. Sometimes, he didn't even need to pass a medical exam.

Suleiman's immediate family, however—his father and uncles—were industrialists. They owned factories producing plastics and fertilizers, cotton-spinning mills, and a vegetable-oil bottling and exporting business. Suleiman managed the Hama branch of the National Insurance Company, a firm for which his family had the coveted license to operate in Homs and Hama. His monthly paycheck of 120,000 Syrian pounds, $2,553 in those days, was about ten times the average.

Rastan was considered so loyal to the regime it was dubbed "the second Qardaha," a Sunni version of the Alawite village that was the Assads' hometown in Latakia Province. Suleiman was proud of the moniker, of the hefty association to power it carried, but he was also aware of his privilege. He was a rich young man drawn to the ideas of communism and socialism, at least as they appeared in his books. He had no illusions about how Syria's socialist model was applied in reality: "The leader is a dictator and the people are his slaves," was how he put it. The Assads ruled Syria, or, more pointedly, Syria was "Assad's Syria." That's what the billboards and posters had declared for decades. Like so many of his generation, Suleiman was conditioned to think that way, raised on secular Baath Party slogans that deified the leader. His school mornings began with robust salutations to "our commander for eternity, Hafez al-Assad!" He'd worn the military-style khaki uniforms mandated as nationwide school attire until other colors and styles were permitted after Hafez's death. Like all the other students, he carried placards and portraits of the president in quasi-military schoolyard parades choreographed by his teachers. He believed that Syrians were "simply like this, that nothing will change here for us." If there were people who thought otherwise, even in the heady early months of 2011, Suleiman didn't know any—or at least any who would admit it to him.

Suleiman couldn't imagine a revolt in Syria. Not in a state built on silence and fear and an emergency law. Under the permanent state of emergency, Assad's Syria banned public gatherings except those officially sanctioned; it arrested people for vaguely defined offenses such as threatening public order and disturbing public confidence; it monitored everything from phone calls to personal letters and censored the media prior to publication. Assad's Syria was a *mukhabarat* state whose intelligence agents didn't bother with the pretense of discretion. They didn't need to. The men in black leather jackets who could make people disappear had legal immunity "for crimes committed while carrying out their designated duties."

Suleiman glanced at the television in that café in Homs, where an image had drawn his gaze away from his date. The screen was set to Orient TV, a Syrian satellite station based in the United Arab Emirates. Shaky footage showed a group of people, no more than several dozen, marching past storefronts. Suleiman assumed it was from Egypt or elsewhere in the Middle East. After about thirty minutes, the clip was replayed. This time, the café owner turned down the music and turned up the television's volume. Suleiman realized he was watching something filmed about an hour and a half south of him.

The amateur video was captured that day—March 15, 2011, the date widely considered the start of the Syrian uprising—near Damascus's famed Souq al-Hamidiyeh. Small protests were also reported in Daraa in the south, Hasaka in the northeast, Deir Ezzor near Iraq, and in Hama. The sun's glare bouncing off the cameraman's lens was strong, blurring some of the images from the *souq*, but the shots, taken from behind the protesters, showed people clapping and walking, including a woman in a white headscarf. "Peacefully, peacefully," they chanted, as well as "God, Syria, freedom, that's all!" modifying the more common "God, Syria, Bashar, that's all!" (Or Hafez, back in the day.)

Orient TV broke with its regular programming. It looped the footage and muted the audio, taking calls live on air from viewers in Syria and abroad. A man from Assad's hometown of Qardaha called in: "This footage that you are broadcasting—what is it? Somebody gathered his brothers and cousins and filmed them. That's it. Don't make fools out of us. The person who filmed this knows that is all it is and everyone is laughing at him. We are all with Assad! We are all sons of Assad! God, Syria, Bashar, that's all!"

Suleiman's date leaned in toward him. "Is something happening here?" she whispered. "Is it really here?"

He didn't know. In Syria, he said, "there was nothing called politics to speak of." No side except the regime's in a one-party state. No politics of opposition in a system bound by razor-sharp red lines every citizen knew not to cross. The rules were clear in Assad's Syria: bread instead of democracy, subservience for state subsidies and a measure of stability and security. Rules enforced by fear. Fear of the state's certain and overwhelming retaliation for any move against it, as in 1982 against Islamists and in 2004 against stateless Kurds. Fear of what would replace a dictatorship that had crushed alternatives. Fear of the kind of wholesale state collapse that propelled more than a million Iraqis into Syria after 2003, and, decades before that, cleaved Lebanon into sectarian militias for fifteen years until 1990. Fear that was less an emotion than a physical presence, a heaviness that burrowed between shoulder blades and lived there, gaining weight. It could steal a person's breath with a single question, an inquisitive glance, an invitation to coffee or tea from the *mukhabarat*—code for an interrogation. It was a fear accumulated over decades, built on the bones of those who dared challenge the country's one-party, one-family, one-man rule.

But Suleiman had just watched a small crowd in the heart of Damascus marching and calling for freedom, and it was broadcast on satellite television. As he left the café and drove his date home, the shaky amateur video kept replaying in his mind, along with a single thought: He knew from his history books that no empire lasts forever. After the images he had just watched, after Egypt and Tunisia and the unfolding events in Libya, Yemen, and Bahrain, nothing really seemed impossible—or certain— in Syria any more.

TWO WEEKS LATER, on Friday, April 1, Suleiman moved with the other barefoot men flowing out of Al-Mahmoud Mosque, near his home, after noon prayers. It was an imposing structure, built by his late grandfather and namesake, with a creamy stone façade and twin minarets stretching into the sky like the gray tips of sharp pencils. He looked at the men around him. Would any of them say or do anything to start a protest like the one a week earlier, Rastan's first? The demonstration on Salibi Street in upper Rastan had lasted no more than ten minutes. Suleiman was in Damascus that day.

The men dispersed. Al-Mahmoud Mosque was one of three main ones in town. Curious to see what was happening elsewhere, Suleiman and an older cousin drove to Al-Kabir Mosque (also known as Abu Ammo), about a kilometer away in the center of town. Men were in the courtyard putting on their shoes, others were streaming out barefoot when a single brazen cry shot out: "We want freedom!" Suleiman looked around. Who had dared utter such words in the "second Qardaha"? A whisper rustled through the crowd, the name floated to Suleiman: Mohammad Darwish. He didn't know him. He would later learn that Darwish was just eighteen, a student from upper Rastan, scrawny, with gelled cowlicks that fell in semicircles on his forehead.

The youngster could have been heckled or beaten and handed over to one of the three *mukhabarat* offices in the town, or to the local Baath Party chapter. Instead, the men outside the mosque, including Suleiman, erupted into the chant. They surged down the main thoroughfare, Revolution Street, named for the 1963 coup that brought the Baath Party to power. Rastan had crossed the regime's red line. All it took after forty-eight years was a student's cry.

Suleiman moved, dreamlike, in slow motion yet accelerated, heart racing ahead of him. Hands clammy. He formed words from thoughts locked deep inside, where no one could report them. They escaped through his dry mouth. He repeated the chants with abandon, felt the strength of a crowd, the unity of people speaking with one voice, the fear and certain knowledge there were informers among them. Goosebumps rose on his skin. The simple act of speaking was subversive. It was intoxicating, empowering, liberating, terrifying.

He didn't need to do it. He hadn't suffered the indignities of a state oiled by bribes at every level of power, the daily humiliations that infected every banal aspect of life for other Syrians—from securing a university placement or a business license to fast-tracking installation of a landline, or getting a job. He wasn't like other young men—unemployed and frustrated, stuck with few prospects and without the means to marry and move out of home. He didn't have family members disappeared by the *mukhabarat*.

He was a rich man with the right name. No personal reason to rebel against a system that had afforded him privileges. No enmity beyond a deep sense of the injustice it meted out to others. For Suleiman, that was enough. His Syria, the one he dared to imagine, belonged to all of its citizens. It was not Assad's Syria. "I knew a lot of people weren't in my situation, that a lot had been harmed by the regime, really harmed to the degree that many families were destroyed, financially or physically," he said. "It all made me say, 'Enough. We need to change this.'" It was as simple and as difficult as that. Mohammad Darwish was the spark, the fearlessness Suleiman wanted to follow, the hope and courage he needed.

Suleiman reached into his pocket, almost reflexively, and pulled out his smartphone, a Sony Ericsson X10. He started filming but was reprimanded by those around him who feared being identified. They recognized and feared this son of lower Rastan from the Tlass clan. Whose side was he really on? He put away his phone and continued walking, but after a while one of his friends yelled out, "*Shabab*, guys, look forward, keep your faces forward, we'll film you from behind!" This time, fewer objected. Suleiman held his phone high and captured a brief snippet of his first protest.

The small crowd walked to the end of the street and then dissipated at a fork in the road near a bakery, unsure of whether to take the slight right toward the statue of Hafez al-Assad at the entrance to the town, or to turn left and loop back toward Al-Kabir Mosque. People peeled away in the confusion. Suleiman and his cousin drove home. He told his parents about the protest, but not that he'd participated. He remembered the footage on Orient TV in that café in Homs. If his town was going to be part of what was happening in Syria, he wanted people to know. He decided to join a protest every week and film it. He saw it as a duty, "like it wasn't even an option to not try and do this, regardless of what it cost."

The next Friday, April 8, Suleiman prayed in Al-Kabir Mosque instead of his grandfather's. After prayers, Mohammad Darwish again shouted a slogan, and everyone followed him. Suleiman captured almost a dozen clips, most of them less than a minute long, and then rushed home to his family villa. It sat on a slight incline with a view of the Rastan Dam. Suleiman and his cousin bolted up the short flight of stairs from the pavement, swung open the heavy black metal gate, and passed the garden on the left with its grapevines and canopy of trees—walnut, apricot, almond, and mulberry. They turned right, into the house designed by a Czech architect, through the high-ceilinged living room with its brick chimney, up the staircase with its wooden railing, into Suleiman's room.

Suleiman had a 1MB DSL line, a luxury in a country of twenty-three million people with fewer than 122,000 broadband subscribers. The line wasn't cheap. It cost 1,950 Syrian pounds a month (about $40 at the time—nothing for Suleiman, but roughly a quarter of a teacher's monthly salary), but it meant he could upload videos in privacy. Internet cafés demanded personal details and an ID card before allowing patrons to log on, and owners had the ability to spy on their customers by sharing their screens without permission.

Suleiman opened his Acer laptop, transferred the footage, and activated the proxy he had used to access Facebook before the government unblocked it. He and his cousin searched for Orient TV, Al Jazeera, Al Arabiya, and a slew of other stations they knew of, as well as others they didn't, like Shaam News Network, or SNN, which they came across during their search. They didn't have contacts at these outlets. They found generic e-mail addresses, created a new e-mail account with a fake name, kept the subject line simple—Protests—and started uploading. The Internet often cut out, forcing them to restart. After about three hours, Suleiman hit SEND. Then he and his cousin watched the inbox, hoping for a response. None came.

AL-KABIR MOSQUE SAT in the center of town, along the socioeconomic border between upper and lower Rastan. Demonstrations occurred there every Friday after prayers. Like elsewhere in Syria, the mosques were launching pads for protests, because, under the state of emergency, they were among the few public places where people could gather. Al-Kabir Mosque on Revolution Street was opposite a State Security office, but the *mukhabarat* agents inside the branch (and their informers among the worshippers) did not openly molest protesters, unlike in the smaller town of Talbiseh, about twelve kilometers south of Rastan. In Talbiseh, protesters were shot dead by security forces. More than once, Talbiseh's men brought their town's victims to Rastan's main square outside Al-Kabir Mosque.

"Look at our dead! Stay sitting! Stay quiet while we are being killed!" they would say through bullhorns.

Talbiseh was appealing to the honor of Rastan's men, seeking to shame and anger them into bolder antigovernment action. Apart from living in "the second Qardaha," Rastan's people had a reputation for being stubborn and escalating even minor disputes into violent feuds between families. The people of Rastan neither forgot nor forgave easily—and they had guns. In Syria, weapons were strictly controlled—unlike in Iraq, for example, and other parts of the Middle East where guns were part of every home's furnishings. Private ownership, licit and illicit, was just 3.9 firearms per 100 people in Syria, a tenth of the figure in Iraq. But in Rastan, most homes had weapons ranging from hunting rifles to Kalashnikovs, a privilege that came with the town's perceived loyalty.

On Friday, April 15, Rastan protested, as it had been doing every week. This time, when the crowd reached the intersection near the bakery, instead of dissipating, it shifted right, toward the statue of Hafez al-Assad. Nobody orchestrated it, there was no one leader. Those behind followed those in front. There was a certain democracy to it in that anyone could yell out a suggestion and people voted with their feet, either following or ignoring. Somebody said, "Let's go to the statue, let's bring it down!" and the mass of chanting men moved in that direction. Suleiman raced ahead to the monument, waiting for the thunder of voices rumbling down the street.

The marble statue of a standing Hafez, a flag draped across his outstretched arms, stood on a white stone platform, in front of a signpost with embossed black lettering that spelt out RASTAN WELCOMES YOU in cursive Arabic script. It was a grand monument, clearly visible to the left of the M5 highway.

The clapping, rhythmic roar neared, but the crowd had thinned. Some men detoured to pick up tools, such as sledgehammers. Others feared what was about to unfold, wanting no part of it. Several climbed the statue and started methodically striking its neck as the space around the monument filled osmotically.

"*Qoloo Allah, Qoloo Allah, shaab il Rastan, mo hayalla!* [Say God! Say God! We are the people of Rastan, not just anyone!]"

Suleiman was afraid. He recognized men watching the crowd whom he knew worked for the intelligence agencies. Some were from his own family. They would not shield him from this act of grand insolence. Insulting the Assads was the reddest of red lines, and the *mukhabarat* no doubt were taking names.

Suleiman slipped his phone into his pocket. Should he walk away? Was he already implicated? Was this revolution worth the risk to him? He had everything to lose, nothing to gain personally. It had happened in Tunisia and in Egypt, he thought. If it had taken weeks there, he figured it would take months in Syria—I can put up with it for that long. He was almost certain the regime would fall just as surely as Hafez's statue. It was just a matter of time and determination. The security and intelligence men in his family would have no power over him then. He resumed filming.

Hafez's marble form was as resilient as the old man had been in life. It mocked the mighty heaves and blows. Tradesmen in the crowd suggested that heat might weaken it, so tires were set alight at the statue's feet. "One! One! One! The Syrian people are one!" the crowd chanted.

The head fell off first. Men pounced on it before it stopped rolling, smacked it with their shoes. It was driven to Talbiseh and paraded through the streets like a corpse, propped on a tire attached by rope to the back of a pickup truck. Talbiseh had goaded Rastan into bolder action, and Rastan had responded with a sympathetic contemporaneous expression of rebellion.

A sturdy metal chain, the kind used to tow cars, was tossed around the beheaded statue as dozens grabbed the ends of it, tug-of-war style, to bring down Hafez. After several hours, the statue suddenly, rapidly toppled from its base to a mighty roar—the crowd whistling, clapping, and shouting *Allahu Akbar!* as it smashed into pieces. Passersby on the highway honked their car horns as hundreds of men rushed toward the splinters. Everybody, it seemed, wanted a piece.

Suleiman and his cousin sped home to upload footage. Once again, he had no response from any of the outlets he e-mailed, but then he found the Shaam News Network's Facebook page. SNN had posted his footage, which was also picked up by Orient TV and broadcast later that night, where Suleiman and his cousin watched it along with his parents. He had spoken in the video, and his parents recognized his voice. His mother scolded him, fearful of the repercussions. His father didn't say a word, but the smile on his face assured Suleiman that he was quietly supportive. "When we saw it on TV, my cousin and I started dancing!" Suleiman said. "We were so happy! It was such a big deal!"

MOHAMMAD

The square eye-level slot in the heavy prison cell door jerked open, metal grating on metal, allowing a shaft of piercing neon light from the corridor into the dim cell. Without a word, the three dozen or so men cramped inside rose to their feet and faced the wall. They knew the drill. This was Military Intelligence, Branch 235, in Damascus, also known as Palestine Branch, a place where nightmares were lived.

Mohammad, a thirty-two-year-old father of two, heard his number called out: 6/15—prisoner 6, cell 15. They never used names. It was sometime after the last of the five daily prayers between sunset and midnight, on March 23, 2011, a week into the Syrian uprising. In the darkness, time was amorphous, but the faint call to prayer from a mosque somewhere in the vicinity anchored the men spiritually and temporally. Mohammad shuffled forward, blinking as his dark brown eyes adjusted to the light. He was going to be interrogated, transferred, or released. He knew the drill.

He'd spent four short stints, or "sleeps," as prisoners call them—a total of less than two years—in various prisons for his suspected Islamist sympathies. The authorities weren't wrong about him, but he was never convicted. Mohammad admired Al-Qaeda and Osama bin Laden, but he was wily and hid his tracks well. He didn't even wear a beard. It was common for suspected Islamists and other political prisoners to disappear in detention, sometimes for years, sometimes forever. Mohammad had gotten off lightly.

His first detention in 2006 occurred because of something he said. A mechanical engineer by trade, he let what he termed his "other self" appear in front of colleagues. He defended the cause of anti-American foreign fighters in Iraq. It cost him three months in the Political Security branch of his hometown, Latakia City, even though at the time his view paralleled that of the Syrian government. Syria's grand mufti, the highest Sunni cleric in the land, Sheikh Ahmad Kaftaru, had issued a *fatwa*, or religious ruling, saying it was obligatory for Muslims to resist the occupying forces in Iraq. Mohammad was arrested anyway. The next year, he spent 111 days in a pitch-black solitary cell in another branch of the security apparatus, Latakia's Military Security. He landed there, in a space just big enough to stretch his legs and stand, because of Western Union transfers of $20,000 to $25,000 each—a fortune in a country where monthly wages were a few hundred dollars. The funds belonged to two childhood friends he considered relatives, smugglers who transported people from as far away as Somalia and Indonesia across the Syrian–Turkish border and sometimes onward to Greece, Germany, and other European states. Mohammad's cut was $40 per wire transfer. His interrogators insisted he was funding an Islamist sleeper cell.

For the first twenty-five days, he was subjected to procedures common in Syrian jails. Doused with water and electrocuted. Hung from the ceiling by his wrists, his toes barely touching the floor as guards beat his sides (they called this *shabeh*). Whipped on the soles of his feet with thick cables until he couldn't walk (the *falaqa* torture method). Then they ignored him. He said that was worse. Alone in the dark, he hallucinated, becoming convinced that his baby daughter was in there with him. He'd bang on the door and ask for a beating, "just to feel something." To Mohammad, being tortured outside the solitary cell "was more merciful than being in it."

He was released without charge or trial, angry about "sleeping" for nothing. The next time he was imprisoned—and he was certain there would be a next time—he wanted it to be for something he'd actually done. So, over the next two years, he set about turning a suspicion into a reality. He introduced sixteen university-educated Sunni men to Al-Qaeda material. He was not yet a member of the group. It was more like a fan club than an

Islamist cell. One of the sixteen was detained, unspooling the clique and landing Mohammad in Palestine Branch on November 28, 2009.

The branch didn't look like much from the outside, a seven-story building with underground levels off the southern interchange in Damascus. Inside, it was a hole so black it served as a CIA rendition site for those America wanted tortured by a state it branded a sponsor of terrorism. Palestine Branch was near Damascus University's Mechanical and Electrical Engineering Department, Mohammad's alma mater, but he considered the prison his "greatest school."

His cellmates belonged to a spectrum of Islamist groups, including Al-Qaeda. He befriended them all but was closest to a man several years his senior who used the nom de guerre Abu Othman. Abu Othman was a *Shari'iy*, or Islamic legal scholar, from the northern city of Aleppo. They looked like a mismatched pair. Mohammad with his dark hair and eyes, impossibly sharp cheekbones framing a boyish face, spry limbs that didn't boast strength but possessed it. Abu Othman was stocky but not muscular, with a bulbous nose, small honey-colored eyes, and a chest-length red-tinged beard. He was incarcerated in May 2007 for membership in the governing council of an Al-Qaeda–linked group called Fatah al-Islam, active in Lebanon—a group that, by Abu Othman's own admission, was heavily infiltrated by the Syrian *mukhabarat*. Abu Othman spent two years cycling through *mukhabarat* prisons in Aleppo before he was moved to Palestine Branch in 2009. He said he weighed just forty-eight kilograms when he walked into Mohammad's cell, such was the pressure he was under during interrogations. Mohammad studied his cellmates. In prison, he said, "you soon learn who wants to work and who has been broken." The men who wanted to work, like Mohammad and Abu Othman, memorized each other's contact details.

Mohammad's first "sleep" in Palestine Branch lasted fourteen months. His family had no idea where he was, or whether he was alive. He was released without charge or trial on January 18, 2011, just in time to watch the Middle East's modern pharaohs teeter and tumble. He was transfixed by the Arab revolutions but doubted Assad would go the way of other leaders without a fight. Mohammad's time outside Palestine Branch was brief. On March 13, 2011, he was snatched off the street outside his home in Latakia City, bundled into an unmarked car, and returned to the branch. He remembered making a pronouncement to the room as soon as the cell door slammed behind him: "Something's changed, *shabab*! There's going to be change, a revolution!" Some of the men cried out in happiness, a few hugged him. Others viewed him with suspicion, wondering whether he was a regime plant.

Just ten days after that, a guard was at the cell door calling his number: 6/15. Mohammad was blindfolded and shoved up stairs to ground level. His eyes uncovered, he stood in front of a uniformed officer seated behind a desk. Mohammad was being released. He didn't understand why he'd been detained, given that he wasn't questioned once in those ten days, but he dared not ask. The officer pushed a sheet of paper toward him. It was a typed pledge that he would not engage in antigovernment actions. It was the first time he'd been presented with such a condition. In the past, he'd been made to sign a statement outlining confessions extracted under torture. He knew not to challenge them. Doing so meant further interrogations and beatings about why the fictions he'd been forced to admit were fictional. "If we catch you again, don't blame us. Expect to die," Mohammad remembered the officer telling him. "Keep that in mind. Expect to die. If you break this pledge, we will kill you."

Mohammad did not doubt the officer's intentions, but he sensed weakness behind his threats. They are trying to scare me because *they* are scared, he thought. He signed the document with no intention of honoring it. He was fingerprinted and handed his personal belongings: an ID card, mobile phone, and 200 Syrian pounds (about $4). It was standard practice in Syrian detention centers to remove a prisoner's shoelaces from his footwear, but Mohammad didn't wait to fetch a pair from a pile he was told to rummage through. He stepped into the chill of a Damascene night on March 23, 2011, in unlaced sneakers. He didn't know it then, but that was his last "sleep" in a Syrian jail. That phase of his life was over, and a new one was about to begin.

. . .

MOHAMMAD WAS BORN on 9/11, September 11, 1979, in Jisr al-Shughour, a city in Syria's northern Idlib Province, near the Turkish border. In the late 1970s and early '80s, it was part of Syria's first, failed Islamist insurrection against Bashar's father, Hafez al-Assad. The seeds of that uprising were planted in socioeconomic policies of the 1960s as much as in the role of religion in the state. At the time, the Sunni Muslim Brotherhood was the spearhead of the political Islamist movement. It had been a democratic political player in Syria since 1946, its ideology based on the notion that Islam was the solution—from the pulpit to the parliament. For Assad's Baath Party, religion had no place in affairs of the state. The Baath's guiding trinity, expressed in its slogan, was unity (of the Arab nation), freedom (from foreign powers and tyranny), and socialism (the instrument for upward mobility regardless of religious, geographic, or economic identity).

Syria's Baath Party, like most of the secular movements sweeping to power in the 1950s and '60s across a Middle East emerging from the trauma of colonialism, had a romantic leftist manifesto that found great appeal. It promised social justice and offered its adherents a larger pan-Arab identity. It told them they weren't just Christians or Alawites or Druze, Shiites, or Sunnis in a majority-Muslim region—they were part of a new Arabism that transcended the confines of a religion or a nation-state. The Baath preached an idealistic egalitarianism, but, like other secular parties governing the region, it birthed a dictatorship.

Like Islamism, Baathism was at once geographically expansive and culturally narrow. Islamism assumed Arabs were Muslims. Baathism viewed Middle Easterners as Arabs. There were, of course, other religions and ethnicities in the region. The Baath and the Brotherhood represented different visions of what Syria should be, and their supporters came from opposite strata of society. The Baath was the party of the downtrodden, stacked with minorities and the rural poor of all sects, including Sunni. The Brotherhood was solidly Sunni, mercantile, middle class, and old bourgeoisie.

When the Baath Party came to power in 1963, it nationalized banks and many large businesses, seized and redistributed land at the expense of the traditional Sunni elite, including the tribes. The Muslim Brotherhood's championship of private property and limited state authority played well to this disaffected constituency. The Baath, quick to recognize and crush a political competitor, banned the Brotherhood in 1964. Its actions spurred isolated riots in Hama that year by some factions of the Brotherhood, in Damascus in 1965, and more widespread instability in 1967.

When Hafez al-Assad seized control of the ruling party through an intra-Baath coup in 1970 known as the Corrective Movement, he achieved several things. First, he ended a tumultuous period of short-lived coups that had consumed the country since independence from France in 1946. He continued to focus on the neglected hinterlands, bringing such infrastructure as schools and electricity to the rural poor, but he also reached out to the Islamist opposition and, more broadly, to the Muslim clerical establishment of *Ulama*, in part to temper the spasms of violence but mainly to secure religious legitimacy for his Alawite community.

The Alawites follow a syncretic religion, a very distant offshoot of Shiite Islam. Most Sunni and Shiite Muslims consider them heretics, not "People of the Book," thus they have been historically persecuted by Muslim leaders of both sects. (People of the Book are followers of Judaism, Christianity, and Islam.) For generations, the Alawites—about 10 percent of Syria's majority Sunni population—were the servant class.

Assad encouraged his Alawite coreligionists to adopt mainstream Muslim rituals that were not part of their esoteric faith, such as fasting during the holy month of Ramadan. He built mosques in Alawite villages. He played to both sides of the Sunni–Shiite divide, manipulating them with a manufactured religious affinity to achieve political goals. His rapprochement with the Sunni clerics and political Islamists ended in 1973 with the introduction of a revised constitution that, among other things, removed the requirement for the head of state to be a Muslim and enshrined one-party rule, decreeing that the Baath led "the state and society." Widespread protests followed, prompting Assad to rescind the article about the president's faith.

The Muslim Brotherhood, although factionalized by deep ideological and personal rifts into Hama, Damascus, and Aleppo branches, was none-theless the main repository of anti-Baathists. Its altercations with Syria's new rulers continued intermittently, especially the Hama faction, fueled by regime corruption, nepotism, and classism through the overt rise of rural Alawites at the expense of the traditional urban Sunni elite.

Since the days of the French mandate in Syria, the military, largely scorned by the upper classes, was an Alawite's main ticket to limited social mobility. Hafez al-Assad—a lieutenant who rose to command the Syrian Air Force by 1963—institutionalized the idea, lifting the sons of the servant class out of society's fringes and funneling them into the military and intelligence services that would underpin his power. The changes did not pass unchallenged. There were sporadic assassinations of Syrian military officers and government officials as well as prominent civilians, both Alawite and Sunni. On June 16, 1979, a militant breakaway faction of the Brotherhood called the Fighting Vanguard entered the cafeteria of the Aleppo Artillery School, separated the Sunni cadets from the Alawites, and gunned down eighty-three unarmed Alawites. Hafez al-Assad vowed punishment. On June 26, 1980, he escaped an assassination attempt, kick-ing away one of two grenades lobbed at him. (A bodyguard fatally threw himself on the other.) The next day, a military unit controlled by Hafez's brother Rifaat stormed Tadmor Prison, in the desert near Palmyra, and massacred hundreds of suspected religious dissidents in their cells. Two weeks after that, on July 7, 1980, Assad issued Law 49, imposing a blanket death penalty on any member of the banned Muslim Brotherhood.

An open, asymmetric conflict followed, a period that would later simply be referred to as the *ahdass*—the events. The Islamists, centered in the cities of Hama, Aleppo, and, to a lesser degree, Jisr al-Shughour, engaged in guerrilla attacks and assassinations. Decades later, Bashar al-Assad would emulate his father in using airpower and artillery against the grounded rebels. On March 9, 1980, helicopter gunships strafed Jisr al-Shughour. Mohammad's family fled to a village on the outskirts of the city, but it was another city, Hama, that would bear the brunt of the anti-

Islamist crackdown. In February 1982, somewhere between ten thousand and thirty thousand people—perhaps more, perhaps less, nobody knows; gunmen and civilians alike—were exterminated. It was mass killing in an information blackout, but survivors remembered where the bodies were dumped and paved over: in the plot under the five-star Afamia Cham Hotel, under the streets of what became a vegetable market in the Hamidi-yeh neighborhood, in a garden near the Bakr al-Sadiq Mosque. Residents of Hama didn't dare pray over the bodies, such was the regime's unre-lenting hatred for its foes, even in death. "If you only knew what is under the hotel," a white-haired, mustachioed man told me when I sneaked into Hama in August 2011. "I know things that I cannot speak of in front of a woman."

Hama's ghosts walked unavenged among the living, a vivid warning of the price of dissent in a nation where memories are long. The 1982 Hama massacre extinguished the Muslim Brotherhood in Syria, but the hunting and hounding of suspected sympathizers continued for years. A generation of Sunni children, like Mohammad and Abu Othman, grew up witness-ing or hearing about the humiliation of their elders at the hands of Hafez al-Assad's regime.

For Mohammad, one particular childhood event shaped his adult-hood. He was seven when it happened. Cars full of *mukhabarat* drove up to the isolated hilltop cluster of flat-roofed homes outside Jisr al-Shughour where he lived. Some of the *mukhabarat* men waited by the convoy as oth-ers raided the home of Abu Ammar, a neighbor whom Mohammad loved like an uncle. Abu Ammar, then thirty-seven, was in the fields threshing wheat. He was dragged into a dirt patch amid the five houses where the families used to park their vehicles.

Although most of Mohammad's distant male relatives, who numbered in the tens of hundreds, were associated with the Brotherhood and the events of Jisr al-Shughour, Mohammad's father could not have been more removed from them. He maintained good relations with the government men in the area. He knew most of the *mukhabarat* agents who loomed over Abu Ammar on that early summer evening of August 5, 1986. There were few other men in the handful of homes. Most were headed by women, their husbands and sons over the age of seventeen rounded up or killed in earlier government raids against suspected Brotherhood members and other Islamists, their sympathizers, associates, friends, family, and even casual acquaintances.

The security men ordered the residents to gather outside, even the children, including Abu Ammar's two sons. They all stood there in silence as the *mukhabarat* took turns beating Abu Ammar. Mohammad watched, frozen in fear, as what seemed like hours passed and Abu Ammar's face and clothes were bloodied. It was quiet, save for the neighbor's cries and the curses of the security men. "Who could dare to do or say anything?" Mohammad's father recalled.

A boy of fourteen pushed through the circle and shoved one of the men doing the beating. The man's colleagues reached for the teenager, but he escaped. They shot at him, chased him on foot. He was caught, shoved into one of their cars, and driven away. The boy was never seen again.

Abu Ammar was not a member of the Muslim Brotherhood, but his younger brother, Abu Hassan, was. In 1982, Abu Hassan helped party members flee the crackdown by smuggling them across the mountainous border into Turkey. He hid their weapons in oil drums he buried along the frontier, and then he escaped to Mosul, Iraq, where he remained until the self-proclaimed Islamic State group took the city in June 2014. (He now lives in southern Turkey.)

Abu Ammar was not the only one punished for the actions of his brother that day. As the sun started its descent, the *mukhabarat* pulled Abu Ammar's elderly mother into the circle. They ripped off her clothes until she was naked, a shocking act in a village where every woman wore a headscarf. They beat her, threatened to rape her. Abu Ammar immediately relented. He said he'd tell them whatever they wanted to hear, he'd confess to anything. He was taken away.

"We went home and nobody said a word about it. My mother didn't say anything," recalled Mohammad more than two decades later. "I can still see it all in front of my eyes as if it's just happening. I still feel that feeling, like I'm in a nightmare. It's impossible to forget, it's imprinted in me. They planted hatred in me that day, it became rooted."

Shortly afterward, Mohammad's father moved his young family to a mixed Christian–Alawite neighborhood in Latakia City, part of the regime's heartland. "The aim was to be forgotten, to get away from everything that might remind me of where I was from," Mohammad's father said. A friend in the government helped him get a job as a civil servant in an arm of the Defense Ministry. It was as different a life from his old one as he could imagine.

Across Syria, the regime sought to deny a base to the Muslim Brotherhood, its offshoots, and other Islamists by eliminating people and intimidating places that might provide them shelter. But for Mohammad (unlike his father), the scorched-earth policy had the reverse effect: "When they imprison my uncle, my cousins—his children—will hate them. I will hate them, my other cousins will hate them, his neighbors will hate them. They did the opposite of what they wanted to do. Instead of uprooting his ties in society, they cemented them."

Abu Ammar was charged with aiding the Brotherhood and spent eleven years in the notorious Tadmor Prison in Palmyra. He returned home on May 30, 1997. By chance, Mohammad was at the older man's house that evening. He was in the guest room late at night when a car rumbled toward the isolated hilltop cluster of homes. Abu Ammar's two sons, traumatized by their father's detention, slept in the hills, afraid of being snatched by the *mukhabarat*, as their father had been, so Abu Ammar's wife asked Mohammad to see who was outside. He opened the door to a man he didn't recognize who was crying forcefully. He threw his arms around Mohammad, planted kisses on his face. "My son, you are a man," he kept saying. "You grew up without me. You didn't deserve to." Mohammad didn't know what to say. All he could do was hug the older man and welcome him home.

Abu Ammar had been released but not really freed. Every month for fourteen years, until the fall of Jisr al-Shughour in summer 2011, the farmer had to check in with the security and intelligence branches in the city, unsure each time whether he'd return home. Bribery became a regular expense, like a utility bill. It all made him feel "confined and humiliated again," but he dared not complain. "The security had eyes everywhere," he said. "I didn't even trust to speak in front of my own son."

MOHAMMAD GREW UP seeking answers to questions that were taboo in Assad's Syria. Questions such as what happened in Jisr al-Shughour, and why an older generation of Sunni Islamists was defeated. It was a dangerous teenage curiosity, one that Mohammad's father tried to smother. His son's questions could land a man—or a high-school student—in jail. Mohammad's older brother, Hossam, didn't care about the *ahdass* of the late 1970s and '80s. The siblings were two years apart, and although they shared the same group of friends, they were very different: Mohammad was sociable, Hossam reserved and apolitical. Mohammad wanted answers, but he knew better than to ask the sheikh at his local mosque.

After the routing of the Muslim Brotherhood and its allies, a regime-molded Sunni Islam filled the void. Hundreds of new mosques and Islamic institutes were seeded, the houses of worship monitored by *mukhabarat*, their Friday sermons approved by the state and delivered by co-opted clergy. Sufism, with its emphasis on mysticism, was traditionally Syria's overarching Sunni dogma. The regime allowed a controlled version of it and demonized the more conservative Salafi branch of Sunni Islam. Salafism preached a return to the purist emulation of the ways of the *Salaf* (the companions of the Prophet Mohammad and their immediate descendants), but it was not monolithic. Its most extreme adherents were the Salafi Jihadis characterized by Al-Qaeda, although most Salafis eschewed both violence and politics. Some believed in subservience to Muslim rulers and silence on political matters. Others advocated nonviolent political participation. Salafism, in all its forms, was fringe in Syria.

Mohammad sought out the Salafi sheikhs despised by the regime. He was still in his late teens when he approached an older Salafi, Abu Barra al-Haddad, one of a handful in Latakia who rotated in and out of prison.

Mohammad didn't tell his father, whose generation he viewed as weak and servile, as if "the Assads had eaten their hearts and replaced them with fear."

Abu Barra al-Haddad was a distant relative by marriage. That was Mohammad's entrée. It was in Abu Barra's living room that Mohammad met men who, once taken into their trust, provided him with CDs of Al-Qaeda propaganda. He viewed it on a desktop computer at home after his family slept. The men on the screen—the *mujahideen*, or holy warriors—filled Mohammad with a pride he craved. They represented "dignity, power, victory"—all the things that the Assad regime had denied an earlier generation of Islamists and that he felt his father had relinquished by taking a job in the Defense Ministry. Mohammad watched the videos and "dreamed of being part of their world."

At university while studying mechanical engineering, he opened a computer café with four used desktops—in part to generate a little income in the evenings, but mainly to view his CDs. In 2000, after Syria was connected to the Internet, he started entering Al-Qaeda online forums, using a program that hid a user's screen from the mainframe at Internet cafés, and another that masked its IP address, a tradecraft he learned from the men who gave him the CDs. The chat rooms included testimonies of fighters from the 1970s and '80s, including from Jisr al-Shughour. Mohammad saved it all to CDs.

Then, September 11, 2001, radicalized his brother Hossam. The once-carefree twenty-four-year-old business administration graduate became eager to identify with a group that had shaken the mighty United States. Hossam's sudden religious awakening was not pious and personal—it was militant, strict, and overbearing, and it clashed with Mohammad's approach. Guided by a young Salafi recently released from prison, Hossam demanded his four sisters wear face-covering *niqabs*, which they refused to do. He insisted that his father, a longtime smoker, stop the habit because ultraconservative Islamists consider it a sin. "He didn't tell him nicely, it wasn't offered as a suggestion," Mohammad recalled. "He wanted to force everything on them, so naturally their reaction was to do the opposite."

Mohammad was pleased when, unlike his family, the brothers' mutual friends readily accepted Hossam's new ideas. Their lifestyle of girlfriends, parties, and trips to the beach ended. The small gang, all university graduates, began watching Mohammad's contraband videos about *mujahideen* with the same enthusiasm they once had for televised Champions League football matches. The Chechen videos were their favorites, especially *The Russian Hell*, which featured the Arab foreign fighter Khattab. The meetings in private homes were dangerous. All it would take was one slipup—a word overheard in public, a misplaced CD, one person to knowingly or unwittingly attract the attention of security and intelligence agents or their informers—to expose them all.

In the same way that 9/11 set Hossam and the group on what they all considered a righteous path, the US-led invasion of Iraq in 2003 defined their destination. President Bashar al-Assad opposed Washington's war on Saddam Hussein, even though Saddam helmed a rival branch of the Baath Party that had a tortuous, acrimonious history with Syria's. For Assad, it was a question of sovereignty—and precedent; he didn't want to be next in line for regime change. So how to hobble an American military force next door that might easily turn to Damascus next? Assad's solution was simple—allow jihadists, foreign and local, to transit through Syria into Iraq, and in so doing achieve two objectives: identify and rid the Syrian regime of potential threats from homegrown Islamists, while at the same time keeping the Americans busy in Iraq. "The idea was we'll send them there [to Iraq], if they die we'll be very happy, if they don't and they come back, we'll arrest them because we don't need jihadists in Syria," Ayman Abdel-Nour said. Abdel-Nour was a senior Baathist and member of the prestigious Baath Congress, as well as one of Bashar al-Assad's college friends, before he defected in 2007 and became one of his leading critics. "We set up training camps in the countryside around Aleppo and near the Iraqi border for them," he said. The operation was overseen by Military Intelligence.

The jihadists, in turn, left Damascus alone. "It was in the interests of Al-Qaeda in Iraq that Syria be a conduit," said Abu Othman, Mohammad's old cellmate from Palestine Branch. At the time, Abu Othman was a member of a small underground circle of senior Salafi Jihadis in Aleppo. "The way we saw it, to us, Syria is a transit point and we won't undertake any work there, in exchange for them [the regime] turning a blind eye to our people, and that's what happened."

The Syrian call to the Iraqi jihad was not secret. It was blessed by the 2003 *fatwa* from Syria's grand mufti, declaring it obligatory for Muslims to resist the foreign occupiers next door. Busloads of volunteers entered western Iraq from eastern Syria. The Americans and their regional allies knew what Damascus was doing. In August 2007, Iraqi Prime Minister Nouri al-Maliki "directly confronted" Bashar al-Assad in Damascus "with details about these camps and infiltration routes, including specific names and places." He told Assad he was "sick and tired of interference in Iraqi internal affairs by Assef Shawkat," according to leaked State Department cables. Shawkat was Assad's brother-in-law and the head of Military Intelligence. In December 2008, CENTCOM commander General David Petraeus told the Lebanese president that "we know for a fact that Syrian Military Intelligence Director [Shawkat] is aware of this issue, as is President Assad." Both the Lebanese president and the head of Jordan's intelligence services warned Assad that "the US knew about these activities and urged him to take action, but their warnings were unheeded." In 2007, in the Iraqi border town of Sinjar, the US military captured more than six hundred Al-Qaeda in Iraq personnel files detailing a one-year period from August 2006 to August 2007. All of the foreign fighters in the records had entered Iraq from Syria. Syrians made up the third-largest contingent of foreign fighters, after Libyans and Saudis, and almost 42 percent of jihadis in the so-called Sinjar records listed at least one contact in Syria. Many listed multiple contacts. At least ninety-five Syrian coordinators were identified by name.

In Latakia, a handful of Syrians facilitated the journey to jihad in Iraq, including Mohammad's mentor, Abu Barra al-Haddad. When coordinators were arrested, Mohammad and his associates would watch carefully when they were released, and under what circumstances—wary of infiltrators, *mukhabarat* spies, and collaborators. Online jihadi forums like Minbar Suria al-Islami warned would-be recruits that if a Syrian facilitator was not operating "in a framework of total secrecy . . . you can be sure [he] is connected to the tyrant's security services and is nothing more than a trap for the *mujahideen*." In 2010, Syria's Intelligence chief, General Ali Mamlouk, boasted to an American delegation that his men infiltrated ultraconservative groups. "We are practical and not theoretical," he said in a leaked State Department cable. "In principle, we don't attack or kill them immediately. Instead, we embed ourselves in them and only at the opportune moment do we move." Some of the would-be jihadis were arrested by Syrian *mukhabarat* posing as facilitators before they crossed the border.

Mohammad knew at least twenty-five Salafis from Latakia who went to Iraq, including his brother Hossam and most of their mutual friends. Hossam slipped away without saying good-bye to anyone except his fiancée (the sister of his Salafi mentor), a week after Mohammad's engagement in early November 2004. Mohammad found a page-long farewell note jutting out of a book atop a chest of drawers. It included short personal messages to his parents and siblings. "He told me that he was certain that this was the right path, and that I should walk along it as well," Mohammad said, but he had no desire to follow his brother. "Instead of going to die in Iraq," he said, "they could have helped establish a base for this thought in our society, to actively propagate it." Hossam's letter ended with a pledge: "We are coming, Bashar. We will return." Mohammad's father burned the note. The father was summoned to several *mukhabarat* branches to account for his son's disappearance. "I told them I didn't know, which was the truth," Mohammad's father said. "I was sure they knew more about where he was than I did. A bird could not fly from Latakia to the Iraqi border without them knowing about it, so what about a man?"

A week later, Hossam called his younger brother. Mohammad had a cell phone with a SIM card that wasn't registered in his name and couldn't be easily traced to him. The SIM belonged to a Somali, a client of Abu Ammar's sons, who had transited through Syria. The sons had made good use of their village's proximity to the Turkish border to smuggle people across the frontier. It was *their* Western Union transfers that had landed Mohammad in solitary confinement for 111 days. Mohammad occasionally helped guide the groups over the border, along routes that would come in handy after the start of the Syrian uprising.

Hossam told Mohammad that he had pledged allegiance, or *bayaa*, to the Jordanian Abu Musab al-Zarqawi's Al-Qaeda in the Land of the Two Rivers, *al tanzim*, the organization, as Al-Qaeda was better known. Abu Barra al-Haddad had helped Hossam get there. From Latakia, Hossam traveled to Aleppo, then east to Deir Ezzor, the border town of Al-Bukamal, and across a vast, sandy frontier into Iraq. After 2011, jihadis would reverse the route.

Mohammad fielded calls from most of the Latakians who went to Iraq. They used code words and offered minimal information—just enough for Mohammad to understand they were okay and to physically visit their families and relay that. Without much effort, he had become a node in a network of foreign fighters that was largely Al-Qaeda.

The Syrians fought in what the Americans called Operation Phantom Fury, the second battle for the Iraqi city of Fallujah, in Anbar Province. It lasted from early November until Christmas Eve 2004 and was the bloodiest battle for US troops in Iraq. It also claimed many of the Latakians. The *tanzim* in Iraq would call families to tell them if their son had been killed. "Sometimes the calls would come through me, but often directly to their families, especially if it was a death," Mohammad said.

He was never contacted by the *tanzim* about his brother. Hossam's last communication was on November 28, 2004. His weeks-long mission to Iraq profoundly changed his family. After his disappearance, his sisters voluntarily did what he had demanded they do, and donned the *niqab*. The family started praying regularly and studying the Quran. Some of his siblings assumed Hossam was killed in Fallujah. Others, like Mohammad, believed he was detained and was in either an Iraqi or a Syrian prison, or was later killed in detention. Hossam's fiancée insists he is still alive, although she has no proof. She is still waiting for him to come home, more than a decade later.

HOSSAM DIDN'T RETURN, but from 2004 onward many battle-hardened Syrian Salafi Jihadis did. Their homecoming coincided with small bombings and shootouts with Syrian security forces, the first incidents since the 1980s. Officials blamed religious extremists and began rounding up suspected Islamist veterans of Iraq. "The Jihadists," as the former Baathist Ayman Abdel-Nour put it, "were supposed to kill Americans, not Syrians."

The Salafis were tossed into the three-story Sednaya Military Prison, some thirty kilometers north of Damascus. Each of its three floors was divided into two wings, right and left, which were each further subdivided into three parts. Several hundred Muslim Brotherhood men detained since the 1970s and '80s were on the second floor. The Salafi Jihadis lived in isolation in most of the third, an area the inmates termed "the black door." Their jailers called it the Al-Qaeda wing. The Salafi Jihadis were divided into two groups—those who adhered to the ideology and had committed what amounted to "thought crimes" but nothing more were on the right; those who had carried arms were on the left.

There were at least four hundred men in Sednaya's Al-Qaeda wing. On March 15, 2011, the start of the Syrian uprising, the day Suleiman was on a date, three hundred additional prisoners, including Mohammad's cellmate Abu Othman, the senior *Shari'iy*, were transferred from Palestine Branch to Sednaya, to join the four hundred. The men behind Sednaya's "black door," and others who were or had been in Palestine Branch, would form the backbone of Salafi Islamist armed groups that would soon participate in a budding insurgency against Bashar al-Assad.

ON MARCH 23, 2011, Mohammad walked away from Palestine Branch as briskly as possible in unlaced sneakers. It was dark and cold. He flagged down one of the ubiquitous Mazda minivans known as *micros* that flitted and careened around Damascus. It was the cheapest form of public transport, at just 10 Syrian pounds a journey. He headed to a bus terminal near Abbasid Square in the northeast of the capital. There he called his father, intending to go home to Latakia City. "Don't come here," his father said. "There's trouble, shooting, go to the village instead."

It was too late to get a ride to Jisr al-Shughour that night. He remembered that one of his cousins lived in the Qaboun neighborhood of Damascus, so he hailed a *micro*. It was stopped at a checkpoint manned by men in civilian clothing. They asked for IDs. When they saw Mohammad's ten-day-old beard and noted that he was from Jisr al-Shughour, they ordered him out. "He's one of the terrorists! He's here to make trouble!" he remembered them saying. One of the men had keys to a realtor's office in a nearby building. Mohammad was hauled in. A *mukhabarat* officer arrived. Mohammad told him he'd left Palestine Branch about an hour earlier. He pointed to his unlaced shoes and held up his indigo-dyed finger, stained with the ink used to sign his confession. The officer called Palestine Branch, confirmed Mohammad's story, apologized, and left. Then the others arrived, from three different intelligence agencies.

It was well past midnight before Mohammad was allowed to continue the few kilometers to his cousin's home in Qaboun. The next morning, he headed to the village outside Jisr al-Shughour. His father told him that Political Security in Latakia was already asking after him. So were other branches. He felt choked and caged, like his old neighbor Abu Ammar. He would not be free until the regime was brought down, but demonstrations would not threaten it; only violence would. He sneaked into southern Turkey along routes he had used with Abu Ammar's sons, bought a pump-action rifle with money he'd borrowed from his cousin in Qaboun, and then later a Kalashnikov. In the weeks that followed, he worked on the fears of a number of young men who'd participated in protests in the area. He pushed them to carry arms he secured from Turkey. "I wanted to implicate them," he said years later. "We all knew people who were detained and slept for fifteen years just because they knew somebody who was Brotherhood, so they knew what it meant to be considered involved. By protesting, we had become like the Brotherhood, we felt we would be treated the same. I wanted them to think this so that they would carry weapons later." Mohammad convinced five men. I knew them all.

ABU AZZAM

In early 2011, before Suleiman filmed a protest, while Mohammad was still imprisoned, Mohammad Daher, better known as Abu Azzam, was a fourth-year Arabic literature student at Homs's Al-Baath University. At twenty-eight, he was one of the older students in class. His education interrupted by the responsibilities of being an eldest son taking on his late father's role as breadwinner in a family of six, and eleven "invitations to tea" from the *mukhabarat* that sometimes led to incarcerations. His first invitation was in high school. He missed exams because he was behind bars and had to repeat the year. He also missed his father's funeral in 2006. Abu Azzam worked in Lebanon after his father's death, polishing floor tiles and doing odd jobs at construction sites for $10 a day, but he longed to return to a classroom.

Abu Azzam was from eastern Syria, from the sunburned tribal plains of Tabqa, near Raqqa, a rural man studying in Syria's third-largest city. He was the first of his family to enter a university, although he came from a line of men and women whose letters were learned in the grand oral tradition of Arabic poetry. He grew up listening to maternal relatives deliver recitals in the rich classical tongue of a language steeped in chameleonic words. He was entranced by the playful sparring of poets at social gatherings, and he longed to be one. He learned the musicality of meter, how to lob puns and jabs in witty prose, and he began writing poetry in the seventh grade, garnering some local acclaim. When he was in his teens, he won a national poetry competition but wasn't permitted to advance to the pan-Arab (regional) level because he was not a member of the Baath Party. The rebuke was the first of many at recitals. He remembered the winning poem and years later could still recite some of its many verses:

A child, whose soul is caressed by smiles,
and whose tears swell easily in prayer.
My features are as pale as autumn,
I am but a mirror reflecting your faces.
I reside within the jinns' palaces,
share the same meals.
Love and prayer join us.
I suffer the fever of the fragile,
I suffer the fever of letters.
From within a thousand wheat spears
I receive but a flake.

O, poem, I came to you an invader
with me are my weapons; a quill and ink
And I crossed over
the other poets behind me
I returned alone
for the rest had passed away
I am the poem's prophet
who preached in my beliefs
what the eraser inscribes
And I am at their throats, a scream
I crossed out all its letters with screams
I am the Euphrates
I came beneath a cloak of two willows
I throw my stick
How hell's seas and ruins
are suffering beneath their brutal leaders

His mother's family infused him with its poetic heritage, his father instructed him in religion. Abu Azzam was raised in the Sufi tradition by an ascetic parent who had no interest in what he considered the "pollution of politics." His father focused on peaceful contemplation and religious texts about prayer, fasting, pilgrimage, and ritual purification. Although Abu Azzam's father was not a mosque preacher, he ran a small after-school workshop from home for the neighborhood children and his own. By the time Abu Azzam started high school, he said he could not only recite hundreds of Hadiths (sayings of the Prophet Mohammad) but also identify the book and page number for a specific Hadith.

His solid religious instruction, and the fact that one of his uncles was in Sednaya Military Prison after fighting in Iraq, cycled Abu Azzam in and out of *mukhabarat* branches on suspicion of being a Salafi. He wasn't—yet. As an adult, Abu Azzam would define himself as a Salafi, but not a Salafi Jihadi whose violence-tainted ideology he despised. He also smoked and shook hands with women, activities from which many Salafis refrained. Apart from that one uncle (a poet Abu Azzam described as "a fanatic," who was killed in Sednaya), none of his other relatives were Salafis. In fact, they opposed them.

Abu Azzam grew up in a family that resented the authorities, especially his mother's side—tribal landowners who were stripped of their holdings by the Baath. Abu Azzam had also learned to fear the *mukhabarat* state. Its interrogations had left his abdomen a mess of linear scars, each between an inch and two inches long, inflicted by razors.

When protests erupted in the southern city of Daraa, Abu Azzam was bedridden, recovering from days-old surgery for a herniated disc he said he had sustained during violent interrogations two months earlier in prison. He was treated in Damascus and returned to Homs, where he watched the televised revolts elsewhere in the Middle East and, like Suleiman, didn't think they would reach Syria, let alone take root. He didn't even think the Daraa protest would extend much beyond the city. But he hoped it would.

When the people of Homs took to the streets in March 2011, Abu Azzam joined them. He hobbled "like a toddler," aided by friends to join protests in Baba Amr, a Sunni working-class neighborhood near his university campus. He enviously watched men jumping and dancing around him. His back injury limited his participation to clapping and chanting.

Abu Azzam was a tank of a man, if that tank were made of something soft. His tanned complexion was dominated by a nose shaped like the flat tip of an arrow. It pointed to full lips framed by a wispy black beard that curled around his jawline. He smiled easily and often—a wide, straight-toothed grin that took up most of his round face. His friends at university nicknamed him "The Sheikh" because of his solid religious education and calm demeanor. It stuck, no matter how many times he told them he wasn't a preacher. He lived near the university campus, Bedouin-style—no fixed address, rotating among a handful of apartments and rooming with other men from eastern Syria, including Bandar, a floppy-haired jokester whose mother was related to Abu Azzam's mother.

Bandar was a few years younger and many times louder than Abu Azzam. He was also a fourth-year language major, but he chose English instead of Arabic. As with Abu Azzam's maternal family, Bandar was from a tribal clan (on his father's side) that mourned March 8, 1963, as the day the Baath seized power and they lost their land. "We grew up knowing who took it," he once said. "It was our neighbors. We are all Sunnis in the village, it wasn't about religion." He remembered several older people, "when they were close to death," asking forgiveness from his family for taking their land. Despite his hatred of the regime, Bandar did not join the protests. He didn't see the point. "Our country is different," he used to say. "Here, they kill people and nobody asks about it. Forget all this human rights nonsense, it doesn't apply to us. This regime won't fall without a war or a foreign invasion." Abu Azzam paid him no heed. He continued to take to the streets, week after week in Baba Amr, as security forces shot into crowds, cordoned and shelled neighborhoods, raided homes, and held hundreds incommunicado, turning a defiant Homs—a city whose people were renowned for their humor and lightheartedness and for being the butt of jokes—into "the capital of the revolution."

Baba Amr, in particular, was targeted for reprisal. The regime considered it a terrorist haven. Abu Azzam remembered hearing gunfire from a home where he was staying, a few hundred meters away from Baba Amr across the railroad tracks. "People were being shot and I was sitting there listening to them die," he said. "I couldn't accept it. I was no better than those being killed, so I decided to go inside [to the Baba Amr neighborhood] and do whatever I could." He recalled something his father taught him as a child, the words of an ancient Sufi master: *Whoever stays silent about the truth is a mute devil.* It cemented his decision.

He moved to Baba Amr in April and stayed with a group of men who talked of arming to protect themselves and demonstrators, especially after the so-called Clock Tower Massacre on April 19, 2011. The day before that incident, a sea of protesters gathered around Clock Tower Square after a mass funeral for fourteen demonstrators. They renamed it "Freedom Square" and vowed to remain until Assad fell. It was the first organized attempted sit-in, but the regime would not cede a public space and allow a Syrian version of Egypt's Tahrir Square or Tunisia's Avenue Bourguiba. Between 2 and 3 a.m., government forces killed and detained an unknown number of people and then hosed down the square as though nothing had happened. Grainy video from that night showed people running from the Clock Tower and the deafening sound of sustained gunfire. "Fuck you and your president!" screamed a young man within view of the soldiers. Others held up spent cartridges as proof the soldiers were firing live rounds. It was a turning point in the struggle for Homs, although years later some of the men present that night would admit that claims of a massacre were exaggerated, even fabricated, by rebel activists to garner sympathy.

After the incident, a bald tobacco trader from Baba Amr named Ahmad Da'bool, who smuggled cigarettes from Iraq, added a few rifles to his inventory, donating them to young men in his neighborhood in early May. There weren't enough to go around. Abu Azzam, as an outsider, wasn't offered one. He volunteered to cook for the small group of armed men and do their laundry. Bandar, meanwhile, focused on the three subjects he needed to graduate. He feared retribution if he participated—not against himself, but his family. "Our regime doesn't arrest one person," he said. "It punishes his entire family."

One of Abu Azzam's friends, a protester snatched from Clock Tower Square, was returned to his family a disfigured corpse, his face burnt, his body marked with gaping wounds. Abu Azzam was horrified—he had never seen such injuries. He decided he would not let that happen to him or to anyone he knew, if he could help it. He went home to Tabqa to check on his family and to buy a gun. "In my heart, I returned to say good-bye to them," he said. On Friday, April 22, the day Syria's revolutionaries dubbed their nationwide protests "Great Friday," in honor of Easter, Abu Azzam was detained near his hometown. At least seventy-five demonstrators were killed across Syria that day, making it the bloodiest to date. With time, triple-digit daily death tolls would become the norm. The tanks rolled into Homs while Abu Azzam was behind bars.

On May 29, 2011, soon after he was released from prison, the poet bought a Chinese Type 56 Kalashnikov and slipped back into Baba Amr. He would not leave it again until he was forced to do so. Abu Azzam would become a commander in an army of young men who hadn't wanted to be soldiers, in a group that would call itself the Farouq Battalions. It would be among the strongest in an emerging franchise outfit known as the Free Syrian Army.

RUHA

The knocking was angry and urgent. Ruha sunk deeper under the bedcovers in her grandmother's room. The nine-year-old didn't want to answer the door. She heard water splashing in the adjacent bathroom. Her grandmother, Zahida, was performing ablutions before dawn prayers. Ruha often slept with her (she liked her electric blanket) instead of in the coral-pink bedroom she shared with her eight-year-old sister, Alaa, in another part of the family complex. Zahida, a widow, was heavyset and moved with difficulty, slowed by illness and her eight decades. She asked Ruha to see who was making a racket outside. Half asleep, the gangly fourth grader rubbed her eyes as she approached the heavy metal door with yellow fiberglass paneling. "Who is there?" Nobody answered, so she cracked it open.

She saw a wall of guns and military camouflage. Her gaze fell on two men in civilian clothing, the informers—*fasafees* or *awayniyeh*, as they were called—their identities concealed behind balaclavas. "Where's your father?" one of them shouted. Before she could answer, her mother, Manal, raced toward her, shielding her eldest daughter behind her back as the column of men stormed into their home. "Where's your husband? He's fled, hasn't he?"

Manal told them he wasn't there. Ruha retreated to her grandmother's living room, steps from the front door. Ruha was from an upper-middle-class family in Saraqeb, a town of forty thousand in Idlib Province's agricultural heartland. The family owned and farmed great swaths of flat, cinnamon-colored earth that unfurled beyond the concrete clusters of their hometown. They planted fields of wheat that Ruha was sure continued forever. The little girl loved the farm, especially cucumber season. She liked plucking the small ones the family pickled onsite and sold commercially.

She crept to a window. She was tall enough not to need to stand on tiptoes to see through it. It looked onto the rectangular open-air inner courtyard that anchored her family's residential complex. She watched the uniforms infiltrate her home, their heavy black boots stomping across the tiled courtyard where she played with her sister Alaa, five-year-old brother Mohammad, and two-year-old sister Tala. She lived in the kind of traditional Levantine residence built for extended families with money. It had a basement and four wings—more like separate apartments—radiating from the courtyard. Her grandmother lived in a three-room section at the front of the complex. Ruha, her parents, and her siblings were to the right. To the left, a gate led to the home of her eldest paternal uncle, Mohammad, and his wife, Noora. It had its own smaller outdoor enclosure, a courtyard within the courtyard, a marble and stone fountain at its heart, climbing jasmine and rose bushes, citrus trees, and grapevines. The fourth and oldest living space was a communal lounge the family called "the cellar" because of its vaulted arched ceiling and thick stone walls. Nobody could remember which generation built it.

Ruha hoped her mother was telling the truth and her father was not home. She was wide awake now, her heart like a breathless bird trapped in her chest. "They're going to take Baba. I won't see my father. That's it, he won't come back." She feared they might take her mother, too, the way she was shadowing the men as they slammed closets, looked under beds, and rummaged through every room. Were her siblings still asleep? If they were awake, were they as scared as she was? Her grandmother prayed aloud for her youngest, favorite son: "Dear God, let Maysaara be safe. Dear God, let Maysaara be safe."

The light of day changed, the storm of military camouflage dissipated. Ruha's father, Maysaara, thirty-nine, was at a friend's house, making plans and placards for that week's protest. He was on his way home when he saw truckloads of security men entering his street. He spun his car around and called his wife Manal, then warned his brother Osama, a doctor who did not live in the family complex. It was too late for Osama.

The dawn raid across Saraqeb on May 1, 2011, netted thirty-eight people, including four of Ruha's uncles—three on her mother's side and her paternal uncle Osama. Her grandmother let out a shriek when she learned he'd been taken. Zahida was hard of hearing but somehow always managed to hear anything about her seven daughters and three sons. Ruha usually chuckled at her grandmother's selective auditory perception, but there was nothing to laugh about that morning.

The little girl's fears shifted to her uncles. She'd heard the adults talk about people killed and tortured in detention. If her uncles survived, would she be able to see them in prison, the way she'd visited her maternal grandfather in 2010? She didn't know why her grandfather was jailed in Damascus, just that he looked older and thinner behind bars. She wondered but didn't ask. The subject made her mother cry.

Her grandfather was arrested on July 27, 2010, after he was overheard complaining about the cost of living and criticizing corruption. He was "invited to coffee" at 9:30 that night by one of the security branches. He didn't return home. The charges against him, filed in a criminal court, included weakening national morale, undermining the state, and—most hurtful to the old man, an avowed secularist—inciting sectarian strife. He was released on bail from Damascus Central Prison in Adra on June 7, 2011. After attending the next court hearing in September, he skipped the following one in November and went into hiding. He was sentenced in absentia to ten years.

This time, Ruha knew why her uncles were in trouble, and why the security forces wanted her father. They were all serial protesters. The men had participated in every demonstration since Saraqeb's first, on March 25, 2011, just ten days into the uprising. It had been a small affair, no more than a few dozen men who walked, faces uncovered, from a mosque partway down the main commercial street, chanting, "No fear after today!" Ruha remembered how excited her father was when he returned home, how his words tumbled out. He was doing something to help Syria move forward, he told her, to secure people's rights. She knew that meant he was against the authorities.

She glanced at the landline in her grandmother's living room. Should she call Baba? She just wanted to know if he was okay. What if he wasn't in a safe place? What if he answered and somebody heard him and he was caught because of her call? She moved between her grandmother's kitchen and the living room, where the adults had congregated, carrying water to the women. Her hands shook, but she didn't spill the liquid. At least her siblings were still asleep. They had been spared what she saw. Grandmother Zahida was in her usual spot, a faded blue couch that time had molded to her shape. She muttered to herself, as she often did, while she fished through a plastic bag of her daily medications. Her eldest son, Ruha's Uncle Mohammad, a sixty-year-old environmental engineer, was on his cell phone, conducting a family head count. He was the elder statesman of the family, slightly built, bespectacled, and mustachioed with salty hair. A man whose voice was never raised but always respected.

Ruha's father, Maysaara, was Zahida's youngest son, the ninth of her ten children, her favorite. He was first to help if his siblings and their families needed it, the heart of every gathering, the one whose stories everybody waited to hear. His sisters teased him that he had more shoes than his wife and was more fastidious about his appearance than she was. His tailored jackets had to be just so, his shirts razor-sharp. He'd laugh at their ribbing but never deny its truth. He doted on all of his children, but his eldest, Ruha, was especially dear to him. He spoke to the nine-year-old like an adult, and she carried herself with that demeanor. She had her mother's graceful long limbs (although she was still awkwardly growing into them), her fair skin, quiet poise, and tight curly brown hair, but she had inherited her father's passion, quick wit, and many of his features. They had the same bold eyebrows framing camel-like brown eyes, thick long lashes, the same full lips, the same feistiness—although that trait surely came from Zahida. Ruha's grandmother had imparted that attitude to all of her offspring, especially her seven daughters, and their daughters. Her sons and grandsons were colloquially known around town by their mothers' names, not their fathers' (as was customary). Maysaara was Maysaara-Zahida. It was a point of pride for the family. So was the fact that all its women were university educated and employed.

Ruha's Aunt Mariam was something of a trailblazer in the neighborhood. A single teacher in her fifties, she had studied in Damascus at a time when many families in Saraqeb wouldn't send their daughters to school in another town, let alone the Syrian capital to live in a dorm. "For those with open minds, who love learning and value their daughters, it wasn't unusual," Mariam said. She lived with her maternal aunt, Zahida's older sister, in a three-room apartment she owned above an underground gym. She taught grades one to four at a local school.

Aunt Mariam was spirited but far less plucky than her mother or her young niece Ruha. Age may have calcified Zahida's joints, diminished her hearing, and creased her delicate features, but it hadn't blunted her tongue or intellect. She was a formidable matriarch, and her home was the heart of the family, the gathering place for birthdays and holidays, especially Mother's Day, Ruha's favorite day of the year, when all of her aunts honored her grandmother. That gaiety seemed distant now. The family was once again gathering around her grandmother that morning in May, because two of Zahida's three sons were in peril. For the first time Ruha could remember, her grandmother looked scared.

The doctor Osama was imprisoned for twenty-one days. He was released, rearrested two weeks later, and fled the country soon afterward. Maysaara could not stay away long. He sneaked home four days later. His children piled on top of him, covered him with kisses. Ruha; Alaa, a sensitive and highly intelligent third grader with anime-like brown eyes and the same tight curls as her older sister; Mohammad, the only son, who was as sinewy as his father; and Tala, the little china doll. Ruha didn't want Baba to leave, nor did she want him to stay. She kept glancing at the door. What if the security forces came back? Would he have time to escape? What if they took him? She didn't know where he had been staying and didn't want to know. She didn't ask. The subject made her mother cry. She wished her father would stop protesting, but she kept that in her heart. Maysaara went into hiding after that visit, and Ruha's life "turned upside down," as she put it. "Baba used to stay with us all the time, then we didn't see him anymore. We used to play on the streets, then we started to be afraid we might be shot."

She was a little girl, but much older than a little girl. "We were fated to learn about things children shouldn't learn about," she said. "I know my parents were trying to hide things from us, but they could not. Everything was happening in front of us."

SULEIMAN

Suleiman's hometown of Rastan was spared direct retaliation for the felling of the statue of Hafez al-Assad, but names were taken. Nobody knew how many, or who was on the lists at checkpoints leading into the cities of Homs and Hama, but dozens of men who were near the statue that day disappeared. Suleiman still worked at the insurance office in Hama, but he changed his route to avoid three new checkpoints, while every week he continued to document the protests.

April 29 was a grim and overcast Friday. After prayers, a man with a megaphone suggested blocking the M5 highway to protest what had become a four-day siege of Daraa. Rastan's men and women marched in the thousands that day. They threaded through streets, their voices rising to the people watching from balconies who showered them with rice and flower petals. "No to the authorities! No to control!" one group chanted, right fists jabbing into the air, as others behind them clapped and repeated a phrase that had brought down dictators: "The people demand the fall of the regime!" Several carloads of protesters from Talbiseh joined Rastan's demonstration.

The route wound past the town's multistory Military Security branch. It looked empty—just a few guards, all locals, standing inside its black metal sliding gate. The branch overlooked a stretch of the M5 that sliced between two hills in a shallow valley. For an hour or so, the protesters sat on the asphalt carpet, eyes toward an impromptu stage, an amplifier and a microphone set up in the back of a Suzuki pickup truck. Dozens of men queued near the vehicle, waiting to clamber onto it and publicly quit the

Baath Party to applause. Then, suddenly, a man pushed in line and grabbed the microphone. "*Shabab*, guys, there are tanks on the bridge!"

A line of armored personnel carriers, dispatched from the army's engineering battalion adjacent to the Rastan Dam, rumbled over a bridge a kilometer north of the gathering. Through his camera lens, Suleiman watched the distant pixelated dots slowly come into focus. He was on the incline above the highway, near the Military Security branch. He saw men below walking toward the oncoming armored vehicles. "Where are you going?" he screamed down to them. "Come back!" others shouted, their voices drowned out by the din of motorbikes buzzing up and down the highway. Tires somehow materialized and were set ablaze, their noxious smoke darkening an already overcast day.

The small group of men reached the armored vehicles and borrowed a chant that had served Egyptian protesters well: "The army and the people are one hand!" Several soldiers emerged from their metal cocoons and were carried on the shoulders of these sons and fathers of military men. A soldier held his Kalashnikov above his head, nonthreateningly, as protesters kissed him on both cheeks. Another joined the chants of "God salute the army!" The men stayed on the armored vehicles like a welcoming procession, thinking the soldiers had defected, as they slowly rattled along the highway toward the crowd.

The quick *pop! pop!* of two shots, followed by an abrupt single volley of gunfire. Suleiman hit the ground. A bullet whizzed past his ear so close he heard it whistle, its sound caught on camera. On his stomach, still filming. Yellow wildflowers obstructed the center of his frame, but he was too afraid to move. He saw the men on the highway start to retreat, slowly at first, and then they ran from the armored personnel carriers.

Pop! Pop! Pop! Shots cracked every few seconds. Panicked cries tried to locate the source of the gunfire. The Military Security branch was what most voices said, so that's where the enraged crowd headed—toward the gunfire instead of away from it. A teenager collapsed in front of Suleiman, his white T-shirt soaked with his blood, as a man on a motorbike scooped him up.

The guards outside the Military Security branch had fled. Stones were hurled at the building, shattering windows. A handful of men, provoked to a frenzy by the gunfire, ripped the heavy metal sliding gate from its railing and tossed it askew like scrap paper. Suleiman crossed the street to get a broader view. He saw a man on the upper floor of the branch open a window and start shooting. From another window, the rat-a-tat-tat of machine-gun fire cut down unarmed men and boys. Suleiman threw himself behind the wall of a house, his heart pounding against its patio floor. He'd driven his mother's older Peugeot 405 that day. It was parked against the wall of the branch. There was no way he could reach it now. Screams and curses and gunfire. He peered around the corner of the house, saw men collapse, saw others on motorbikes braving bullets to rescue them, saw men who'd fetched their guns and returned. They climbed onto the flat rooftops of adjacent buildings, apartment blocks that were taller than the Military Security branch. From their rooftops, the small group of armed men heaved brightly colored gas canisters, the kind found in every Syrian kitchen, onto the grounds of the branch below, igniting the gas by shooting the canisters in midair. Others hurled traditional Molotov cocktails.

Suleiman had to get away. One of his aunts lived nearby, in the direction away from the branch, so he sped on foot toward her home. He passed people peering from their front gates, imploring him to tell them what was happening. He ignored them. He was trying to process what he'd witnessed. "They were cut down! They were in the beginning of their lives, young men like flowers, every youth had a story, a family, had parents who worked hard to raise him, had a life!" He was sure the regime men inside the Military Security branch would not survive the wrath of Rastan's sons, because "there were now martyrs. There was blood."

At the time, there were some in town, including one of Suleiman's uncles, who were trying to reconcile protesters with the regime. They urged them to present written demands to local authorities instead of voicing them in the streets. Across Syria, Baath Party officials made efforts at the town level to open dialogue with protesters, but many distrusted the regime. Suleiman was certain the Rastan reconciliation initiative, never strong to begin with, was now dead. It took him about ten minutes to reach his aunt's house. He borrowed a car and rushed home, opened his laptop, and uploaded his footage. The acoustic obituaries soon began, echoing from Rastan's minarets. Gunfire continued intermittently throughout the night.

By sunrise on April 30, Rastan had been "liberated" from government control at a cost of twenty-six dead—twenty from Rastan, six from Talbiseh, and many multiples of those numbers wounded. Loyalists in the Political Security and State Security branches, as well as those in the Baath Party office, withdrew without a shot during the altercation at the Military Security branch. For Suleiman and many others, time was now marked as either before or after the bloodshed at the Military Security branch. "After that day," he said, "there was no turning back at all. Ever."

The toll of the night's fighting on the government side was unclear. Three armored personnel carriers entered the grounds of the Military Security branch and evacuated an unknown number of dead and living. Suleiman didn't see them. He arrived at the branch around 7 a.m., after they'd left. His mother's Peugeot 405 had taken four bullets in its metalwork, and its windows were shattered.

Smoke poured through the blown-out windows of the branch. Orange flames leapt from its roof. The scorched carcasses of at least four vehicles lay in its grounds. Suleiman covered his mouth and nose with the collar of his shirt and, smartphone recording, stepped into the building's hazy interior. It was the first time he'd been inside. Glass crunched under his feet. People were leafing through documents that survived the flames, mainly intelligence reports, shouting out the names of those surveilled. Papers were carried outside and burned in the courtyard.

A similar scene played out at the Political Security branch, a two-story white villa that was still smoldering by the time Suleiman reached it. BASHAR THE DOG was freshly spray-painted along its wall and on a green dumpster, near a framed portrait of the president thrown into the street.

In all three of Rastan's intelligence branches, Suleiman found reports on his late grandfather, uncles, and father but not on himself—just the heads of the families. Meticulous accounts of the men's movements, who their friends were, cafés they frequented, what they owned, and other elements of their daily life. Suleiman took the papers home.

That afternoon, a funeral tent was erected outside Al-Kabir Mosque, where the dead were to be mourned collectively. The fathers or closest male relatives of the deceased sat in a row of white plastic chairs, portraits of Bashar al-Assad at their feet. The event morphed into a rally, a pattern replicated across Syria. A few chants or speeches turned a funeral into a political gathering, one the state would violently suppress, resulting in new deaths, new funerals, new demonstrations. But Rastan was free of security forces. It could voice its pain and anger without fear of immediate reprisal. Mourners took turns at the microphone, highlighting divisions within the opposition that would later fracture it. A young man in a tan leather jacket implored those around him to "purify" their spirits and return to God to take on "this infidel party."

Najati Tayyara, a prominent human rights activist and intellectual, pleaded with the men to stay peaceful, to not fall into what he warned was a regime trap to portray its opponents as violent. "Syria is for everybody," he said. "Religion is for God and the homeland is for all!" The mourners got to their feet, applauding and repeating the secular statement with fervor.

Almost two weeks later, on May 12, regime agents snatched Tayyara from the streets of Homs. He was released on January 17, 2012, and fled to Jordan the following month. He became a member of the Syrian National Coalition, a political body of exiles formed in late 2011 that would be widely despised by those still inside Syria for its petty bickering, ineffectiveness, and corruption. Tayyara's voice, like that of many others in exile, did not travel far across the border. Syrians were deaf to those claiming to represent them from the safety of elsewhere. Inside, other voices prevailed.

FOR A MONTH, from April 29 to May 29, Rastan was untethered from the state, a "liberated" island free of the regime's uniformed men (but not its informers). Suleiman settled into a double life. During the day he was a wealthy, law-abiding citizen from a prominent family who managed an insurance office in Hama. After hours, he was an opposition activist using the pseudonym "Rastan Free." He was enmeshed in two parallel activist groups: one on the ground, the other in cyberspace. The virtual network was masked in anonymity, with fake names and Facebook accounts, a place where messages were always typed, never spoken. Voices could identify and incriminate.

For Suleiman, the heart of that matrix was the Shaam News Network, or SNN. The network never contacted him, never sought to verify his footage or to ask him how he obtained it or what happened before or after the snippets he filmed. It simply took what he uploaded and posted it. It was at his initiative that he dug out SNN's Skype address one day and typed a short message: "Hello, I'm filming from Rastan." A typed response followed, instructing him to upload his footage to YouTube and then paste the link in a Skype chat. It was easier than what he'd been doing—sending videos as e-mail attachments. SNN didn't ask who he was (he feared their knowing), and he didn't know who they were or where (it didn't matter to him). They were simply people distributing footage he wanted seen. And besides, none of the other media outlets responded to him.

THE PERSON RECEIVING Suleiman's Skype queries was a man named Bilal Attar. A Syrian exile in his thirties from Hama, Attar set up the SNN platform on February 22, 2011, with a childhood friend, Abulhassan Abazeed, an exile from Daraa. Both men were from Muslim Brotherhood families who had fled the crackdown in the 1980s to settle in Jordan, where Abazeed and Attar grew up together. The pair relocated to Yemen as adults. In 2011, before the start of the Syrian uprising, Abulhassan Abazeed was an IT manager at an information technology consulting firm based in Sanaa. Bilal Attar, an accountant, had moved from Sanaa to Brussels, Belgium, where he applied for asylum. The pair created a Facebook page and a YouTube channel to post links to media reports about Syria, including old television interviews with Syrian opposition figures in exile.

There were several other anti-Assad Facebook pages in early 2011. "The Syrian Revolution 2011" was the most prominent, the site that had called for "days of rage" in February. "The Syrian Revolution 2011" was run by eight people, including Bilal Attar's brother. "The truth is, we all knew each other," said Attar, years later in Istanbul. "We were wary of infiltrations by regime elements, and of trusting people we didn't know who claimed to be revolutionaries. We were the sons of the Brotherhood but not Brotherhood. In fact, we didn't like them."

Attar despised the Islamist group whose failed insurrection was the reason for his family's exile. So Attar and Abazeed decided that if there was going to be an uprising in Syria, they wanted no ties to the past. "We felt very strongly that we didn't want to work with anybody over the age of forty," said Attar. "They had their turn in the last era. They failed. We wanted to be different."

The other SNN cofounder, Abazeed, was from the same clan as most of the Daraa youths detained for antiregime graffiti in February 2011. Through his family in Daraa, Abazeed connected with activists in the southern city and told them he would disseminate their footage. The activists were close enough to Jordan to tap into its cell-phone network and bypass the Assad regime's strict controls. Footage was also physically transported to Jordan on flash drives and uploaded from there. The images trickled into SNN, two or three videos a day, but by mid-2011 the platform was receiving up to six hundred videos from across Syria every Friday. The footage, stamped with SNN's logo, was often picked up by international news agencies, increasing the site's visibility. Donors in Saudi Arabia and the United Arab Emirates took notice. They funded about forty Inmarsat and Thuraya satellite telephones, devices banned in Syria, that were smuggled into the country overland in commercial buses. Other donations helped finance 264 Astra 1 satellite devices, as well as rechargeable 3G accounts for activists in areas that still had cell-phone service and DSL Internet.

In August, SNN received an e-mail from a little-known Lebanese Shiite politician, Okab Sakr. Sakr belonged to the Future Movement, a Lebanese political party founded by the late Prime Minister Rafik Hariri, who was assassinated on Valentine's Day 2005 in a one-ton car bomb in Beirut that killed twenty-two others. In the months before his murder, Hariri had challenged Syria's almost-thirty-year political and military domination of its smaller neighbor, Lebanon. Hariri's killing was widely blamed on Damascus and prompted hundreds of thousands of Lebanese to demand Syria's departure from their country. After two months of sustained protests, and intense Western pressure, the Syrian army withdrew.

Rafik Hariri's son Saad inherited the leadership of the Future Movement and sharpened its anti-Assad rhetoric. He blamed Bashar for his father's death. In early 2011, when Bashar's kingdom of silence and fear cracked, Saad Hariri and his Future Movement wondered, Why not help it crumble?

Okab Sakr was the party's designated sledgehammer, the messenger. In his e-mail, Sakr had asked to meet with SNN. The first rendezvous was in August, at a café in Paris. "Sakr said, 'How can we help you?'" Attar recalled. The SNN cofounder asked for satellite Internet devices. Sakr said cash was easier. At their next meeting, at a café in Brussels (where both Sakr and Attar lived), the Lebanese politician slipped a thick wad of crisp 500 euro notes across the table. They fit neatly in Attar's pocket.

Okab Sakr was interested in sending all sorts of messages to the Syrian regime. Soon, Sakr and SNN's two cofounders, Abazeed and Attar, would help lay the foundations for the organized arming of the uprising in Syria.

But Suleiman didn't know any of that, didn't know Attar or Sakr. He just knew that SNN had set up Skype chat rooms for each of Syria's fourteen provinces, linking protesters who were connected only by the Internet. He was added to SNN's "Homs room," where activists shared tips and information. That's where he learned about live-streaming sites like Justin.TV and Bambuzer, and how he obtained direct contacts to Al Jazeera and Al Arabiya.

Suleiman's other network, on the ground in Rastan, was also developing. Suleiman and his cousin added Maamoun, a video activist and mobile-phone repairman, to their group. They didn't know him but knew his older brother. That was enough to trust him. Maamoun brought to the arrangement more than just video skills. He owned a small mobile-phone store (and a DSL line) near Al-Kabir Mosque, which Suleiman would later use to livestream demonstrations. Others, too, were emerging as natural organizers in the protests, telling stragglers to keep up, suggesting chants, and maintaining a general sense of order. Some served as unarmed lookouts. They all soon came together, a core of about ten men. They called themselves the town's Local Coordination Committee (LCC), or *tansiqiya*. *Tansiqiyas* were emerging across Syria, anonymous clusters of local activists who pushed through tight media control to directly disseminate information. They were the seeds of a grassroots civil society, young Internet-savvy volunteers working in their hometowns and learning as they went.

ON MAY 29, a foggy Sunday morning, the regime's tanks, military trucks, and armored personnel carriers rumbled into Rastan. Suleiman was in Homs at his sister's home. He woke to his phone ringing. "All hell is breaking loose over here," an uncle told him. "Don't come back, stay where you are." Suleiman tried contacting his parents but couldn't get through. He dialed and redialed every relative's number he knew. The telephone and Internet lines were cut. After several hours of trying, a cousin answered, a lawyer named Samer Tlass. Samer was on a hill east of Rastan. He suggested a rendezvous point: a gas station on the road to Salamiyeh at the intersection leading to the town of Umm al-Amad. He said he had important videos.

The spot was flat, brown, agricultural, treeless. Nowhere to hide. Suleiman pulled into the gas station. So did five trucks full of soldiers and four Peugeot 505s (along with the 504, the cars of choice for the *mukhabarat*). Paranoia set in. Were they looking for him? Had they eavesdropped on the call? Were the *mukhabarat* really that good? I'm done, Suleiman thought. If Samer arrives now, we are both screwed. He considered driving away. It might look suspicious, but then so would loitering. All they had to do was ask for his ID and see that he was from Rastan to haul him in for questioning, especially on that day. Just act normal, he told himself, but he couldn't. He turned the ignition and drove up and down the road. He saw the convoy head out just as Samer arrived. The cousins embraced. Samer slipped a memory card into Suleiman's hand and left.

The videos were mainly of injured children in hospital beds. A quiet girl in a pink T-shirt, her head wrapped in bandages. Another child, this one whimpering, her shoulder covered in a cast, a sling around her right arm. They were on their way to the Rawafidh School when their bus came under fire sometime between 7 and 7:30 a.m. The driver was shot but survived. A first lieutenant from the Tlass family who was traveling back to his military service wasn't so lucky. He died, along with a schoolgirl named Hajar al-Khatib who had turned eleven that day. Hajar's body was released to her father, despite his refusal to sign a paper saying she had been killed by terrorist gangs. Her devastated father said, "I told them, if that's what they wanted they could keep her body."

On May 31, the state-owned *Tishreen* newspaper reported both deaths. It said the pair were "martyred" in an attack by "extremist terrorist groups" and that their flag-draped bodies were honored as they left Homs Military Hospital. A few years later, in January 2014, at the opening of Geneva peace talks between the Syrian government and the opposition-in-exile, the head of the Syrian rebel delegation would begin his speech by recounting the story of Hajar al-Khatib and calling her the first female child martyr.

SULEIMAN WATCHED the videos on Samer's flash drive with horror. Children had been shot! The images provided proof of the security forces' indiscriminate fire. He needed to upload them to SNN, but his sister in Homs didn't have DSL. He didn't know anyone in the city who did. Anger clouded his judgment. He walked into an Internet café, handed over his ID (as was obligatory), and started uploading the videos. It was impossibly reckless, but no one noticed. Luck was on his side.

That same desperation and luck drove him to run the gauntlet of checkpoints back to Rastan a week later. He had no idea if his name was on the lists of the wanted. Dressed in a suit and tie, Ray-Bans affixed to his clean-shaven face, and driving an expensive car, he figured he didn't look like somebody the low-level loyalists would stop to question. He was right. He wanted to be home to document what was happening, but he had another reason to return: One of his relatives, a twenty-four-year-old first lieutenant named Abdel-Razzak Tlass had defected from the army in response to its attack on Rastan. He was one of the first officers to break from the regime, a split steeped in symbolism. He was a relative of former Defense Minister Mustafa Tlass, defecting from Daraa, birthplace of the revolution, where he served with Division 5, Brigade 15, Battalion 852.

In an emotional statement aired on Al Jazeera on June 7, Lieutenant Tlass said he'd witnessed officers he named killing peaceful protesters. "Is the army supposed to steal and protect the Assads?" the young mustachioed man asked. He sat in what looked like a tribal tent, dressed in battle fatigues and cap, two yellow stars on each lapel. "The honor of Rastan is under attack! Rastan is being destroyed by artillery, mortars, and tanks! Where are you, honorable officers of Rastan? Where are you?" Lieutenant Tlass called on them and others to defect. "Where are your consciences? You did not join the army to protect the Assads!"

Rumors swirled that Abdel-Razzak Tlass had slipped into Jordan from Daraa after making the video, but it was shot in al-Zafarani, a town in the Homs countryside, and uploaded by activists who would become part of the Farouq Battalions. Suleiman knew his relative wasn't in Jordan. The officer's father had contacted Suleiman and, using coded language such as, "Meet me where I last saw you at the family barbecue," arranged a rendezvous. Suleiman drove straight to the location. Abdel-Razzak Tlass had sneaked home to Rastan and was hiding in a farmhouse on its outskirts. He planned to organize an armed uprising to defend and take back his hometown, and he wanted Suleiman's help.

MOHAMMAD

Mohammad was bringing in guns from Turkey. Pump-action shotguns for 7,000 Syrian pounds each that he sold for 8,000. Profit was not his motive. Once a man carried a weapon, "he was almost forced to continue in this path," as Mohammad saw it, because, "regardless of whether he had a light weapon or a tank, it was the same thing to the regime." Mohammad was in his hometown of Jisr al-Shughour. He watched its peaceful protests, weekly events since mid-April, but didn't participate. He had other plans. He enlisted a small group of Salafi friends from Latakia who, along with the few local men he'd armed, overran half a dozen small police stations in villages dotted around the city. The first raid was in mid-April, the same time as Jisr al-Shughour's first protest. Mohammad said he let the six policemen go, and netted nine Kalashnikovs and ammunition. It wasn't hard.

The Baath regime was largely absent from the countryside that had once formed its social base. Local police stations (and informers) were about the extent of its presence. The instruments of the state were concentrated in the big cities. To the urban elites of the largely Sunni mercantile class that decades earlier had sided with the Muslim Brotherhood, the *mukhabarat* state offered limited economic liberalization in exchange for loyalty, ensuring that the old elites were stakeholders in the survival of the new. Sect mattered less in this arrangement than politics and interests and making money—but only for those closest to the regime and others it wanted to woo. Family came first, and Bashar's maternal cousins, the Makhloufs, became the richest and most powerful businessmen in Syria, with monopolies in telecommunications and other industries. Former Defense Minister Mustafa Tlass's family wasn't far behind. It meant that classism, rather than sectarianism, was a stronger revolutionary driver for many of the regime's opponents, coupled with the long-suppressed hatred of those whom it had harmed. Like the people of Jisr al-Shughour.

ONE FUNERAL CHANGED the course of events in Jisr al-Shughour and had ramifications beyond it. Basil al-Masry, a twenty-five-year-old father of two, was killed on June 4 as he attacked a security outpost near the Jisr al-Shughour railway station. Few outside his family knew that he had picked up arms against the state. He was not part of Mohammad's circle.

The Masrys had man-size holes in their family tree, entire branches snapped off in the 1980s, and every subsequent generation knew who had done the pruning. Thousands attended Basil al-Masry's funeral, including people from nearby villages. The story circulating among the mourners was that he was killed, unarmed, at a regime checkpoint. Masry's wooden coffin, adorned with olive branches, was carried through the streets of his hometown. "Heaven, open your doors," the mourners chanted as they streamed across a bridge over the Orontes River toward the cemetery. The crowd returned to wait in a public garden near the post office, to pay condolences to Masry's family in a funeral tent erected nearby. On the roof of the post office were government snipers. Mohammad watched the crowd from the balcony of a friend's home. He had concealed his Kalashnikov and brought it with him. His men also had guns hidden in their cars. They retrieved them and fired at the post office. The snipers responded indiscriminately, killing five people in the crowd and wounding dozens more, some of whom were rushed twenty kilometers north across the Turkish border to a hospital. In the hours that followed, entire generations of families fled to the Turkish border.

Mohammad's men weren't the only armed men present. There were others from surrounding villages. A young, unarmed mourner named Fouad saw groups of men grab guns from cars. He heard the first shots but didn't know their source. He hid near the post office and watched security forces shoot unarmed protesters. A man he didn't recognize threw a Molotov cocktail through the wide double doors of the post office. Fouad was a twenty-five-year-old small-business owner. His family, like many in Jisr al-Shughour, bore scars from the 1980s, when his father and uncles were imprisoned for their ties to the Muslim Brotherhood. He hated the regime. The day Hafez al-Assad died was cause for a secret celebration in his home. His sick, elderly father danced in the living room when he heard the news. Fouad had protested every week since mid-April and took pride in his peaceful resistance. Crouched behind a car, he now watched gray smoke escape from the post office. A man who worked in a quarry to the north of the city propelled an incendiary device through the building's double doors. The explosion ignited a mighty fireball that belched thick smoke and shards of glass that clinked delicately as they showered the street. Men rushed into the building. Both Fouad and Mohammad saw eight blackened bodies slumped in two rooms.

As in the 1980s, helicopter gunships took to the skies over Jisr al-Shughour, emptying antiaircraft ammunition into people, bullets that split skulls. The State Security and Political Security branches were within walking distance of the post office. The personnel there handed over their guns and were given safe passage by the armed men, who numbered a few hundred. Military Security, however, refused to surrender. Some attackers hurled dynamite into the building, others shot at it but missed, killing at least four people on their side. "For God's sake, enough!" someone yelled. But the armed men weren't done. A bulldozer rumbled toward the Military Security building, a barrel of explosives in its blade. The barrel detonated, paving the way for men to move inside.

Fouad entered a wide corridor. "There was no place for me to step except on the dead," he said. Sickened, he walked into a room at the end of the hallway. A man in khaki was still alive. He was a customer at Fouad's store and pleaded with Fouad to save him. "How can I get you out?" Fouad asked him. "It's either you or me. I will get in trouble for you. How can I do it?"

"I have never hurt anyone," Fouad remembered the soldier saying. Before Fouad could respond, a man with a hunting rifle walked in, shot the soldier in the head, and walked out.

Fouad ran out of the building, screaming. He hated the regime, but these armed men and their actions did not represent him. He went home, bundled up his mother and younger siblings, and headed straight to the Turkish border. The sons were exacting revenge for crimes against their fathers and grandfathers, he thought, but he knew it would not end there.

The regime sent 120 reinforcements who were intercepted and killed by armed groups before they reached Jisr al-Shughour. Assad's dead in the Military Security branch were buried in mass graves. "We filmed them as if they were mass graves full of the regime's victims," Mohammad said years later, "but they were mass graves of their members. Those who oppressed us for thirty years were killed, nobody else."

Thousands of families from Jisr al-Shughour hugged a strip of territory ringing the foothills of the Turkish border, on the outskirts of the Syrian village of Khirbet al-Joz. The lucky ones had cars or pickup trucks to sleep in. Some fashioned shelters from burlap bags, sheets of plastic, tree branches. Most just sat in the dirt of plowed fields and orchards of apple, plum, and flowering pomegranate trees, with little more than the clothes they wore. Many had fled after the shooting in the garden near the post office, or the following day. Food and clean water were scarce. There were no bathrooms, no showers, no privacy. A young woman rinsed a baby bottle in the flowing water of a nearby stream. Others tried to wash the mud out of their clothes. Young men plied old smuggling routes into Turkey and returned with as many bags as they could carry of bread, bottled water, and clothing. They told each other to say, "*ekmek*," Turkish for bread, if they were stopped by border patrols.

While the families cowered in the fields, columns of tanks headed to Jisr al-Shughour. A Syrian government spokeswoman said the people of Jisr al-Shughour hadn't fled but were just visiting relatives in or near Turkey. At the same time, Syrian state media said its forces were on their way to rescue civilians used as human shields by armed gangs and terrorists wearing stolen military uniforms. "If the people of Jisr asked for the army, we wouldn't be here, living like this, would we?" said a young woman in her twenties. She sat on a plastic mat in the mud, cradling her two-month-old daughter. Her family had been outdoors for a week. Her older brother was scared of crossing into Turkey. "People are saying we might be targeted in Turkey, that Assad's men can still find us. Is that true?" he asked. "Should we go from one hiding place to another?"

Thousands crossed and were housed in an old, disused tobacco factory in Yayladağı in southern Turkey, which became the first Syrian refugee camp there, known as Yayladağı One. Every night around 6 p.m., Turkish soldiers stood near a small clearing in the thick scrub, where the coiled razor wire marking the border was pulled away. They supervised Syrians walking across a two-meter gangplank over a shallow ditch into Turkey and directed them to waiting minivans that took them to the camp. One night, at around 9 p.m., there were still hundreds of people at the unofficial crossing. A grandmother in a black *abaya* and firmly fixed *hijab* sat on a rock near the opening. "It's like in the 80s: they are burning our houses, showering us with bullets," she said. The old lady had left on the day of Basil al-Masry's funeral. She started to cry. "How can I go to Turkey and I don't know where my sons are? They said they would follow us, but we haven't heard from them. The telephone lines are cut. I don't know what's happening."

The armed men, including Mohammad's group, knew what was happening and set the narrative. They had just provoked the first major armed insurrection in the Syrian uprising, an inconvenient truth that played into the regime's line that it faced armed opponents, not peaceful protesters like Fouad. And so, a story about a mutiny was devised, one I was first to hear.

I'd spent a rainy night in the Syrian fields with families near the Turkish border. The next morning, a *moqadam*, Arabic for colonel or lieutenant colonel, sat cross-legged in the damp soil, wearing a borrowed plaid short-sleeved shirt and pale green trousers. He said his name was Hussein

Harmoush, and he produced a laminated military ID card. He was the highest-ranking defector to date. A twenty-two-year military veteran, he split from the 11th Armored Division of the Syrian army's Third Corps. He said he burnt his uniform in disgust, starting with the rank designated on his epaulets, then the rest of it. He struggled to speak. Men gathered to listen. After a long pause and many deep breaths, the *moqadam* with the thinning salt-and-pepper hair said he defected from Homs on June 3 with thirty of his men and was joined by other defectors who arrived in Jisr al-Shughour after June 5 to defend civilians from loyalist troops. "I feel like I am responsible for the deaths of every single martyr in Syria," he said. Harmoush began to weep. A man sitting next to him put his arm around him. At least half a dozen other men, most with graying hair and weathered faces, also began to sob. At the time, it seemed like their grief overpowered their pride. Did they know Harmoush was lying?

The distant wail of an ambulance from over the Syrian hills grew louder. It carried an old man shot in the abdomen and the hand. He walked with difficulty to the opening in the coiled razor wire, and although the crossing was closed until the evening, the Turks let him through. Harmoush followed him in. Within weeks, Harmoush formed the Free Officers' Movement, which called on the Syrian military to back the people, not the Assad government. It was the precursor to the Free Syrian Army.

The contrivance about a mutiny worked. There was no mass defection, yet the story was repeated dozens of times by wounded men evacuated to hospitals in the southern Turkish town of Antakya, and by some families in the fields. Some men admitted they'd shot at regime soldiers but insisted there was also a mutiny. Farmers spoke of seeing soldiers shoot other soldiers. Even the regime described men "in stolen military uniforms" shooting its soldiers. Human rights organizations carried the witness testimonies, and I, along with most of the world's media, reported the claims. "We invented the story about the defections," Mohammad told me much later, a claim admitted by others. "We made a liar out of Hussein Harmoush. We had to explain how the regime men were killed."

On September 15, 2011, a disheveled Harmoush appeared in Syrian custody, paraded on prime-time Syrian state television in a sit-down interview. It was the first sighting of the officer since he disappeared on August 29 from a Turkish refugee camp where he lived with his wife and four children. Harmoush was tricked into returning to Syria by an undercover regime agent posing as a weapons dealer, and detained there. It's not known what happened to the officer after the interview. In it, he said there was never a band of defectors. "The truth is, it was all an act," Harmoush told the interviewer. "We said that there were soldiers protecting the people, but it was all a lie, an advertisement." Few believed him.

ABU AZZAM

Abu Azzam didn't know how to use a gun. As a university student in Homs, his conscription was deferred until graduation. Some students would purposely fail in order to delay their service, or (like Suleiman) pay their way out of it. Every man above a certain age in Syria, with the exception of only sons and bribe payers, had military training, so those who had completed their twenty-one-month compulsory stint taught Abu Azzam how to assemble and disassemble a weapon. It wasn't that hard, he said: "Just aim at the target and shoot." Although he'd been in the Homs neighborhood of Baba Amr for months, living under regime fire, it wasn't until August that he pointed a gun at a human silhouette and squeezed the trigger. He didn't know whether the bullet met flesh. Or perhaps he did and didn't want to admit it. It was easier that way. He'd tried protesting. It didn't produce results as far as he was concerned, except dead protesters. He figured these were the regime's last days anyway. It would soon be over, and the gunman would revert to being an Arabic literature student.

That same month, Abu Azzam was joined by Bandar's older brother, Bassem, who was as keen to join the revolution as Bandar wanted to keep it at bay. Bassem had protested every week since he'd returned to Syria in February from Libya, where he worked as a laborer. Like Abu Azzam, Bassem also was a poet. He was outraged by regime reprisals against Baba Amr, and he vowed to join Abu Azzam there. He kept his plans from Bandar. He just turned up one day near his younger brother's apartment and told him he was entering Baba Amr with or without his help. Bandar called his mother and begged her to lie and tell Bassem she was sick so that he would return home to the east. He did, but Bassem was back in Homs four days later. He was going into Baba Amr, he told his brother, through its checkpoints if he couldn't skirt them, come what may. "He didn't know the area, he'd be arrested," Bandar said. "I wouldn't let any harm come to him if I could help it, not to my brother. He had a white heart, you know. His mind was made up, so I had to help him." Bandar sneaked his brother inside. Bassem, it turned out, was pretty good with a rocket-propelled grenade launcher. The pair of poets became a team—Bassem manning the RPG and Abu Azzam serving as his assistant, carrying the rockets.

Baba Amr was besieged that summer, choked by armored personnel carriers, checkpoints, and tanks that cruised its streets, mutilating homes with a randomness that sickened Abu Azzam. "They didn't care who or what was in the homes, they'd just fire, fire, fire, without even checking," he said.

Artillery plowed streets. It sliced open houses, pockmarked walls. Abu Azzam marveled at the mess a single bullet could make. Its often neat, precise entry wound, the splatter of scarlet and crimson and rosy reds at its exit point—if it exited. He stopped squirming at such palettes. His nights were disturbed. The wind howling through empty windowpanes, or a cat creeping on shattered glass, would jolt him awake. He'd inspect his surroundings in the dark—a light would have given away his position. He was surprised how quickly he got used to the sounds of war. At first, he'd flinch at the thunder of shelling and fire that could split open the darkness. What frightened him the most was the tank-mounted Shilka antiaircraft system with its four-barrel guns, each one pounding eight hundred and fifty to a thousand 23mm rounds a minute into bedrooms and kitchens. Then, he said, he stopped feeling anything: "It became almost routine."

Abu Azzam and the other armed men in Baba Amr called themselves *majmoo'at*—groups—using descriptive names that offered practical information. Abu Azzam's *majmoo'at,* for instance, was named after a school in its vicinity. *Majmoo'at* Tayba was near Tayba Patisserie. Every member of *Majmoo'at* Omari was from the Omari family. They weren't yet calling themselves battalions or brigades. They didn't see themselves as soldiers, just local men banding together, looking for protection and to protect. They soon ballooned to more than two dozen groups, the smallest just five men, the largest up to eighty-five.

Abu Azzam's *majmoo'at* was tasked with helping others take out a snipers' nest in Hanadi Tower, a building on Brazil Street in the nearby neighborhood of Insha'at. They moved at night, always at night, when they hoped their chances were better against the sharpshooters. The tower had once been a benign landmark, just a tall building, but urban warfare unspools cities. It defiles their meaning. Shopping strips become fronts, mosques and their minarets targets, and the rooftops of university dorms regime sniper positions.

There was a camaraderie in Baba Amr born of overwhelming danger. It was the "happiest time" of Abu Azzam's life. His group shared chores and pooled their money (he had 12,000 Syrian pounds, about $240). Civilians welcomed them, fed them, and offered them moral support, even as the armed men reciprocated when they could. "All of Baba Amr felt like one family," Abu Azzam said. "I felt like the warrior poets I'd read about [in Arab lore and Islamic history]. I was doing something I totally believed in, not because I was carrying a weapon but because I was convinced that I was working against a tyrannical government that was killing all these people. My duty was to stand with the people who were my family and my friends' families. We entered this mess and couldn't get out of it, but I was happy." The closeness of death made him feel more alive for cheating it.

Soon, families who had anywhere else to go fled. As the siege tightened, food became scarce, foraging for it more lethal. The men of Abu Azzam's unit fasted, eating once a day to ration their supplies. They scrounged for food in abandoned apartments. Pasta and onions, with their long shelf life, were prized finds. So too was a copy of Sun Tzu's *Art of War*, which Abu Azzam stumbled across in a living room. It became his indispensable guide to this new world of soldiers and weapons, with its rawness, its lack of protective layers, its upturning of order. Parents buried children. Vegetable stalls were military targets. A pair of poets had become warriors, just like their Arab and Islamic ancestors, men of words and weapons. Abu Azzam got used to burying men with whom he'd had breakfast that morning, men whose real names he often didn't know. They were all using pseudonyms—Abu this and Abu that—afraid there might be informers among them who would retaliate against their families. Abu Azzam would catch himself wondering whether he'd die before his friends did, and how many more of them he would bury. Would he see his hometown of Tabqa again? How quickly life could drain from a man, pooling in a puddle, only to be mopped up and thrown out like dirty water. "We were crying all the time, seeing *shabab* die, but we could not stop," Abu Azzam said. "What was happening would not let us stop. It made us more insistent to fight."

Adrenaline and faith took over at the sharp crack of bullets. He was not fighting for Islam, but inspired by it. "If God has written that I will die at a certain hour, I won't die a minute before," he told himself. Religion was a refuge, a means to quiet the fear and panic of combat. A way to order chaos, to believe that whatever happened on this street, in this neighborhood, this city, this country, this life and the turn it had taken, was not the end. If Abu Azzam survived, he survived. If he died, he believed he'd die a martyr, so he'd "win either way." He stopped worrying about whether he could kill a man. He focused instead on making it harder for men to kill him. Move. Don't stay put. Aim. Shoot. Move. Don't stay put. The enemy wore the uniform of his national army. Some were conscripts, obliged to serve. He knew that. One of his two brothers, the middle one, was a conscripted soldier with Brigade 112 in Nawa, in Daraa Province. Abu Azzam knew that soldiers could not easily defect without fear of retaliation against their families, or being detained or killed in the attempt. They had to figure out how and where to flee, and it was the same for their families. For some, it was easier to remain in their posts and feed the opposition intelligence. (Abu Azzam's brother later defected.) But nuance and hesitation and thinking are inconvenient on a front line where there is only one rule—shoot or be shot, and do it quickly. The enemy in Abu Azzam's crosshairs was "a person killing children and women in the president's name, not a Syrian," he said. "I could not see him as a Syrian."

. . .

BANDAR WATCHED the tanks crushing Baba Amr from his nearby apartment. He heard the same sounds of war from the guilt of safety. His brother Bassem had stopped taking his calls (the landlines still worked). If Bassem wouldn't come out of Baba Amr, Bandar decided, he was going in. He cleared his phone of images of demonstrations and snippets of revolutionary songs (they were enough to get a person detained). He uploaded pictures of Bashar al-Assad in case he was stopped and searched by soldiers, and stole over a wall into the shattered neighborhood.

Bassem had been in Baba Amr for a month. "He looked weaker and slimmer, he looked strange," Bandar said. "I asked him to leave. I told him Mother wanted to see him, but he didn't listen. He told me I'd lied to him once before about our mother. He was happy doing what he was doing." After less than thirty minutes, Bandar left, but he was so haunted by the changes in his brother's appearance that he tried again ten days later. This time, his brother didn't even speak to him. "He just looked at me. He wasn't angry, he loved me, but I kept telling him to leave. I mean, they were about twenty guys! What could they do? A demonstration was more effective because at least large numbers demonstrated."

Bandar was too frightened to stay. The shelling and gunfire were relentless, although his brother hardly seemed to notice. "I told him this issue is bigger than you and me, we can't change anything," Bandar said. Bassem listened, calm and unmoved. "He didn't say a word to me," Bandar said. "Not a single word."

SULEIMAN

The three motorbikes twisted around sharp turns, bumping over pot-holes as Suleiman and the other riders navigated the alleyways of Rastan with their lights off. They plowed into the inky fields beyond their town, bouncing over uneven earth, toward a farmhouse where Abdel-Razzak Tlass and other defectors were hiding. As soon as they passed populated areas, they unsheathed Kalashnikovs wrapped in sacks and towels. Suleiman was unarmed. They continued in the dark to avoid detection by Syrian security forces encircling the town, and informers inside it. "Make sure your safety is off," the lead driver told the others. It was 10:40 p.m. on a breezeless night in August, the holy month of Ramadan. The safe house was still forty minutes away.

Rastan had become a parking lot for tanks and armored vehicles, with eighteen checkpoints. Its three-story sports center was repurposed into a military base. Two tanks idled at the stump where the statue of Hafez al-Assad once stood. "The tanks are always in the streets," Suleiman once said as he drove past them. "I think if they want to get a pack of cigarettes, they take the tank to the store."

Suleiman was still helping organize and film the demonstrations, and disseminating information through his Twitter handle @rastancoor, and his YouTube channel, Rastanfree, but he was also moving between the defectors' safe house and the town—transporting food, money, and phone credits to the men in hiding.

The safe house was a two-room dwelling in an orchard. It sheltered eight defectors, mainly first lieutenants in their twenties who still wore their uniforms. They called themselves the Khalid bin Walid Battalion, named for a famed commander buried in Homs whose Islamic army conquered Syria in the seventh century. They were the first group to publicly declare themselves a *katiba*, or battalion. They sat in a semicircle on plastic chairs in a room. Each man produced a laminated military ID and stated his name, age, unit, and the place from which he'd defected. Like Abdel-Razzak Tlass, most had been stationed in Daraa, but some had served in Damascus, Aleppo, and even Quneitra, near the Golan Heights. They wanted to be heard. They wanted to make it clear that soldiers were blinkered. Their only source of information—beyond what they could see—was Syrian state television, with its talk of armed terrorist gangs, foreign conspirators, and Salafi Islamist instigators. It didn't cover peaceful protests, except pro-Assad rallies. Satellite television was forbidden to soldiers.

The men all spoke of the difficulty of defecting, of seeing colleagues killed or imprisoned for trying, or for refusing to shoot into crowds. It was one reason why there were never mass defections of entire units. The men wouldn't say whether they'd killed people. They aimed at legs, or above heads, they said. Lieutenant Ibrahim Ayoub, a wiry officer with two yellow stars on each slender shoulder, said he had witnessed the rapes of both men and women. "I imagined a soldier doing those things to my family in Rastan," he said. He defected on July 6. They all said they saw soldiers loot homes and senior officers—whom they named—kill detainees. "If we went into a house looking for somebody and the person wasn't there, we'd ransack it, ruin it, shoot it, burn it, demolish it," one of the officers said. "They'd take everything, even a phone charger, even the taps."

The Khalid bin Walid Battalion wanted to be the seed of an army of defectors. The young officers didn't want armed civilians like Abu Azzam and Bassem with them, fearing the chaos of men not used to a chain of command. They were disappointed with senior officers who had fled to Turkey, like Hussein Harmoush, who had led the Free Officers' Movement until he was detained, and Riad al-Asaad, a colonel who defected on July 4, 2011, and established the Free Syrian Army on July 29. (In September, Harmoush's group was folded into the Free Syrian Army.) "What is the point of being overseas?" asked Lieutenant Amjad Hamid, the Khalid bin Walid's leader. "We need them here in Syria." In Rastan, the men of the Khalid bin Walid made and followed their own orders. "We have no communication with officers outside Syria," said one of the eight. "We are officers. We are supposed to protect our people here."

Outside, crickets chirped, foliage rustled in the darkness. Inside, a small gas burner hissed as water bubbled and coffee brewed. The eight defectors were jumpy, hypervigilant to sounds around their hiding place. They had reason to be: Forty-eight hours earlier, there had been nine of them. The nine had publicly announced their defection as a group in a brief video statement that Suleiman shot and uploaded to YouTube. It was aired by Al Jazeera on August 6. The officers made individual videos, too, which Suleiman also filmed, such as a forty-eight-second clip showing First Lieutenant Fady Kism, a tall, bearded man with dark eyes and plump lips, announcing his split from the Syrian army's Third Division. "I'm doing it because of the destruction that I saw in Rastan, and in Homs, in Daraa and Hama," the twenty-three-year-old told the camera.

The next afternoon around 1 p.m., shortly after his mother watched the video of Rastan's defectors on Al Jazeera, Kism was dead, killed in an ambush by loyalist soldiers traveling in a blue van with tinted windows. The soldiers tricked the defectors into thinking they wanted to join them. A firefight broke out. The next day, the official Syrian Arab News Agency ran a short piece about "an armed terrorist group" that had "set an ambush four kilometers east of Rastan city, opening fire on a convoy carrying officers to their workplaces." An officer and two soldiers were killed, the report said, adding that three loyalists were also wounded. "We only protected ourselves," Lieutenant Ibrahim Ayoub said. "We are not interested in attacking unless civilian lives, or our lives, are in danger."

At 5 p.m., just hours after he was shot, the announcement of Kism's death was broadcast from the loudspeakers of Rastan's mosques. Suleiman's mother opened the window of her living room to hear it: "The martyr, the

First Lieutenant Fady Abdel-Jalal Kism, may God have mercy on his soul, will be buried today," it said, followed by melodic Quranic verses. She kept the window open and stood there for a moment to hear the prayers. "The blood made us hate him," she said, almost to herself. She was talking about Bashar al-Assad. "Before that, we loved him. I loved him, to be honest. We were content. People lived and worked in peace." She lamented Assad's first speech on March 30, two weeks into the uprising. If only the president hadn't chuckled as he spoke while blood spilled in the streets. If only he'd apologized for the killings and for detaining and harming the Daraa youths blamed for the graffiti. If only he'd addressed the real reasons people were in the streets, instead of stoking sectarian fears and talking about sabotage, sedition, foreign and local conspiracies. Suleiman's mother gestured toward the villas, not far from her home, of the former defense minister, Mustafa Tlass, and his sons. "They are traitors," she said. "I don't know how we can reconcile with them. They aren't planning ahead for when Bashar falls. They don't think that he will."

Just before sundown, the body of Fady Kism was lowered into the ground in jeans and a blood-soaked army-green T-shirt. The men of the Khalid bin Walid remained in hiding, but hundreds of others poured into the spaces between the tall white headstones, the sun's dying rays painting the hillside cemetery a warm golden hue. Dusty hands tossed gritty dirt into the grave.

"To Heaven we are going, martyrs in our millions!"

"Death but not humiliation!"

"Syria is ours, it's not for the Assad family!"

"There is no God but God!"

Kism's dazed mother rocked back and forth as she sat on the concrete floor of her home in upper Rastan, mourning the eldest of her four sons. "May their hearts burn the way they have burnt mine," she said. "There are a lot of informers here, they must have informed on him." Her son hated the army, she said. He defected five days earlier to avoid being sent to Deir Ezzor in Syria's east. "He told me he wanted to join the free officers, that he'd rather die with them than have to shoot people," she said.

She put her head in her hands and burst into tears. Kism's first child was due in weeks.

Outside Al-Kabir Mosque, firecrackers exploded just before 10 p.m., as they did every night during Ramadan, signaling the start of another demonstration after *taraweeh* prayers. Friday was protest day, but across Syria during that Ramadan, every day had become Friday. Al-Kabir Mosque was opposite the once-dreaded State Security branch, where Suleiman had found reports about his family. The building's beige concrete walls were now plastered with antiregime graffiti: BASHAR IS A DONKEY, BASHAR IS A TRAITOR, BRING DOWN BASHAR!

Suleiman and his friends in the *tansiqiya* set up lights and speakers in the square between the mosque and the former intelligence building. They all contributed to buy a professional sound system, a microphone, and bullhorns. A donated projector beamed Al Jazeera or Al Arabiya, whichever channel was broadcasting live protests, onto a screen stitched from several white sheets and hung against the wall of the mosque. The images were a reminder that Rastan was not alone.

Tanks surrounded them, eighteen checkpoints harassed them, informers walked among them, yet thousands of men, women, and children still filled the square, their faces softly illuminated by strings of lights hoisted above them. Some waved flags—the two-starred, red-striped flag of the state as well as the three-starred, green-striped flag of the revolution. They held cheeky placards. One mocked General Maher al-Assad, the president's younger brother and commander of the feared elite Republican Guard and Fourth Armored Division. He'd reportedly said that he hadn't even put on his uniform yet, meaning the regime's opponents had yet to see the full force of his response. IF MAHER'S IN HIS PAJAMAS, WE'RE STILL IN OUR BATHROBES! the placard read.

A large, eight-panel cardboard banner moved through the crowd: THE FALL OF THE REGIME SERIES, EVERY NIGHT AFTER *TARAWEEH* PRAYERS, PRODUCED AND DIRECTED BY THE HEROES OF THE REVOLU-TION. This year, Ramadan's traditional epic TV dramas were playing out on the streets, not on the screen. Songs of defiance, including the anthem of the revolution, roared from the speakers, loud enough for the soldiers in their tanks streets away to hear:

> *Hey Bashar, hey liar.*
> *Damn you and your speech, freedom is at the door.*
> *So come on, Bashar, leave [*Yalla Irhal ya Bashar*].*
> *The martyrs' blood is not cheap.*
> *So come on, Bashar, leave [*Yalla Irhal ya Bashar*].*

On the balcony of the intelligence building stood the members of the *tansiqiya*, including Suleiman, who was livestreaming through Justin.tv, using the DSL line in Maamoun's store next to the mosque. Suleiman panned the crowd, waved to friends who caught his eye. "What a dream, a beautiful dream!" he said. Mohammad Darwish, the eighteen-year-old who shouted "Freedom!" and prompted Suleiman's first protest, took the microphone. Darwish, his back curled, right foot on the balcony's shin-high ledge, leaned toward the crowd below. "We salute the hero Fady Kism!" he yelled. A mighty cry of pride and anguish, anger and defiance rolled back to him. Framed portraits of the dead, black ribbons in their corners, were held high. On that night, Fady Kism's image joined them.

"What happiness, what *Eid* [religious festival], when every day we have a *shaheed* [martyr]" Darwish sang. The crowd clapped along, a thunderous rumble that shifted in rhythm and intensity as Darwish switched between chants. "One, one, one, the Syrian people are one!"

"We salute the free Alawites, the free Christians," shouted another man standing at the microphone. "We salute them!" the crowd responded, fists pumping into the air.

The energy was infectious, exhilarating, the crowd electrified, the mood more festive than fearful, despite the security forces streets away. Protesters defied them with their joy, their music, their dancing. Their faces were uncovered. Drummers set the beat as small groups danced and twirled and jumped and hugged, working themselves into a sweaty frenzy. They chanted in solidarity with other towns and villages under attack.

Their threats were one, their experience shared, their demands the same: to bring down a regime that had ruled them for almost five decades—and, as some were now chanting, the execution of the man at its helm. The crowd of thousands sat down. "The people demand the fall of the regime," they whispered, rising to a crouch. "The people demand the fall of the regime!" they repeated a little louder, standing a little taller. "The people demand the fall of the regime!" they screamed, jumping into the air, hands clapping above their heads, arms stretched toward the sky.

The crowd was pressed together tightly. Many had stories about a brother, a daughter, a neighbor, a friend who was killed or wounded or disappeared. They wanted to be heard. Modesty was discarded as clothing was edged away to reveal scars, electrical burns, or the red-raw anger of bullet wounds. Mobile phones, like so many fireflies, lit up with grisly images of corpses that were once loved ones.

"Listen!" a twenty-year-old man in the center of the throng yelled, his arms outstretched as he turned and gestured around him. "We shattered the barrier of fear with our voices!" He was proud that he had to shout to be heard, and certain this was the only path available to Assad's opponents. "To stop now is harder than to continue and to go forward, because to go back means certain death. We will be hunted," he said. "We can't turn back. Everybody here is a martyr in waiting. Either we die free or we die." And besides, he said, he was sure the international community would soon demand an end to the violence: "They can't stay quiet forever as we die, can they?"

ABU AZZAM

The seeds of Abu Azzam's Farouq Battalions were planted that summer, in a nighttime meeting in an orchard in the town of Al-Qusayr, in western Homs. About twenty men—farmers, businessmen, students, and a thirty-six-year-old lawyer named Osama Juneid (better known as Abu Sayyeh) met with defectors from Rastan, including Suleiman's relative Abdel-Razzak Tlass and others from the Khalid bin Walid Battalion. Many of the men assembled in a two-room farmhouse along the Orontes River were strangers to each other, brought together by the owner of the farmhouse, an activist who helped smuggle weapons from Lebanon into Homs.

They had been selected because some had picked up arms, and others were at the forefront of peaceful resistance in their areas. They came from neighborhoods in Homs, including Baba Amr, and towns around it, such as Talbiseh, Rastan, and Tal Kalakh. It took them four hours to agree to coordinate their armed efforts, although there was no talk of forming a single battalion or naming it the Farouq. That happened later, in a Skype call in August among three men from Homs: the lawyer Abu Sayyeh, who was present at the farmhouse meeting; a wealthy sheikh named Amjad Bitar; and a realtor-turned-activist, Hamza Shemali, also known as Abu Hashem. "We all agreed that we must do something organized and military, to form a battalion," Abu Hashem remembered, "and we needed to call it something symbolic. The first battalion to form was Khalid bin Walid, it took an important name. Homs was called the city of Khalid bin Walid, so we needed something bigger for our battalion."

They chose a name weighted in history and ambition, and with clear sectarian overtones tied to Assad's alliance with Shiite Iran. The Farouq Battalions were named for Farouq Omar bin al-Khatab, a *sahaba* or companion of the Prophet Mohammad, political architect of the caliphate and the second caliph who conquered the Sassanid Persian Empire, among other territories. "We wanted to be called Farouq as an indication of our desire to confront Persian ambitions in our Arab lands," the lawyer Abu Sayyeh said. They wouldn't use the name, the Farouq Battalions, until November 2011, when Suleiman's relative, First Lieutenant Abdel-Razzak Tlass, would publicly announce the formation of the group in Baba Amr.

ABU OTHMAN

The clues were accumulating, seeping through the prison walls where Mohammad's old cellmate, the *Shari'iy* Abu Othman, collected them. Something was stirring outside. It wasn't a premonition or similar fancy but a conviction, one cemented by the arrival of three teenagers in Abu Othman's cell in Palestine Branch in early March, before he was transferred to Sednaya Prison. The teens from Daraa were among the two dozen youths detained and accused of writing anti-Assad graffiti on school walls. They were brought to Abu Othman's cell number 12. "They looked scared," said Abu Othman. "It was natural, they were young, sixteen, seventeen, eighteen. Their fingernails weren't pulled out or anything. They'd been beaten and tortured, but nothing more than normal."

Mohammad Ayman Alkrad was one of the three. In Palestine Branch, he became 10/12: prisoner 10, cell 12. He was eighteen, about to graduate, and he intended to follow his father, a retired judge, into law. He lived in the Dam neighborhood of Daraa City and played football every night with a group of friends in the concrete yard of Quneitra School, near his home. On February 22, a day before the protest outside the Libyan Embassy in Damascus, Alkrad noticed fresh graffiti on the school wall: IT'S YOUR TURN, DOCTOR, it said, and LET THE REGIME FALL. He didn't know that similar slogans had been written on other schools, and that other boys had been picked up a week earlier. "I saw it and thought, It has nothing to do with us, let's play, so we did," Alkrad said.

He went home after the game. He had just stepped out of the shower when an agent from the local Military Security branch knocked on the front door. His father answered. Out of respect for the retired judge, his son wasn't dragged from home but instead told to appear at the Military Security branch in Daraa that night. Neither father nor son knew why. "I swear to God if I tell you I had any idea what it was about I'd be lying to you," Alkrad said. "Nothing at all because I hadn't done anything, and I was keen to go and explain that. It wasn't as if I was scared."

He was scared when the handcuffs snapped across his wrists, when he was hooded and bundled into an Opel sedan and driven thirty minutes away to a Military Security branch in the city of Sweida. He was scared when he entered what he called "the corridor of torture," when he saw the metal pipe running along the ceiling with handcuffs. He hung from it for days, spun like a rotisserie chicken during those thrashings. He was scared when he realized what he was suspected of: "You're the one who wants to ruin the nation? You dare to write on the walls about the doctor? What has the doctor done to you?" He was scared when he was squeezed into a tire and beaten with thick cables, doused with cold water in the middle of winter, and electroshocked. He hadn't done anything. Then he wasn't sure. "I started thinking to myself, Have I done anything?" After those sessions, his small, dark solitary cell felt like a refuge. The opening of its door did not mean release, the closing of it did.

After six days in Sweida, Alkrad—bruised, swollen, seared by electric cables, his wrists raw from handcuffs—walked into Abu Othman's cell with two others: his cousin Shukri Alkrad and a young soldier from the Abazeed clan, one of eleven detained from that family. Alkrad realized the other two were also implicated in the graffiti. He had thought he was the only one. He looked at the men in cell number 12. "There were about thirty of them staring at me. I didn't know where I was, so I asked them. They told me I was in Palestine Branch. They were all Brotherhood, Fatah al-Islam, Al-Qaeda."

Writing on a school wall. Abu Othman had heard stranger reasons for landing in Palestine Branch. The youths denied the claim, but Abu Othman didn't believe them. "I was thinking that they may have done what they were accused of, but it was natural that they wouldn't admit it. They were young and new. I told them to be careful, not to speak too openly, because there were spies in the cell." The teenagers told the *Shari'iy* about protests in Egypt and Tunisia, about dictators toppled and others threatened, about a new pan-Arab battle cry shaking the region: The people demand the fall of the regime. Abu Othman was buoyed by the news.

Abu Othman's conviction that something was stirring in Syria only grew after he was transferred to Sednaya Prison on March 15, 2011, along with the three hundred or so other Islamists from Palestine Branch. (The three teenagers stayed behind. The Daraa youths, all two dozen of them, were released and returned to a hometown rocked by protests in late March.) Sednaya Prison allowed monthly family visits. If a man was detained on the seventeenth of the month, his family was permitted to see him for thirty minutes on the seventeenth of every month. "So every day, somebody had a visitor," Abu Othman said, "and they'd share what they heard with us." That's how the inmates learned about the pardons.

The Syrian regime issued new amnesty laws, including Decree No. 61 in May 2011, which covered "all members of the Muslim Brotherhood and other detainees belonging to political movements," and another in June, as well as Decree Nos. 161 and 53, which ended the decades-long state of emergency and abolished the Supreme State Security Court, respectively. Sednaya housed pretrial detainees nabbed under the state of emergency laws, awaiting sentencing, and those on whom the court had passed judgment. Sednaya and Palestine Branch were emptied of Islamists and filled with protesters. "I can't give you names, but we were told by brothers with lots of experience [in jihad], who had spent a lot of time in Sednaya, that upon our release we should sit and not work," Abu Othman said. "Just sit and wait."

Abu Othman was released on June 20, 2011. He went home to Aleppo, to his wife and two children, but it didn't take long before he and his fellow Sednaya "graduates," as they called themselves, started quietly mobilizing. "When I was detained, I knew four or five or six, but when I was released I knew a hundred, or two or three hundred. I now had brothers in Hama and Homs and Daraa and many other places, and they knew me,"

Abu Othman said. "It took just a few short weeks—weeks, not a month—for us, in groups of two or three, in complete secrecy, to start."

The Islamists were certain that the Assad regime offered the amnesties while knowing full well the "graduates" would take up arms against it. "If an Islamist brother was going to act, he was going to do so with weapons to face the security [forces]. It would be jihadi, and this would allow the regime to say to the world, 'Look at the terrorists.' We were aware of this, we didn't give the regime that justification," Abu Othman said, "but in secret, we were working."

Abu Othman bought four guns from the town of Sarmada in Idlib Province, plus "sprays that would put you to sleep" from Turkey. "It was the time of the civilian protest movement," he said, "with no ability to do much more than basic preparations." His "basic preparations" involved working in a jihadi intelligence cell in Aleppo, which at that point was still a firmly controlled bastion of the regime. His job was to monitor government soldiers and *shabiha*, the paramilitary pro-regime thugs. He passed the intelligence to colleagues, who would detain or kill the suspect. "When we started, I have to admit, I can't deny that Al-Qaeda was basically finished in Syria," Abu Othman said. "So when we started, we did so without instructions or orders. We started to gather ourselves, to vouch for each other and for others." In Sednaya, they had been told simply to wait for their new leader—so wait they did.

THE LEADER, a Syrian who went by the nom de guerre of Abu Mohammad al-Jolani, arrived in August, the Muslim holy month of Ramadan. He stole across the Iraqi border one night with five colleagues—their beards trimmed, explosive belts fastened, pistols and grenades concealed in their clothing. They navigated berms and trenches, traversing two-way smuggling routes used to ferry cigarettes, livestock, weapons, and jihadis to enter the northeastern Syrian province of Hasaka, where two Syrian colleagues were waiting for them.

Jolani and his team were part of Abu Bakr al-Baghdadi's Islamic State of Iraq, the latest name and incarnation of an Al-Qaeda affiliate founded by the Jordanian Abu Musab al-Zarqawi after the 2003 US invasion of Iraq. Jolani was also a prison graduate—of the US-run Camp Bucca, in the sunbaked sands of Iraq's southern desert near Kuwait. He spent six years there, misclassified by his American jailers as an Iraqi Kurd from Mosul. The future ISIS leader Abu Bakr al-Baghdadi, and men who would become his senior lieutenants, were also in Camp Bucca, although Jolani didn't know Baghdadi inside the wire. They would meet later.

The Camp Bucca inmates, in their bright yellow and orange jumpsuits, passed their time painting, playing table tennis outdoors, and being "re-educated in Islam." There was a mural at the entrance to the prison called *The Road to Freedom*. In five illustrated steps, it outlined a prisoner's path out of Camp Bucca—health services, Islamic discussion, "freedom schooling," workshops, and court, which all led to a blue "happy bus." The jihadi leaders, cocooned in Bucca from the worst of the sectarian bloodletting ravaging Iraq, took the happy bus and regrouped outside the wire. Camp Bucca was to Al-Qaeda in Iraq what Sednaya Prison was to become for Al-Qaeda in Syria—a recruiting pool and ready-made network of vetted men.

Jolani and his colleagues, eight men in all, spent their first night in Hasaka, Syria, in the home of a former Sednaya inmate who was originally from Hama. Three of Jolani's team were Syrian, two of whom met him on the Syrian side of the border: Saleh al-Hamwi and a man with three aliases—Abu Ahmad al-Shami, a.k.a. Abu Ahmad *al-hudood* (of the borders), a.k.a. Abu Ahmad *al-idari* (the administrator). A third Syrian, Naseem *al-a'lami* (the media officer), had traveled with Jolani from Iraq. Also part of the group were a Saudi named Abu Imad; an Iraqi, Abu Khadija; and two Jordanians—one known as Abu Samir, and another, Abu Julaybib, who was a brother-in-law of Al-Qaeda in Iraq founder Abu Musab al-Zarqawi.

They were the founding fathers of a new Al-Qaeda franchise that hid its lineage, one Jolani was authorized to set up by Baghdadi and Al-Qaeda's central command. It was called Jabhat al-Nusra l'Ahl as-Sham, or the Support Front for the People of the Sham, the latter word referring to

Damascus, Syria, and/or the Levant. At the time, Al-Qaeda looked like a spent force. Osama bin Laden had been killed months earlier. His successor, Ayman al-Zawahiri, had bin Laden's passion but none of his charisma, and the Middle East was in the throes of revolution, experimenting with peaceful protests rather than violence to effect change. Jolani's nighttime crossing would recast all of that. Jabhat al-Nusra's first unpublicized operation was a December 27, 2011, attack on a State Security branch in Damascus. Almost a month later, on January 23, 2012, the group announced its presence in an audiotape broadcast on a well-known Al-Qaeda platform.

RUHA

Ruha didn't tell any of her friends what was happening at home, that Baba—Maysaara—didn't live there anymore, that she didn't know where he was, that he'd steal visits when he could. She even kept it from her best friend, Serene, with whom she walked to school every day. Serene lived at the foot of Ruha's street, at the bottom of its gentle incline.

Ruha loved Serene, a tall, fair-skinned girl with long blonde hair, but she didn't trust her. Even children had picked sides in the conflict, and Serene was not on Ruha's. That wasn't the problem, because, as Ruha saw it, "everyone can have their opinion," but she thought it safer to keep hers from Serene. "I knew that if I spoke, somebody might tell their parents and might harm us, so I didn't say a word to anyone."

The blonde girl regaled Ruha with details of the pro-Assad rallies she attended. She'd recount the chants, what she wore, the route, and how much she loved the president. Ruha didn't tell her that she'd twice marched with the other side, that she had covered her face with a scarf and walked with women who wore *niqabs*—not because they were religiously conservative but because they wanted to conceal their identities for fear of retribution. "I knew what I was doing," Ruha once said. "We are children. If we were to speak of these things, we'd become enemies from a young age. That's wrong. I didn't want enemies." As a child, she had everything she wanted, but she knew older people didn't, so she marched for them. It was her decision. "When Baba participated, I decided to participate too. Maybe if I was older, I might have been against him, on the other side, but I was young, so I walked with him."

Maysaara's absence affected her deeply. Her grades dropped. She didn't care for Arabic, her favorite subject. She couldn't focus in class. At night, her dreams left her afraid to close her eyes. She'd wake screaming that she had to hide Baba. The nightmares were always the same—angry knocking at the door, uniformed men swarming into her home, finding Baba, then shooting him dead in front of her. In late spring, her school was shelled during the last lesson of the day; it was English class for Ruha, math for her eight-year-old sister, Alaa. "It sounded like a rocket," Ruha said. "In the beginning, there were bullets," Alaa recounted, "then rockets." Soon there would be helicopter gunships and warplanes and barrel bombs and chemical weapons. It was the fate of their town, Saraqeb, to be crucified at the crossroads of two key national highways: the south–north M5, which linked the capital Damascus—through Abu Azzam's Homs, Suleiman's Rastan, and Saraqeb—to Abu Othman's northern city of Aleppo, and the west–east M4, which connected Aleppo to Mohammad's coastal city of Latakia in Assad's heartland. Saraqeb was smack in the middle of land supply routes for the Syrian military.

Alaa remembered diving under her desk like all the other children the day bullets pierced the window of her classroom. "Hide so you won't be shot!" her teacher yelled. Alaa found it odd that she was shivering, even though it was warm. Her hands couldn't blot out the ugliness of things breaking around her, even though she was pressing them as firmly as she could against her ears. Ruha and her classmates rushed to their teacher: "She hugged as many of us as she could. We were all gathered around her in a circle, screaming, standing in the corner. I was terrified. I emptied my lungs of air."

That was the sisters' last day at school. After that, their mother and aunts taught them. Ruha was happy to be home. It felt like an extended vacation, but it also meant she couldn't escape household chores. In between lessons, Aunt Mariam, the schoolteacher, taught her how to knit a revolutionary-flag design onto scarves and headbands—black, white, and green horizontal stripes with three red stars. Ruha wore the headbands around the house, especially when her father sneaked back on visits that only raised the little girl's fears that he would be captured at home.

But when the Syrian army's tanks stormed through Saraqeb's streets at dawn on August 11 during Ramadan, Maysaara was still in hiding. They were looking for protesters. Gunfire shattered the quiet shortly after *suhoor*, the predawn meal ahead of the daily Ramadan fast. "To the cellar!" shouted Ruha's mother, Manal. The children ran across the courtyard and into the vaulted room with thick stone walls. It was the farthest place from the front door. Manal helped her mother-in-law, Zahida, into the room. They were joined by Noora, Ruha's aunt, whose husband, Mohammad, had gone to the farm early that day. There was no way to warn Uncle Mohammad or Maysaara. The electricity, cell-phone network, and Internet were all cut that morning ahead of the sweep. The cellar door was left ajar to let in light, but it also let in sound.

A hailstorm of metallic pings got closer. Ruha's skittish aunt, Noora, prayed aloud, the same words over and over: "Dear God, don't let them come in. Dear God, keep everyone safe. Dear God, protect the men." Ruha's mother flinched at every bullet, every bang, every scream. The little girl was frightened by the fear of the older women. "If we're going to die," she whispered, "at least we will die together." She knew that the regime was detaining children to lure their wanted fathers. It had happened to a three-year-old cousin on her mother's side. Let them take me, she prayed, and leave my brother and sisters. Her grandmother, Zahida, drew her youngest grandchildren, Mohammad and Tala, into her soft belly and covered them with a blanket. "Mohammad was screaming, 'Leave me, I want to fight them!" Ruha recalled. "We all told him to shut up."

ACROSS TOWN in her three-room apartment, Ruha's Aunt Mariam heard wailing. Her neighbor's son was being dragged from his home. She approached the window, parted the curtain slightly, but heard more than she could see. Her elderly neighbor was begging for his son's release.

"Get inside, old man! It's none of your business!"

Aunt Mariam crawled along the floor of her living room, afraid her silhouette would draw the men inside. She crept up the stairs to her flat roof, peered over the edge, and saw two buses in the middle of the street, soldiers moving in and out of homes, as well as *shabiha*, paramilitary regime thugs, dressed in jeans and sneakers. She couldn't tell what was in the buses. "I saw what I thought were pillows, they were white shapes. It took me a while to realize they were men who had their undershirts pulled over their heads."

She held up her mobile phone and tried to film the buses, but she couldn't focus the image. Her hands were shaking. Where were her brothers? Where was Maysaara? Where were her nephews? Were they among the "pillows" in the bus? "God is with us," she murmured, "and anyone who remains silent against an injustice is a mute devil." The least she could do was bear witness, and pray for the men in the buses.

RUHA FROZE. Banging on the front gate. Her heart at her feet. Her mother opened the front door and uniformed soldiers swarmed in. Ruha and Alaa screamed when the men entered the cellar and upended furniture. They took her late grandfather's decorative 1910 musket. It was only the first of two incursions that day. The afternoon call to prayer was echoing when the second group of strangers, these men not in uniform, marched into Ruha's home. They were the *shabiha*. Some had their faces covered. "They said ugly things to Mama that made her cry," Ruha said. "They were very mean and nasty, they swore at me. They told me to shut up and stop crying. I don't know how, but I stopped. I was worried about Mama. They told Mama, 'Tell your husband to surrender to us because when we find him, we will step on his neck and break it. We will kill your brothers, too.'" They left with Manal's jewelry, but Maysaara had once again eluded them. Ruha's Uncle Mohammad, however, was snatched from the farm.

Uncle Mohammad was one of about 130 men detained in Saraqeb

that day. He was penned in a warehouse with hundreds of others from across Idlib Province. There was just one bathroom, which constantly flooded, and not enough room to lie down. The environmental engineer was embarrassed to say that he was stuck near the toilet. He slept while seated, couldn't stomach the stench to eat, and said he lost twenty kilograms in the thirty-six days he was there. They insisted he had demonstrated, even though, unlike his brother Maysaara, he had not. "I was one of those who wanted dialogue with the regime," Mohammad said after he was released. "If the regime thinks that it can finish off the demonstrations by force, it is delusional, and if the opposition thinks that it can bring down the regime, it is delusional. We need to talk. I believed in that when I went to jail, and when I came out, my brother Maysaara had bought a gun."

Maysaara had done so reluctantly. "I didn't want the fall of the regime," he said. "For five months [until the August 2011 raid in Saraqeb], I didn't want its fall, just its reform, but its actions forced us to demand it. There was no armed opposition the first time the army entered Saraqeb. Nobody fought it, but after the *shabiha*, people bought guns with the idea that we wouldn't let a thug take us or anything we had."

Maysaara financed the purchase of guns and ammunition for the men of his family and his friends and neighbors. As in Abu Azzam's Baba Amr, that was how a battalion was born: a man, his brothers, cousins, nephews, friends, and neighbors armed themselves, and with time adopted the military nomenclature. Maysaara was also part of an informal underground network to help military defectors flee. It was as strong and as fragile as a spiderweb. House to house, car to car, skirting checkpoints along back roads, town to town. Maysaara befriended another railroader, a businessman named Abu Rabieh, from the hills of Jabal al-Zawya in Idlib Province. Abu Rabieh was gray-haired, clean-shaven, and a decade older than Maysaara. He had the LG electronics franchise in Idlib Province. They became inseparable—a pair of well-off businessmen turned revolutionaries.

. . .

MAYSAARA WAS DRIVING his red Toyota HiLux pickup truck, Abu Rabieh beside him. A box of syrupy sweets slid gently along the backseat. It was just before sunset on January 24, 2012. Maysaara had pulled out of a gas station that was out of gas. He drove slowly, looking for one of the many roadside fuel sellers who sold gallons of varying quality out of plastic containers. A driver in a three-car convoy stopped him to ask directions.

Ruha was in the *souq* with one of her seven aunts, buying toys for her sister Alaa, who had just had an operation on her legs to correct in-toeing. Ruha was debating whether or not to buy a Barbie. The dolls never lasted more than a week in her home. She didn't even bother to name them, such was their short lifespan. They'd break or disappear into a cupboard Maysaara had built especially for his daughters' many teddy bears and toys. Suddenly, a bolt of sustained gunfire. It frightened the little girl, but her aunt told her it was on the outskirts of town. Ruha returned to examining the toys on display.

Maysaara saw their faces before he was pepper-sprayed. He put the truck in reverse, and, temporarily blinded, floored it toward Saraqeb as forty-eight bullets pierced the vehicle's metal skin. Drivers honked at him but swerved out of his way. He felt a searing pain in his back. "Quicker! Quicker! I'm hit, I'm hit!" Abu Rabieh kept saying. Maysaara drove until the gunfire stopped. Eyes burning, he cradled his friend's head in his lap, as Abu Rabieh died in his arms.

Ruha and her aunt walked back to her grandmother's house, along with an adult male cousin they had seen at the *souq*. A neighbor stopped the cousin. "How is Maysaara?" he said. "God willing, he hasn't died has he?" Ruha's feet buckled. She collapsed in the street, inconsolable. Her cousin carried her to a house that sounded like it was in mourning. Grandmother Zahida was wailing. The old lady had said she had felt like a stone was sitting on her chest all day, that something wasn't right with one of her children.

A bullet had lodged in Maysaara's back, another sliced through him near his spine. His bloodied pants, sport jacket, and white striped shirt were returned to his family that night, but it was days before they saw him. It was raining shells when he came home, his family cowering in the cellar. Ruha's father was carried in by two men. His feet dragged behind him. He could not stand. He could barely speak. He stayed just long enough to kiss every member of his family and then was whisked away. It wasn't safe for him to linger.

SULEIMAN

Rastan's *tansiqiya*, the group of local activists, had two regular meeting spots—the back room of a store that sold small household appliances near Al-Kabir Mosque, and a one-story home at the dead end of an isolated alleyway. Both belonged to Merhi Merhi, a father of two in his early forties, who was responsible for general coordination in the *tansiqiya*. His graying hair, the deeply etched crow's-feet around his blue eyes, and prominent nasolabial furrows, made Merhi look like the old man of the *tansiqiya*, an impression accentuated by his quiet gravitas. It endeared him to the other members of the all-volunteer group. Rastan's *tansiqiya*, like most across Syria at the time, paid their own expenses and were not funded beyond donations from community members.

They would gather on Merhi's front porch after wiping their feet on the sliver of flat, squarish marble he used instead of a welcome mat. It was a remnant of the statue of Hafez al-Assad that once stood at the entrance to Rastan. They sat on blue-and-white plastic mats spread over a cool tiled floor, veiled by a grapevine's laden foliage, perfumed on summer nights by climbing jasmine that twirled around the porch and the scent of fruit-flavored tobacco from *narghilehs*. They'd often return there after protests. Suleiman and Maamoun, the mobile-phone repairman, would transfer and organize their video footage. Suleiman's cousin, the lawyer Samer Tlass, was usually there too, along with several other lawyers. They were all using aliases at the time.

"If Bashar had only asked for a minute's silence for Daraa, we wouldn't have gotten to where we are now," Merhi said one night. "At the end of every battle, the solution must be political, but what will it take to get to that point now?" He was fond of saying that he didn't have political ambitions, that he'd only finished ninth grade and didn't care who was president as long as he wasn't trying to kill his people and he treated them with dignity.

"Who are we going to have a dialogue with?" one of the men asked. "A tank? Our crimes now are possessing USBs and mobile phones. What do we say to the parents of the martyrs? The best solution is a coup, that the army says, 'Enough blood.' The other option is we enter the abyss."

They picked at plates of grapes, figs, and watermelon as they wondered how the revolution would end. Suleiman listened as he organized snippets of video on his computer. One showed homes being shelled by the army. He'd bought it for 5,000 Syrian pounds ($103) from an active-duty soldier. Another was of an emaciated male corpse, a piece of masking tape across his bare chest that said CORPSE #5. There were other grisly videos of bodies, some with missing eyes, lacerations, burns, gunshots.

"An Apache," Samer Tlass blurted. "A strike on the presidential palace is the solution, because if there is no Western intervention, the regime will not give up. Iran will not allow the regime to give up."

Another lawyer in the room predicted a long war. "The Syrian people have made the decision to bring down Assad and his regime, and the regime is determined to bring down the people," he said. "These are the only options. Peaceful solutions are over. I anticipate war—civil and regional."

"No!" said Merhi, shaking his head. The Syrian people would not be drawn into a deeper conflict, or fall into the trap of sectarianism. His Alawite friends in the loyalist camp, whom he still spoke to, were coming around to the idea that Assad and his generals would probably flee, and they would stay behind. "We have to find a way to live together," he said.

Suleiman looked up from his laptop. "The revolution must stay peaceful," he said. He was helping the Khalid bin Walid Battalion with its media work, but that was the extent of any crossover. "Military work is separate from ours," he said. "The defectors are responsible for protecting the demonstration, but that's it. We are peaceful. We can't give Bashar an excuse in front of the international community to suppress this revolution. We're like the dog from that old joke, remember? That's why we're doing this."

The men nodded, a few smiled. The joke dated back to Lebanon's civil war in the 1970s and '80s. It was about a hungry, shabby dog in Lebanon that, tired of the war, escaped to Syria—only to return to Beirut months later, surprising its friends. The dog said it was treated well in Syria, groomed and petted, and fed so much it put on weight. "Then why did you come back?" the other dogs asked.

"Because I want to bark and howl."

THE TANKS AND the armored personnel carriers in Rastan weren't actively attacking the townsfolk, although there were frequent rumors and false warnings of another offensive. On September 27, after days of shelling, the tanks in and around Rastan stormed the town. Soldiers fanned out, going door to door apprehending thousands of suspected protesters. Homes were burned and looted. The Khalid bin Walid Battalion countered, but it was overwhelmed and outgunned. The military converted an orphanage built by Suleiman's grandfather into a base. It was down the street from Suleiman's home. His parents urged him to leave Syria. He had recently learned that his name was on a leaked list of thousands of wanted, and that three intelligence branches—Air Force Intelligence, Military Security, and Political Security—were looking for him. It would have been easy for Suleiman to slip into Turkey or Lebanon, but he refused to leave Syria. His parents were adamant that he at least leave Rastan. Reluctantly, he agreed.

On September 28, in the darkness before dawn, Suleiman and three friends in the *tansiqiya,* including Merhi, bundled into his car and, headlights off, moved along back roads and agricultural tracts. Suleiman's cousin, Samer Tlass, stayed behind. They were still in Rastan's eastern farmlands when Merhi demanded that Suleiman stop the car. "*Khalas*, enough. I'm going to stay here!" Merhi said. Even as the wheels still turned, he opened the car door. "Get in the car, for God's sake!" Suleiman pleaded as he slowed down. Merhi could not be convinced. He said a quick good-bye and disappeared on foot into the farmlands.

Suleiman and the other two activists hid at a relative's home in an industrial area of Homs, and from there they moved to Hama. The army was in Hama, but Suleiman had a strong network of friends there who offered him refuge. Merhi used a satellite phone to stay in contact with Suleiman. Both Merhi and Maamoun, the mobile-phone repairman, continued filming and sending Suleiman raw footage over phone lines that still worked in the northern part of the town near the Rastan Dam, where they were in hiding, as well as via couriers who, at great personal risk, would sneak through the tightening blockade to deliver the footage. Suleiman edited, polished, and published the clips and disseminated other news about Rastan to the media and larger activist networks. He was his hometown's megaphone.

On October 3, the Khalid bin Walid Battalion announced its withdrawal from Rastan—to safeguard the local population from continuous shelling, according to a statement it released. But it didn't move far. Abdel-Razzak Tlass and a group of men remained in the fields on the outskirts of town. Despite the crushing military presence and its checkpoints, protests resumed in late October in what some locals took to calling "occupied" Rastan.

In early November, Abdel-Razzak Tlass and most of the Khalid bin Walid Battalion escaped to Baba Amr in Homs, where Tlass became the face of Abu Azzam's Farouq Battalions. Tlass announced the formation of the Farouq on November 6—just days after he'd left a battered Rastan—in a short video staged to look spontaneous. In the clip, armed men crowded the back of a spotless white pickup truck (they weren't yet smearing mud on their vehicles to hide from airborne predators) as it crawled down a dead-end alley. Tlass stepped out of the passenger seat to clapping, flag-waving civilians chanting, "God salute the Free Army!" "In the name of God, the most merciful and compassionate," Tlass began, "we are the Farouq Battalion, part of the Free Syrian Army, created on

November 5, 2011, to protect innocent protesters in Baba Amr, and to protect innocent civilians."

Merhi remained in his hiding place near the Rastan Dam. He often called me from there, usually between 1 and 3 a.m. Sometimes, he just wanted to talk to somebody who lived outside his claustrophobic shelter, to be reminded of what "normal" used to mean. More often, he had other questions: Could I get him weapons? Did I know any suppliers? Could I connect him to anti-Assad Lebanese politicians like Saad Hariri? He stopped asking those questions after I made it clear I was a reporter, not an activist. His queries then changed. Was information getting out? Did the international community understand that people were being killed with no accountability? Perhaps it just didn't know, he would say. If it did, it would surely act, wouldn't it? And then one day, his calls stopped.

At 5:30 a.m. on November 24, the military swooped in on Merhi's hiding place, a farm named Mazraat Tlel in the western fields on the edge of the Rastan Dam. Most of the remaining *tansiqiya* was sheltering there, along with several defectors. A rebel spotter got word to the men in the farmhouse shortly before the soldiers arrived. Merhi and his friends were trapped between the water and the army. There was one raft. It wasn't big enough for everyone. Maamoun, the mobile-phone repairman, was one of seven men who first crossed to the other side of the dam. The raft returned, picked up another six men, then headed back. It needed two more trips. Maamoun watched the soldiers on the other bank creep up to the farmhouse. They unleashed two RPGs into an empty room before opening fire. They were there to kill, not to detain. The raft, laden with men, furiously paddled toward Maamoun. Merhi was on the bank near the farmhouse, hiding in the brush. Maamoun heard the muted pings of bullets piercing the liquid's gleaming surface, along with his friends' cries. The raft froze in place, halfway across the dam. Merhi was stuck on the other bank. Maamoun looked at him. There was nothing he could do for his friend. The soldiers saw Merhi, too. Maamoun ran away, to the sound of sustained gunfire. He dialed and redialed Suleiman. It was nearly 6 a.m. The call connected while Maamoun was still running. "Suleiman," he said, "the *shabab* are dead! I saw them, at least seven. About twelve of us got away. Everybody we left behind is dead!" The final toll, Maamoun and Suleiman would later learn, was sixteen killed, including a number of defectors.

Suleiman was crushed, split in half. Suleiman the friend wanted to grieve and scream and cry, but Suleiman the activist took over. Like an automaton, he went through the motions of trying to verify the information, then he published an account of the raid and named his dead friends. Merhi was dead. Three brothers from the Tlass family were dead. Mohammad Darwish, the eighteen-year-old who had led Rastan's chants, who had sparked its first protests, was dead.

2012

ABU AZZAM
JANUARY 2012

The poets, Abu Azzam and his relative Bassem, were stationed near a mosque in Baba Amr, in a sliver of territory the Farouq Battalions called Lira Plaza. Its name came from a discount one-lira (dollar) store in it. Regime solders were based in a school across the street. Homs, the opposition's "capital of the revolution," was cleaved into pro- and anti-Assad neighborhoods, streets, and street corners. Its government-controlled parts were still the old country: rubble free, with working Internet and electricity, cafés and restaurants along tree-lined boulevards, portraits of the president. There were tanks there, too, mainly outside security and intelligence buildings, but their guns were at rest. Lira stores there were still just lira stores.

Baba Amr was Syria's first rebel stronghold. Three square kilometers of defiance, the pride of a revolution that declared it would kneel only to God. Tank treads gnawed alleyways cratered by artillery. Gunmen in tracksuits stood guard behind eye-high stacks of sandbags or piles of broken cinderblocks. Words, some crossed out, clashed on walls sliced by shrapnel.

> THE LIONS OF ASSAD PASSED HERE.
> LEAVE, LEAVE, LEAVE, LEAVE YOU DOG!
> YOU MUST GO AWAY, MUST NOW! [in English]
> THE FAROUQ WAS HERE.

That January, there was a bread crisis in Baba Amr. Regime soldiers wouldn't allow flour in. No bread for five days. Clapping women and children walked along a rain-soaked street: "O God, your people are defenseless," they chanted. "O Arabs, do you feel with us? Dear God, quicken your salvation."

Syrians described their movement as an orphaned revolution —weak, leaderless, abandoned by an international community learning Syrian geography with each new atrocity. They asked why the mere threat of a massacre in Libya's rebel-held Benghazi rallied an international coalition, when in Syria, actual massacres didn't. Despair can sharpen religiosity. Blood and desperation and trauma can radicalize it. On January 22, Baba Amr's besieged protesters marched in the streets and demanded the declaration of jihad. The next day, by coincidence, Jabhat al-Nusra announced its presence in Syria and the world heard the first digitally altered words of its leader, Abu Mohammad al-Jolani: "The voices rose, calling for the people of jihad, so the only thing for us to do was to answer the call."

Others heard the call, too, or claimed to. There were Arab League monitors in Syria that January to study a peace proposal. They had been to Baba Amr once before, in December 2011, and returned the following month. Baba Amr's women broke through cordons of fear and Syrian government minders to reach the Arab officials. "We want the detainees, brother, we want the detainees!" one woman pleaded. "Yesterday they took six from our street. We want the detainees!" A mother of five ran out of fingers counting the *mukhabarat* branches she'd approached looking for her husband. "We were all in the kitchen, trying to stay warm near the stove, when they took him. Please, brother, they're returning our men as corpses. If he's dead, alive, I just want to know." Within weeks, the Arab League suspended its mission. Syria was too dangerous for peace. The regime's tanks and armored personnel carriers came out of hiding. Metallic rain resumed.

Abu Azzam had acclimatized to his new world. The student poet who didn't know how to use a gun was now confident enough to offer tactical suggestions during meetings, but he felt negligent on another front. Abu Azzam, the eldest son, had abdicated the responsibilities of his old life. He was in Baba Amr protecting other families and wondering about his own. Were his mother and siblings safe? Were they being punished by the *mukhabarat* for his actions—the way Bandar feared his family would be if he participated in protests? One day, Abu Azzam found a working landline in an abandoned apartment and called his mother. He wanted to hear her voice but feared what she might say, that she'd cry or beg him to leave or question his decision. She did none of that. She told him she was proud of him. "She lifted my spirits a lot," said Abu Azzam. "She is a strong person and I took strength from her."

His brothers-in-arms, like his classmates, took to calling him "The Sheikh," and, like his classmates, they ignored his protestations that he wasn't one. Anyone who knew the Quran the way he did, who could offer advice based on its passages, was clearly worthy of the title. And besides, they'd joke, he looked like a sheikh with his long, curly beard. "Who has time to shave?" he would counter. "Your beards aren't shorter! Have you seen yourselves?" In the bleakest hours, when they were hungry and cold and grieving yet another friend, Abu Azzam recounted tales his father taught him about historic Islamic conquests against unjust rulers, or recited his poetry. Bassem contributed verses of his own, like one he titled "Down with the Regime."

> *The magi's reign has ended*
> *the old face has been smashed*
> *Syria has risen*
> *it has returned to us [. . . .]*
> *Today in the land of truth*
> *a tangible truth in a tangible life*
> *we are entering the future clear-eyed*
> *demanding that history testify and that our grandchildren know*
> *that Muslims, rightly named, spoke and acted*
> *Those who knew, who know, that if they spoke they would die, acted.*

When the head of the group in Lira Plaza was killed in a firefight, Bassem and the other men asked Abu Azzam to take his place, and Abu Azzam the commander was born. He wondered how it had come to this. "I took to the streets as part of a revolution, I didn't think one day I'd become a commander," he said. "I didn't start this to be one. Nobody thought it would last long, or that we would get to the point of even taking up arms. We just want to end this."

His group now included a small number of defectors who had switched sides in Baba Amr. Abu Azzam was proudest of them because, he said, "their defections delivered a message that our goal wasn't to kill. We treated them as our brothers, and they started fighting with us. They were heroes." He remembered calling the father of one defector, a sniper from Daraa they nicknamed "Agile," to inform him that his son had died fighting alongside the rebels. "God have mercy on his soul," Abu Azzam recalled the father saying, "I am proud of him. I have another son who will stand in his brother's place if you want me to send him to you."

Baba Amr's sons were the Farouq and the Farouq were its sons, regardless of where they came from. The blood had made them brothers. Suleiman's relative, the defector Abdel-Razzak Tlass, was a military commander in the Farouq. He was often described as the battalion's leader, although in reality there were four: Tlass plus the three civilians who'd been on that Skype call in August 2011—the lawyer Abu Sayyeh, the realtor Abu Hashem, and the sheikh Amjad Bitar. Opposition media activists pushed the idea that the Farouq and the broader Free Syrian Army were largely comprised of defectors, but they were mainly armed civilians.

Abu Azzam thought the attempt to create an equivalency, even a lopsided one, was wrong. "We are a civilian revolution, not a revolution of defected soldiers against their colleagues," he said. "There is oppression, and there are people coming out against the oppression. It is a revolution against a dictator."

Abu Azzam never fought alongside Abdel-Razzak Tlass. They were in different sectors, but, like many Syrians in the opposition, he viewed the young, handsome, charismatic officer with the hefty name as a hero.

Tlass's impassioned speeches, broadcast widely on Gulf satellite channels, drew in donations to the Farouq from across the Arab world. (By the summer, Tlass would be felled by a cybersex scandal.)

The Farouq's local leaders in Baba Amr were all civilians. The former cigarette smuggler, Ahmad Da'bool, procured weapons from Iraq (via the eastern desert) and Lebanon (the easier, shorter route across shallow streams and orchards). His younger brother, Mahmoud, and a man named Ammar al-Buqai (nicknamed *il-Gider*, "the able") smuggled ammunition from Lebanon, transporting it in batches small enough to hide in their cars. Sheikh Amjad Bitar provided the bulk of the funding, but the Farouq also had an international financier—Saad Hariri, head of the Lebanese Future Movement, via his messenger Okab Sakr, the young Shiite Lebanese politician who was also slipping wads of euros to the media platform SNN.

The Farouq representative assigned to meet Sakr had never heard of him. He had to Google him before their first meeting in late 2011 in a hotel in Istanbul. "I had a lot of questions about him," the representative said. "Like why do you want to help us? What do you want? Do you want us to hold a banner in your name? He said no. We have a history with this regime and we want to support you. If this revolution succeeds, we all succeed, and if it doesn't, we are all affected."

The Future Movement's Lebanese political rivals, the pro-Assad Shiite militant group Hizballah, had made the same calculation: If Assad fell, their group would be sandwiched between a hostile Israel and a predominantly Sunni and less-friendly Syrian neighbor. The two Lebanese parties extended their political dispute across the border into Syria. The Iranian-backed Hizballah sent its men to fight alongside Assad. The Saudi-backed billionaire head of the Future Movement, Saad Hariri, sent his money to the Farouq via Okab Sakr. "There wasn't an envelope that would hold the amounts we were getting, it was in bags," the Farouq representative said. It was never less than $50,000 a day, for months, as Baba Amr morphed into Syria's Stalingrad.

By late January, shells were tearing through the air every few seconds in the neighborhood. The regime's gunners were on a schedule: 6 a.m. to

6 p.m., with an hour lull for lunch. Aid agencies were denied access. Foreign journalists died, others were wounded and trapped with the people sheltering them. The living cowered underground in the neighborhood's few basement shelters, while the dead rotted above them. Corpses were dragged into homes until it was less dangerous to bury them. Rubble and shell casings rendered streets impassable to cars. Those who escaped did so on foot. Food was scarce. The taps ran dry after rooftop water tanks were targeted. There was no electricity.

On January 28, the day the Arab League suspended its mission to study a peace proposal, Abu Azzam and Bassem were fighting kilometers apart. The Farouq intended to advance on four regime checkpoints in a coordinated dawn offensive. Abu Azzam remembered a light snow falling as he and his men charged and uprooted the first post. By midmorning, Bassem's unit fought its way to Abu Azzam, but Bassem wasn't with them. "The guys were crying. I asked them where Bassem was. They cried harder. Then, they took me to him."

Abu Azzam didn't have time to bury his relative. He and the men around him were called to the defense of a pocket near the orchards. When they returned, Bassem was deep in the earth. "For a long time, every time I remembered him, I'd cry for him, but then I envied him," Abu Azzam said. "He had died a martyr. It had ended for him."

The Farouq Battalions' Kalashnikovs, hunting rifles, and rocket-propelled grenades were no match for the Syrian military's awesome firepower. On March 1, the Farouq's Abdel-Razzak Tlass announced a "tactical retreat" from Baba Amr. Abu Azzam withdrew to Al-Qusayr, in western Homs. A symbol of the armed rebellion had fallen.

BASSEM'S BROTHER BANDAR had fled Homs for his village in the east, and later moved to Raqqa City. He learned of his brother's death on Facebook. He read and reread the post. It was wrong, it had to be. The page was administered by a Syrian in Saudi Arabia—what did he know? Bandar dialed Abu Azzam and other Farouq men. Their phones were dead.

Days later, he heard from Abu Azzam. "God have mercy on his soul, he's gone," he told Bandar. Bandar didn't believe him. He wanted proof, so Abu Azzam sent him a photo. The bullet wound above Bassem's left eyebrow was evident in the image. It dyed his face red. His arms were folded across his chest, his wrists tied in preparation for burial. "He was wearing my green woolen sweater," Bandar said, "that was how I first recognized him." He blamed himself. He should have tried harder to convince Bassem to leave. Why didn't his older brother listen? Why did he have to die? Then, slowly, Bandar accepted it. "Bassem had a good life, but he died for a cause, and in that I found peace," Bandar said. "He went to help people who were being killed. Is there a cause more beautiful?" After Bassem's death, Bandar stood in his brother's stead and joined the protests.

Bassem had left a will, bequeathing his two most valuable possessions— a jacket and a pistol—to friends in his unit. Abu Azzam didn't write a will. He had nothing to offer except his words, an ode he penned to Homs. In one verse, he wrote:

> *She stood proudly before death, trying to stem the bleeding of her children*
> *In the country of fear, in the uncertainty of a refugee tent in a*
>   *freezing December*
> *They have woken from their slumber and in caravans they are pounding*
>   *toward life*
> *Summer is the heat of bombs and limbs buried under ruins*
> *Doves in the shadow of Baba Amr's doors, their wounds mocking their killer*

TWO FRENCH JOURNALISTS, reporter Edith Bouvier and photographer William Daniels, were trapped in Baba Amr. Two of their colleagues, the Spaniard Javier Espinosa and British photographer Paul Conroy, had escaped. Two others, Marie Colvin and Rémi Ochlik, were dead, killed days earlier on February 22, when four rockets slammed into the makeshift media center where they were all hiding. The four survivors had attempted to escape the same way they'd entered—through a 2.5-mile underground water pipeline, just 1.6 meters high, which ran under Syrian army positions. It was the only route into and out of Baba Amr. Bouvier, wounded in the leg and unable to walk, was strapped to a stretcher carried by Syrians. As all four journalists scurried through the tunnel, explosions rocked one end of it. The army had discovered it. Espinosa and Conroy, quick-footed and well ahead of the two French journalists, made it out and were smuggled across the border to Lebanon. Bouvier and Daniels were forced back into Baba Amr. Thirteen Syrians died trying to get the foreign journalists to safety, in a rescue effort overseen by the Farouq Battalions in coordination with civilian activists. By March 2, Bouvier and Daniels were safely in France. Shortly after that, the Farouq's Abu Hashem, the former realtor, and several of his men, were invited to the French Embassy in Beirut. "They offered us three million dollars. It was a check, a thank-you check," Abu Hashem said. "We returned it."

The Farouq needed money, "a lot of it," as Abu Hashem put it, but its image was more important. "We were people with serious demands and not a gang saving journalists for money, and not the terrorists Bashar said we were. We weren't like those Bashar had let out of Sednaya," Abu Hashem said. The gesture earned the Farouq political capital with anti-Assad Western and Arab diplomats that it would later cash. "It was a huge boost to our reputation," Abu Hashem said. "They realized what we were."

The Farouq had custody of another group of foreigners whose release later in 2012 would also serve it well. In late December 2011, the Farouq captured seven Iranians. Abu Sayyeh remembered looking up from his sweet tea at around 6 a.m. one day in Baba Amr to see five Iranians trailing in with his men. The Farouq claimed they were soldiers; Iran said they were engineers working at a Syrian power plant in Homs. Two more Iranians, who both sides agreed were civilians, were captured after they went looking for the other five. They all remained with the Farouq until June, when Abu Hashem released them into the custody of Turkish authorities— except for two who died when the regime shelled a Homs school that the Farouq had turned into a barracks. Iran, the Lebanese group Hizballah, freelance negotiators, and Turkey offered the Farouq up to five million dollars to release the Iranians. "If we had taken that amount, we would have been considered a kidnapping gang, but when we handed them over, we won international relations that enabled us to get weapons later," Abu Hashem said. "It opened doors for us."

THE DEFECTORS who claimed to lead the Free Syrian Army were sequestered in an isolated refugee camp in southern Turkey's Hatay Province, living in white canvas tents surrounded by flat green fields. Hours-long power cuts were common at the site, preventing officers from following the news of a Syrian uprising they purported to lead. Egos ballooned in the defectors' bubble as rivalries deepened. The colonel at the helm of the FSA, Riad al-Asaad, who defected in July 2011, refused to cede his position to a major general, Mustafa al-Sheikh, who defected in November 2011. The major general outranked the colonel in the old system, but defection dates determined the new hierarchy. Military men counted the weeks and months since they had switched sides like children stating their exact age.

Fighting men inside Syria learned to rely on themselves (and God). They learned to film their exploits—realizing that YouTube clips served as advertisements, that a good explosion caught on camera could fetch a million Syrian pounds if it impressed the right private sponsor. They learned that they needed to test bullets before buying them, that some were blanks, that rocket-propelled grenades smuggled from Iraq were unreliable. They learned that they could buy weapons and ammunition from some of the same corrupt men who were trying to kill them on the other side. They learned that they should give their battalions and brigades Islamist names if they wanted to impress sheikhs in the Gulf with huge fundraising capabilities. Adnan Arour was the sheikh most rebels wanted to attract—a gray-bearded Salafi from Hama who had fled to Saudi Arabia in the 1980s and had his own show on Saudi satellite television. Not because they agreed with Arour's hate-filled speech against Alawites and minorities (some did), but because the sheikh could rattle a tin and fill it. The appearance of piety helped attract Salafi donors. Salafi beards—with shaved mustaches—became fashionable. But while Syrians took Salafi money and pledged loyalty, the cash hadn't necessarily bought their support or belief, just temporary gratitude.

Rebels met and planned and organized in small groups under the banner of a Free Syrian Army that offered them little beyond a name and an affiliation. Southern Turkish border towns such as Antakya, Gaziantep, and Şanlıurfa became logistical hubs for the revolution. Places where donors met fighters, where refugees arrived, nonlethal supplies were purchased, the wounded were treated, where men placed their families before returning to the Syrian battlefield, where foreign fighters made their way, smugglers fished for clients, and later kidnappers hunted for foreign prey such as aid workers and journalists. Stores proliferated, selling all manner of combat uniforms, including the Afghan-style *shalwar kameez* not worn in the Levant but preferred by jihadis.

There were safe houses here and there, closer to the border, where weapons deals were negotiated and campaigns planned, and other safe houses where weapons were manufactured. One workshop, an old two-room stone house in an olive grove in Syria's Idlib Province, manufactured IEDs that rebels called the *jineyee* (Arabic for genie, or crazy female). It was operational in February 2012. The bomb-maker, a short bearded man in civilian clothes and latex gloves who looked to be in his early forties, puffed on a cigarette as he prepared what he called his special recipe in a safe house he referred to as his kitchen. He didn't give his name or even a pseudonym. He'd learned his trade in the military, he said, where he'd been an explosives engineer, "another lifetime" ago. His creation, a rust-colored metal tube, stood at about 60 centimeters and contained two kilograms of yellow granular explosive material, hooked up to a trigger device (using nine-volt batteries and phones), remotely detonated. "We haven't been doing this for very long," said a defector, a young captain in the kitchen. "It took a few tries to get it right, the mix of materials. It was trial and error, and looking some things up on the Internet." The bomb-maker scooped up explosive material and poured it into a cylinder, shooing the captain and others out of the room. "Excuse me," he said, "I've got a lot of work to do."

IN MARCH, far from the public eye, the Saudis and the Qataris started choosing their teams within the Syrian armed opposition. The Qataris wanted to deal with defectors but not the Free Syrian Army's purported leaders—the squabbling major general and the colonel. They chose other interlocutors. Major Abdulrahman Suwais was one of three defectors present at the first meeting between the Qataris and defectors, in Ankara's Marriott Hotel. The Qataris asked for a list of Syrian factions to support. "They made it clear that *meem tah* [antiaircraft missiles] and *meem dal* [antitank missiles] were out of the question," Suwais said. The defectors were to take whatever weapons they were given. Suwais extracted from the Qataris a promise of 100,000 euros, money he used to set up a brigade in his hometown of Homs.

Unlike the Qataris, the Saudis sidelined all of the defectors. They relied on Okab Sakr. Okab Sakr in turn relied on four men who formed the core of what would come to be known as the Istanbul Room, a secret clearinghouse for distributing arms and ammunition. The Farouq's Abu Hashem, who was now the Farouq's foreign liaison, was one of the four. He joined the two SNN cofounders, Bilal Attar and Abulhassan Abazeed, who were now also part of the Farouq Battalions. The fourth man was known as Abu Fadel, a defector's son from Haffeh in Latakia Province. The quartet met Sakr in mid-March at a hotel in Istanbul. Sakr asked them for names—of people who represented armed factions inside Syria. In early April, more than two dozen of those names were flown into Istanbul's Ataturk Airport from southern Turkey and chauffeur-driven to a seaside resort, the Renaissance Polat, for a three-day meeting to organize a unified rebellion. The men represented each of Syria's fourteen provinces except Tartous and Sweida. Almost half were from Latakia, because Abu Fadel couldn't decide on a two-man team from his province.

Okab Sakr walked into the hotel conference room flanked by an Arabic-speaking Turk in his thirties from the National Intelligence Agency

(MIT), the only man in the room to keep his phone. Everyone else had to hand over his communication devices at the door. "I am Okab Sakr, a Lebanese Shiite, but don't be shocked. Not every Sunni is with the revolution and not every Shiite or Druze or Christian is with the regime," Sakr said. His words were like a cluster bomb. The room exploded in conversation so disruptive that Sakr allowed a thirty-minute recess. "We wanted to know who was this Shiite who said he was going to support us?" one of the eleven Latakia representatives said. "I'd never heard of him."

When the session reconvened, every man was asked to introduce himself and to specify who he represented inside Syria and how many fighters he had. "Naturally, all of the numbers were fake," the same Latakian recalled. "The problems started from the beginning. It was a game, but we had to play it to get something to liberate our lands. Everybody was sizing up everybody else, asking, Who are you? Why are you here? What have you done? It was chaotic."

Sakr promised guns. He said they were from private sources, not states, and the Syrians were to take what they were given. No requests. "He told us there are lots of weapons in Libya. We'll buy them through various ways, and you'll receive them in Syria. Don't ask me about the details," another participant said. "We didn't care about the details. I didn't care where it came from. I just wanted guns."

In late April, the first batch of weapons slipped into Syria, under cover of darkness, from three points along what was still a regime-controlled border with Turkey—one place led into Latakia, the other two into Idlib. Abu Fadel, one of the four core members of the Istanbul Room, was responsible for the route into his home province of Latakia. Turkey's "red light" on the border, Abu Fadel said, had turned green. Boxes were carried across the frontier at a place known to locals as "the intersection of the two rivers," not far from the first refugee camp in Turkey, Yayladağı One. It was an all-night operation. Once inside Syria, the goods were transported in cars with armed escorts who checked in with spotters hidden along the route to avoid regime ambushes. The boxes contained bullets, what the rebels called NATO rifles (Belgian FALs), and rocket-propelled-grenade launchers, each launcher equipped with no more than ten rockets—not enough for even a short day's fight. "It was all brand new, straight from the factory," a rebel who was there said. "But it wasn't large quantities. They provided just enough to hook us with the promise of more."

The Farouq's Bilal Attar and Abu Hashem scouted the two other locations that led into Idlib Province: One was opposite the Syrian town of Atmeh, the other near the Turkish village of Hacıpaşa. They cut the barbed wire at Atmeh and sneaked through it, ferrying boxes on foot. At one point, Bilal Attar snagged his head on razor-sharp metal that left a 13-centimeter scar. Atmeh was nothing more than an olive grove at the time, a place where, Attar said, "dogs feared to tread." The weapons and ammunition were emptied into small trucks and covered with cinderblocks, sand, and other construction materials and then smuggled to Homs along back roads at night. They were stockpiled in rebel neighborhoods in "the capital of the revolution" for a few weeks until May, when the Farouq Battalions set up clandestine transportation routes to Hama, Idlib, Daraa, Deir Ezzor, and the Damascene countryside. Bilal Attar's SNN partner, Abulhassan Abazeed, was intercepted and detained by the regime while delivering one of the first shipments in May. His fate remains unknown.

Abu Azzam was enlisted to help. The Farouq Battalions assigned him to Uqayribat, a flat dustbowl of ochre earth in Hama's eastern countryside. It was tribal territory, and Abu Azzam, as a tribal man from the east, was tasked with recruiting a battalion of locals to secure and transport weapons and ammunition through his patch of the distribution network. The guns traveled in a small truck sandwiched between cars of discreetly armed escorts. The speck of a town sat along a knot of well-worn smuggling routes through the desert to Iraq. "My responsibility," said Abu Azzam, "was to secure the weapons and transport them to Yabroud and Qarah," towns in the Damascene countryside. He turned an old, disused school into a warehouse. "There were still schoolbooks, exam papers, a few broken desks. We cleaned it out. The dust was so thick. We used it when we needed to, and sometimes the weapons weren't unloaded— they continued directly on their path."

Okab Sakr tasked the Farouq with the Syria-wide distribution of the weapons and ammunition that came through the clearinghouse operation known as the Istanbul Room. The Farouq's cut was a third. The Turks trusted them (because of the Iranian hostage negotiations), as did the Europeans, thanks to the French (courtesy of the journalists' rescue). It was all done in secret. The Farouq began to look the part of an organized battalion, dressing in uniforms emblazoned with their logo—a black shield bearing their name, bordered by crossed swords and a three-starred Syrian revolutionary flag fluttering from the barrel of a Kalashnikov. They even developed an anthem. The Istanbul Room operation expanded. The Saudis and the Emiratis provided weapons and ammunition, including cluster bombs made in the United Arab Emirates. The Qataris, despite their separate deal with the army's defectors in the officers' camp, also doled out cash in the Istanbul Room. It was supposed to be a command-and-control center. It would prove to be neither.

SULEIMAN

Suleiman felt guilty. He was alive. He had escaped Rastan and that raid on the farmhouse near the dam. He should have been with his friends that day, he was one of them, a member of the *tansiqiya*, but they were dead and he was alive. Alone, afraid, angry. He couldn't stop now. To stop meant betraying his friends' blood. His work was more urgent. He quit his job in Hama. The city was besieged by the military. So, too, was Rastan. Its eighteen checkpoints had become thirty. But his parents refused to leave. The family had scattered. His only brother was in Hama, his two sisters in a Homs that was under attack. He was a fugitive. Syria suddenly felt claustrophobic. His parents begged him to escape, but he could not forsake the revolution.

To elude his enemies, he hid among them, at a friend's chalet just south of Tartous, in regime heartland, where there were fewer checkpoints. It was winter, off-season, the beach resort practically empty. He was communicating with Rastan's new *tansiqiya* and the few surviving members of the old one. His cousin, the lawyer Samer Tlass, was still there. He wasn't in the farmhouse that morning, either. Samer had a new task now—to send information and footage to Suleiman to edit and upload. Suleiman used his own money and also gathered donations to buy cameras, satellite equipment, and food and to pay men who could get into Rastan to smuggle it inside. He waited for the videos of blood and shelling and tanks and death to disseminate them to a world he wasn't sure cared.

He then moved to Aleppo, which was also regime held, with fewer checkpoints and lower chances of raids. He got a job at a branch of QNB bank through an uncle who was a board member and shareholder. One of his cousins rented an apartment for Suleiman, keeping Suleiman's name off the lease. In February, one of the videos Suleiman received from Rastan showed his family home being shelled. His parents were in Homs at the time, visiting one of his sisters. Suleiman had to tell his father the news. "My father said he was prepared to lose everything as long as his children were safe," Suleiman said. His father repeated a common Arabic saying: "*Kuloo be yit'awad* [Everything can be compensated]." Suleiman's parents moved in with him in Aleppo.

He started work on February 1, 2012, in the bank's customer support office, keeping a low profile and not socializing with his coworkers. He thought he could resume the double life he once led in Rastan. He was wrong.

A CUSTOMER at the bank was asking for Suleiman by name. It was early, around 10 a.m. on May 23, 2012. Suleiman was at his desk, sipping coffee. He ushered the customer in and served him a strong Turkish brew. The man was in his early thirties, clean shaven in a suit and tie. He said his name was Mohammad al-Homsi, a Syrian expatriate living in Saudi Arabia, who wanted to open a US dollar account.

"Why did you ask for me by name?" Suleiman said. "How do you know me?"

A mutual acquaintance, the customer replied. The name was unfamiliar. Suleiman asked for the customer's identification papers to open an account. They were in his car, the man said. He would come back tomorrow with the paperwork. The day ended like any other. Suleiman offered to drive two female colleagues home. They were still in the car when he slowed to stop at a cigarette stall by the side of the road. As he did so, a white Kia Rio swerved in front of him. Four armed men in civilian clothing, including his visitor that morning, rushed toward him.

Suleiman didn't have time to lock his door. A hard rifle butt slammed into his face. Dragged out of the car. Arms twisted behind him. Handcuffs biting his wrists. Shaken into a rag doll. A blindfold. Darkness. Screaming, the women were screaming. "Get out!" somebody yelled. Silence. Shoved into a backseat, sandwiched between two men. Heart hurtling. That's it, I'm done. Today is the last day of my life.

He surrendered to God, whispered the *Shahada*, the declaration of faith, under his breath, the last words a Muslim should recite before death: "There is no God but God. Mohammad is the messenger of God." He thought of his parents. He should have been married by now and given them a grandchild. At least these regime agents didn't know where he lived, since his rental contract was in a cousin's name. But his papers were in the Samsonite briefcase in his car! How could he have left them there?

Focus. Think. Where were his two phones? One was in his suit jacket, the other near the handbrake of his car. His recent calls on Skype included his relative the Farouq commander Abdel-Razzak Tlass. What else? The videos! Maamoun, the mobile-phone repairman, had sent him about two dozen videos, which he had intended to upload when he got home. There were images of rebels making the victory sign near burning tanks. That's it, I'm done.

Who were these men? Which *mukhabarat* branch? Why had they bothered with that charade in the morning? They didn't need to. They could have dragged him from the branch in front of everybody. Why didn't they? Did they think he was one of the pro-regime Tlasses, a close relative of the former defense minister? Perhaps they weren't sure. Who had informed on him? It must have been that coworker he had pelted with his sandwich a month ago. The man had said he wished Bashar al-Assad would burn Homs and Hama and Idlib, and, without thinking, Suleiman tossed his sandwich in his face. The man had apologized; he said he forgot Suleiman was from an "affected" area. Suleiman said he had lost his home. He thought that was a reasonable explanation. It must have been that man. That incident. That damned sandwich, and now he was stuck between two *mukhabarat* agents. Who were they? It didn't really matter, but he wanted to know.

"May I just know who has taken me?" he asked.

"Don't be afraid. We are Air Force Intelligence, and we are still in complete control of the situation, don't think otherwise."

Air Force Intelligence. The most feared. The most ruthless.

"Don't worry," one of the agents said. "It won't take more than half an hour, then we'll let you go."

THE WHEELS STOPPED. Suleiman was led out of the car, still blindfolded, directed by an agent. Turn right. Stairs. Five steps. Left. Stairs. Stop.

Blindfold removed, handcuffs unlocked. He was at the door of Air Force Intelligence in Aleppo, standing in front of a guard who looked no older than twenty. The guard was handed Suleiman's car keys and his second phone, and then he led his prisoner down a long, brightly lit corridor into an empty room on the left. He handcuffed Suleiman to a radiator and gave him a pen and a four-page application form.

Name. Father's name. Mother's name. Birthday. Occupation. Primary School. Secondary (if applicable). Baath Party membership and level. Family members. Relatives serving in the security forces. And so it went. Suleiman was a member of the Baath Party—it was obligatory for career advancement. He listed relatives serving in the military and ignored the defectors. The phone burned in his pocket. He had to remove its SIM card. He glanced at the guard sitting behind a desk in the hallway opposite the open door. He asked to go to the bathroom. His request was denied. The guard turned his head, so Suleiman reached for his phone.

"Get your hand out of your pocket!"

Suleiman obliged but soon tried again.

"Take your hand out of your pocket! We are still treating you with respect!"

The guard was in the room. He unshackled Suleiman from the radiator. "Empty your pockets now. I'll search you and I don't want to find anything."

Suleiman handed over his phone, ID card, a silver Omega watch, a silver necklace, and a wallet with 2,300 Syrian pounds (about $35 at the time). He was told to unlock his phone. He feigned opening it, said he'd forgotten the passcode. "Now or later, but you will give us the code," the guard said. He itemized Suleiman's belongings, placed them in a large brown envelope, and led him down another hallway, this one dark and silent and lined with doors on each side. Opaque light peered in through a dirty slit of a window at the intersection of wall and ceiling, as if it knew better than to enter.

The guard stopped outside a door marked COMMUNAL FOUR. The key turned. The sound of scampering. The smell of stale sweat and urine as Suleiman was shoved into the rows of men facing the wall. The door closed.

"*Marhaba, shabab* [Hello, guys]," Suleiman said.

"Shh!"

"Where are you from?" a voice whispered.

"Rastan."

"Rastan? Then come and sit next to me!"

There was a hierarchy in the cell, determined by seniority based on time spent inside. Newcomers were crushed in the center, forced to sit cross-legged in the overcrowded space. Veterans were also cross-legged, but around the perimeter, where they could at least lean against a wall. They were all in their underwear. Suleiman soon understood why. The heat was suffocating in a room with no ventilation, no light, no toilet. Speaking was forbidden.

Suleiman picked his way among the bodies toward the voice that called him. It belonged to the *shawish*, a term that designated a cell leader, the person who served as an interlocutor with the guards, if they asked for one. "I thought you were an officer in your suit and tie!" the *shawish* joked. "Just don't let them break you, and be careful who you speak to. There are spies in the cell."

The key turned, the men scrambled to their feet and faced the wall.

"Suleiman Tlass!" the jailer said.

"Present."

"Your number is one."

The door slammed.

What did that mean? The inmates said it meant Suleiman was first for a beating that night. You'll be okay, he told himself. You're strong. You're fit. You'll be okay.

The door opened again—after minutes or hours, Suleiman couldn't be sure. It was all the same in the darkness.

"Suleiman Tlass!"

"Present."

"Prepare yourself. You're going to be on Ad-Dunia television."

Ad-Dunia was a regime mouthpiece that often aired so-called confessions of captured men and women it described as terrorists who "confirmed" the regime's narrative that the revolution was a foreign conspiracy led by extremist Sunnis and hatched by Syria's enemies to weaken it against Israel and America.

Suleiman felt panic rise in his bones. He was going to be paraded on television to betray the revolution. That was surely worse than any beating that lay ahead. What would he say? What would his parents think? At least they'd know why he hadn't come home and maybe where he was. How could he praise a regime that had killed his friends, and then say that he was deluded and duped, like the other confessions he'd watched? Some of the inmates tried to console him: If they put him on television, one said, they might pardon him and let him go. He was, after all, a Tlass.

The violence of the heat and body odor made him nauseous. He stripped to his underwear and fixed his eyes on the door. He dozed off and then woke to the bustle of men hurrying to their feet before the door opened.

"Suleiman Tlass, come here!"

"Can I just get dressed?"

"No."

He wore handcuffs and a blindfold and was told to address the interrogator as *sidi*—sir. He was led barefoot into a quiet room. He sensed the presence of people. Was he being filmed? Would he be forced to betray the revolution on television in his underwear?

"You have 20 seconds, you son of a bitch, to open the phone," a voice said calmly. "Take him outside to unlock the phone."

He was walked out, his eyes uncovered, and handed one of his phones, an Android HTC. He told the guard there'd been too many attempts to open it and that it had shut down. He was blindfolded and led back into the room.

"It seems you're a real son of a bitch," the interrogator said. "Take him down."

Pushed to the floor, bent at the waist, his legs and upper body forced through the hollow of a car tire, his hands still handcuffed behind his back, his eyes covered. He was in the *dulab*, the dreaded tire, immobilized, unable to see the blows to brace for them. He couldn't tell how many hands lashed him with thick flexible rods that he heard slicing the air. Hard blows on his back, his feet, his head. The air stolen from his lungs. He couldn't speak but begged them to stop. He felt the heat of pain, the warmth of his blood.

"Abdel-Razzak Tlass, eh? You like the whores in the Turkish camps?"

So they had viewed the photos on his memory card, probably on a computer.

"Get up, you bastard!"

He was kicked out of the tire. "What's the code? Open the phone!"

"*Sidi*," Suleiman said, "the phone is locked. I need to enter my e-mail to unlock it. I need Internet."

"Get him out of here! Let this dog open the phone and bring him back!"

He was led up a flight of stairs, blindfold and handcuffs removed. He hit the hard-reset command to delete Skype and Facebook. He couldn't do anything about the photos. The guard didn't seem to realize what Suleiman had done. The phone restarted and the guard led his prisoner back into the room.

The interrogator lingered on the photos of Suleiman's female friends in Turkey, describing their physical details with a lewdness that disgusted Suleiman. The interrogator wanted their names. Suleiman made up fake ones. He had photos of Rastan's defectors, too, but they were images available online. At least he hadn't posed with any of them. He was asked to account for the photos.

"I downloaded them from the Internet, *sidi*," Suleiman said. "I follow the news about my country and that's why I have them."

"You really are a son of a bitch, aren't you?" the interrogator said. "Take him down!"

He was back in the tire.

"Focus on his feet until you strip the skin off his soles."

He didn't know how long it lasted. He didn't know he could scream like that. That he could hurt like that. That he could survive that. His feet, his spine, his backside, his head. His body throbbed.

"Stand up!"

"*Sidi*, I can't."

"Stand up!"

He rose on bleeding feet.

"Okay, now we can begin," the interrogator said. "What is your role in these events?" It was an open-ended question. No clue about what he knew or wanted to know.

"I swear, *sidi*, I don't have a . . . ." Swish. The flexible rod again.

"*Sidi*, I participated in a protest!"

"A protest, you son of a bitch? Bring the electricity."

A splash of cold then heat slicing through him. Tingling. Numbness. He drifted in and out of consciousness, grateful for the periods of darkness. Revived with water, the cycle was repeated, how many times he couldn't tell.

"Four demonstrations, *sidi*!" he eventually said.

"You still haven't confessed, you son of a bitch. What was your role in filming? Who did you finance?"

So he knew. Suleiman pleaded ignorance. He did what he said he wouldn't do. He blamed his dead friend Merhi Merhi. He said Merhi duped him into filming a protest once. They'd already killed Merhi, they couldn't hurt him any more, but they could stop hurting Suleiman.

"Get out!" yelled the interrogator.

Suleiman walked out on the bloody, sluffed soles of his feet. He tried standing on his tiptoes, but that hurt even more. He didn't yet know that four of his toenails had been yanked out. He was in another room, hand-cuffed to another radiator, sitting on the floor with paper and a pen to write his confession. His blindfold removed, he saw his blood. It dripped on the paper. The guard wasn't happy about that. He handed Suleiman clean sheets. Suleiman bled on them, too. He filled the first page with biographical information, the rest with lies. He stuck to his story of four protests and being tricked into filming them by his dead friends and others whose names he made up. He didn't want to hurt anyone. He also didn't want to be asked for more information. He was allowed to rinse off some of his blood before being led back to the communal cell, where he collapsed on the floor.

"Nobody talks to this dog!" the guard told the room. "Nobody asks him any questions or does anything for him."

The door slammed. Suleiman felt the prisoners lifting him. Some of the men stood, offering their patch of floor so that Suleiman could lie down. They raised his legs against the wall to try and stem the bleeding. Somebody placed clothes under his head like a pillow. They gently wiped his feet with the scraps that remained of their own clothes. Somebody massaged his hands and whispered into his ear: "The important thing is you're still alive," the voice said, over and over. "Others died on their first night. You are still alive."

MOHAMMAD

Mohammad stopped running guns. Others could do that. He switched to smuggling Islamist foreign fighters, or *muhajireen*. The first one he stole across the Turkish border into Syria was a Moroccan, in September 2011. Then Tunisians, Libyans, Lebanese, Egyptians, and other Arabs. Europeans and Americans followed. Many came to implement Sharia in a cosmopolitan land the Quran said was blessed. For some, religion was an afterthought, for men searching for purpose, power, adventure, or refuge from trouble back home. Others were simply sick of watching Muslims dying and begging for help. Syrians, in their abundant hospitality and desperate pragmatism, accepted them, but not necessarily their ideas.

Mohammad grew up idolizing the Chechen *mujahideen*. He helped sneak some of his heroes across the border. They didn't have far to travel, since most were refugees and migrants who'd fled Russian aggression years earlier to settle in Turkey. By mid-2012, the Chechens aggregated in the towns of Doreen and Salma, a patch of Latakia Province that the Free Syrian Army had freed of Assad's troops. The battlefield reputation of the Chechens was unparalleled: "Martyrs would fall in front of them and they wouldn't stop, they'd keep pushing forward, on the offensive, pushing, pushing," Mohammad said. "We aren't like that. After seeing them, I was determined that we must have *muhajireen* [foreign fighters] like them fighting with us."

The *muhajireen* were aided by a Turkish policy that for years focused less on who went into Syria than who came out, and even then the policy was lax. The foreign fighters were easy to spot on domestic flights from Istanbul to southern Turkey—men with scant luggage, long beards, and short pants worn above the ankle in the manner of the Prophet Mohammad. One overheard them at airports, discussing plans in various Arabic dialects and Western accents.

Several Turkish airports were jumping-off points to different parts of Syria: Hatay was the gateway to Idlib and Latakia Provinces. Gaziantep led to Aleppo, andȘanlıurfa was on the road to Raqqa. The 822-kilometer Turkish–Syrian frontier, in all its variegated beauty, was a sieve. Smuggling routes, like those used by Mohammad, predated the Syrian revolution. Many were so well known they had names: *the barrel*; *the fishery*; *the olives*. They varied in length, difficulty, and terrain. There were goat tracks etched into pine-covered slopes, grassy clearings with no tree cover (you had to sprint through those sections). Routes through foliage so thick it could whip you in the face if you weren't careful. Steep climbs that tested footing on loose stones and dirt. Streams crossed via fallen logs or by climbing trees.

After Syrian border posts with Turkey fell in mid-2012, it became easier. A person could walk through the formal crossings—even without a passport if it was a one-way trip into Syria. Some illegal routes operated in full view of the Turkish military. In the Turkish village of Hacıpaşa, where a constriction of the Orontes River marked the border, it was like a game. Smugglers on the Syrian side openly waited and watched soldiers on the other bank. When the Turkish armored personnel carriers drove away, the smugglers ushered clients into a round metal tub, and, guided by rope strung from tree to tree, crossed the river. From there, it was a tractor ride to the main road. Getting to Atmeh, a border town in Idlib Province visible from Turkey, meant dashing across flat red earth under Turkish guard towers and stepping over coiled razor wire or through a hole in the chain-link fence into an olive grove near a field of cucumbers. A good smuggler would time the dash to coincide with personnel shifts in the towers. (Atmeh and Hacıpaşa were the two sites where the Farouq's Bilal Attar and Abu Hashem first smuggled weapons into Syria.) Night crossings were hardest—relying on the light of the moon in darkness so intense it was difficult to see the person ahead. Turkish border guards either were willfully blind or shooed people back. Sometimes (especially at night), they unleashed dogs. Some expected bribes. The polite ones didn't specify amounts. A guard once allowed me to squeeze into Turkey through the vertical bars of a locked border gate. It cost less than $10.

Mohammad focused on trails into his area of operations—Idlib and Latakia Provinces. He checked every *muhajir*'s references, or *tazkiya*. It was part of Jabhat al-Nusra's mandatory vetting process for foreigners—somebody within Al-Qaeda had to vouch for the recruit. "If a man came without formal *tazkiya*," Mohammad once explained, "I'd contact somebody I knew from the same country who was working and tell him that I wanted a background check on him before I brought him in." He didn't turn away those lacking *tazkiya*—he sent them to his old prison friends who now headed battalions in a Salafi armed group called Ahrar al-Sham. Some found their way independently to other Islamist fighting cadres, or, less commonly, to units of the Free Syrian Army. Sometimes Mohammad sent them to a small camp of foreign fighters near Atmeh run by a Saudi-born Syrian dentist, an "Afghan Arab" who had trained with Al-Qaeda in Afghanistan. The man, Firas al-Absi, was independent of Al-Qaeda in Syria. Mohammad didn't get along with him. He met Absi twice and twice rejected Absi's offer to join him. "There was an ideological dispute between us," Mohammad said. "Absi believed that what he'd liberated was Islamic land and the rest was the land of disbelievers, whereas our view was that it was all Islamic land that needed to be liberated. He was ideologically inflexible."

Absi was ISIS before there was ISIS. On July 19, 2012, he strutted along the broad boulevard of Bab al-Hawa (Gate of the Wind), the first Syrian border post with Turkey won by rebels. Clad in a white short-sleeve shirt under an ammunition vest, a green camouflage cap hiding his bald spot, Absi casually carried his rifle upside down, flanked by three armed men and a fourth waving the black flag of the Islamic State of Iraq. Absi made a proclamation at Bab al-Hawa that day: "Praise be to God, we triumphed over the dogs, the dogs of Bashar and their allies," he said.

"We, the *mujahideen*, announce from here the establishment of an Islamic state by the will of Almighty God. We will rule by Sharia and will not disobey the commands of God on his earth."

He wouldn't rule anything. Abu Azzam's Farouq Battalions would see to that.

MOHAMMAD DID more than smuggle *muhajireen* across the border and farm them out to battalions. He was a hustler. Street smart, ruthless, calculating, and—until 2013—covert. The *muhajireen* with whom he interacted knew he was Jabhat al-Nusra and Al-Qaeda. That was, after all, why they contacted him. But others, including Syrian rebels in the political and armed opposition, didn't know who he really was—not even that he was with Jabhat al-Nusra. He had honed the practice of hiding what he termed his "other self."

Mohammad infiltrated rebel circles in Turkey and Syria to gather intelligence on what others ostensibly on the same side were doing. One summer night in mid-2012, he attended a meeting of two British diplomats and several Syrian aid workers in a hotel lobby in Antakya. Mohammad was there posing as a refugee with fresh details about conditions inside Syria. The aid workers had learned shortly before the start of the meeting that the diplomats weren't bringing a translator, and they asked me to interpret. The British pair did not know I was a journalist.

In theory, the diplomats—a political officer and a military attaché—were there to discuss donating humanitarian aid, but their questions over three hours were about Jabhat al-Nusra and other armed groups. The aid workers tried to steer the conversation back to humanitarian issues, but the diplomats wanted an exchange—intelligence for food and tents. The Syrians resented what was asked of them. Mohammad smirked more than he spoke. He wasn't impressed with the diplomats' shallow knowledge of the Syrian battlefield. He rarely attended meetings after that. Instead, he developed moles, men he equipped with cameras concealed in shirt buttons, pens, eyeglasses, and watches. He ordered the devices via the

Internet and used *muhajireen* traveling from Europe as mules. "If they were going to spy on us," he later told me, showing me the devices, "I was going to spy on them."

MOHAMMAD WAS ONE type of Jabhat al-Nusra operative, Saleh was another—a young Syrian graduate of Sednaya Prison who was part of the group's inner leadership circle. Saleh wasn't impressed with his new Nusra colleagues. He didn't even think they were really *tanzim*, Al-Qaeda, because "they weren't strong, they weren't what I expected, they seemed like regular guys." Saleh was an aide to Jabhat al-Nusra's number two, an Iraqi named Abu Maria al-Qahtani who served as the group's lead *Shari'iy,* or religious official. Abu Maria was based in Saleh's hometown, the eastern Syrian city of Deir Ezzor, where the Nusra *Shari'iy* had lived since 2010 after he crossed into Syria for medical treatment. Saleh had been with Abu Maria since late 2011. "I understand you don't believe that we're really Al-Qaeda," Abu Maria told his aide one day in spring. "We are part of Al-Qaeda in Afghanistan, but we came via Iraq. They sent us. If you like, go to Iraq and meet the *shabab*."

Saleh had tried to meet the *shabab* before—in 2005, when America was in Iraq. He was not quite nineteen at the time, a first-year university student in the health sciences, when, along with about a dozen of his friends, he decided to fight the Americans in Iraq. The men didn't make it across the border. An informer landed them all behind Sednaya's black door. Saleh didn't pray regularly, let alone consider himself an Islamist before he was imprisoned, although he'd started reading banned Islamist literature. Six years in Sednaya made him a Salafi Jihadi. He was released on April 28, 2011, with no formal charge, as part of Assad's amnesty.

In spring 2012, Saleh accepted Abu Maria's invitation to meet the *shabab* in Iraq. He spent May in Mosul and the Anbari desert, the last patches of Islamic State of Iraq's fading influence, an authority exerted through extortion and violence. "They were very weak in Iraq at that time, poor things," Saleh recalled. "Very weak, but they still controlled areas." The Iraqi border guards he regularly encountered seemed weaker. "They could see us in our [Toyota] HiLux pickups. We were armed, they were armed. They'd turn off the lights and pretend they didn't see us. They must have been scared. Why would a soldier want to die? We were either smugglers or *tanzim*."

Saleh returned to Syria in mid-June, convinced of Jabhat al-Nusra's still-secret pedigree. Abu Maria dispatched him to Damascus to work with Nusra leader Abu Mohammad al-Jolani, or *al-sheikh al fatih*, the conqueror sheikh, as Jolani was called. Saleh joined Jolani's inner circle, a group of men so young "none of us have any gray in our beards."

Jolani and his deputy, Abu Maria, were soaking up cells of Sednaya men already active and those waiting for something like it to emerge, through word of mouth and handwritten letters delivered by couriers. The Sednaya graduates knew Nusra was Al-Qaeda, but the group was careful to hide its lineage from others, as per instructions from Al-Qaeda leader Ayman al-Zawahiri. It wasn't the first time Al-Qaeda had set such a condition. Its founder, Osama bin Laden, once counseled Somalia's Al-Shabab group to hide its ties to his organization because, "once it becomes declared and out in the open, it would have the enemies escalate their anger and mobilize against you."

Bin Laden knew Al-Qaeda had an image problem—attributed, among other things, to the methods of its rogue Iraqi affiliate. The group founded by Abu Musab al-Zarqawi imposed harsh diktats on Iraqis, beheaded enemies, bombed marketplaces full of civilians, and killed Muslims as indiscriminately as others. In January 2011, according to a letter retrieved from Bin Laden's Pakistani hideout in Abbottabad after his death in May 2011, the American jihadist Adam Gadahn had advised Al-Qaeda's leadership to "declare its discontent with the behavior . . . being carried out by the so-called Islamic State of Iraq, . . . otherwise its reputation will be damaged more and more as a result of the acts and statements of this group, which is labeled under our organization."

Jolani did not intend to replicate his Iraqi parent's methods or be sullied by its reputation. He had plans to ingratiate Jabhat al-Nusra into the Syrian uprising without the baggage of its heritage. Syria would serve as the stage for an Al-Qaeda reboot, using as foot soldiers the graduates of Sednaya Prison and Palestine Branch. "We will show our values, deal with people well," Saleh remembered Jolani saying, "and then after a while we'll tell them, 'The Al Qaeda that was smeared in the media? This is it. We are it. What do you think of us—Jabhat al-Nusra?'"

In July 2012, Jolani left his base in the Syrian capital, accompanied by aides including Saleh. They shuffled between Nusra positions in rebel-held parts of the northern provinces of Idlib and Aleppo, traveling at night, without headlights and guided by GPS. Jolani appraised his men incognito, often using the alias Abu Abdullah and telling local Nusra commanders that he was an emissary of "the conqueror sheikh." He micromanaged his organization and followed up his visits with detailed handwritten letters to commanders, lauding a certain man or suggesting others be dismissed.

Jolani was calm and confident, disciplined, a man who listened intently and thought strategically. He often hid in plain sight of the regime, at one point taking a public bus to Deir Ezzor to see his deputy, Abu Maria, and at another renting an apartment in Kafr Hamra—a town in the Aleppan countryside that was still controlled by the regime—to escape intense bombardments raining on rebel-held territory. Like Abu Maria, Jolani was always armed with a pistol and an explosives belt, even in the bathroom, even when Saleh said they were "very safe."

Jolani's travels made it clear to him that he needed a higher caliber of commander. He could rely on the Iraq veterans among the Sednaya graduates—they at least had experience, but many others didn't. He asked Iraq to send battle-hardened senior men, and Abu Bakr al-Baghdadi obliged. The second wave of leaders entered Syria in the last days of Ramadan 2012, a year after Jolani's trek. They came in two batches. The first included the Iraqi emir of Mosul, as well as a young Syrian firebrand named Abu Mohammad al-Adnani, who hadn't been home to Binnish in Idlib Province for a decade. Adnani arrived with a title—Baghdadi had appointed him Nusra's general *amni*, or security official, essentially responsible for Nusra's version of the *mukhabarat*.

The second group, an eight-man team, was met at the Syria–Iraq border by Jolani himself, and Saleh. It was led by Abu Bakr al-Baghdadi's deputy, Hajji Bakr, a former colonel in Saddam's army. Jolani had asked Iraq for reinforcements, but he could not have foreseen the impact the new arrivals would have on his organization. "They came," said Saleh, "and our troubles began."

BY MID-SEPTEMBER 2012, Jabhat al-Nusra established a more organized system of bringing foreign fighters into Syria, naming an "emir of the borders" to facilitate their entry. The emir, or commander, Abu Ahmad *al-hudood* (of the borders), was part of Jolani's original group of eight in August 2011. Al-Qaeda's central command in Afghanistan pitched in with details of coordinators in Tunisia and the Arabian Peninsula who sent men to Turkey. The *muhajireen* were picked up outside Hatay Airport, never inside it, to avoid security cameras. Nusra dedicated two cars to the airport run. "On the slowest day, there'd be five; the busiest day, fifteen," said a Nusra insider with knowledge of the operations. Four halfway homes were rented in Hatay: two in the main city, Antakya, one in Reyhanlı (not far from the Bab al-Hawa border crossing), and one in Kırıkhan, in the northeast, each location functioning as a separate cell, unaware of the others. There were seven phone numbers (changed every few weeks) solely for the *muhajireen* project. There were so many Tunisians they had their own line.

Mohammad was a cell leader within the operation, focused on border crossings, but he was otherwise unaware of others doing the same thing. It was a common practice within covert groups to run independent cells oblivious of each other so that if one should be compromised, it could not endanger others.

Saleh watched the influx with concern. The *muhajireen* weren't heeding Nusra's instructions to tone down their appearance at airports. The foreign fighters "were coming with long beards, it was obvious what they were there for," Saleh said. "Some of these people, how were they living in the West? They were so backward."

But the Turks didn't seem to care. Nusra sent more than fighters into Syria from Turkey. It transported satellite communication devices, phones, and fertilizer (for use in improvised explosive devices). Saleh once even sent bullets through the official Bab al-Hawa crossing. "The Turks didn't even check," he said. "They didn't care about what you were taking into Syria, just what you were bringing out." And even then, they were lax.

SALEH WAS CAREFUL never to be photographed with Jabhat al-Nusra, never to appear in any of the group's video or audio recordings. He had a fake Syrian ID for entering Turkey and could blend into a café in Istanbul as easily as into a Nusra training camp. Jolani made him an *amni*, a security official, one of Nusra's many, to work under Adnani, the man Baghdadi appointed to head Nusra's *mukhabarat*. Saleh was tasked with gathering intelligence on "people who had issues with the *tanzim* in Iraq, people who had defected" and fled to Turkey. He filed his reports to Jolani and Adnani. The two men had different ideas about what to do with the information. Adnani wanted defectors in Turkey assassinated with silenced pistols. Jolani forbade operations across the border. "The sheikh [Jolani] used to say, 'Do not fire a single bullet outside of Syria,' " said Saleh. He ordered his men to disarm before entering Turkey, a rule Saleh disliked: "I wanted to enter Turkey with my [explosive] belt and weapons, I couldn't go in naked, but [Jolani] would not hear of it. He said he didn't want problems with Turkey."

Saleh had issues with Adnani, who had ordered him to assassinate an Iraqi defector Saleh had tracked to Aksaray in Istanbul—an order Saleh knew couldn't have been approved by Jolani. He reported it to Jolani, who instructed Saleh to ignore Adnani but to lead him on: "Say yes, yes, but don't do it."

The rift within Nusra's senior leadership over working in Turkey soon blew open. The Syrian political opposition was due to hold a conference in a Turkish hotel. By chance, the Turkish caterer was the friend of a Turk who supplied Nusra with security cameras and manufactured the remote detonators for its IEDs, devices Saleh took into Syria. The Turk asked Saleh to deliver a message to Jolani: "He said a friend was going to set up a conference room for a meeting of the Syrian political opposition, and he wanted to know if the brothers in Syria were interested in doing anything about it. It could be arranged."

Jolani said no. "He said we don't want to blow something up there, Turkey is our lungs. We don't want the security services there to turn on us, they will paralyze our movement," recalled Saleh. Jolani cited Al-Qaeda leader Ayman al-Zawahiri's orders banning attacks inside Turkey, given its role as a major conduit for men, money, and munitions, as well as its anti-Assad policies.

Jolani mentioned the opposition meeting to a senior Iraqi Nusra leader he revered like a father. The Iraqi was Abu Ali al-Anbari, a veteran of both the Afghan and the Iraqi jihads. Abu Ali al-Anbari wanted to blow up the Syrian political opposition in Turkey. So did Adnani. Jolani refused. Word of Jolani's intransigence quickly crossed the border to Iraq. It did not please Abu Bakr al-Baghdadi.

EVEN THOUGH NUSRA's inner circle was bickering, on the ground the new Syrian Al-Qaeda prototype had smoothly become a key player in the armed uprising. The Sednaya men were its backbone. The Turkish border was open. Nusra's Iraqi parent paid half its bills, while the rest of the funding came from private donors and war spoils. Jolani was organizing his cadres. His Al-Qaeda background remained hidden. Jabhat al-Nusra was disciplined, effective, spearheading some of the most audacious attacks against the regime, using methods like suicide bombings, which few others employed. Its Iraq veterans manufactured IEDs that worked, copper-lined shaped charges that could penetrate armor—the same IEDs they'd once used against Americans. Its men fought alongside others, including the Free Syrian Army, but, after battle, kept to themselves. They were religiously conservative but initially didn't impose their beliefs on civilians. Later, toward the end of 2012, they began interacting with local communities only to provide social services like distributing flour to bakeries, to keep bread in Aleppo at its prewar price of 15 Syrian pounds. The group avoided indiscriminate civilian casualties and even made an effort—as in one video claiming responsibility for a blast on March 20, 2012, and telling local Christians they were not the target—to reassure the broader population outside its Sunni base. Still, some of its sectarian language was harsh, especially against Alawites, and would only get worse. Nusra considered non-Muslims infidels, but, as a Nusra commander once told me, "That doesn't mean that if he's an infidel I should kill him." But it did afford the person a form of second-class citizenship. That summer, Jabhat al-Nusra's flag—a stylized *Shahada* (declaration of faith) above the group's name—was more often printed in black lettering on white, instead of the black flags of Nusra, ISIS, and other Islamist groups that would soon become ubiquitous. The colors were reversed, one of the printers told me, "so that people don't think we have Al-Qaeda here."

For many of Syria's fighting men in rebel-held areas, it became a status symbol to be accepted into Jabhat al-Nusra's vaunted ranks, given that would-be recruits were routinely turned away—unlike other armed groups that accepted anyone, keen to beef up their numbers and their profiles on YouTube. "We pay a great deal of attention to the individual fighter, we are concerned with quality, not quantity," a Jabhat al-Nusra commander in Aleppo once told me. Men who didn't pray were rejected. So were smokers (because smoking was a sin). More interested in a man's mind than his military prowess, Nusra worked on both. A potential recruit undertook a ten-day religious-training course, "to ascertain his understanding of religion, his morals, his reputation," and, only after that, a fifteen-to-twenty-day military-training program. Successful recruits swore *bayaa*, or a pledge of allegiance, to Jabhat al-Nusra, essentially a religious vow to follow the chain of command. The Free Syrian Army had no such means to enforce discipline.

In December 2012, the United States designated Jabhat al-Nusra a terrorist organization, identifying it as an alias of Al-Qaeda in Iraq. The terrorist label did not isolate the group within Syria. Instead, anti-Assad

Syrians rallied around what was one of their most effective fighting forces, a group that still hid its Al-Qaeda lineage. On December 14, the first Friday after the designation, Syrians across the country marched under the slogan THE ONLY TERRORISM IN SYRIA IS ASSAD'S. Dozens of rebel groups publicly declared, "We are all Jabhat al-Nusra." Even the leadership of the political opposition in exile—which Nusra didn't recognize—condemned the terrorist label. Just a year after it had announced its presence in Syria, Jabhat al-Nusra had achieved what Osama bin Laden had dreamed of— a formidable force with strong popular support.

RUHA

Ruha's father, Maysaara, returned home to Saraqeb on July 15, 2012. He'd spent months in hiding, recuperating from gunshots sustained in an ambush that killed his friend Abu Rabieh. He'd been in the desert flatlands between Idlib and Raqqa under the protection of a tribal sheikh, and then eight weeks in Turkey. The three-car Free Syrian Army convoy of relatives that escorted him from the Turkish border honked like a wedding procession when it turned into his alleyway. Ruha and her siblings—Alaa, Mohammad, and Tala—waited outside their front door like coiled springs, pouncing on their father when he stepped out of the car. He scooped up his two youngest and walked into his mother's living room. Zahida was in her usual spot, the faded blue couch. Maysaara knelt before his mother and kissed her cheeks. She took his bearded face in her hands: "Why have you come back?" she asked.

He laughed. "Is that any way to greet your son?"

"I'm happy to see you, but I'm afraid for you. You should leave."

Saraqeb was disfigured, broken, changed after a four-day military assault in March. Twenty-four civilians had been executed and more than a hundred homes torched in fires Assad's men lit and fed with liquid flames, including Aunt Mariam's apartment. Another eleven homes were destroyed by tank fire, forty-six more damaged but still livable. In the *souq*, the corrugated-metal store shutters were peppered with bullet holes, blown out, and twisted into macabre art by the heat and force of explosions. No two looked alike. It had all happened as Kofi Annan, the United Nations Special Envoy to Syria, had peddled a six-point peace plan. Assad said he backed Annan's initiative, even as Syrian troops stormed Saraqeb and other towns in Idlib Province.

On March 27, the military withdrew from Saraqeb but left four outposts behind. A dairy factory in the northern neighborhood and an olive oil factory in the southern neighborhood became barracks. A checkpoint called Kaban was created, and snipers were planted at the Iza'a (a radio communications tower). Four Free Syrian Army groups in Saraqeb opposed them, including one Maysaara helped finance, as well as non-FSA Islamist groups and a small contingent of Jabhat al-Nusra fighters who kept to themselves.

Ruha's mother and siblings, her grandmother, and her Uncle Mohammad and his wife Noora fled to their farm during the incursion, living in its supply room. Ruha's Aunt Mariam stayed in town with one of her sisters, haunted by "ghoulish" cries that kept her awake and the sounds of storefronts being smashed and looted.

Mariam lost everything in the March fire. Her white plastic chairs and kitchen table melted into smooth, hard puddles. She couldn't tell whether the heaps of ash were once her clothes, cushions, quilts, or books. Her ceiling fans drooped like wilted flowers. She remembered thinking they looked beautiful. She walked out of her home with a partially melted coin collection in a metal box. That was all she kept. Her neighbors weren't allowed to put out the fire, although one tossed a hose from his kitchen window through hers. "One of my neighbors asked the security forces, 'Why are you burning the home of an old lady and her niece?' They said, 'You don't know anything. Terrorists visit her home.' They were talking about my nephews and brothers, and brothers-in-law."

Mariam suspected that a neighbor's son had informed security forces about her family visits. She'd tutored him in the ninth grade. "I am not annoyed or upset," she said. "God compensates the oppressed. I forgive them. If it will stop here, I swear I do. Let them burn the house, we'll build something better, as long as nothing happens to any of us. We are two single women who had never protested and they burned our house. If they did that to us, what is going to happen to Syria?" Mariam and her frail aunt, Zahida's older sister, moved in with her mother, Zahida.

Ruha wore one of her best dresses—pink with yellow polka dots—the day Baba came home, but she quickly changed into the new Turkish clothes Maysaara had bought his children. She didn't even pause to take off the tags. The house was full of aunts and cousins. It felt like Mother's Day. For the first time, Ruha was relieved, not afraid, that Baba was home. "I wasn't scared because I saw that he was carrying a gun, he could defend himself a little bit," she said. "Before, he had nothing except his voice."

She knew her father was part of something called the Free Syrian Army. She'd heard the adults talk about it. She had worried that his injuries might have incapacitated him, but he looked the same, except for the Kalashnikov that never left his side, his green ammunition vest, and the grenade he carried at all times, even during meals and when he played with his children. "I'd rather die a thousand deaths than be captured by them," he'd often say. It was a common refrain. One of his adult nephews walked around with a plastic bag full of grenades that bulged like lemons. Maysaara may have looked the same as before, but the murder of his friend Abu Rabieh hadn't merely changed him—he said it destroyed him. "It is like a piece of shrapnel lodged in my heart," he said. "I wanted them all dead."

WAR ARRIVES SUDDENLY, uninvited, and brings with it a new normal. It has its own cadence, its own logic. It is the mundane experienced through heightened, sometimes supercharged emotions. The daily rhythm of life goes on, as it must, but with a constant undercurrent of tension, a baseline permanently shifted with the knowledge that a single abrupt event at any time—a knock on the door, an artillery shell, a sniper's bullet—can upend everything. The commonness of death cheapens life. Mourning periods—typically weeks, months, and years long, depending on a person's relationship to the deceased—become abbreviated. Otherwise, as Mariam said, much of Saraqeb would be draped in black. The town's rebels called ahead to the gravedigger before they went on a mission. Some paid his fee of 2,500 Syrian pounds in advance, so their families wouldn't have to. Government snipers were stationed near the graveyard, hunting the bereaved. To avoid them, townsfolk often buried the dead at night, hastily and with little ritual.

There were daily power cuts now, sometimes for nine hours, sometimes for two. Ruha's family switched from an electric burner to a gas stove, although the gas cylinders that once cost 275 pounds were now 3,000. Bread remained at its prewar price, but the fresh produce in the market—onions, potatoes, beans, and cucumbers harvested nearby—were inflated by a factor of at least three. The family could still afford what it didn't grow. Others couldn't. Cell-phone and Internet coverage had been out since October 2011, but the landlines still worked. Indiscriminate artillery fire was the new background noise. Doors were kept open so they wouldn't blow off their hinges from the force of the blasts, windows were slightly ajar to not shatter against each other. After every round of shelling, Ruha's Uncle Mohammad would conduct a family headcount by phone to check on everyone and try to locate the strikes.

The town had become a canvas, a character telling its own story. Cinderblocks—added to already high fences around homes near snipers—spoke of terror. Those streets had new names, too. One was dubbed "Moharram [Forbidden] Street," because, after 8 p.m., regime snipers made it too dangerous to cross. Families still lived there. Where else would they go, mused one woman—to the humiliation of a refugee camp or to burden relatives? Walls displayed great blasts of color, through painted murals and graffitied messages, especially around Saraqeb's cultural center. WHERE WERE THE ISLAMISTS WHEN THE REVOLUTION STARTED? appeared on one wall. The response, beneath it, was equally curt: IN PRISON. Spongebob Squarepants marched across a wall carrying a Syrian revolutionary flag. Handala was there, too, the iconic image of a barefoot Palestinian refugee child in tattered clothing, hands clasped behind his turned back, strands of thorny hair sprouting from his head. He faced a brick wall above the phrase I SWEAR, WE HAVE PAID ENOUGH. The poetry of Palestine's Mahmoud Darwish was magnified in sweeping calligraphy: AND WE LOVE LIFE, IF WE FIND A WAY TO IT. One wall, in

black and red, bore a simple message: THE BEST OF HISTORY IS WHAT HAP-
PENS TOMORROW.

Yesterday's neighbors, meanwhile, had become today's enemies, as
differences—social, economic, religious, tribal—were magnified to confirm the otherness of the other side. One morning, a sticky bomb, a small
explosive attached to a magnet or adhesive, was planted on the car of an
alleged regime informer. He lived a few streets from Ruha's home. The
blunt boom wounded but didn't kill the man. The women of the family
looked up from their morning coffee when they heard the noise. "This is a
revolution of the streets," one of Maysaara's sisters said after the target was
identified, "and the streets know each other."

One of Maysaara's nieces and her teenage daughter, Lama, lived in
Saraqeb's closest house to the Iza'a and its resident sniper. "He's our
new neighbor," Lama joked. The sniper had shattered their windows.
They repaired them with fiberglass. He shot that, too. Lama would
crawl through the bedroom she shared with her single mother, certain
the man with the gun could see them. He'd emptied seven bullets into
their bedroom door. One night, he kept firing at the thin electrical
wire that attached their home to the grid until he snapped it. "I think
he was bored," Lama said. After a direct rocket strike splintered a
door and crushed a wall, mother and daughter moved out and into the
family complex.

Mariam lived in fear of men storming their home. She took shorter
showers lest she be caught naked or inappropriately dressed. Like her sisters and nieces, she slept fully clothed, including in a headscarf. But not
everything changed. One afternoon, Mariam and the other women of the
family sat in the inner courtyard, joking and laughing as they picked the
leaves off bundles of green *molokhia* stalks spread out on blankets in front
of them. Ruha and Alaa helped, too. The leaves were left to dry for days
before being stored for the winter *mouni*, or supplies, in a small room near
the laundry. The men watched from the adjoining cellar. "Why are they
bothering?" Maysaara asked. "Will we live till the winter?" One of his
brothers-in-law said he no longer allowed his family to gather in the same

space when thuds intensified. He scattered his children in different rooms so that if a bomb fell, somebody, he figured, might survive.

Ruha's mother, Manal, stepped away from the courtyard and into the kitchen to do the dishes. Her eldest daughter followed her, just as a bullet hit the outer kitchen wall. Manal shuddered. "It's just a sniper," Ruha told her mother. She knew it meant one shot, not a fusillade. "Mama is so scared of bullets," she said, smirking. She was embarrassed that her mother had flinched.

ON WEDNESDAY, JUNE 18, just after lunch, one of those things happened—a single abrupt event that could upend everything. It took the form of an audacious, unprecedented attack on the heart of the regime in Damascus. By chance, there was electricity and the television was on, so Mariam heard the breaking news that several members of Assad's inner circle were killed in an explosion during a meeting at the National Security Bureau in the capital. Defense Minister Daoud Rajha, Deputy Defense Minister Assef Shawkat (who was also Assad's brother-in-law), and the head of the president's crisis management office, Hassan Turkomani, all died instantly. A fourth official, the director of the bureau Hisham Ikhtiar, would later succumb to his wounds. Mariam let out a shriek, lifting her shaking hands to her cheeks. "Thank God, thank God," she said. "Does it mean it is nearly over?"

Celebratory gunfire erupted even as some fighters in town admonished their comrades to save the bullets. "We will need them!" To which came the reply, "Not today!" Gunfire intermingled with cries of "*Allahu Akbar!*" from the town's mosques, and a message to loyalist troops in the four outposts was broadcast over a mosque's loudspeaker: "Your leaders are dead. You are our brothers! Join us! We will open our homes to you."

On Arabic satellite channels, reports poured in of defections elsewhere, of checkpoints overrun, their booty of tanks, weapons, and ammunition falling into rebel hands. "What is wrong with us? Why haven't we done anything yet?" asked one of Mariam's nephews. "Is it real? Is it really almost over?" another in the Free Syrian Army asked his aunt. "I'm so sick of guns, bullets, bombs."

It wasn't over. Shortly before 11 p.m., a rocket plowed the street outside the home of the Brek family. Minutes later, a house painter was outside a base of rebel fighters. He was still in his beige work clothes, splattered with dark green and white paint, and blood. He fell to his knees, red-faced and sweaty, and unfurled a bloody white blanket with pale blue stripes. "People! People! Dear God! Somebody, anybody! Look what they have done! Look! Dear God, oh my God!"

The fighters ran outside. A toddler was wrapped in the blanket. She was wearing a blue T-shirt and white shorts, barefoot, with patches of blood on her pudgy legs. She no longer had a face, her head a squashed blob of flesh. "She's not the only one!" the painter screamed. He collapsed, deflated, near the child, sweat and tears streaming from him. The young fighters tried to console him with words about God's will that he didn't want to hear. They told him to take the child to the town's hospital, for what he didn't know. She was dead.

At the hospital, the little girl's mother lay dead on a stretcher, her deep red clothes soaked in bright red blood. Young men screamed, *"Allahu Akbar!"* in sorrow and anger. One swept up body bits from the floor. The rocket had killed the little girl, her mother, her brother, two aunts, and another woman from the Brek family, and wounded several others. A child in a long lilac shirt lay on the bloody floor. Her right arm was bandaged and she lay motionless, her eyes open. She looked dead. With great effort, the little girl raised her left hand and made the "V for victory" sign.

THURSDAY, JULY 19. Saraqeb's rebels had been preparing for what they feared would be an imminent attack by loyalists. State media had laid the groundwork for an offensive, reporting that Saraqeb's townspeople were asking the regime to free them of "terrorists" nested among them. Then, Wednesday's strike on Assad's inner circle reversed the momentum. Saraqeb's rebels, buoyed by a sense of invincibility, or perhaps inevitability, decided to attack the Kaban Checkpoint, one of the four posts in their town.

The battle began at 6 p.m. The first regime tank shell landed on the home of an Assad supporter—a good omen, the FSA men said. Their smugness turned to laughter when a man drove the white fire truck to put out a blaze near his home. "He's not from the fire department," a rebel said. "It's self-service."

Then, the sound of a thousand cars backfiring. Graceful arcs of red tracer fire, like a string of broken pearls, reaching toward the clouds, falling well short of the helicopter gunship circling overhead, arrogant in its altitude. Mortars unbuilt concrete without any warning until seconds before impact. Shells crashed and thudded into residential streets. The helicopter gunship unleashed its rockets with a whoosh. The electricity was out, but, an hour into the battle, several young activists fired up a generator, hooked up an Internet connection, and called nearby FSA units via Skype. "Listen, brother, the power is out here, so the line might cut. We need RPGs—two, three, as many as you have. Brother, it's a very difficult situation now! Mortars, tanks, and there's a helicopter too. Whoever can come, come!"

Armed men on motorbikes roared through empty streets. Most families, including Ruha's, hid in their homes. A crowd stood outside the Hassan Hospital, waiting to receive the wounded. Men shouted for stretchers as cars disgorged bloodied passengers. There weren't enough stretchers, so armed locals, many in mismatched military attire and civilian clothing, carried in their wounded colleagues, or their neighbors. A man died on the street outside. His bright red blood formed a thick pool in a dip in the asphalt, as the sad, angry, frantic crowd around him cried out, *"Allahu Akbar!"*

"Tell the people that there is no more room here!" a man yelled from the hospital steps. "Send them to Shifa [Hospital]." The cars kept coming. Broken bodies carried in, others carried out, mainly the dead. Grown men cried openly. The hospital floor was a mess of bloody footprints. The foyer was bursting with armed men trying to find out who was hurt, who was dead, even as the few remaining doctors shouted at them to get out to ease the overcrowding. Women asked about their sons.

A man hobbled in, unaccompanied, looking as though he'd been dipped in soot. Two children—a little girl, her head bandaged, and her younger brother, also wrapped in white gauze—walked out of the hospital, both covered in a fine concrete dust. Their tears had mixed with the dust, creating pasty rivulets from their eyes to their jawlines. Within two minutes, more than a dozen people were carried in. There weren't enough gurneys, so they lay on the bloody white tiles.

A woman in a striped burgundy-and-navy floor-length, long-sleeved dress made her way up the few broad steps to the hospital entrance. "Where is Saddam?" she screamed to anyone, to everyone. She turned from one man to the other with the same question: "Where is Saddam? I have lost his father today, I cannot lose him, too! I want my son!" She could barely stand. She seized on Khaled, a tall, middle-aged fighter with graying hair who wore a black ammunition vest and a Kalashnikov across his back. "Where is he?" she yelled. She grabbed him by his black vest. Khaled did not respond, could not even look at her. She slapped him across the face. "Where is my son?" Khaled turned away from the mother. Twenty minutes later, Saddam's mother ran out. "He's dead! He's dead!" she shouted. "My boy is dead!" She crumpled on the street outside the hospital, next to a pool of blood. But Saddam's mother would turn out to be wrong: A bullet had grazed her son's head, covering him in blood and leaving him unconscious, but he was alive.

"Empty the area, empty the area! Three tanks are moving toward us now!" The crowd outside the hospital scattered. Two teenage boys stood rooted in place, waiting with an empty orange stretcher.

Back at an FSA outpost at a school, armed fighters trickled in from the front and the hospitals. The Kaban Checkpoint was destroyed and the fifteen or so soldiers manning it all killed. "Nobody expected this kind of retaliation," a young fighter said. "They knew where we were, why didn't they come after us instead of the families? They are cowards."

At 9 p.m., the Hassan Hospital was still receiving wounded. A young girl, no older than four or five, was carried in by her father, followed by an older woman on a stretcher and a middle-aged man. "Get out!" the doctor told an armed man who had followed them in, sobbing like a child. "She is my aunty, this is my uncle," he said, pointing to the middle-aged couple, who were bleeding onto the floor.

The little girl begged for her mother. A nurse searched for a pair of scissors to cut away her blood-soaked pink T-shirt. "Don't be scared, my darling," the male doctor told her. The child had shrapnel in her bloodied left eye and at least two small pieces lodged in the left side of her neck, which was spurting blood. Her short black hair was in two ponytails tied with pink bands.

The base of the child's head was sliced open. The hospital generator hummed and sputtered and cut out three times within twenty minutes. The doctor paused, waiting for the power to come back on, before he resumed stitching the scalp at the base of the little girl's skull. There was no anesthetic.

By 10 p.m., the death toll was twenty-five. It would climb to thirty-five. Nobody counted the wounded. The armed men outside the hospital were angry, hyped up, ready to head back and fight, but in Ruha's home, her family questioned whether the attack on the checkpoint had been worth it. "Too high a price," Mariam said, shaking her head. "So much blood. Too much blood."

The mortars and whistling rockets continued well into the night. At 12:04 a.m., one of the town's mosques broadcast a message. This time, it wasn't directed at the loyalist troops surrounding Saraqeb, urging them to defect. It was for the townsfolk. "People of Saraqeb, there is a wounded twelve-year-old boy in the hospital. We don't know whose son he is."

FRIDAY, JULY 20. Another single abrupt event occurred, the kind that could upend everything, this one also relayed in a news flash, this time just before midday. The Russian ambassador to France had declared that Assad was ready to leave office "in an orderly way." Celebratory gunfire erupted in Saraqeb, just as it had two days earlier.

Families cooped up in their homes breathed in the streets. Neighbors congratulated each other. "Thank God, it's over," an old man in a red-and-white-checkered headdress said to himself. Women ululated. Teenage girls threw rice on fighters as they paraded through the streets. Young children dodged between vehicles to pick up spent cartridges and to gather candy tossed into the crowd. A parade snaked around town, skirting neighborhoods with active snipers before returning to the main street near the *souq*. Women sprayed the crowd with water from garden hoses, providing relief from a searing midday sun.

Before an hour was up, there would be whispers that perhaps the news wasn't true, that the Syrian Information Ministry had denied the comments by the Russian ambassador. Some would murmur it, but nobody, it seemed, wanted to broadcast it openly in the crowd. The war-weary people of Saraqeb needed something to celebrate.

Basil, a member of Maysaara's Free Syrian Army unit, leaned on the wall of his post along the main street, puffing on a cigarette. He rested his Kalashnikov on the ground and watched the celebration. "I am crazy with happiness!" said the twenty-nine-year-old. "You know, I only picked up this gun because I was sick of hearing something called 'peaceful' while our people were being killed. I felt it was impossible to beat Bashar peacefully. Weapons were the tool, but our strength came from our community." He was a welder before he became a fighter. He said he didn't like guns, but he wasn't ready to let go of his just yet. "My gun will stay with me until we are certain that he is gone," he said. "After that, I have two options—either I keep my weapon for my son so that he won't need to beg for a gun like his father did, or I will wait and see what becomes of this army. I will hand in my gun to the army—not Bashar's army, but the army of the Syrian Arab Republic, and I hope to never carry a gun against a Syrian again."

After forty minutes or so, the gathering thinned. People headed to the mosques for Friday prayers. Reality reasserted itself. Shelling resumed in the near distance, the discordant, symphonic cadence of war.

That evening, Mariam sat outside the family's front door watching her three nieces—Ruha, Alaa, and Tala—play in their street. The little girls crouched in their starting positions, each placing one leg in front of the other, ready to pounce on the count of three: "One, two, three!" Mariam said as the sisters raced, giggling, to the top of their sloping narrow lane before turning around and sprinting back toward their aunt.

The night was near pitch-black, the day's heat trapped in the air. The electricity was out, as usual, so the family moved outdoors into a timid breeze. Mariam watched her nieces play, thinking about the Brek family, who had suffered the rocket attack days earlier. "They were sitting here just like us," she said. "It's frightening what we have gotten used to. Death will find us if it wants to, if God wills it, but we are changing, becoming harder as human beings."

"Will you be with us at zero hour?" Mariam asked me.

"What does that mean?" Ruha said.

"It means when we've run out of time, when Annan's initiative and all the demonstrations mean nothing. When our fate will be decided," Mariam replied.

Ruha nodded. She had understood.

ABU AZZAM

Assad was losing the border posts. In late July, within days, rebels captured three crossings with Turkey and one with Iraq. Bab al-Hawa was the first, captured on July 19, the same day Saraqeb's rebels uprooted the Kaban Checkpoint and the town paid such a bloody price.

Firas al-Absi, the Islamist who was ISIS before ISIS, set up camp at Bab al-Hawa's so-called new gate, opposite Turkish border guards. Within weeks, the Farouq Battalions were based at the old gate, several kilometers deep inside Syria. Absi ran the black Islamic State of Iraq banner up the flagpole. In response, the Turks shut their end of Bab al-Hawa. The banner angered the Farouq and other rebels. Who was this Islamist tainting their revolution with an extremist symbol? It did not represent them. Even Mohammad, the Jabhat al-Nusra fighter funneling *muhajireen* into Syria, thought Absi's actions were foolish. "He was too quick to put up the black flag. It was too early," Mohammad said. He thought Absi should have moved on from Bab al-Hawa. "There was nothing more for him to do there, and his presence was an obstacle to others. It wasn't smart."

Nusra's leadership shared Mohammad's view. "Who did Absi think he was?" Saleh said. "He had about twenty men, that was it. Firas al-Absi was nothing. He didn't occupy a minute of our thinking, and he wasn't part of us. He started acting as if he was a representative of Al-Qaeda in Syria when he wasn't. Everybody was against his raising of the black flag. We, as Nusra, were against it. We didn't want a confrontation with the Turks."

Abu Azzam was transferred from Uqayribat, where he was securing and transporting weapons and ammunition along his stretch of the

Farouq's secret nationwide distribution network, to Bab al-Hawa, where he was appointed the Farouq's commander at the crossing. The battalion's leaders outlined his new mission: "They said there is this guy called Absi," Abu Azzam remembered. "We want you to try to come to terms with him, given your religious background."

Abu Azzam, clad in his Farouq military uniform, waited until nightfall before approaching Absi. It was Ramadan, when the lethargy of the dawn-to-dusk fast, coupled with an August heat, slowed everything. Absi had a cool arrogance, a calmness that only amplified the fearsomeness of his words. Abu Azzam appealed to history. He told Absi that the Prophet carried four flags—white, yellow, black, and red—and that none were inscribed. The problem wasn't the *Shahada* or the color of the banner over Bab al-Hawa, Abu Azzam said, "but why this flag that has come to symbolize Al-Qaeda?" It didn't represent Syrians who had yet to decide the shape of their post-Assad state.

For Absi, there was nothing to decide except when to implement Sharia. God had decreed rules and laws and a system of governance. It was not a matter of choice. As far as he was concerned, the black flag would remain and Bab al-Hawa would serve as the first outpost of an Islamic state.

Abu Azzam believed in both Sharia and a democracy that he said meant "nobody is forced to think anything." Democracy did not contradict his Islam. The imposition of Sharia—or anything else—did. "I won't put a gun to somebody's head and ask him, 'What do you think, should we apply Sharia or not?'" he told Absi. "But you and others, in the way you are imposing your ideas and expressing them, you are turning people away from Islam, even Muslims." The Farouq commander reminded Absi that the Quran they both followed decreed that "there is no compulsion in religion." Absi branded Abu Azzam an infidel and the Farouq Battalions Western agents. Both men, Absi and Abu Azzam, were Islamists, both Salafis, both Syrians, but they had nothing in common beyond those labels.

ABU HASHEM, the realtor-turned-Farouq-foreign-liaison, gave the order to remove Absi. The jihadi was alone when he was seized one night in the no-man's-land between Turkey and Syria at Bab al-Hawa. His body was found in a ditch near the crossing on September 5, days after he disappeared. The Farouq neither confirmed nor denied a role in his death. Absi's murder was the first shot fired by rebels against ultraconservative Islamists ostensibly on their side. Privately, Abu Hashem said he had no regrets: "We got rid of him and imposed the Farouq's control of the border crossing. It had to be done." The black flag came down.

Absi's men vowed revenge. His brother, Abu Atheer al-Absi, a Sednaya graduate fighting in Homs, took over his group. Later, Abu Atheer would pave the way for the rise of Islamic State, becoming the first commander in Syria to pledge allegiance to it, but that summer Abu Atheer was focused on settling a score. He issued a "wanted list" of sixteen members of the Farouq he suspected of involvement in his brother's murder, including Abu Azzam.

Abu Azzam was in Atmeh with Abu Hashem overseeing a shipment of weapons from Turkey the night Absi was snatched. "I wasn't there, but I wasn't against what happened to Absi," he said. "God bless the hands that removed him. We should have killed them all, every one of them who thought like him, the beards who tried to hijack our revolution. That was our mistake."

THE ISTANBUL ROOM wasn't a physical space with an address. It was more a concept, a label, a mess. The Lebanese politician Okab Sakr, representing Saad Hariri and the Saudis, was at its core, alongside a Turkish intelligence official and a civilian Syrian representative of Qatar (not a defector). The three distributors were a level below: two members of the Farouq—Bilal Attar (formerly of SNN) and Abu Hashem—and the Latakian Abu Fadel. The next level down were civilian middlemen, about two dozen, drawn from all of Syria's fourteen provinces, who, along with the trio of distributors, chose the recipients of free weapons and ammunition.

The middlemen were cycled in and out of the program. Some were accused of accepting bribes to add an FSA group to the list of beneficiaries, or demanding pledges of loyalty. Others sold the weapons and pocketed the funds. The bigger and higher-profile an armed group, the more likely it was to be a recipient, so commanders inflated their numbers.

Meetings were held in hotel conference rooms. Cell phones were always confiscated at the door. Those who challenged Okab Sakr—or his three distributors—weren't invited to subsequent gatherings. At one, a middleman from Latakia accused Abu Fadel of setting up his own patronage network. Sakr told the accuser to leave. "You're kicking me out? You get out! Syria is my country, not yours," the middleman said. "Who are you to order us around? To tell us where weapons should go and who should get them? You get out!" The Turkish intelligence agent, who rarely spoke during the proceedings, intervened. "Whoever says a wrong word about Okab Sakr," he said in perfect Arabic, "I am prepared to throw into prison until he rots." The message to participants was clear. "Either we follow them, and get lots of weapons, or we don't and die," a middleman from Damascus said.

Except there were never lots of weapons. The Istanbul Room was established to funnel supplies to men on the ground, and in so doing assert leverage over them. But the supplies, when they came, were inconsistent and insufficient, prompting fighters to look elsewhere. Rebels found private sponsors, bought weapons from inside Syria, smuggled them from abroad, manufactured their own, or joined non-FSA Islamist groups that generally had stronger support.

The FSA tried to establish the infrastructure of an institution. It formed military councils, one per province, to gather all the FSA groups in a particular area under its command. The military councils became part of the Istanbul Room operation, in a bid to organize it, although once again, the FSA's squabbling leaders in exile—the major general and the colonel—were not involved. The Idlib military council, for instance, had sixteen groups under its wing that summer. "We were asked to unite in order to get support," the defector heading the Idlib council, Colonel Afif Suleiman, said at the time. "The support didn't come, so people are saying, 'What did you give me so that I should stay with you?'" By August, there was another complication. The Istanbul Room's sponsors, Qatar and Saudi Arabia, fell out over which armed groups to support. The Qataris focused on the military councils but also had strong ties to the Syrian Muslim Brotherhood. The Saudis, via Sakr, were vehemently anti-Brotherhood. Sakr started handpicking battalions within each military council to support. He selected three of the sixteen in Idlib, infuriating the Idlib council chief so much that he complained directly to the Saudis. "We clarified the issue to our Saudi brothers about Okab," Colonel Afif Suleiman said. "They promised that there will be no support, either military or financial, except via the councils." That didn't happen.

Battalions started aligning with either the Saudis or the Qataris, or with private sponsors from Kuwait, the UAE, and elsewhere. The Americans scrambled to try to grasp the complexity of the battlefield. In an August trip to Istanbul, then–Secretary of State Hillary Clinton met with a group of Syrian civil activists in a bid to understand who was who on the ground. "She said, 'We want you to tell us who we should deal with and who we should avoid,'" one participant said. "I laughed. I swear I laughed. Can you imagine the US secretary of state saying that to a small group of activists, most of whom are under twenty-five? The US has no idea."

At the time, Washington was not dealing directly with the armed opposition but had authorized a nonprofit organization, the Syrian Support Group (SSG), to fundraise for the Free Syrian Army. The SSG comprised Syrian exiles in the United States and Canada as well as a former NATO political officer. "I used to talk to the Americans often over Skype via the Syrian Support Group," said Ahmad Zeidan, the nom de guerre of a member of the Idlib military council. "They used to say, 'Unite and we will support you.' This is empty talk. The truth is foreign states each want people who will work the way they want them to. They want to choose our future leaders. We won't allow them to. This is against democracy anyway, isn't it? We are fighting to have a democratic country, not so that we can install people with American or European or Saudi agendas."

Political money and foreign agendas split rebel ranks, even as those same states urged the men on the ground to unite. Some private sponsors, including ones in exile, tried to dictate operations down to which checkpoints to hit. Despite the mayhem, the Istanbul Room's supplies between May and September 2012—there were no more than half a dozen shipments—helped turn huge swaths of northern Syria into rebel territory. The Syrians hoped that with a de facto "liberated" zone in northern Syria, the international community would implement a no-fly zone over the area to ground Assad's planes and helicopter gunships. The territory could then serve as a space for hospitals to operate unmolested by air strikes, where the political opposition could base itself and establish the institutions of a new state, where thousands of displaced could seek refuge instead of fleeing the country. The no-fly zone never happened.

The Farouq Battalions took support from all who offered it—private donors, Syrians in the diaspora, sheikhs in the Gulf, the Saudis, the Qataris, the Europeans, the Turks—with the aim of being beholden to none of them. Ask any two Syrians who funded the Farouq and you'll get three answers. "We refused to politicize our rifles," Abu Sayyeh, the former lawyer and one of the group's four leaders said. "We were not aligned with any party, local or foreign."

The Farouq—given its control of Bab al-Hawa and its role as the Istanbul Room's distributor—worked closely with MIT, the Turkish National Intelligence Agency. The Turks denied any role in arming or allowing other countries to arm Syrian rebels via Turkish territory, but that's precisely what they facilitated. Convoys of arms and ammunition, overseen by MIT, routinely crossed the Turkish border into Atmeh—never through the official Bab al-Hawa crossing—in operations conducted between midnight and dawn. Once inside Syria, the Farouq convoys faced attack by regime forces as well as ambushes by renegade rebels and criminals looking to intercept the supplies. The Farouq was also accused of faking strikes on its own vehicles in order to keep the cargo. It issued receipts upon delivery, the vouchers outlining the inventory and including a pledge, signed and fingerprinted by the recipient, that the goods were a loan to be returned to a future Syrian state. But what state? And who would enforce such an agreement? The documents didn't even bear a letterhead. In the end, it didn't really matter. The Istanbul Room would be short-lived and the pledges not worth the paper on which they were written.

RUHA

Ruha didn't like being stuck in the cellar, with its thick stone walls and arched ceiling, the oldest part of their family complex, but she hated the basement more. At least the room they called the cellar was above ground. The basement was the family's new go-to refuge when the jets screamed and things crashed around them. That occurred most days now, and more than a few nights. On the worst nights, the family slept down there, in a space crowded with neighbors, aunts, and cousins. There was little safety beyond the illusion of it, only solidarity in numbers. The women of the family had swept the dusty space clean, pushed its knickknacks against a wall, and placed a pile of thin mattresses in the center of its uneven concrete floor. The men had installed a toilet and a kitchenette. Ruha's grandmother, Zahida, proud and stubborn, refused to "cower like a rat" in the basement. If she was going to die, she'd often say, she'd die in her bed or on her faded blue couch.

Ruha wished she could stay with her grandmother, but she wasn't allowed to. The little girl wasn't good at sitting still, not for hours that ran into days. She felt suffocated in the airless underground room. "What if it is shelled and we are stuck under rubble?" she asked one day. "At least outside or above ground we might have a chance to get out, to get away or something, but under ground? And under rubble underground? We'll die for sure. Isn't that true?"

Ruha's younger sister Alaa didn't mind the basement as much. She was calmer and more solitary by nature, but the sudden change in atmospherics would frighten her. "The air, something happens to it, I feel like I am dying," she said. She was too young to know that explosions could suck the air out of a room, but not too young to feel it.

The little girls had learned the vocabulary of war, new words like *katiba* (battalion), *qannas* (sniper), *hawen* (mortar), *shazaya* (shrapnel). They knew the sounds that accompanied some of the words and how to tell them apart. They fashioned new games from the new words. They made paper planes—pretend planes to shoot down the real ones above them, to pretend they weren't powerless and stuck in an underground space their parents pretended was safe. Their mother would hush them, promise them sweets if they were quiet. War or no war, she didn't want her girls thought of as ill-behaved. Manal was more or less raising the children on her own. Maysaara had pulled away from his family. He wanted his children to get used to living without him, in case one day they had to. He also stayed away from them because, he said, "Children can make a man weak. They make a man a coward. I try to keep them at a distance from my heart, from my eyes. It is negatively affecting the children, I know it is, but we have a duty. We're talking about the fate of a country."

He was still helping finance an FSA group mainly comprised of relatives, as well as smuggling medical supplies and satellite communication devices from Turkey. He transported the goods in black duffel bags he and his nephews carried on their backs across the border. He'd pour the jumble of medical packaging in a heap on the basement floor for Ruha and Alaa, their mother, and Aunts Mariam and Noora to sort through. The women placed like with like: packs of gauze, blood bags, intubation tubes, sachets of hemostatic agents, and other items whose use they couldn't divine.

Manal feared what the war was doing to her children. "They are used to the sound of rockets, it doesn't scare them," she said. "I don't know if it's because they don't understand the consequences of the sound, that if a rocket lands near us we would, God forbid, die or be chopped to pieces," she said. "They don't understand this."

Except they did. Alaa devised a game around it, one she played in the basement. She explained the rules one day. "I hear what they're saying about who died. I memorize it as if I'm recording it on paper. I record it in my mind. I count who died, who has lived, who has left." When asked why, she just shrugged and repeated a word that was her default answer to what was happening around her: "It's normal."

Alaa's other game, the one she played with her sister when they were allowed above ground, was collecting *shazaya*, shrapnel. "They are like my toys. I like them, they are unusual shapes." Alaa displayed them on windowsills until Manal scolded her, afraid of the sharp edges and the possibility of explosive residue in the remnants. The sisters gathered the pieces in a plastic bag they hid on the stairwell leading to their flat roof. Another game involved pretending to man a checkpoint and asking passersby for identification. "Are you with the revolution or against it?" a child asked as he stood at his front door. The local version of cops and robbers was now *thuwar* (revolutionaries) and *shabiha* (regime thugs). Nobody wanted to be the *shabiha*.

For Ruha, the open-air inner courtyard where she used to play had become her great fear. She'd dash across it, whispering prayers under her breath, certain the sniper a few streets away and the ones she imagined nearby could see her. The family's rooftop water tank was shot, so she knew her house was within range. She also knew that being a little girl was no protection. The sniper at the Iza'a had severed another little girl's spinal cord. Her name was Diana, and Maysaara had helped her get to a hospital in Turkey. Ruha saw a photo of the girl in a hospital bed, so she knew it was true, not just something her parents told her when she complained that she wasn't allowed to play in the street anymore.

In Saraqeb, there were new neighbors as parks became cemeteries and the dead moved closer to the living, or the displaced sought refuge there because it was safer than what they were fleeing. Ruha's Aunt Mariam cleared out her blackened apartment and allowed a displaced family to squat in it.

The adults, like the children, were trying to figure out the new rules. The regime's hold over towns like Saraqeb had disintegrated, but its replacement was unclear. Criminals exploited the instability across rebel-held northern Syria, kidnapping people for ransom and carjacking civilian vehicles. Every man with a gun was becoming an authority. Ruha's Uncle Mohammad was carjacked twice in one month at fake FSA checkpoints. He accepted the loss of his first vehicle (he refused to pay the 400,000 Syrian pounds, $6,225, the criminals demanded), but not the second. Within ten days of its being stolen, Maysaara retrieved the second car, "by force of guns, not kind words," as Uncle Mohammad put it.

Syria's revolutionaries wanted to bring down the Baathist regime but not the Syrian state. How to untangle the two? How to dissect a regime from institutions that were a reflection of its corruption and paranoia? Was it enough to remove senior officials and leave the rest? How much of an institution could be hollowed out and replaced without sacrificing competence for politics? And how to bring the various armed rebel groups under a new civilian control (an impossibility but still a hope)?

Every town in rebel-held Syria struggled with the same questions. Each one had become an independent republic, responsible for its own governance. Saraqeb's approach was to retain some elements of the old order. Staff at the *baladiye*, or municipal council, still showed up for work and drew state-paid salaries. Other government offices, like the records of births, deaths, and marriages and the agricultural office (which dispensed subsidized fertilizer and other staples), functioned as per normal. The headquarters of the Baath Party, however, was burned, because, as one young activist said, "It didn't serve a purpose."

Older, more traditional forms of power like religion and tribal authority, once repressed, now rebounded to fill the governance void. Sharia courts emerged to try to impose order on lawlessness. The traditional pyramidal structure of the tribes was reconstituting. Assad's Syria did not entertain alternative sources of power, so it weakened the vertical authority of the tribal chieftain at the apex (whose word was once law) by elevating other lower members whose power came from their close ties to the Baath and hence their ability to get things done. But the old, broken lineages of power were being restored.

Across the rebel north, *tansiqiyas*, Local Coordination Councils like the one Suleiman had joined in Rastan, became the main founts of budding governance systems based on friendships, local reputations, and the size of one's family or tribe. Non-FSA Islamist battalions like Jabhat al-Nusra also had their own social-service arms that often competed with *tansiqiyas* and, with time, would develop their own courts and schools. Saraqeb's *tansiqiya* was beset with problems of its own making. By August, it suspended its activities because of a 1.2 million Syrian pound ($18,700) bill accrued by its two free medical clinics. False receipts—a lot of them—were suspected of being issued by some members. The *tansiqiya* relied on donations, mainly from Syrians in the diaspora, but the influx of money was irregular. One month, it was 10 million Syrian pounds. The month before that, only one million.

A restructuring of Saraqeb's *tansiqiya* was proposed. The body's nine elected positions would expand to forty-five, to include representatives from all of the main families—to spread the responsibility and accountability and expand the body's activities. On a warm summer night, Maysaara and his brother, Mohammad, hosted a meeting in their cellar to discuss the new plan. Current and former members of the *tansiqiya,* the town's notables, and FSA fighters were in attendance. Ruha's Uncle Mohammad opened proceedings by saying he resented being told what to do by younger members of the *tansiqiya* in a society where elders made decisions.

"What did your generation do for us against the regime?" one of the younger men asked. "We fought it, you didn't. You can't tell us what to do now! How many people over forty-five are involved in the revolution?"

Not many, Uncle Mohammad said, because they had family responsibilities. "It's not like we told Maysaara not to get involved. We are three brothers. If something happens to us all, what happens to the family?"

"If everybody thinks, 'I have family responsibilities,' nobody would have moved," the young man countered.

"That's our problem!" another man said. "We argue with each other more than work together. Look at the Islamists and their discipline! I don't blame people for thinking they are cleaner than we are."

"The longer it takes, the more extremists there will be," said Uncle

Mohammad. "There weren't armed foreigners in Syria before, now there are. If only Bashar had introduced reforms, it would have been okay. I'm a democrat, a believer, I pray five times a day, but I'll drink whiskey or beer," he said. "These extremist groups can't dominate Syrian society. We are the majority, our way of thinking will prevail."

"When we finish with Bashar, we may need to get rid of them," a former *tansiqiya* member said of non-FSA Islamist groups. "Even if the regime falls, the harder battle will be forming a new country. We will sacrifice a lot more to create a new country than we will to bring down the regime."

"I don't accept, even now, that Syrians are killing each other," Maysaara said quietly.

"Didn't I tell you that you're not suited to be a military commander?" his brother teased.

Maysaara nodded. "We want a new Syria," he said. "They've tried to kill me many times. I hope I'll get to see it."

RUHA AND HER SISTER ALAA may have seemed to their mother a little too unafraid, but their baby sister, three-year-old Tala, wasn't. She was sick with a strange hormonal imbalance that one of the few doctors left in town said was precipitated by fear. The toddler needed to see a specialist, but there weren't any—they had fled or been killed. There were endocrinologists in government-held areas, but that was another country, an internal frontier more dangerous and difficult to cross than an official border between states. Turkey was an easier option, but how to get there? There were four ways a Syrian could enter Turkey: with a passport; bleeding in an ambulance; approaching border guards and being sent to a refugee camp; or illegally smuggled in. Ruha's family didn't have passports. Maysaara said he couldn't bear to put his wife and children in a refugee camp. They really only had one option. Maysaara told his older daughters to pack for two weeks.

"We're going to Turkey! We're going to Turkey!" Ruha shouted as the sisters hugged and jumped in their coral-pink bedroom. They'd never been beyond Syria's borders. Ruha put more hair clips and bracelets in her purple backpack than clothes. Alaa picked two of her favorite outfits and a selection of T-shirts and shorts. She folded them neatly into her pink schoolbag and then stood in front of the closet full of teddy bears. "Which one should I take?" she asked Ruha.

"What for? We'll be back soon."

Alaa nodded and shut the closet door. Their brother Mohammad was just as excited as they were. His sisters laughed when he walked into their bedroom with his blue schoolbag and showed them what he'd packed. "He's put his dirty clothes in there!" Ruha said.

"It's my bag, I can take whatever I want!" he answered.

"Fine. Get in trouble," Alaa said, but neither of the sisters told on him.

The house was full of aunts and cousins who saw the family off, but it didn't feel like Mother's Day to Ruha. "When will I see them again?" she asked me. "Do you think we'll leave before the nighttime shelling?"

Maysaara pulled away from the curb a little after 8 p.m. Ruha cried and waved to her aunts and cousins standing outside their front door until they faded from view. A pickup truck mounted with a 14.5mm antiair-craft gun moved ahead of Maysaara for protection, and also because one of its two passengers, Maysaara's nephew, was going to drive the family sedan back home. Little boys cheered, "God salute the Free Army!" as the truck passed.

"We're the Free Army?" Alaa giggled.

Little Mohammad fell asleep in the backseat. Tala clapped to revolutionary songs playing through a USB device.

> *Paradise, paradise, paradise.*
> *Our homeland is paradise!*
> *Beloved homeland, your soil is sweet, even your fire is paradise.*

They passed towns that looked deserted, saw garbage as proof of life. In one place, children too young to remember parks and swings and slides climbed miniature hills of rubble where nothing grew, their little hands and shoes coated in a fine, gray dust. Streets of disemboweled apartments, barely an exterior door or window untouched by weaponry. A bedroom wall peeled open, revealing its private interior. The mirror of an almond-colored dresser dusty but not cracked. In another town, a field of stalls—vegetables in purples and oranges and reds and greens. Shoes of different sizes in neat rows along the pavement. "Look, it's normal life," Alaa said. "Is this opposition too?"

They wove between ribbons of asphalt and dirt roads to stay on rebel-held tracts. They entered an olive grove. Maysaara slammed on the brakes and turned off the headlights. He'd noticed tank treads in the soft earth. The question was, regime or rebel? The pickup truck had detoured. They were alone. Ruha prayed quietly. "I'm scared," she whispered. Regime or rebel treads? Maysaara relayed the question over a walkie-talkie to FSA units in the vicinity. The answer was inconclusive. There were two routes out, a voice crackled—a shorter one laced with army snipers or a much longer one with a few checkpoints to skirt. Both were dangerous. Maysaara wondered what to do.

"Baba," Ruha whispered, "do we want the easier road or the safer one? Take the safer one. We don't want to be caught and beaten."

Without a word, Maysaara and Manal turned and looked at their ten-year-old and then at each other. "*Tikrami ya sitt* [As you wish, madam]," said Maysaara. He took the longer route. The pickup truck was waiting for them near the Turkish border. Mohammad woke as the family piled into its backseat.

"Is this Turkey?" Mohammad asked.

"No, we've gone back to Saraqeb," Alaa teased.

They drove to a line of tall trees, then it was on foot from there with a jumble of schoolbags and backpacks. Coiled razor wire glinted in the moonlight. There were silhouettes ahead with plastic bags that rustled, giving them away and prompting commands shouted in Turkish. The silhouettes recoiled. Ruha and her family watched and waited. A ghost approached the wire. Shots were fired into the air, military camouflage came into view. "It's blocked," whispered Maysaara. The family retreated.

The pickup truck had gone. Maysaara called a smuggler, and we waited in the dark until he arrived. Seven of us squeezed into the smuggler's car. "It's a bad night," said the smuggler. "The Turks have moods and tonight they're not blind."

"Does this town get shelled too?" Ruha asked. It blurred past. Another point along the border. Shots fired. No way across. It was already past midnight. Back in the smuggler's car to another jumping-off point that looked promising. The family stepped onto the uneven ground of plowed fields, the ridges and troughs tricky to navigate in complete darkness. Maysaara walked ahead, carrying Tala and several bags. The smuggler lifted Mohammad over his shoulder. Alaa shrieked as we fell into a muddy irrigation ditch. "Shh!" Ruha told her sister as she landed in the ditch too. "Don't even breathe!" Wet up to our waists and thighs in brown sludge. Manal's black robe caught on the coiled metal teeth of the line delineating the border. She took it off to free herself. Still kilometers to the Turkish road and a waiting car. Streetlights beckoned along the horizon. "Border guards!" the smuggler said. "Into the cornfield!" Waiting, resting, then moving, the tall stalks hiding our approach. Rustling. Others were there, too. A Syrian man crashed into Alaa. The little girl screamed. Maysaara ran to her. "I'm here, I'm here, we're almost there," he whispered. She clamped her hand over her mouth to prevent herself from screaming again, but she couldn't stop shaking. Nobody moved. Had the border guards heard Alaa? "That's it, we're caught," Ruha whispered. She wanted to go home. She'd had enough of Turkey already. It was too hard to get into. Waiting in the cornfield. The smuggler made calls. A group of people had been caught sneaking a large shipment of hashish into Turkey. That's why the guards were on higher alert, he said. Maysaara carried both Alaa and Tala. Several Syrian men, strangers, helped with the family's bags. The cornfield ended and a clearing began. "Run!" the smuggler said, as he stayed behind. Little legs moved as fast as they could. Manal brought up the rear to make sure all her children were in front of her. An old sedan, driven by the smuggler's partner in Turkey, came into sight. Its engine sputtered, its fumes nauseating. The family bundled into the backseat as it rattled toward Reyhanlı. That was as far as the smuggler would take them. Then, it was a taxi ride to Antakya, to an apartment that housed several injured fighters from Maysaara's Free Syrian Army unit.

The two younger children fell asleep immediately. Turkey that first night was a cramped room with two mattresses and a couch. Ruha and Alaa changed out of their mud-caked clothes and collapsed on one of the mattresses. They fell asleep as refugees.

SULEIMAN

In the darkness of a Syrian prison cell, time is measured by the meals. Flat Arabic bread and a single communal bowl of *labneh*, a yoghurt spread, meant another day had begun. Lunch was boiled, gritty cracked wheat (bulgur) without seasoning, served in the same bowl, a few spoons per man. Another morsel of bread and a dozen or so boiled potatoes, shared by the 90 to 120 inmates in the space, meant that the sun had set beyond the prison walls.

Suleiman felt his strength ebb, his body wilt, even as his wounds slowly healed. He prayed that he wouldn't be interrogated before he could withstand new blows, but, ten days after his first session, he was summoned again. "Do you really think that the beating you got from us is a real beating?" the jailer said to him. "Do you see this slab?" He pointed to the floor of the corridor outside the cell. "I can remove it now and bury you under it and no one would say anything."

Suleiman was back in the tire. The jailer said Suleiman had forgotten to write that he was an eyewitness. To what, he didn't know. It didn't matter. "Whatever you want, sir," Suleiman said, but the jailer didn't have any questions. He stopped when he was panting. Suleiman couldn't walk for a month. He temporarily lost feeling in his right hand. He'd lean on inmates to get to the bathroom. Some guards would allow him to be carried; others would beat men who helped him. He'd crawl. There were two toilet breaks a day. Bathing wasn't allowed. He thought of all the things he'd taken for granted—fresh air, sunlight, cleanliness, to feel sated, space to lie down, a bathroom. He got used to the smell of men who had soiled themselves, to the heavy heat that made it hard to breathe, to being in close proximity to so many unwashed bodies in an unventilated room that was never cleaned.

He marveled at the artistic cruelty of his guards. Who thought up these things? To handcuff a man to a pipe running across the ceiling in the corridor and keep him there, suspended above the floor, body weight borne by aching shoulders and wrists until something—his wrists, his shoulders, his mind snapped. One of the inmates was hung upside down for days until his body weight sawed through his ankles, exposing the bone in both legs. He was tossed back into the cell, developed gangrene, and died. So did two other men Suleiman saw.

Surviving the interrogations was part of the misery, staying human was harder. Learning to fall asleep to the sounds of men wailing. Suleiman spent his days entombed like the other prisoners, sitting in silence, arms wrapped around his knees, shoulder to shoulder in the permanent night, picking lice off his body. He used to be so meticulous. A man who wore labels effortlessly, and not for show. The filth sickened him. He became obsessed with tracking time in the timeless dark. It was his way to stay sane, to maintain a link to a reality the blackness intended to obliterate. He would not give them that. His body was trapped, but his mind was free. He memorized details of his conditions as if he were preparing a report to disseminate. To remember was to resist. Men around him hallucinated. One talked to an imaginary little girl, his daughter. Another went to the bathroom where he sat, unaware that he was in a cell with others. Suleiman sank once, although he didn't remember it. The other inmates told him what happened. They said he cried, shook uncontrollably, and talked to his mother: *Don't think I'm weakened, Mama! I'm strong. I'm not a coward! I can bear this and everything. Don't be afraid for me, Mama!*

After sixty days, the door opened before dinner one night. "Suleiman Tlass, I haven't forgotten about you," a guard said. Suleiman was thrown into a solitary cell. He counted the 40-centimeter floor tiles. Three by five. After the overcrowding of the communal space, this one felt like a reprieve. At least he could lie down.

A week later, he was back in the communal cell. The guards would open the door every now and again and order "that dog Abdel-Razzak Tlass's relative" to approach. He had to stand there and take the beatings. They usually used a thick pipe. Once, he counted thirty hits in a row. A human body can bear so much force, he thought. How am I still alive? How has my head not exploded? Really, the human being is a strange creature.

He felt singled out. Others weren't subjected to that routine treatment at the door. He didn't know that his father had gone to the bank and that the two women in the car had told him what happened. He didn't know that his mother had crushed his computer under her feet when she heard. He didn't know that his well-connected uncle, the one with shares in the bank, visited every security branch in Aleppo until he learned where Suleiman was. He didn't know that same uncle requested a meeting with Major General Adib Salameh, the head of Aleppo's Air Force Intelligence branch. He didn't know that his uncle turned up at the meeting with the son of Syria's grand mufti, the highest regime-affiliated Sunni cleric in the country. He didn't know that Major General Salameh told his uncle that if it were not for the presence of the mufti's son, he'd be joining his nephew underground. He didn't know that his uncle soon afterward fled Syria for Egypt, and later Turkey.

On August 6, 2012, Suleiman heard his name called, along with names of about two dozen others. It was before breakfast. The men were blindfolded, handcuffed, and led onto a bus. The wheels stopped at what sounded like an airport. The handcuffed prisoners were linked by a chain and led up the ramp of a military cargo plane. Suleiman smelled hair burning. A man screamed that his beard was alight. Suleiman felt a thunderbolt of electricity. Others were also being Tasered. The plane was in the air. Somebody vomited on Suleiman's suit jacket and pants. He wasn't wearing a shirt. He'd used it to tend his wounds. A soldier kicked him and mocked "the doctor" in a suit. Suleiman tasted blood. The treatment continued until they landed. On the ground, Suleiman and the other "sons of his chain," in prisoner parlance, were greeted with blasts of water that left Suleiman shivering in the middle of summer. He opened his mouth to try and catch a few drops. He was hungry and thirsty. The water pressure felled men, which pulled on the others in the chain gang. Another bus ride. Suleiman was barefoot. He stepped out onto a loose, pebbly surface. He flinched at gunshots.

"So these are the ones to be executed?"

"Yes."

He was more angry than scared. Why didn't they execute us in Aleppo? Why torment us and bring us here? Then a calm numbness. He saw his parents waiting for him at the dinner table, his sisters in the garden of his home in Rastan, sitting under the fruit trees. Suleiman surrendered, whispering the declaration of his faith as the chain gang was walked several hundred meters. He waited for a bullet. It didn't come. Suleiman and the sons of his chain were directed downstairs, where their blindfolds were removed. They were in a corridor at Air Force Intelligence in Mezzeh, near Damascus, one of the most notorious of Syria's many dungeons. The bureaucracy of torture dictated that Suleiman sign a typed pledge. The paper read as follows: "I, the detainee Suleiman Tlass Farzat, declare that I will not interact with detainees or give them my telephone number or address, nor take from them their telephone numbers or addresses, or any spoken or written message, and I will inform the head of the prison if any detainee attempts to give me his telephone number or any message to pass along. I bear full responsibility for any breach of this."

Suleiman signed the document and inked his fingerprint. It smudged. He was taken to solitary cell 10. There were a dozen men inside, in a space that measured 1.2 meters by two. They numbered themselves. The first six stood while the other six sat, knees to chest. They were all protesters. The routine here was similar, although breakfast included a few olives, and the cell was allowed one three-liter bottle of water a day—250 milliliters per man. Here, the men weren't taken out in twos and threes to the bathroom, as in Aleppo. The entire cell had until a guard's count of ten to be done. There were only two toilets.

The days became months spent in hunger, boredom, filth, and fear—fear of another beating, fear of disease, fear of being forgotten. An inmate from Abu Duhoor in Idlib Province developed a fever and died one day. Another succumbed after an interrogation. Suleiman and the others knocked on the cell door and waited for the guards to remove the corpse. Skin became occupied by scabies and lice. Diarrhea could kill a man. Most of the inmates were down to their underwear—they'd used their clothes to clean themselves. Only one man was released alive. He was from Hama and—pledge be damned—memorized the details of his cellmates' last known addresses, telephone numbers, whatever details he could to find their families and tell them where their sons, brothers, and fathers were buried alive. He contacted Suleiman's father, who went to see him in Hama. Suleiman's father paid security agents, politicians, local officials, people who claimed to be mediators for information about his son. He paid and got nothing in return.

Suleiman prayed to hear the guards call his name, even if it was just for another beating. It might mean that in some way his case was moving forward. Six months later, on December 9, 2012, the door opened and Suleiman's name was called. He was walked to a larger communal cell containing at least a hundred men. The door closed. He felt a gentle tap on the neck. He spun around to see two of his relatives, Osama Mattar and Ahmad Farzat, both defectors with the rank of captain. Like a child, Suleiman threw himself into their arms. He was no longer alone.

ABU AZZAM

Abu Azzam set his delicate hourglass teacup on the coffee table in front of him. 10:34 p.m. Another heart-piercing screech of incoming artillery. He didn't react beyond eyeing the sweet tea. It rippled but did not spill, as a blunted boom crashed into a field beyond a glassless window. Fresh vertical thunderclouds rose from another shallow crater outside. The strikes were getting closer in time and space. Three in ten minutes. Then another three in less than half that. Abu Azzam and a handful of his men watched and listened from the Farouq's ground-floor headquarters in a semidestroyed building. It was once a border police station, its two upper floors now partially collapsed and pancaked on top of the room where the men sat. It was early October, and they were at the Tal Abyad border post, opposite the Turkish town of Akçakale. The Farouq had won it less than two weeks earlier, on September 19, with a smattering of other groups—two, seven, eight, or seventeen—everyone rushed to claim credit. Abu Azzam had moved east, pushing toward Tal Abyad soon after the murder of the Islamist Firas al-Absi at Bab al-Hawa, leaving that post under the command of his deputy, Thaer al-Waqqas. Four of the seven main crossings on the Turkey–Syria border were now in rebel hands. The Farouq controlled two of these—Bab al-Hawa and Tal Abyad—where Abu Azzam was also in charge.

The shelling had kept Tal Abyad's two pale-gray sliding metal gates locked, but it was an easy four-minute walk from Turkey into Syria through flat, sun-scorched terrain alongside the post's high wall. REVOLUTION UNTIL VICTORY was spray-painted in English along a concrete divider in the middle of the closed border post. Abu Azzam's old roommate, Bandar, and I crossed in a night dark enough to move unseen, in an artillery storm fierce enough for the Turks to perhaps think few would try to sneak across. Bandar was on his way back from Turkey to regime-controlled Raqqa City, where he lived with relatives.

Abu Azzam and Bandar had not seen each other since Bassem, Bandar's brother, was killed in Baba Amr. The pair forcefully embraced in the Farouq's headquarters—Abu Azzam in a navy blue Adidas tracksuit, Bandar in a crisp white *galabiya*. A long, tearful, silent hug. The ground shook again. Another round of incoming, this one audible only in the flash before it exploded on impact. The farther a shell from the observer, the louder it whistled through the air. Death by artillery was often silent. Several of the Farouq men in the room rose and scurried to the basement. Abu Azzam stayed put. He sank into a gaudy armchair, its fabric a mix of the same sandy browns and beiges and pale greens as the landscape outside. "It's normal, normal," he said of the strikes. "It's their way of saying, 'Welcome!'" He took another sip of tea. The shelling, he said, was from a regime position, "17,850 meters away—to be exact."

THE FAROUQ WAS at the height of its power. A source of rebel envy and pride. The group had expanded nationwide, with units operating from Daraa in the south near Jordan all the way up to the northern region bordering Turkey. It claimed to be a force of some twenty thousand. Its fighters dressed like a professional army. Its sharp multimedia arm produced slick videos of the Farouq's exploits in clips that opened with its anthem. Most other FSA and non-FSA battalions and brigades also had press officers, logos, and flags, but the Farouq had the sheen of emerging from Baba Amr, symbol of the revolution's first liberated (and lost) territory. The Farouq's detractors weren't sure about its ideology—was it Salafi, so-called moderate Islamist, or secular? Its men were a mix of all of those things. But mainly, it was the Farouq's growing clout that most concerned its critics, and its control of the border posts.

In a home on the outskirts of Raqqa City, a group of local rebel commanders discussed how to take control of Tal Abyad from the Farouq just weeks after it fell. "The border posts are like gold," one of the men said. "If somebody wants to send you weapons and [the Farouq] control all the border posts, can they do it except under the Farouq's conditions? How will you get weapons in? Does anyone cement their door closed?"

A single fan whirred, blowing warm air around a room full of agitated, chain-smoking rebels who accused the Farouq of smuggling diesel fuel, cement, and hashish across the Turkish frontier. "The Farouq has great people who made sacrifices," one commander said. "There are many clean Farouq, but tell me, why did the Farouq leave Homs and come to the Turkish border? They're interested in money, in the smuggling, not the fighting anymore." It was an accusation repeated more than once by more than one man in more than one meeting.

ON SEPTEMBER 29, 2012, a new FSA command structure was announced, and some within it quickly angled to take on the Farouq. The Joint Command for the Revolution's Military Councils was a Qatari-influenced, defector-heavy, publicly announced body that replaced the covert Istanbul Room. The Joint Command, as it was known, was tasked with overseeing the Free Syrian Army's fourteen provincial military councils.

The Joint Command was based just inside Syria in Atmeh, in a school near an olive grove. It was led by a barrel-chested, gray-bearded defector from Rastan named General Mithqal Ibtaysh, who had split from the military just three months earlier. He sat behind a glass-topped desk in the principal's office, while FSA commanders and the heads of military councils waited like anxious students to see him. The Joint Command had promised salaries—$150 a month per fighter—and the principal's office was bustling with men signing up to get paid. They didn't know it then, but it would be a one-off payment.

The general gestured to his colleague, a mustachioed, bespectacled man who introduced himself as General Doctor Engineer Salim Idris, a defector from Al-Qusayr, in the Homs countryside, who left his regime post in July 2012. General Idris produced a spreadsheet of armed groups under the Joint Command's wing, boasting of how many factions were joining them. "I was personally requested at a meeting with the crown prince of Qatar, I met him two weeks ago," said his colleague General Ibtaysh. "All he asked for is unity. Qatar has blessed this move."

The Joint Command was less than a week old at the time, but it had already made clear its intent to take Bab al-Hawa—and Tal Abyad—from the Farouq. "We don't want the Farouq to be present at Bab al-Hawa," General Idris said. "It's a difficult time to discuss this now, but we are working on it." What the generals didn't reveal until years later was their plan to wrest the covert distribution of arms and ammunition from the Farouq. General Ibtaysh asked Major Abdulrahman Suwais, one of the trio of defectors who first met with the Qataris back in March, to take over the Farouq's transportation role. Suwais did not accept the offer. "Farouq was well established," he said later. "They were the heroes of Homs, so how could I? Even if I wanted to act clever and deliver the weapons, the Farouq controlled the routes."

The Joint Command was receiving arms and ammunition, most of it gathered from Libya, every week via Atmeh. Rather than deliver the goods, General Ibtaysh told beneficiaries to travel to Atmeh and pick up their own supplies. "The Farouq was responsible for the transportation. I took that from them," said General Ibtaysh, "because they used to charge transport fees—a third. That is why I eliminated their role."

The Joint Command's new system was plagued by old problems, the same ones that had handicapped the Istanbul Room. "What do you think we get?" General Ibtaysh asked. "Sometimes twenty thousand rounds, sometimes one hundred thousand rounds. What does that do for an army with fourteen military councils? Imagine that a commander would come to me from Damascus, the distance he'd crossed and the danger, so that I could give him four thousand bullets. How many bullets is that per man and how long will it last?"

As with the Istanbul Room, state sponsors and private donors soon bypassed the Joint Command's distribution mechanism to supply their favored rebels directly. This weakened the Joint Command, just as it had weakened the Istanbul Room, and fomented rebel rivalries. "This matter is the reason why we were no longer listened to," General Ibtaysh said. "I told sponsors, even if it's a gift from you to a group—inside or outside the FSA—let it come through us. But to give it to them directly while we are present? It was insulting. I wanted to enforce a chain of command, make groups on the ground reliant on us, but the foreign sponsors and other internal forces did not want that. They wanted it to fail," he said. "May God not forgive them."

ABU AZZAM HEARD the whispers in Tal Abyad, felt the rivalry and discontent of some of his allies just as surely as he could feel the ground rumble with every explosion. He had grown used to the physical brutality of war but not its bloodless scheming. Weren't they all supposed to be on the same side? He didn't want to be dragged into what his late father had called "the pollution of politics." What an apt description, he thought, for the machinations of men. Why were some of the other rebels so distrustful of the Farouq? He knew some didn't like the fact the battalion took a cut for delivering arms and ammunition. As far as he was concerned, "we should have taken two-thirds, given the work we were doing." He heard about smuggling across the border, by his men and others. "Transgressions occur—I'm not telling you we're angels," he said. The Farouq didn't charge fees at the borders it controlled, unlike the group overseeing Jarablus, for example, a small outpost about 120 kilometers from Tal Abyad. But the Revolutionary Council in Jarablus—which controlled that border—was composed of locals and didn't face local opposition. Members of the Farouq were considered outsiders in Bab al-Hawa and Tal Abyad.

Abu Azzam had no intention of staying in Tal Abyad. He was in talks to establish a civilian committee of locals to oversee the crossing while he pushed inward toward Raqqa City. He was soaking up local armed groups—some seventeen had joined the Farouq within days of Tal Abyad's fall—but Abu Azzam still felt "attacked from more than one side." How much simpler things were in Baba Amr, he thought, when they were fighting for God and country and each other. What had happened to his revolution? He had seen rebels clash over war spoils. "They raised their weapons against each other," he said. "Can you believe it? For what?" The revolution had gone on too long. It had devolved into anarchy. Rebel groups competed with each other for foreign funding, for territory, for the power and reputation of certain commanders. Perhaps nowhere was the chaos more evident than in the great northern metropolis of Aleppo. The city was in many ways the anti-Homs, dragged into the uprising in July 2012 like a hostage by men who were not its sons. The rebels who pushed into Aleppo were from the poorer, more religiously conservative countryside around it. A band of rivals, not brothers, who weren't welcomed by locals—men with little camaraderie, undisciplined groups, some of which looted the homes of civilians they claimed to be protecting.

Abu Azzam stroked his neat, Salafi-style black beard and exhaled slowly—a deep, regretful sigh. "Every three men are now calling themselves a battalion and five are calling themselves a brigade," he said. It was approaching midnight, the shelling had abated, the regime's gunners done for the day. Abu Azzam asked one of his men to make coffee, before Bandar and I continued toward Raqqa. I asked Abu Azzam about General Ibtaysh's request that the Farouq cede the border posts. He smirked. "When somebody other than the Farouq liberates an area, then he can make such a request," he said. "We are the ones who spilt our blood here, who are sleeping under artillery bombardments."

As Bandar and Abu Azzam said their good-byes, the Farouq, along with another group of rebels stationed at Tal Abyad, prepared to head out on a mission. The men tied white headbands to their foreheads to recognize members of their own side. The thin strips bore the *Shahada*, the declaration of their faith. The men gathered in a circle. "We will step on them, we will crush the house of Assad," they sang. They clapped and danced and then moved out toward the regime position that had been shelling them. It was 17,850 meters away—to be exact.

FOR THE FAROUQ BATTALIONS, the beginning of the end did not come in the rubble of battle amid cries of men at war but rather in a marble-floored Turkish resort overlooking Antalya's shimmering turquoise waters. The hotel was the setting for the so-called Antalya Conference in early December, a meeting called by foreign backers of the rebels to unify nonextremist armed factions. More than 550 defectors and civilian revolutionaries attended, as well as security and intelligence officials from Saudi Arabia, Qatar, the UAE, Jordan, Turkey, France, the United Kingdom, and the United States. The Joint Command's General Ibtaysh was not present. "No one informed me," he said. "I was in Syria working." The Farouq delegation included its three founders—the foreign liaison Abu Hashem, the lawyer Abu Sayyeh, and the sheikh and donor Amjad Bitar—as well as the former SNN co-creator and Istanbul Room distributor Bilal Attar. Abu Azzam traveled from Tal Abyad to attend.

On the first day of the conference, the Saudis presented a plan to divide Syria into five geographic fronts, an idea they'd floated a month earlier. It was an attempt to replace the Qatari-backed Joint Command and weaken Qatari influence in the armed uprising. Syrians were expected to pick their regional team. "I was shocked in Antalya to see how the brothers were so entrenched in these regional camps—Saudi and Qatari," said Abu Sayyeh. "Honestly, we weren't in either—we were Syrians, that was it."

Okab Sakr told the Farouq he expected them to vote for the Saudi plan. The Farouq leaders met and decided not to do so. The Joint Command was a Qatari–Turkish initiative. It had challenged them and stripped them of their transportation role, but it was backed by Turkey, rebel Syria's logistical lifeline and the Farouq's strategic partner along the border. The Farouq did not want to antagonize the Turks, but its leaders refused to plant themselves in the Qatari–Turkish camp, despite the protestations of the sheikh. Amjad Bitar pushed strongly for aligning not only with Qatar and Turkey but also with the Syrian Islamists—from the Muslim Brotherhood to hard-line Salafi groups, including Ahrar al-Sham—supported by those states. "I completely rejected this, to follow the Brotherhood track," Abu Hashem said. So did Abu Sayyeh: "There was deep enmity between us and the Brotherhood that remains," he said. The Farouq refused to pick a regional team. "Whoever wasn't standing in a particular line behind a regional player at that time lost out," said Abu Hashem. "It was that simple."

By the third and final day of the conference, the 550 rebels in attendance selected a group of 261, who in turn voted for a thirty-member Supreme Military Council to oversee the Five Fronts. General Doctor Engineer Salim Idris, General Ibtaysh's former colleague, was elected chief of staff of the Supreme Military Council. The command was divided into five zones, based on geography. The Farouq's Abu Sayyeh was elected assistant deputy chief of staff for the Homs front. The mighty Farouq Battalions had only one position out of thirty in the new Free Syrian Army command structure. Months later, Abu Hashem was elected Salim Idris's deputy, and Abu Azzam would be appointed to the eastern front, but it made little difference to the Farouq's declining fortunes.

The Antalya Conference exposed rifts among the Farouq's founders. "The disputes became clear then between the three of us," said Abu Hashem. "Me and Amjad and Abu Sayyeh. It reached the point that we cut things off between us. We couldn't accept each other anymore." In early 2013, the Farouq asked Sheikh Amjad Bitar to resign. "Amjad Bitar was like a bank," said one of the Farouq's original civilian leaders in Baba Amr, "and when he was removed, the bank of the Farouq collapsed."

After Antalya, "the Farouq was left blowing in the wind," Bilal Attar said. "The Saudis—because we rejected the Five Fronts—didn't look at us. The Qataris chose Ahrar al-Sham to replace the Joint Command [as a recipient of their support], and we weren't friends with Ahrar." The Turks also backed Ahrar al-Sham.

Abu Azzam watched the politicking at Antalya with disgust. The conference "was a conspiracy against the revolution," he said, a "project cooked up by foreign states and fed to us." He left Antalya grateful to head back to the chaos of the battlefield. At least he knew its rules. He had learned them in Baba Amr—shoot or be shot, and do it quickly. But he wasn't in Baba Amr anymore, where danger was from only one source. Now it was everywhere.

2013

RUHA

In Turkey, there was no gunfire or nighttime shelling. No snipers real or imagined for Ruha to fear. She could play in the street again outside her temporary home, a fourth-floor walk-up the family shared with wounded Free Syrian Army relatives from Saraqeb. In Turkey, the parks were still playgrounds, not new cemeteries. Ruha hadn't been on a swing or a slide for almost two years. Her mother, Manal, would sit on a bench and watch her children laugh and run and play without fear of something falling from the sky and exploding. Fifteen days came and went. Ruha's baby sister, Tala, had pending medical appointments, but away from the war, the tod-dler's strange hormonal condition seemed to be slowly clearing up on its own. Turkey's playgrounds were nice, but they weren't home. Ruha kept asking Baba when they would return to Saraqeb. She cried when she learned they were staying. "We came to treat Tala," Manal told her eldest daughter, "but now the planes are as permanent as the birds in the air. We can't take you back to that. We have to try and keep you safe."

"Nobody dies before their time," the little girl replied. Submitting to God's will—a ready-made phrase intrinsic to her faith and her best argu-ment for going back. It didn't work on her parents. She'd cry when she spoke over Skype with her Aunt Mariam, her grandmother Zahida, Uncle Mohammad and his wife, Aunt Noora. Her father, Maysaara, had bought the relatives in Saraqeb a satellite Internet device. It was their only con-nection to the world outside their war zone. Their landline coverage did not extend beyond the limits of Idlib Province, disconnecting them from the rest of Syria. Mother's Day 2013 was difficult for the little girl. It was

usually Ruha's favorite day of the year. "We'd make sweets, give my grandmother gifts, we'd all play," she remembered. "I love my grandmother. I
know that I'm spoiled, that she spoiled me. When will I see her again?"

In Turkey, the children developed a new habit. At bedtime now, the
lights had to stay on. They feared being in the kind of pitch-black of that
cornfield the night they sneaked across the border. Ruha and her siblings
spent their days watching cartoons on an old laptop, or with crayons and
coloring books. They made friends with the Turkish children in their
building. They couldn't converse, but somehow they understood each
other the way children often do. Maysaara didn't enroll them in school.
"How can I put my children in school, as if life is normal, when there are
children in Syria who can't go to school?" he said. "My children are no better than those in Syria." It was his form of survivor's guilt.

Ruha was happy not to be in school, but the apartment was cramped
with the recuperating FSA fighters. The young men were often edgy,
impatient to heal and return to the battlefield. "These guys bore me,"
Ruha would say. "They sit in front of their computers all day, following the
news." Her mother recognized that the young fighters were "emotionally
very tired," as she put it. She didn't want her children disturbing them, so
she sometimes confined Ruha and her siblings all day to one of the apartment's two bedrooms. "The children cannot speak, yell, cry, run, some
of the *shabab* get agitated," Manal said. "I try to keep them quiet, but this
is a form of pressure on the children." For Ruha, it was suffocating, like
being stuck in the basement back in Syria but without the fear. She wasn't
good at sitting still.

They were refugees now, but business-class refugees. Ruha and her siblings didn't have to hawk packs of tissues or bottles of water on Turkey's
streets. They weren't reduced to a pair of hands in a sweatshop, or forced
to live in the refugee camps, unable to come and go without Turkish permission. Ruha's parents could afford rent and food, but Maysaara was
always away as though at work, busy helping other families, with little
time for his own. Manal was again raising the children alone.

When Maysaara wasn't illegally sneaking into Syria—which was often—to bring in medical supplies, communication equipment like satellite Internet, and donations from wealthy members of Saraqeb's diaspora, he was visiting his hometown's wounded in Turkey's hospitals. One day he was busy sourcing a large quantity of flour and trying to figure out how to get it across the Turkish border. "The people need bread," he said. "The bakeries have all been hit [by warplanes]. The women will bake, but they need flour." He called representatives of the Syrian political opposition in exile and pleaded for money or for their intercession with the Turkish border authorities. "Our political opposition is like, what can I call them? They don't care, they don't ask!" he said. "They're too busy at their conferences! They want to go to Doha and other world capitals, they should go to Hell! There's a war and people are focusing on conferences, on YouTube videos advertising themselves. What about the people inside?" After several days, with the help of Turkish friends, he managed to get a truckload of flour over the border, paid for by donations from Syrians in the diaspora. The political opposition did not help him.

Ruha's parents turned their apartment into a halfway home for anyone from Saraqeb who needed a place to stay—for those who had accompanied wounded loved ones to Turkish hospitals, or recent refugees unsure how to navigate their new life in a new country with a new language. Ruha took heart from the visits. "It makes me feel like I am a little closer to home," she said, "even if the people visiting us from Saraqeb aren't related to us." For her mother, the guests and their stories had the opposite effect. They compounded her survivor's guilt. "We are physically here but mentally there, worried about family and friends," she said. "This is not normal life. It is not normal to live alone in isolation, away from your family and community, to live in limbo. We are living a half-life, permanently unsettled, unstable, temporary." It affected all of her decisions—from whether or not to buy furniture ("What for? We're going back soon") to how her children spent their days ("They'll go to school in Syria. We will return").

It was the knowing what was happening in Syria, the not knowing, the wondering. Air strikes on Saraqeb meant people would be wounded, some of whom would try and make it to Turkey. Maysaara was often told of impending arrivals. He'd rush to the border to meet the injured and accompany them in the ambulance, or he'd wait for them in the hospitals. It wasn't unusual to see people staying in their apartment who were discharged from Turkish care but still too weak to cross the border back to Syria. Manal would cook for everyone. One day Ruha walked into the living room to see a man with a ghastly lower-leg wound lying on the couch as her father changed his bloody bandages and cleaned the injury. She didn't look away. "If, God forbid, you are wounded," the man told Maysaara, "I will not let anyone clean your wounds except me."

"Brother," another man in the living room said, "the line in front of you is long."

Ruha was eleven now, and she understood why her father was rarely home, and why he seemed preoccupied when he was. "Baba has to do it," she told me. "He has to help. Do you think that the people who left their studies and their country wanted to? What does your country, your home, your street mean to you? That's what it means to me. Would you like to leave the home you grew up in? Your family? Who wants to leave those things? If we knew we wouldn't die if we stayed in our home, we wouldn't have left Syria."

AUNT MARIAM RATTLED a small canister of diesel. It was almost empty. She'd been waiting all winter for free supplies promised to the townsfolk by either Jabhat al-Nusra or the secular *tansiqiya*. Mariam couldn't be sure and didn't much care which group had made the pledge. She just needed heating fuel. It cost 150 Syrian pounds a liter, as much as 200 pounds in some places—it used to be 25. She poured the thick liquid into the *sobya* heater by torchlight. There was no electricity, as usual. It came for only two hours a day now, shortening already-truncated winter light. Ruha's grandmother, Zahida, had gone to bed soon after sunset, as she often did that winter. There was no point freezing in the dark.

The *sobya* slowly drew out the dampness in the air. Mariam was in her mother's living room with several of her sisters, nieces, and grand-nieces. The women rested on thin mattresses and cushions placed around the perimeter of the room. "Do you know the joke about the genie in the lamp?" one of Mariam's nieces asked. "A man found a lamp, rubbed it, and summoned its genie. 'Your wish is my command,' the genie told the man. 'Great,' the man said. 'I need a bottle of cooking gas.' The next day, the man rubbed the lamp again, summoning an irate genie. 'What do you want?' the genie asked. 'I've run out of diesel,' the man said. 'Couldn't you have waited a few days?' the genie replied. 'Now I've lost my spot in the queue for the cooking gas!' "

Laughter warmed the room. Most of the women had stopped using gas cookers. Firewood was cheaper. Meat was a luxury. Vegetables were more than triple their old price, even after adjusting for currency inflation. Water shortages were common because of the lack of electricity to pump the groundwater. "What can we do except laugh?" one of Mariam's older sisters said. "Praise be to God. We are better off than many, but there's no work, no money. I miss greens! I went to the market yesterday, a man was selling okra. I bought a handful just to taste it. That's all I could afford—650 pounds a kilo! But at least he priced it in pounds. Nobody talks about pounds anymore because it fluctuates so much, it's all in dollars. Imagine, dollars!"

Another sister lamented the flour shortages. "My granddaughter keeps asking for cake, she's used to me baking cakes. Where am I going to get flour?" She'd asked a relative in Turkey to send her four kilos. "I don't care how much it costs," she said, "and I paid for transportation too."

The room was dim, lit by a thin LED strip hooked to a car battery that bathed the women in a grayish hue, just enough to see each other. Their nightly gatherings had become a ritual—air strikes permitting—like an informal therapy session. One night, they recounted the new revolution-inspired baby names in town. A couple had called their son Baba Amr, after the neighborhood in Homs where Abu Azzam had fought. An Arab child was named Azadi, a Kurdish/Iranian word for freedom. A baby girl was called Thawra, Arabic for revolution. Two of the younger women, Mariam's nieces, said their friends were marrying foreign fighters from

Jabhat al-Nusra. "Why are they doing this?" one of the younger women asked. "We haven't run out of Syrian men yet. Bashar is trying his best, but we still have *shabab*."

One of Maysaara's sisters said a foreign fighter told two of her sons to snub out their cigarettes because smoking was a sin. "They just ignored him," their mother said. One of her sons told the fighter, "Who are you to tell me what to do? You are a guest in my country."

"They're fighting here for us," Mariam said. "I won't cover my face for anyone, but who else is helping? At this point, I don't care if the devil intervenes." It was one of her most commonly used phrases. "We just want to finish this. Enough."

Mariam's niece Mayada, a young, strong-willed English-literature major, said that in her heart she wanted an Islamic state, but she recognized that in Syria, a multiethnic and multisectarian society, that was unlikely. An Islamic state would be "more just," she said. Her Aunt Sarea, who was just a few years older, snickered at her remarks. She wouldn't live in an Islamic state, Sarea said. Unless that state was modeled on Turkey, it would be an excuse to lock women in their homes.

The women debated the issue for hours. The Quran was clear on the rights of women and minorities, said Mayada. "Clerics will find a thousand Hadiths to counter it," Sarea replied. In the end, both women agreed that an Islamic state was not the best option—not because Islam doesn't grant rights to women but because the male clerics who interpret the religion could not be trusted.

Another of Maysaara's sisters retold the story of how her home and car were damaged when two rockets landed nearby at lunchtime one day. "It felt like the sky was raining fire," she said. A neighbor's young daughter died. A displaced family living a few doors down lost a child, while another of its children was left without upper limbs. "I didn't know where to go," Maysaara's sister said. "To the basement? The glass was shattering. To the bathroom? I could hear the yelling outside and the announcements from the mosque, then my daughter called and said, 'Mama, a barrel has landed on my in-laws' house.' I put on my headscarf and ran out to see if

I could help. What could I do? Their house was on top of them. People screamed, 'The Mig is coming!' I ran back home. Smoke was everywhere. They retrieved my daughter's in-laws in clumps."

"We're sick of it, we're so sick of it," she said. "My grandson, my darling, he hemorrhaged so much when their front door was blown to pieces. We're scared about his eyes. They're still pulling out shrapnel from his body. Every day, it seems they find something new, he's peppered with it. The warplanes just won't stop! They're always in the air. Don't they take breaks?"

SULEIMAN

Suleiman was in one of the most feared detention centers in Syria's *mukhabarat* state—Air Force Intelligence in Mezzeh, near Damascus. He was in a communal cell with two of his relatives, Captains Osama Mattar and Ahmad Farzat. The two defectors had been reduced to numbers—1501 and 1502—but Suleiman was still permitted a name. One day, he heard a guard call it. His relatives remained behind as Suleiman was handcuffed and tied to other men, the sons of his chain. The detainees were beaten with thick cables as they were marched, heads bent, eyes to the floor, onto a bus, then driven a short distance to a hangar within the Mezzeh complex. The hangar gate slid open. Suleiman saw hundreds of men squeezed into the space. They sat in six rows.

Suleiman was assigned to line number one. It was a good location, near a wall he could lean against. He couldn't cross his legs. Knees-to-chest was the only position for sitting, for eating, for sleeping. After the permanent darkness of his cell, the brightness of the hangar's neon lights hurt his eyes. Suleiman looked around. He recognized prisoners who had bid him farewell in Aleppo—men who had said their good-byes, thinking they were being released. That's it, he thought. Nobody gets out of here. Transferred maybe, but nobody will get out of here.

Every line had a *shawish*, a prisoner assigned to organize trips to the bathroom (there was one toilet for the hundreds of men) and to distribute food to his row at mealtimes: a piece of bread per man and a handful of either boiled bulgur or olives, sometimes a lick of jam or the yoghurt spread *labneh*. The line masters had another duty, too—to provide names every night for predawn beatings. Failure to do so would result in the *shawish*'s beating—it was either he or the other prisoners. Suleiman's days were spent in fear of being summoned at night. Still, he sympathized with a *shawish* whom other men in his line came to hate. It wasn't the *shawish*'s fault, he thought, that the regime had turned one of us against us. Suleiman felt alone in the crush of bodies. He wondered about his parents. Where were they and what had he put them through?

Speaking was forbidden, but Suleiman and his neighbors sometimes whispered to each other to pass the time. On the floor around him, he found stiff wire broom bristles and some loose threads. He sharpened the ends of the bristles by rubbing them on the concrete floor. He saved his olive pits, polished them smooth on the concrete, then carefully, slowly pushed the makeshift needles through the soft center of each pit, fashioning them into a string of prayer beads. He'd never been religious before. He attended the mosque every Friday and fasted during the holy month of Ramadan, but that was about it. Now he silently prayed five times a day and recited verses from the Quran that detainees in other cells had taught him. The prayer beads became his talisman, a reminder of a force Suleiman believed stronger than the prison guards and the regime they represented. "Who is your God? Who is your God?" the guards would yell. There were only two acceptable answers—Bashar al-Assad, or you, *sidi*. They were not Suleiman's god.

He was down to his boxers, but on a palm-size scrap of soft, thin denim that he had kept from another cell, he embroidered a wish: *Your blessings, Mother*, followed by his name and that of his parents. It reminded him that he was not a number or a faceless prisoner, another piece of bruised flesh buried alive. He was Suleiman Tlass Farzat, a Sunni Muslim from Rastan.

The hangar seemed to be a holding pen. There were no interrogations, just the predawn beatings that left some inmates dead. The overcrowding meant there were plenty of bodies each *shawish* could choose from. Suleiman was summoned only once. It was winter. He stood barefoot in a thin layer of snow as guards lashed him and the other men with silicone rods and thick cables before turning a hose on them. Suleiman bled, and shivered, and prayed for it to end.

MARCH 28, 2013. Just after breakfast, the guards were shouting out names. Suleiman's heartbeat quickened when he heard the names of several of his former cellmates from Aleppo. He lifted himself off the floor a little, as though it would somehow help him hear better. He closed his eyes and listened: Diaa al-Absi. Ahmad Moaamar al-Zein. Suleiman Tlass Farzat. He jumped to his feet.

"Get your things!" a guard shouted. Suleiman didn't have any things. He was barefoot in his boxers. The line *shawish* tossed him a pair of fleecy black pants that had been lying near the wall. They were damp and many sizes too big. An inmate from Hama gave Suleiman the shirt off his back— it was white with blue stripes. Suleiman left behind his underwear. There were men who could use it, he figured. Some were naked. Names were shouted, inmates scuttled toward the hangar gate. Suleiman turned to the man who sat behind him in line number one. His name was Abdel-Kareem Mohammad Mansour, and he was from Qalaat al-Madiq in Hama. Suleiman pressed his prayer beads into his neighbor's hand, as well as the half-piece of bread he'd saved that morning to stave off hunger pains later in the day. He kept the scrap of denim. The pair embraced. "I'll pray for you!" Mansour said. "Please find my family!" He repeated his last known address, shouting it out in the mayhem, regardless of the consequences, as Suleiman, holding up his damp pants, rushed toward the hangar gate. It slid open.

"Get out, you animals, and get on the bus!"

Sunlight on his skin. The guards hadn't bothered to blindfold them. The detainees were driven a few hundred meters back to where Suleiman had been processed on his first night. He walked down a flight of stairs into an office. One of the two mobile phones he had when he was arrested sat on a table, near a clear plastic bag containing his belongings. He signed and fingerprinted a receipt for them. The guard didn't return his mobile phone. To hell with it, Suleiman thought. He considered asking about his car but decided against that, too. "It wasn't worth it. I'm being released! They've returned my things, don't upset them now."

He was ordered to wait near a minivan, to squat like the other detainees while he was handcuffed and blindfolded. He heard vehicles arriving and people alighting, and, after a while, names were called to board buses. Suleiman froze when he heard one: Samer Tlass, his lawyer cousin who had been part of Rastan's *tansiqiya*. Suleiman knew Samer had disappeared before he had—Samer vanished on Valentine's Day 2012 while trying to smuggle flour into Rastan. Starving towns into submission was an overused tactic in Assad's war, one some of his opponents also employed on a lesser scale. Rastan had been besieged for almost a month, its bakeries low on supplies, when Samer ventured out to try to secure food. Nobody knew what had happened to him. The cousins were both in Air Force Intelligence's Mezzeh detention center at the same time. Suleiman's name was called soon after Samer's. "So he knows I'm here too. We are both being released on the same day, at the same hour, the same minute, and are probably sons of the same chain!"

Suleiman boarded the bus. Was Samer near him? He wanted to whisper his cousin's name but knew better. Speaking was forbidden. The detainees sat with their heads bowed as a guard walked the aisle. "Who among you is a Sufi?" the guard demanded as the vehicle drove away. None of the detainees responded. "Nobody?" the guard asked. "This week, the Sheikh Mohammad Ramadan Said al-Bouti was martyred by armed terrorists." Bouti, eighty-four, was a senior pro-regime cleric killed in a bombing on March 21 as he delivered a lecture in a Damascus mosque. A few of the detainees murmured, "May God rest his soul." Suleiman couldn't muster that. He hoped the sheikh would rot in Hell. But he was intrigued—what was happening in Syria? How had rebels reached a regime stalwart in Damascus? The bus suddenly swerved to avoid what sounded like artillery. "You see! All the time you spent inside, now you're out and you are about to die!" the guard laughed. "Tomorrow, don't go back to your business in terrorism and then come back to us here, because we won't let you out alive."

Suleiman stifled a smile. So they really were being released! The bus stopped. The detainees were ordered out, their blindfolds removed, but the handcuffs stayed on. Suleiman looked around him. A sign indicated he was at the Military Police branch in Qaboun, Damascus. He scanned the inmates. His eyes found Samer.

Samer was as shocked to hear Suleiman's name as Suleiman had been to hear his. He was certain he'd misheard. When was his cousin detained and how? His younger cousin, the one who had always been so well groomed, now stood across from him. "He looked like a ghost," Samer remembered, "a shadow."

Suleiman stared back at Samer. His older cousin was thinner, his skin sallow, his hair long and matted, his beard thick and unkempt. Suleiman just wanted to embrace him but dared not move. For the second time in his incarceration, Suleiman cried. He could see that Samer, too, was crying.

TWO DAYS LATER, the cousins and some of the other men were crowded into a windowless vehicle the guards called "the meat-fridge truck." It barreled through the land of the living before stopping at Damascus Central Prison in Adra, northeast of the capital. The facility was better known simply as Adra. It was the place where Ruha's grandfather had once been incarcerated, and where she had visited him. Suleiman and Samer were not being released.

They spilled out of the truck and were ordered to strip naked before entering the prison. Suleiman was glad to be rid of the oversize fleecy black pants he had struggled to hold up. He was handed a black-and-white-striped prison uniform and sent straight to the barber. His lice-infested locks tumbled around him. A guard gave him a bar of soap and led him to a communal bathroom. Suleiman hadn't showered in almost a year. It had been just as long since he could go to the toilet without sharing the seat with other men and having until a guard's count of ten to be done. He felt like a caveman emerging from a filthy hole. He turned the tap. Hot water! It cascaded over his scars and infections. He tried to scrub and scald what defiled him, but he feared he was hallucinating. Had he lost his mind? Was he still in a dark, dank cell, acting out like some of the men he had seen?

He was led along clean, wide, and well-lighted corridors to an office where he was registered, fingerprinted, and photographed. The mugshot on his laminated prison ID showed a man whose once-cherubic face was hollowed thin, expressionless sunken eyes rimmed by dark circles. He was assigned to cell 608. Samer was in 704.

Cell 608 was clean and bright, with two rows of beds facing each other. The beds were assigned by the prisoners according to a seniority based on time spent in the cell. Suleiman was directed to a patch on the floor, but he didn't mind. At least he could lie down and even stretch out his body. Adra was part of the civilian prison system, a place for the sentenced and those awaiting trial—unlike the *mukhabarat* dungeons Suleiman had just left, with their violent interrogations and harsh conditions. To Suleiman, Adra felt "like being pulled out of Hell and entering Heaven," he would later write. In Adra, detainees could walk between the cells. There was even a common area with stalls selling clothing, footwear, food, and other items. The prison had natural light and electricity in the cells. Inmates were allowed to converse, and to use the bathroom. Suleiman still had the 2,300 Syrian pounds from when he'd been arrested. The currency had devalued so much that the amount only bought him two tubes of toothpaste—one for him and one for Samer. He couldn't afford a toothbrush or slippers or underwear. A new friend, a cellmate from Rastan whom Suleiman didn't know back home, bought those items for him. The man had been detained in the army's October 1, 2011, raid on their hometown.

In Adra, prisoners were allowed family visits once a week and a three-minute phone call every fortnight. Each prisoner had a designated visitors' day—Suleiman's was Wednesday. His new friend from Rastan was expecting his mother the next day, a Sunday. Suleiman asked if the friend's mother would contact his family. He scribbled four telephone numbers on a scrap of paper—his mother's, an aunt's, and numbers for two uncles. (He didn't know one uncle had been murdered by regime thugs and the other had fled Syria.)

The following Wednesday, Suleiman was called to the visitors' hall. He sprinted through the corridors, scanning the noisy crowd on the other side of the metal mesh until he saw his mother and aunt. He couldn't stop the tears. Couldn't find the words. The reunion seemed to last mere moments. A bell sounded. They had barely talked. Suleiman took the patch of cloth he'd embroidered in the hangar and pushed it through a hole in the wire mesh to his mother. She held it to her heart as a guard walked Suleiman back to his cell. His mother had brought him a care package—they were permitted in Adra—with clothes, a blanket, bedsheets, a towel, 25,000 Syrian pounds, and the earplugs and eye mask he once needed to sleep. He tossed the mask—he never wanted to see another blindfold. In cell 608, his cash provided its own form of seniority. He "rented" a bed from a cell-mate for 3,000 pounds a week, paid back his new friend from Rastan, gave Samer a portion of the money, and purchased an exercise book and pen. It was a child's notebook, pink with a green border, with a sad blue elephant on its cover holding multicolored balloons. It took Suleiman months to find the nerve to write.

RAQQA CITY

Saleh, the aide to the Jabhat al-Nusra leader, drove into Raqqa City the day after it became the first of Syria's fourteen provincial capitals lost by Assad. The takeover in the first week of March was more of a surrender than a battle, one that lasted just three days. After that, nothing in Raqqa would be as easy as its fall.

Saleh was in the city to see an old friend and Nusra colleague named Abu Loqman. They had been cellmates in Sednaya Prison. Now, Abu Loqman was the new power in Raqqa. He had appointed a local metal worker, Abu Saad al-Hadrame, as Nusra's emir in the provincial capital.

The city was won by men who called themselves *mujahideen*, not revolutionaries. Abu Azzam did not participate in the fight. He stayed in Tal Abyad, a hundred kilometers away, although his middle brother, the defector, was killed wearing a Farouq uniform in battles on Raqqa City's outskirts. The lead Islamist groups largely locked out the Free Syrian Army during and after the fall of Raqqa City, although a few small groups were present. They didn't want to replicate the chaos, looting, and lawlessness of Aleppo. Raqqa was supposed to be the anti-Aleppo.

The city's streets were swept clean, its two churches untouched. Even some of Assad's portraits remained in place. Graffiti signed by Jabhat al-Nusra warned against stealing. The group's fighters, their faces covered, stood guard outside banks and other institutions. A Nusra pamphlet dated March 17 invited civil servants back to work. An eleven-point manifesto, plastered on store walls and other public places, outlined what Raqqa's new leaders considered the collective responsibility of the city's people. "Do not dwell on the past and disputes between individuals," read the first point. "Act with Islamic morals and forgive rather than maintain enmity. Stand in line outside bakeries. Report suspicious parked cars or objects in the street. Pray and seek God's forgiveness and guidance." The list included a complaints hotline: 117.

The sky-blue sports stadium was the place where rebels, civilian activists, and a representative of the political opposition were trying to forge a new order. A handwritten cardboard sheet taped to the entrance asked *mujahideen* not to bring their weapons inside. Civilian activists sat at plastic tables arranged in a circle, laptops open, a printer purring in a locker room two floors underground. They called themselves the Raqqa Media Center and debated options for a logo. A few doors down, in a closet of a room, a bald, mustachioed lawyer with closely shorn gray patches over his temples sat behind a desk near a fax machine. Abdullah Khalil wore a slate pin-striped suit, white shirt and tie, three-starred revolutionary pin on his lapel—looking as out of place among the bearded men in military camouflage as the fax machine was out of date. Khalil was part of the Syrian political opposition and the head of the new provincial council. In reality, he *was* the council. The size of his office reflected the (non)importance the battalions afforded him. He mainly dealt with complaints.

Khalil the politician insisted the Free Syrian Army had a commanding role in Raqqa City and that Jabhat al-Nusra would not change social mores, even though the group was distributing glossy pamphlets of what it considered appropriate female attire. A red X near trousers, wrist-to-ankle *abayas* cinched at the waist, and buttoned-up long overcoats. The only clothing worthy of a green tick was an amorphous black floor-length sack and a headscarf extending to a woman's thighs that covered her face and eyes. Raqqa's Muslim women wore jeans, tight shirts, and *hijabs*; *abayas* embellished with diamantés and other adornments; or colorful long-sleeved, ankle-length dresses paired with bold headscarves. Khalil the politician was adamant that Nusra's ideas would not stick. "The people who are bringing down Bashar Assad can bring down anyone else," he said. But he and his ilk didn't bring down Bashar al-Assad in Raqqa. Nusra and its allies did.

Jabhat al-Nusra was headquartered in the governor's former seat of power, a sand-colored, multiarched building in a square lined by palm trees. A bronze statue of Hafez al-Assad in the square had been felled, and a man's dress shoe was attached via a flexible wire to its head—for those who didn't want to use their own shoes to beat "Hafez" around the face. TOMORROW WILL BE BETTER was spray-painted on the statue's back. Nusra had raised a massive black flag in the square and distributed flyers calling for replacing the three-starred revolutionary flag with a black one bearing the *Shahada*.

Several hundred people publicly protested the move, while others, like Bandar, Abu Azzam's old university roommate from Homs, who lived in Raqqa City, complained inside the privacy of their homes—and, in Bandar's case, to a visitor from Jabhat al-Nusra who had come to see me.

The Nusra fighter, a twenty-one-year-old former literature student, knocked on Bandar's door and then stood several meters away from it, his back turned to avoid seeing the lady of the house should she open it. He wore a gray *shalwar kameez* and a black scarf wrapped around his head. Only his eyes, brown and bespectacled, were visible. Bandar and his friend Abu Noor, who was also in his twenties, answered, then called me to the door. Bandar came back with the Nusra flyer about the flag.

"What is this?" Bandar asked the Nusra fighter standing in the stairwell. "We were just talking about it, we don't like it."

The masked man, who was unarmed, smiled through his face covering. "And what don't you like about it?" he asked. "We are all Muslims, so what is the problem with a flag that bears the *Shahada*?"

"We are not all Muslims," said Abu Noor. "You and I are, but there are Christians here, too. You have insulted them. And besides, what gives you the right to change the symbol of the revolution?"

"We protected the churches," the Nusra member said. "The Christians came to [Nusra emir] Abu Saad. He said, 'You are protected, you can return to your homes.' Let's not talk out here. The neighbors will hear us. Do you have coffee?"

The men walked into the living room. Two gray-haired men, Moayad and Ahmed, rose from sky-blue couches to greet their guest.

Abu Noor, a wiry young man who worked in a pharmacy by day and at night volunteered to guard the post office near his home against looters, was concerned the flag would invite US drone strikes. "They'll think we're extremist Muslims!" he said.

"There is no moderate Islam or extremist Islam," the Nusra member said calmly. "There is only Islam, and Islam is under attack in the West, regardless of whether or not we hoist the banner. Do you think they're waiting for that banner to hit us?"

Ahmed, an older man in a tan leather jacket and a white *galabiya*, interjected: "What we're saying is, put the flag above your outposts, not in the main square of the city. We all pray, we all say, 'There is no god but God,' but I will not raise this flag."

"We are not forcing anything on anyone," the Nusra member said. "We offered it as a choice. We did not take down the revolutionary flags in the city—even though we could have."

Outside, the night air was cool. Warplanes, which had been continuously rumbling over the city during the day, retreated, prompting bakeries, shuttered because of the threat of air strikes, to open. Long queues, segregated by gender, formed as night fell, just as they did every night, guarded by armed men with black scarves covering their heads and faces.

"With this banner, you have cleaved us from our country Syria," Moayad said. "Why is it here? We are not an Islamic emirate; we are part of Syria. This is a religious banner, not a country's flag."

The Nusra member leaned forward and looked the older man in the eyes. "This is a lack of self-esteem, something we were conditioned to feel toward our religion by a regime that didn't let us practice it," he said. "Do you know how many people a day come to pledge allegiance to us, to try and join us?"

At that, Moayad lost his temper. He stood up, moved a few steps across the room, and wagged a finger in the masked man's face: "The Syrian revolution rose up to step on Bashar's neck, but I swear I am with Bashar against this flag!" he yelled. "That is how strongly I feel about it! You are causing *fitna* [discord]!"

The young man remained seated. "What did you do for the revolution?" he asked.

"I used to transport ammunition smuggled from Iraq to towns in Raqqa Province."

"That's great, thank you," said the Nusra member, taken aback by an answer he didn't seem to have expected. "But why do you say that this flag will cause *fitna* and all of the problems of the Free [Syrian] Army—the thieving and the looting—aren't *fitna*?"

The comment only enraged Moayad, whose relatives were Farouq fighters, although he kept that from the masked man. "Whoever wrote this is a Zionist!" he said, grabbing the leaflet.

Things quickly escalated. "You have blasphemed because you accused somebody of being an infidel!" the Nusra member said, raising his voice for the first time. "I know the man who made this flyer; he is not an infidel!"

"God will judge me, not you!" Moayad said. "How old are you, anyway? I can't tell with that scarf covering your face. Where are you from? I don't want to know your name or see your face, but where are you from?"

"I am a son of Syria," the young man said.

Ahmed, the older man in the tan leather jacket, spoke up: "We are all Muslims. Who are you to force a flag on me? I am Syrian, and I have a flag."

Moayad sank into his armchair. One of the men cracked open a window. Another went to check whether the coffee was ready. The Nusra member calmed things down. "Do you want the Quran to be the constitution in a future state?" he asked the room. All the men said they did.

"I apologize for all of this. We are angry," a chastened Moayad replied.

"It's okay, but I tell you that you haven't convinced me of your arguments," said the young man.

"I'm telling you that you will lose all the support you have because of this flag," Ahmed said.

Coffee was served, along with pitted dates on small round plates. The talk shifted to the men they all knew from various brigades, Islamist and otherwise: where they were fighting, who had been killed, and who had switched battalions. "Look, mistakes happen," the young masked man said. "We weren't all trained. I was a student before all of this." He still hadn't touched the dates or even the coffee he had requested.

"You're going to starve to death if you keep wearing that thing," Ahmed said, referring to the black scarf.

All the men laughed, including the Nusra member—but he did not, at any time, take it off.

THE FACE COVERINGS were Abu Loqman's idea. While Nusra fighters elsewhere, as well as rebels from many groups, sometimes donned scarves to conceal their identities, in Raqqa it was a rule—Abu Loqman's, not Nusra's. "He wasn't in line with Nusra's general policies," Saleh said of his old friend. It went beyond the scarves. Abu Loqman's seven to eight hundred fighters set up checkpoints in and around Raqqa, sparing no one—not even other members of Nusra—from searches. "That wasn't our policy," Saleh said. "That was one of [Nusra leader] Jolani's edicts. He didn't want checkpoints on the road so that we didn't create problems with the civilians or other factions, but in Raqqa, there were checkpoints like the *mukhabarat*, and they covered their faces. So every time a brother passed by Raqqa, honestly he'd complain to the sheikh [Jolani]. The complaints were piling up." Jolani told Abu Loqman to fall into line. Abu Loqman ignored him.

Abu Loqman held court in Nusra's headquarters near the fallen statue of Hafez al-Assad, where Saleh often visited him. His old friend, Saleh said, was "a control freak," one who infiltrated and spied on other groups in the city and the wider province—all the way up to Abu Azzam's Tal Abyad. Abu Loqman didn't like the Farouq's control of the border post. He considered the Farouq arrogant, sitting on both the Tal Abyad and the

He wasn't in a Farouq uniform that day. He was dressed in indigo jeans, a dark-green crew-neck sweater, a black leather jacket, and navy boat shoes. He reached into his jacket for a pack of Winston Silver cigarettes, then turned to his mother. "Just so you don't hear it elsewhere, they planted an [improvised explosive] device in my car yesterday," he told her. The IED consisted of several sticks of TNT wired to the ignition of a BMW Abu Azzam often traveled in. A neighbor alerted the Farouq commander to the presence of the device. Um Mohammad put her hand up to her mouth. She had already lost one child, her middle son, on February 20, in the battles for Raqqa Province.

"May God protect you," she told her eldest son.

"Nobody dies before his time," Abu Azzam said. "I know that I am going to be killed either by the regime or by the Jabhat [al-Nusra]. There is no difference, they are both dirty."

Men on the same side were killing each other. Abu Azzam's former deputy at Bab al-Hawa, Thaer al-Waqqas, whom he'd left in charge of the border crossing, had been assassinated on January 9. The murder was considered payback for the Farouq's killing of the Islamist Firas al-Absi, the man who was ISIS before ISIS. Absi's faction was independent of Jabhat al-Nusra, and Abu Azzam now feared he was in danger from both groups—Absi's and Nusra.

The Farouq commander rattled off the names of towns and cities he said the Farouq had helped clear of Assad's forces. "What did they liberate?" he said of Nusra. "They are just here to try and impose their rules on us." He held up his cigarette: "They threatened to label me a *kafir* [infidel] because of this," he said. Bandar and other men who had just returned from Raqqa City relayed details of Jabhat al-Nusra's smear campaign there against Abu Azzam and the Farouq.

"They're calling us Farouq *sarouk*," one man said. (*Sarouk* roughly translated in this context meant "thief.") "Some of them say that we are nonbelievers."

Lunch was spread on a black plastic tablecloth on the floor—store-bought kebabs, grilled tomatoes, and roasted green peppers. "This is the first thing I've eaten all day," said Abu Azzam. It was almost 4:30 p.m. The men seated around him, including Bandar, were all university friends from Homs. They recalled those days with fondness. "I've lost so much weight in this revolution," Bandar said, laughing. "Do you remember how we used to cook in Homs?" Abu Azzam's specialty was *molokhia*, green leaves carefully picked and turned into a viscous soup served with chicken and plain rice.

One of the men recounted an incident that had happened earlier in the day in Raqqa City. He had parked his white pickup truck at a street-side coffee stall while everyone in the vehicle placed orders. The truck was flying a generic black flag inscribed with the *Shahada*. Three young women crossed the street—two in *hijabs*, skinny jeans, and tight sweaters that clung to their thighs, the third in a black *abaya*. The third girl stared at the armed men in the truck and midstreet brazenly took off her *abaya*. Under it, she was dressed like her friends. The men in the truck whooped and whistled and applauded the young woman. "She must have thought we were Jabhat [al-Nusra] because of the flag and wanted to make a point!" the driver said proudly. "So I turned up the music so she would know that we weren't! See, these are our women! This is Raqqa, and the Jabhat thinks it's going to control it?"

Lunch was cleared and the men said their good-byes. Bandar and his friends returned to Raqqa. Abu Azzam's deputy, Abu Mansour, who was also his cousin, walked into the room, bade his cousin farewell, and told him he was going to check on his family just across the border in the Turkish town of Akçakale. Abu Mansour walked the short distance home. His niece had just served him Turkish coffee when one of his two cell phones rang. "What? Where are you? I'm coming now!" he said, before rushing out the door. It was a little before 5 p.m., and Abu Azzam had just been shot.

Minutes earlier, on the other side of the border, Abu Azzam had also received a call. It was from one of his men. Jabhat al-Nusra had set up a random checkpoint at a spot dubbed "Liberation Roundabout," on the main road in Tal Abyad, and was detaining and trying to disarm Farouq fighters. Days earlier, eleven Farouq men in town had been picked up by Nusra and were still in its custody. Abu Azzam grabbed a PKC machine gun and ran out the door to intercede on behalf of his men. According to his mother, he didn't ask anyone to accompany him, although two of his men followed him anyway. He had just reached the roundabout and stepped out of his car when a Nusra fighter tossed a hand grenade in his direction, and then opened fire. It was over within minutes. Abu Azzam and other wounded men were ferried by passersby to the border crossing into Turkey, where Abu Mansour waited to rush his bloodied commander in a taxi to the local hospital in Akçakale.

The hospital foyer was crowded with unarmed Farouq fighters in plain-clothes. Um Mohammad paced up and down, carrying a blue garbage bag containing her son's clothes. She held up his bloodied indigo jeans, stared at the tear above the right knee. Abu Azzam was shot three times, twice in his left abdomen and once near his heart. Both his hands were bandaged from shrapnel wounds that also peppered his legs, as well as just above his right eye.

A phone rang. It belonged to one of the Farouq men. "Don't do anything until we get men and ammunition," he told the caller. "Calm down! Calm the men down! Here, speak to Um Mohammad and do whatever she says."

Um Mohammad took the phone. "Please, you are all my sons. This is not the time for rash decisions. We must be smart. Calm down. We are all angry. This has become personal, but we don't want unnecessary loss of life. Please calm the men down, I'm counting on you."

Abu Azzam was taken into an X-ray room. His mother leaned forward through the crowd to cover his naked shoulder with the mauve bedsheet. Another gurney was wheeled out of the emergency room toward the elevator. The crowd in the foyer gathered around it as the bedsheet was lifted, revealing a dead man. He had shoulder-length hair and looked to be in his early twenties. Um Mohammad and members of the Farouq didn't recognize him, but a short man with a close-cropped, graying beard did. He said the dead man was a member of Jabhat al-Nusra, and he even knew his name. Um Mohammad started crying. "He's so young, may God rest his soul," she said. "I buried a son weeks ago. May God help his mother."

Another dead man was wheeled out, also identified by the short man as a member of Jabhat al-Nusra. "They have eyes and ears everywhere," Um Mohammad whispered, looking at the short man. By 6 p.m., four policemen were guarding the entrance of the hospital and using a handheld metal detector to check everyone coming through the doors.

Abu Azzam was transferred to a larger hospital in Şanlıurfa, some fifty-three kilometers away. He let out a cry as he was wheeled into an ambulance. A thin stream of fresh blood escaped from under the large bandage over his right eye. Later that night, Abu Azzam's sister and other female relatives crossed into Turkey in the dark, along with their children. They were taken to Abu Mansour's home. Two Farouq men sat outside the front door, guarding it, although they were both unarmed. "If this is what it has come to—us fighting each other—then I want to sit at home and support Bashar," one man said. His view was not shared by most of the Farouq, who were itching for a fight. In a bid to calm tensions, Nusra released the eleven Farouq fighters, along with twenty-two others it had detained. "The problem is that they have forgotten that we are all fighting Bashar," Abu Mansour said of Nusra. "They want an Islamic emirate. They say that they are Islamists and we are apostates, but we will not accept that they have any sway or authority over us or others. Their fight is not to liberate Syria or against Bashar. It's to control Syria. May God heal Abu Azzam, that is the main thing, but in every province now, we will fight them."

SALEH

To Nusra foot soldiers like Mohammad, the leadership presented a united front. Mohammad wasn't privy to the machinations of the group's senior emirs. He didn't know that Nusra's Iraqi parent, Abu Bakr al-Baghdadi, wasn't happy with what his moles in Jabhat al-Nusra's inner circle were telling him. There were two principal informers, both of whom were part of the second group of leaders Baghdadi dispatched from Iraq to join Jabhat al-Nusra in Ramadan 2012, a year after the first expeditionary band headed by Jolani. The pair were Abu Ali al-Anbari, the jihadi veteran whom Jolani revered like a father, and Abu Mohammad al-Adnani, the young firebrand general *amni* Jolani didn't see eye-to-eye with.

Baghdadi's Syrian franchise was doing well—too well, his informers told him, and its leader Jolani was popular—too popular. Nusra's disciplined fighters were enmeshed in a local armed movement focused on Syria. Its men, including *muhajireen,* were encouraged by the leadership to marry local women to further integrate beyond the battlefields into communities where they were based. Baghdadi's Syrian spawn threatened to overshadow his own less-successful organization across the border. It didn't even need his money anymore. He'd once paid half its bills. Now Jabhat al-Nusra sent *him* funds—including a one-off gift of $2 million— in crisp US bills stuffed into bags and transported to Iraq in Toyota Land Cruisers. In late 2012, Nusra began paying monthly salaries: $200 for a married fighter, $100 for singles. "We had so much money and wealth, we were trying to figure out how to get it to Khorasan to support it," Saleh said, using the term jihadists apply to Afghanistan and Pakistan, where Al-Qaeda leader Ayman al-Zawahiri was based.

The money came from several sources. In mid-2012, Jabhat al-Nusra robbed a state bank in the eastern city of Mayadeen, netting the equivalent of about $1.63 million in Syrian pounds and some $108,000 in foreign currency. Aleppo, Syria's commercial heart, served as a steadier source of income, and later, so did the oil and gas fields of eastern Syria. Nusra stripped Aleppo's multimillion-dollar factories bare and sold their equipment in Turkey for millions. It overran regime bases and added Assad's military stockpiles to its own. "We had everything," Saleh said. "Power, wealth. I would drive around and people would fall over themselves just to tell me *Salam alaykom* [Peace be upon you]. Men were throwing themselves at us, just for us to allow them to join us. In Iraq, Baghdadi and his group had none of this. They were not liked. We were loved."

Baghdadi's moles in Nusra, Abu Ali al-Anbari and Abu Mohammad al-Adnani, cared less about popularity. They were cut from vintage ISI cloth—work alone, trust no one, be feared rather than loved. "They started trying to control things, to remove emirs from their positions, bring in others," Saleh said. "They weighed a person's worth based on his loyalty to Iraq." They weren't pleased with him, said Saleh, because "they knew I wasn't on their team."

Jolani sensed a growing threat from Adnani, but not initially from Abu Ali al-Anbari—not until Jolani's moles in Iraq informed him of the reports Abu Ali was filing to Baghdadi. Each leader—Jolani and Baghdadi—had spies in the other's inner circle. Baghdadi sent Jolani letters via couriers, demanding he reveal his group's lineage. Jolani demurred. He discussed splitting from Baghdadi with several trusted aides, including his deputy, the Iraqi *Shari'iy* Abu Maria al-Qahtani, as well as Saleh. Abu Maria strongly urged Jolani to split from an Iraq-based group that he said didn't have policies or a strategic plan beyond "assassinations, mass killings, silenced pistols. They kill without planning or thinking through the consequences. It's a hobby for them." Baghdadi and the ISI leadership weren't "the type to run a *dawla*—a state," Saleh remembered Abu Maria saying.

"They will ruin what we are setting up," said Abu Maria. "In the history of the *tanzim*, its strongest period is now, here in Syria, with what we are doing. This is not an opportunity to be wasted on people like this. We cannot afford to lose it."

Jolani considered seeking the counsel of Al-Qaeda leader Ayman al-Zawahiri somewhere in Afghanistan, but communications were poor. The *tanzim* still relied on letters sent by personal couriers. A reply could take months. That winter, Baghdadi got wind of Nusra's discussions and summoned to Iraq the Nusra leader Jolani, the lead *Shari'iy* Abu Maria, Adnani, and the Saudi Abu Imad, who was one of the original group to cross into Syria with Jolani. "I saw Sheikh Jolani when he returned," Saleh said. "He was really agitated. I saw him in Al-Bab [in the Aleppan country-side]," along with several other senior Nusra leaders, including the emir of Aleppo. Jolani told his men: "I went thinking we could get rid of Adnani, that he'd stay over there; instead they lauded him." Saleh laughed. Nusra's emir of Aleppo had asked for permission to assassinate Adnani and others like him. "If we kick them out, it's a problem, if we keep them, it's a problem," the emir of Aleppo had said. "Let's finish from them. They are threatening everything we've built." Jolani refused.

As tensions rose that winter between Jolani and Baghdadi, the ISI leader relocated to Syria in early 2013, moving between Al-Bab in the Aleppan countryside and Nusra's largest training camp in the area, in Ras al-Hosn, Idlib Province. Another small group of men—veteran Al-Qaeda fighters from Afghanistan and Pakistan—traveled to Syria during the same period, to link up with Jabhat al-Nusra. The group was sent by Ayman al-Zawahiri, men from Khorasan who would come to be known as the Khorasan Group, a cell the United States accused of plotting attacks in Europe and the US.

In a message hand-delivered by a courier, Zawahiri ordered Jolani to help the men from Khorasan reach Europe. They were not in Syria to fight the Assad regime, and their mission was to remain highly secretive, the letter said. Jolani hid the small delegation, but Baghdadi—through the Saudi Abu Imad—learned of their presence and confronted Jolani about it. "Why didn't you tell me that you have emissaries from Khorasan? You have a relationship with Khorasan independent of me?" Baghdadi said. Jolani replied that his orders from Zawahiri were clear—the issue was to remain between Jabhat al-Nusra and Khorasan. "And what is Jabhat al-Nusra?" Baghdadi asked. "It is part of us."

Baghdadi demanded to see the Khorasan cell. "It's not a question of 'you must see them,' we have our orders," Jolani said. "We were ordered to prepare them with passports and money, provide them with a few brothers with experience, and send them all to Europe. They aren't affiliated with us or you, they are from Khorasan."

Baghdadi refused to back down. So Jolani relented and took him to the group from Khorasan. They were in Aleppo's Eye Hospital, which also served as a prison where foreign journalists, among others, were held. (Nusra, and other rebels, had been kidnapping journalists since at least 2012).

Soon after, Baghdadi called for a general meeting of all Nusra's senior emirs. Jolani insisted it was difficult and dangerous to gather the leadership in the same place, but Baghdadi didn't care. The meeting was held in a basement that Nusra had built under its training camp in Ras al-Hosn. The proceedings were interrupted at one point after Baghdadi learned that a Syrian army general was a prisoner at the camp. Baghdadi wanted to see him. He walked the general above ground, shot him dead, and returned to the meeting.

Jolani felt threatened by Baghdadi's presence in Syria, and his new direct lines of communication with Nusra emirs. In late March and early April, Jolani embarked on a tour of key Nusra bases throughout Idlib and northeastern Syria, including Raqqa City, to shore up his support. Unlike his earlier field trips, this time he did not hide his identity—he told his men who he was. In Raqqa City, Jolani met Saleh's old Sednaya cellmate, Abu Loqman, the power in the province, and the local Nusra emir, Abu Saad al-Hadrame. Both men greeted Jolani warmly and renewed their pledges of allegiance to him. Jolani left Raqqa at 3 a.m., continuing to Deir Ezzor farther east, while Abu Loqman headed straight to Baghdadi in Al-Bab.

Three days later, on April 8, 2013, Abu Bakr al-Baghdadi publicly released an audiotaped bombshell. For the first time, he revealed Jabhat al-Nusra's ISI and Al-Qaeda lineage, and he announced that he was merging ISI and Nusra into one entity—the Islamic State of Iraq and As-Sham (ISIS)—under his command. Jolani was blindsided. He heard the news in the media like everyone else. Saleh was still in Raqqa City. Abu Loqman had not yet returned from Al-Bab. Jolani rushed back from eastern Syria in a six-car convoy toward Idlib and Aleppo, his power bases, accompanied by Nusra's lead *Shari'iy*, Abu Maria. The convoy retraced its path. At Tabqa, Jolani switched cars, as he often did, stepping out of a black Toyota FJ Cruiser into a Honda Accord. The FJ Cruiser blew up an hour later, killing the Syrian and two *muhajireen* in it. The vehicle had been fitted with a sticky bomb IED, most likely at its previous stop in Raqqa City. The Nusra leader quickly released his own public audiotape, rejecting the merger and, for the first time, publicly pledging allegiance to Ayman al-Zawahiri, while requesting the Al-Qaeda leader's mediation.

It took Zawahiri two months to respond to the feud, in a private letter leaked to Al Jazeera. When he did, Zawahiri rejected the merger, telling Baghdadi to stick to Iraq and Jolani to stay in Syria. He decreed that Jabhat al-Nusra was the official branch of Al-Qaeda in Syria. Baghdadi ignored him. His supporters argued that they weren't bound by such a decree, since Zawahiri's division of Iraq and Syria effectively recognized a colonial border, and they pounced on it as proof that the Al-Qaeda leader had gone soft.

Saleh heard Baghdadi's announcement in Raqqa, where he was waiting for his old friend Abu Loqman to return. After three days, Saleh decided to head back to Aleppo to join Jolani. He intercepted Abu Loqman on the road.

"Where have you been?" Saleh asked him.

Abu Loqman remained in his car. He said he'd been in meetings with Baghdadi. "Did you hear the statement? What do you think?"

"It's upsetting," Saleh replied. "They've ruined what we've built."

"No, no, it's a good move," Abu Loqman responded.

The pair argued about who was right—Baghdadi or Jolani. "Listen, brother, understand something," Abu Loqman told Saleh. "I am *Dawla*, *Dawla*, *Dawla* [Arabic for state—what ISIS called itself]. I will not change. Come, join us. Let's stay together."

Saleh shook his head, got back into his car, and drove straight to Jolani. It was the last time he saw Abu Loqman, who was soon appointed the ISIS emir in Raqqa Province. Saleh found Jolani upset but calm—a little too calm, he thought. The crisis was a test from God, the Nusra leader told him. "We expanded quickly and people liked us and money was coming, weapons," Saleh remembered him saying. "We didn't imagine it would happen so quickly." Jolani said that he expected trouble within the organization, "like drones, deaths of commanders, but not that we would fall into a dispute with Iraq."

Jabhat al-Nusra's six thousand or so fighters split. Some stayed with Jolani, while others, especially the more conservative *muhajireen*, followed Baghdadi's edict and joined ISIS, leaving Nusra more Syrian almost by default. The effect was profound: "All of Nusra became *Dawla*, and we were few in number," Saleh said.

Baghdadi was at a farmhouse in Al-Bab, accepting pledges of allegiance. The troublesome Adnani was appointed ISIS spokesman. Abu Ali al-Anbari also joined Baghdadi. Of the men who originally crossed into Syria from Iraq with Jolani back in Ramadan 2011, only one—the Saudi Abu Imad—became ISIS.

In the Latakia countryside where he was now based, Mohammad heard the news like everyone else. He lost twelve *muhajireen* from his unit to ISIS. Mohammad regretted bringing them into Syria. His former cellmate in Palestine Branch, Abu Othman, the *Shari'iy* from Aleppo, called him. "What do you think?" Abu Othman asked him. "What are you going to do?"

"I'm Nusra, and you should stay where you are, too," Mohammad said.

Abu Othman didn't take his old friend's advice. He joined ISIS, where he served as one of the group's Sharia judges in Aleppo. "I am with them because the *tanzim* [Al-Qaeda] was a tool for an aim, and the aim is an Islamic state, and it happened," Abu Othman told me, explaining his reasoning. "Baghdadi's view, his ideas affected me. We have reached the end point for a *tanzim* and the beginning of a *dawla* [state]. The time has come."

IN MAY 2013, ISIS began wresting Raqqa from the forces, including Jabhat al-Nusra, who won it in March. By August, it had consolidated its grip and would soon make the city its de facto capital. The group called itself "*ad-Dawla*," the state, which is exactly how it viewed itself—as a sovereign state and not an armed faction among many fighting the Syrian regime. It considered the Arabic acronym for ISIS, *Daesh*, a derogatory term, because it implied that it was a group like any other whose name could be abbreviated.

ISIS began setting up its state in Raqqa City. It looked much like the one its earlier incarnation had established in Sunni parts of Iraq after the US-led invasion in 2003. It imposed its austere interpretation of Islam on locals. It removed Christian symbols like crosses from the city's churches and turned them into *dawa*, or proselytization, centers. The female dress code Jabhat al-Nusra had suggested was imposed, the city's women forced into the amorphous black sacks and face coverings. The five daily prayers were made obligatory, and *hudud* (Sharia punishments, such as cutting off the hands of thieves) were publicly enforced. Conspirators were crucified, others were decapitated, their heads placed on the spikes of a fence that enclosed a grassy traffic roundabout called *Naem* (Paradise), which locals renamed *Jahim* (Hell).

ISIS, *ad-Dawla*, was quick to pronounce other Muslims infidels. It filled its jails with anyone who opposed or questioned it or was perceived to be engaging in anti-Islamic activities. Abu Loqman jailed Abu Saad al-Hadrame, the Nusra emir he had appointed. Civilian activists, including some of those in the basement of the sports stadium, were detained. Others fled or went underground. The stadium became an ISIS detention facility known as Point 11. Abdullah Khalil, the lawyer-turned-politician who registered complaints in a closet of a room, was arrested by ISIS. His fate is unknown. The Nusra fighter who had argued with Bandar and his friends over the raising of the black flag laid low for months and then fled to Aleppo, where he remained until the fall of rebel-held parts of the city in 2016. The two gray-haired men who challenged him escaped with their families to their hometowns on the outskirts of Raqqa City. The two younger men, Abu Noor and Bandar, stayed in Raqqa. Bandar spoke to me as often as he could during that period, addressing me in the masculine so that, should anyone overhear him, they would not know he was speaking to a woman who was not a relative. Communications were generally limited to ISIS-approved Internet cafés or private satellite devices the group allowed some residents to use. Bandar called me one day, turned on the camera to reveal ISIS's black flag on a wall behind him so I'd know where he was, then leaned into the screen and whispered, "Don't come back here, anywhere near here. They'll kill you."

"Bandar!" somebody shouted. He turned abruptly. The line went dead.

ABU AZZAM

General Doctor Engineer Salim Idris was frustrated. He sat in the lobby
of the plush Ottoman Palace hotel in Antakya one spring day, dressed in
a gray suit, sky-blue shirt, and navy tie, black shoes polished to a shine.
He looked like a businessman, not the head of the Free Syrian Army's
Supreme Military Council trying to arm an uprising. For twenty-seven
days after he was elected in December at the Antalya Conference that had
proven so disastrous for the Farouq, Idris didn't receive so much as a bullet
from the revolution's Arab and Western backers, undermining his cred-
ibility with Syria's fighting men before he'd even begun. "I have no influence over the suppliers," he said a month later. "I must beg."

He'd moved the FSA's military command to the Bab al-Hawa border
crossing, but he was often in southern Turkey meeting with donors and
diplomats. He was expecting an American shipment of nonlethal aid later
that afternoon—helmets, flak jackets, ready-to-eat meals. That's not what
he wanted. "They can keep them," General Idris said. "We need between
500 to 600 tons of ammunition a week. We get between 30 to 40 tons. So
you do the calculations."

He wanted to organize the armed uprising but wondered how he could
succeed where the Joint Command and Istanbul Room had failed. If he
could only bring half of the men under his command, he said, he'd consider it a success. The problem was that, by his count, some 70 to 80 percent were armed civilians, not defectors used to taking orders. "Bashar is
not better than us at organizing his men, but he has the power of a state.

He can bring that to bear and punish a man who won't follow orders," the general said. "It's not easy."

The general had become a lightning rod for the rebels' anger, his phone a millstone with constant calls and visits from rebel commanders complaining about the lack of supplies. "Sometimes, they come to me, they are very angry, they want to eat me," Idris said. "There are officers and revolutionaries who ask me why they personally are not getting ammunition. I can't work on supplying individuals! I must work via operations rooms to supply fronts."

He had set up an operations command center that sent senior defectors to monitor battlefields and report who fought where and how, who abandoned their posts, who responded to advice, who worked well with others, and who sat back, watched, and waited to move in and snatch the war booty. He intended to withhold support from ineffectual groups. Take Commander X, Idris said, who in the past, to impress his overseas or local patrons, "goes and fires a few rockets, creates a bit of dust, films it, and puts it on YouTube so that he can say, 'See, I worked.' Now, it's no longer like that." Commander X won't be supplied by the Supreme Military Council or included in future battles, Idris said. He'd inform the commander's patrons, too. The problem was that Commander X, like most fighting men in Syria, knew not to rely on one source for anything.

Idris was under pressure to prove himself worthy of his title. "People rose against oppression, to talk, to speak up, and now they won't stop," he said. "Everybody is an analyst, from a fighter to a commander to the refugee."

ABU AZZAM WAS frustrated. Stuck in Turkey. He had survived the assassination attempt, his wounds healing, but fear of another attack had made him a refugee. He was a member of the FSA's thirty-man Supreme Military Council headed by General Idris. Abu Azzam represented Raqqa, but it wasn't the frontline. For the first time since 2011, Abu Azzam was in a safe place, and he hated it. It was May 22. He was in Istanbul at the seaside

Ataköy Marina Hotel for a two-day meeting between the FSA command and Saudi representatives. It was the first gathering between the two parties since Saudi Arabia had nudged Qatar aside earlier in the month to take over "the military file" and become the main funnel of arms to the FSA. The Saudi delegation was led by Prince Salman bin Abdulaziz al-Saud, then defense minister and future king, and attended by the Lebanese politician Okab Sakr. The Qataris (and their representatives) were not invited.

The commanders expected a working plan to come out of the meeting, and tangible support, but by the end of it, only one front—Al-Qusayr, near the Lebanese border—was earmarked for 300,000 bullets and an undisclosed number of rocket-propelled grenades and tank shells. The Saudis distributed envelopes containing $5,000 cash to each participant to cover personal expenses.

Abu Azzam returned to his ground-floor room with an envelope. He sat on the balcony, stared trancelike at the manicured lawn, then closed his eyes and turned his face up to a bright, cloudless sky. He was in dark jeans, the same navy-blue boat shoes he was wearing when he was shot in Tal Abyad, and a gray polo shirt. "I'm in shock. I'm embarrassed to go back to my men empty-handed," he said. "I need ammunition. What am I going to tell my men? It's always promises, promises, but this time I was hoping for something more from the Saudis. Sometimes the Qataris offer you support immediately."

The Farouq had splintered after losing its foreign donors, leaving its leaders bickering. The Supreme Military Council had shut off its taps to them, but Abu Azzam still had men on the fronts fighting in the Farouq's name. Some Farouq commanders headed to the eastern oil fields of the city of Shaddadi, hoping Syria's black gold would make them self-sustainable. Assad had lost the city in February 2013. Jabhat al-Nusra sat on Shaddadi's refineries, while the Farouq had the oil wells in the countryside. One was little use without the other, but the two groups would not cooperate. Nusra snatched the wells from the Farouq, and Shaddadi's oil (as well as that of other towns) became a major source of income for the group. Nusra sold the valuable liquid to local traders, who set up makeshift refineries in rebel-held areas. Nusra also transported it to Turkey and even traded with the regime. "We have to sell it to the regime because we need money," a Nusra emir in Shaddadi once told me. "What are we going to do with it if nobody buys it? Drink it? A sea of oil is worth nothing if you can't sell it."

Abu Azzam's phone rang five times in fifteen minutes. He put it inside his hotel room within earshot and returned to the balcony. A smile, sad and regretful, spread across his face. "My phone used to ring before," he said. "Sometimes it was a girl asking me to go for a walk. Now it's all requests for ammunition, to help the wounded, or news about a battle." He reminisced about his university days in Homs. He did that often now. He remembered his friends like Bandar sitting in the cafeteria, talking and laughing, while he wrote poetry. "Sometimes I was so broke I didn't have money for a cup of coffee, but I was happy. I'd tell my friends, 'Let's go for a walk.' I didn't like being by myself back then, but now I just want to be alone." He was quiet for a moment. "Now, I've aged. I feel like an old man." He was thirty. Burdened with responsibilities he hadn't asked for. Tormented by the fear of not meeting them. "Our revolution was beautiful, but political money entered and dirtied it," he said. "Now I must wear a fake smile, grit my teeth, and kiss the feet of donors and tell them they are the crowns on my head, because men rely on me. I am tired."

He began reciting his poetry but stumbled—he couldn't remember the words. "My head is full of so many things." His phone kept ringing. He would not ignore the calls. Agitated, he sank into his chair. His polo shirt lifted slightly, revealing an abdomen disfigured by traumas old and new—angry red wounds from the assassination attempt near paler lines, dozens of them, cuts from his regime interrogations. His thoughts were as random as the scars on his abdomen. There was a girl he liked at university, he said. He smiled at the memory. "I'd scoop her up in front of the whole cafeteria, I didn't care. I'd shock my friends. They used to call me 'The Sheikh,' because I was religious, and there I was, publicly showing my love for this girl. I don't know where she is now. I hope she's still alive."

By the summer of 2013, the once-mighty Farouq Battalions simply withered away.

RUHA

Ruha's Uncle Mohammad and his wife, Noora, weren't home when the artillery crashed into their upper floor on April 25, the rocket wounding walls and raining rubble into their courtyard fountain. No one was hurt, but days later, elsewhere in Saraqeb, much nastier projectiles claimed more than concrete.

It was a cloudless day, the sky a bright blue, when the chemical weapons tumbled from a helicopter gunship, white smoke trails mapping their paths to three locations. It happened shortly after the noon call to prayer on April 29. A fifty-two-year-old mother, Mariam Khatib, died after one of the tear-gas–type canisters landed in her garden. An autopsy performed in Turkey under UN observation "indicated signatures of previous Sarin exposure" in her organs. Seven more victims, all foaming at the mouth, with constricted pupils, nausea, and vomiting, were treated in Saraqeb with atropine and recovered.

One of the canisters did not explode. It fell intact in a shallow, muddy pond near several homes. Local activists photographed, measured, and weighed it and then informed senior members of the opposition, who connected them to the Organisation for the Prohibition of Chemical Weapons (OPCW). It was the third chemical attack in Syria since August 2012, when US President Barack Obama had warned that the use of such weapons was a red line that could prompt retaliatory US military action. The Saraqeb attack would not be the last.

The OPCW didn't conduct an investigation in Saraqeb or take custody of the unexploded weapon. "They said they couldn't if they didn't pick it up themselves," an activist from the town said. "What are we supposed to do with it? After months, they told us to hide it in a cave underground and don't tell anybody that you have a chemical weapon."

The activist, an economics graduate in his twenties, was left to dispose of weaponized Sarin. He had no idea whether or not it was still live or how to deal with it. He feared its being discovered by rebel groups and used against other Syrians as much as its leaking its contents. On July 18, in the golden hue of dusk, the young man walked up a hill on the outskirts of his hometown, a desolate place populated with little more than rocky outcrops and scattered olive trees. He put down his smartphone but continued recording as he rummaged through his backpack, and pulled out a large plastic jar—the type used for homemade pickles—and a ziplocked bag containing the rusted canister. He put the ziplocked device in the jar and then cushioned it with household sponges—yellow, green, and pink. He placed the jar deep inside a tight crevice at the foot of a rock formation, as deep as his arm allowed him, then he piled stone upon stone to conceal its opening. "We thought that if we reveal the existence of the canister, that would end the regime because of Obama's red line and international laws against chemical weapons use," he said. "I had hope that the time will come and the proof will be ready, here in the cave, but nobody cared." To the activist and many like him, Obama's red line meant nothing. "I was very, very, very shocked—I can't tell you how much," he said. "Nobody cared about us or about international laws and forbidden weapons. It made me want to just wait for a barrel [bomb] to fall on me."

SARAQEB EMPTIED after the chemical attack, but Ruha's relatives stayed in their home. Aunt Mariam sat in her mother's living room one day with a younger sister, exchanging the town's news. It was early May, less than two weeks after the chemical assault, and the air strikes were ferocious. One had recently killed people and charred their bodies. A man had to be identified by a piece of his shirt. A father lost his wife and four children. "They say that every night he puts out his children's pajamas, expecting them to come back," Aunt Mariam said, "because the corpses were unidentifiable." Some of Saraqeb's families fled into the fields around their town. An NGO distributed tents to them from a bakery still under construction. Ruha's Uncle Chady, her mother's twin, was volunteering to help build the bakery. He said the bereaved father turned up there one day, asking for a tent to house a family he no longer had. Nobody had the heart to deny his request.

The shelling, once unpredictable, was now as regimented as a television viewing guide. Syrians called it "the nightly schedule." It began a little after 11:30 p.m. one night with the screech of incoming artillery crashing near Ruha's home. A second, then a third strike, each louder and closer, amplified in a night black because of the lack of electricity and otherwise nearly silent in a neighborhood emptied of families.

Hiss, whoosh, boom! 11:40 p.m. Another shell. Ruha's Aunt Noora shrieked and, flashlight in hand, led her fourteen-year-old niece Lama (whose house had been next door to the sniper at the Iza'a) out of a darkened living room toward the basement. Ruha's Uncle Mohammad cracked open the front door in case neighbors still present sought refuge with them, and then he joined his family downstairs. Grandmother Zahida stayed in her bed—as usual.

Another three rockets just minutes apart. What was the target? Like Uncle Mohammad's house, most of the washed-out, low-slung, flat-roofed concrete homes were already disfigured by earlier attacks. There were no rebel bases among them. Saraqeb's rebels had been firing Grad rockets at regime forces all afternoon from outside the town's limits, along a stretch of highway they'd won months earlier. Were the regime's strikes retaliatory, the family wondered, the word—*retaliatory*—denoting a reaction, implying a starting point. What was the starting point for that night's barrage? The Grads? The regime's air and artillery strikes before them? The formation of rebel groups? The decades of corruption and dictatorship that pushed protesters out into the streets?

11:53 p.m. Manmade thunder so close it sounded just above the room. The blast dislodged gray snowflakes from the basement's unpainted ceiling that floated down onto Uncle Mohammad and Noora, Aunt Mariam, Lama, and me. "Dear God!" screamed Noora, covering her ears with her hands. A television news report about a faraway battle could send her into a panic and her relatives into a fit of amusement at her expense. They'd sweetly chide her and remind her that even children had adapted to the sounds of war. Noora never did. She leaned against a vertical concrete support beam. The glow of several flashlights illuminated particles of dust suspended in the stuffy airlessness of the room. Insects scurried across its untiled floor. The ceiling was about thirteen feet high, the room some four yards underground, a single doorway for an exit, two narrow slits of sturdy glass just below street level—too small to crawl out of.

Mariam silently mouthed prayers. Mohammad held a black walkie-talkie up to his ear, trying to hear screechy rebel messages, but the words were muffled, drowned in static and noise. Noora wailed at every crash and thud. "It's not that bad," Lama repeated, her voice sturdy but her hands shaking. "Remember that night when we stopped counting at a hundred and fifty? It's not that bad."

11:55 p.m. Another artillery strike, then mortars and rockets in each of the next two minutes. "Whose homes are they landing on?" Noora asked.

There was no outgoing fire, only incoming—a sound heard with the entire body, not just ears. Limbs and muscles and heart and mind tense as the enraged projectile rushes along its arc. Breaths held. Where will it fall? Passive prey in a basement with only one exit. Luck the only difference between a direct hit and a near miss. The projectile lands. Exhale. Breath shallower, faster. It exploded somewhere else, perhaps on somebody else. Limbs and muscles and heart and mind relax, then tense again. The room echoing and shaking to booms reverberating in chests. The time between shells measured in heartbeats—getting quicker, stronger, melding into a single, terrified throb. Hiss, whoosh, boom!

"Maybe we should leave tomorrow," said Noora. "I can't take much more of this! What time should we leave? 5 a.m., 6 a.m.?"

"Don't worry," Mohammad said, gently patting her knee. "Bashar's pilots sleep in. We'll have plenty of time."

"Who is counting?" Lama asked. "How many is that now? It's not that bad. It's not that bad."

Mariam tried to lighten the mood. "One of my friends has a new washing machine," she said, laughing so hard she could barely get the words out. "She calls it '*auto eed, auto ijir*' [a hand-and-foot automatic]"—that is, she was washing by hand. Even Noora laughed.

12:05 a.m. A few moments of quiet, then the sound of a car outside. The family listened for the wail of ambulances. There were none. "Thanks be to God," Noora said.

12:17 a.m. The few neighbors still around ventured outside, calling out to each other to make sure everyone was accounted for. Uncle Mohammad yelled back that they were fine. On that night, the strikes tore through empty houses, not flesh and blood.

The family did not escape the next morning. They couldn't leave Zahida behind, and she couldn't—or wouldn't—travel. The next afternoon, at 1:30 p.m., just as a lunch of peas and rice, mint and cucumber salad was being laid out, a warplane screamed overhead. The women prayed loudly, Lama put her shaking hands up to her temples. The jet passed without dropping its payload. But later that evening, the familiar nightly schedule got underway—a little earlier this time, at 11:11 p.m. The family once again scurried to the basement, accompanied by the hiss, whoosh, and boom of things exploding around them.

"Why isn't anyone helping us?" Noora screamed. "Why doesn't anyone care?"

SARAQEB WAS HIT with twenty-two barrel bombs one day in July, improvised explosives packed into water heaters or barrels full of metallic fragments and dropped from helicopter gunships. The barrel bombs were crude, unguided weapons, directed only by gravity and the wind. One of the barrels exploded at the foot of Ruha's street, demolishing the home of her best friend, Serene, the young Assad supporter Ruha used to walk to school with. Serene's grandfather had invited his children and their children to lunch. Serene was the only survivor. She lost an eye in an attack that claimed fourteen of her relatives. Ruha, far to the north in Turkey, cried for her friend. The barrel bomb did not respect childhood or even politics. It didn't care that Serene's family members were closeted loyalists.

After that attack, Maysaara rushed to Saraqeb and insisted that the family members vacate to their farmhouse on the outskirts of town. His mother, Zahida, complained but did not deny her favorite son's demand. Maysaara and his brother, Mohammad, began building extra rooms and bathrooms in the farmhouse. The family complex was abandoned.

Ruha's parents enrolled their children in school that September, in an overcrowded Syrian-run facility in Antakya that offered Arabic-language instruction and Turkish lessons. They could no longer ignore a hard truth—the regime was not about to fall and they were not going home anytime soon. Ruha cried on the first day of school, but then she did that every year. "Honestly, it doesn't matter how old I get," she said, "it's a habit." She was almost twelve, and happy to be with Syrians her own age. "Now," she said, "I have somebody to talk to, to empty my heart to. To take out my frustration."

The school ran in two shifts, morning and afternoon. The older girls, Ruha and Alaa, didn't get home until 7 p.m.; their younger brother Mohammad had the earlier shift. Little Tala, who had recovered from her hormonal disorder, started kindergarten. Manal was happy to see her children regain a sense of normalcy that eluded her. Although still living "a half-life" in two worlds, she was relieved the family had moved to the farmhouse and proud that her twin brother, Chady, was helping build a bakery. She followed news of its construction as closely as her children's homework assignments.

In early October, Maysaara surprised his wife and children with a trip to Syria to celebrate the Muslim Eid al-Adha holiday. Ruha was ecstatic. She shopped for days, picking out gifts for her cousins. They returned home on October 12. The next day, Uncle Chady was killed in an air strike on the bakery. He was thirty years old. His sister was inconsolable. A shy, soft-spoken woman, Manal retreated deeper into herself. Ruha was devastated. "I wanted to see Uncle Chady before he was buried," she said. "They wouldn't let me. I wasn't allowed to go and sit in condolences, either. What do they want to protect me from? This thinking is wrong. A child should learn everything, not be told to go to the next room when adults talk. No! We need to know about the situation we are living in, to understand what is happening, to not be frightened by it."

It was dangerous to stay in Syria, Ruha knew that, but she still threw a tantrum a week later when Maysaara said they were leaving. "When I came back from Syria after that Eid, I started wishing to die," Ruha said. "I didn't want to live in Turkey. I'd rather live in Syria, even if I might die. At least I'd be in my home with my grandmother and family. We die when God wants us to, at a time of his choosing, isn't that right? So what do we think we are running from?"

Back in Turkey, Ruha voluntarily did more of the housework, quieted her siblings, helped cook. "I felt like my siblings' mother after Uncle Chady died," she said. Maysaara stayed home more. He took Manal and the children on day trips to the beach, to the mountains, to the mall as often as he could, but none of it seemed to draw his wife out of her deep sadness. Manal struggled with a grief made heavier by its invisibility. "In the beginning, they used to say the names of the martyrs," she said, "then the martyrs became numbers. The day Chady died, his name was not mentioned. He was a number, one of thirty-six people who died in Syria that day. Nobody is talking about us as people. On top of the oppression and the war, we are also dehumanized. We are people."

MOHAMMAD

Mohammad the Nusra fighter was based in the Latakian countryside, part of the sweep of territory known as the *Sahel*, or the coast. The *Sahel* extended from the twin mountain chains of Jabal al-Akrad and Jabal al-Turkman, near Turkey, down to the glistening waters of the Mediterranean and the country's two main port cities of Latakia and Tartous. It was Alawite heartland, the only place in Syria where the demographics were reversed and sectarian minorities were a majority, not Sunnis. The area included Assad's ancestral hometown of Qardaha.

Mohammad was based in the village of Doreen. Salma and Doreen were the two closest rebel towns on the cusp of regime-held territory. "A bullet in the *Sahel* is like a rocket to the regime," he once said, explaining the area's importance. If Assad lost the *Sahel*, he lost the war just as surely as if he lost the capital, Damascus. It formed his support base. In Doreen alone, seventy-five men had signed up to be suicide bombers to help push rebel forces deeper into the *Sahel*. The prospect of killing Alawites also drew foreign fighters to the area in droves. (There were foreigners on Assad's side, too: Lebanese Hizballah, Iraqi Shiite militias, Afghan mercenaries, Iranian and Russian military advisers and, later, Russian pilots.) *The muhajireen* waited with Syrian fighters—including Mohammad and Jabhat al-Nusra—in Salma and Doreen, facing sleepy Alawite villages, until August 4, 2013, when, in a predawn raid, they seized eleven Alawite villages—and 106 Alawite women and children.

· · ·

EIGHT-YEAR-OLD JAWA couldn't sleep the night she was kidnapped. An odd smell drew her out of her bedroom sometime after 3 a.m. She wondered why anyone would burn something outdoors at such an hour.

Jawa lived in the Alawite village of Blouta with her mother and siblings: two sisters—Lojayn, thirteen, and Hanin, ten—and a three-year-old brother. Nothing much happened in Blouta, which is exactly why the family was there. Jawa's father, Talal, sent his wife and children to the village after several car bombs targeted their street in the Damascus suburb of Mezzeh 86. As the breadwinner, Talal stayed behind in Damascus to run his cosmetics and perfume store.

Jawa watched cartoons in the living room. Her sister Lojayn, also roused by the unidentified smell, joined her after shutting off the gas canister in the kitchen, thinking it had leaked. Their mother woke to drink a glass of water and urged her daughters to go to bed. She was still in the living room when the lights went out, the television darkened, and gunfire erupted outside. "Hurry, gather in the corridor!" she told her children as she scooped up her sleeping son. "Mama, let's escape!" Jawa whispered. There was just one window, a small one in a bedroom, that wasn't covered in security grills. "Mama, let's go through that window," Jawa said. Her mother shook her head. "I can't fit, and your older sisters can't fit through it. I don't want to lose you. What if they take you?"

The front door burst open and armed men with covered faces barged in. Talal's wife fell to the floor, covering her baby son with her body. Lojayn locked herself in a bathroom, Jawa dove under her bed, while Hanin hid under her parents' bed. The men were in the corridor. "Kill me but don't harm my children!" Talal's wife told them. "If there are children, bring them to me," a man replied. Talal's wife didn't respond. The rebel fighters spread out through the house, shooting at shadows. Talal's wife panicked. "Okay! Okay! Stop shooting!" she yelled. She called her children to her. The family was marched onto the verandah. Hanin struggled to walk—she'd been shot and was bleeding. A rebel tank was outside their home. Gunfire and screaming in the streets. Jawa's mother asked her to go back into the house and get their shoes. She didn't want her children stepping on empty cartridges. Jawa returned with shoes for everyone except her mother.

The men with the guns told the family to join the neighbors and relatives walking in their nightgowns and pajamas toward one of the larger houses in the village. Jawa was terrified of the armed strangers, of the gunfire, of Hanin dying because she was bleeding. She felt guilty that her mother was walking barefoot because she hadn't been able to find her slippers.

They entered a house crowded with neighbors, relatives, and screaming, crying children. The house shook from explosions and Jawa shook with it. Windows shattered. A neighbor who was a nurse began treating the wounded, but she had little more than cotton wool and disinfectant. Jawa saw the woman cover a young girl's bloody face with a blanket. She didn't understand the child was dead. Jawa hid behind her eldest sister. An armed rebel distributed boxes of biscuits to quiet the children. Another asked Lojayn for coffee. "How do you take your coffee?" Lojayn asked him. "It's not to drink," the fighter said, "it's to put on wounds. Bring me the container."

Jawa watched the fighter pour coffee grounds on Hanin's thigh to stem the bleeding. Then he wrapped the wound with fabric he tore from a curtain. His face was covered. Only two or three of the armed rebels revealed their faces, with bushy beards. One of the bushy beards stepped out onto the balcony of the house and in a loud, strong voice began proclaiming, "*Allahu Akbar! Allahu Akbar!*" to a shower of gunfire. A rebel with a walkie-talkie and a Kalashnikov walked into the house. He seemed to be in charge. He told the children to go outside, the women to stay. Jawa walked behind Lojayn, who carried their baby brother.

"Put him down and stay with the women," an armed man told Lojayn.

"He won't be quiet except with me and his eldest sister," Talal's wife said. "Leave him with me."

"No," the armed man said.

It was left to Jawa to carry her baby brother outside and help her sister Hanin, who was leaning on her. The children were directed toward an Alawite shrine not far from the house. It was desecrated. Rebels were still inside, smashing images and wiping their dirty boots on religious texts. Other rebels brought the children jam, chocolate, and biscuits before herding them into a truck. Jawa's baby brother sat in her lap, her sister Hanin behind her with several of their cousins. There were bags of bullets at Jawa's feet. She was scared to step on them. Two girls told the two armed men in the truck that they wanted to say good-bye to their mothers. "Go and see them for a minute," one man said. The girls came back crying, their faces blood red. "They're all dead!" screamed Zahra, one of the girls.

"Liar!" Jawa yelled.

"Jawa and Hanin, your mother was shot in the mouth and heart and stomach."

Jawa didn't believe her. "The armed men said they'd let our mothers follow us," she said. "I thought maybe Zahra was saying that just to frighten us. I didn't think it was true, but I wasn't sure." The truck started moving. Hanin, an asthmatic, faded in and out of consciousness. The children whispered among themselves. Whatever happens, they told each other, wherever they take us, we'll stick together.

TALAL'S LIFE CHANGED with a single sentence. His cell phone was set to *silent*. He didn't hear the eighteen attempts to rouse him in the early hours of August 4, 2013. He woke at a quarter to six, just as his brother's wife was calling. "She said that armed men had entered my village and killed my wife and children and everyone in it," he explained. "That was how the information first reached me."

The forty-three-year-old father called his wife's cell phone. Somebody answered but didn't speak. Talal heard screams, cries of *Allahu Akbar*, and then the line went dead. He dialed and redialed. The calls were unanswered. He sent text messages. *For God's sake, answer,* he wrote. *Tell me what's going on.* No response. He drove toward his village of Blouta, one of the eleven seized by rebels, but he could get no closer than a military checkpoint three kilometers away. The Syrian army was shelling his hometown, backed by air support from warplanes and helicopter gunships. So much gray smoke, like vertical clouds that obscured the houses.

Talal's panic deepened. He remembered what his wife had told him: If there was trouble—and she had time—she would hide their children in an atticlike storage space above the kitchen. The father pleaded with a soldier at the checkpoint. " 'Please, sir, don't let the planes hit my house, there's a 99.99 percent chance my children are still in it,'" Talal recalled telling him. "I don't know if he listened."

THE CLIMB WAS TOUGH, uphill through a parched orchard of plum trees with yellowing leaves and fruit the color of a dark bruise. Instead of using the orchard's well-worn paths, Mohammad clambered over four-foot-high stone terraces cut like a staircase into the hillside. It was no time for a leisurely stroll. Warplanes howled overhead. It was 1:40 p.m., August 15, and the jets had already undertaken eleven sorties, accompanied twice by helicopter gunships, in a bid to win back the eleven Alawite villages. There was a smell of burnt trees, set ablaze by firepower. Mohammad extended the barrel of his Kalashnikov rather than his hand to help me up the hill. He would not touch a female who was not a close relative. He did this twice before realizing there was a bullet in the chamber.

The hilltop afforded a panoramic view of the battlefront. Three peaks, each a regime position, rose behind. In front, the captured Alawite villages were tucked into Latakia's hills and shallow valleys. ISIS and a group of mainly foreign fighters called Suqoor el Ezz had spearheaded the predawn rebel raid on August 4, when Jawa and Hanin and the other Alawites were captured. Units of the Free Syrian Army were also there, but not in the lead.

Mohammad pointed to smoldering houses in one village. The FSA, he said, was tasked with taking the territory but managed to secure only half of it. "The Free Army can't even take one village. That's how effective it is. We are the ones taking ground."

He despised the FSA, especially its defectors, who he said were "raised on Baathism." To Mohammad, the enemy was everyone who was not like him—the regime, Alawites, the FSA, Sunnis fighting with the Syrian military (most of the army was Sunni, given that more than 70 percent of Syrians were Sunni), even other Islamists who weren't as conservative as he was. "The decision-makers in this country will be those with military power," he said. "If they"—the FSA and the Syrian political opposition— "want a secular state and have the military power to create one, let them. If they are going to confront us because of our project, we will confront them. We are fighting for religion, what are they fighting for?"

TALAL'S MIDDLE DAUGHTER, Hanin, the wounded ten-year-old, called him on his landline in Damascus five days after she was kidnapped. It was the first contact he'd had with his family. Hanin told her father that her siblings and mother were with her.

"Where are you?" Talal asked.

"In Aunty's lap."

"Which aunty?"

"Aunty Ghada."

She didn't have an Aunty Ghada. A man with a Syrian accent took the phone. He told Talal that his wife and other children were dead. "You only have her left," he said. "If you want her, go to Latakia and tell the head of the Military Security branch to negotiate with us. We won't speak to anyone else."

The men holding the 106 Alawite women and children wanted a prisoner exchange with the regime. Talal, along with other families, tried and failed to get an audience with Latakia's head of Military Security. They saw his deputy, who brushed off their concerns. They approached other officials. The head of the local Baath Party chapter offered to arm the families. "After what?" Talal asked him. "After the gangs entered the area, killed who they killed, kidnapped who they kidnapped?" The governor of Latakia asked the families what the armed men wanted. "He was asking me!" Talal said. "If a dog is lost in Europe, they set up an operations room to find it. I told him, 'Am I supposed to tell you the news?'" Talal left the meetings dejected. "They don't feel with us," he said. "They're officials who are just there like a framed photo. We mean nothing to them."

The only things Talal was sure of were that one of his children, Hanin, was alive, because she'd called him, and that he'd fallen between two fires—rebels who viewed him as an extension of the regime just because he was an Alawite like President Assad, and a regime that didn't seem interested in helping him. Blouta didn't receive special government attention because it was Alawite, he said. "Our villages were neglected, poor. We have unemployment, too. I swear to God, I carried a bag on my back for three years and went from pharmacy to pharmacy and to hairdressers selling cosmetics and perfume. I worked as a night guard, as a construction laborer. Why didn't they [the rebels] think that some of us have problems, too?" He ruled out approaching the Syrian political opposition for help. "It's impossible," he said, "because these members of the opposition, whoever they are, are killers and partners in the deaths or kidnappings of our children—without exception." Talal viewed the opposition the way Mohammad and many fighters on the other side of the Latakia front viewed him.

On August 12, the first images of the Alawite detainees were released in a three-minute, eleven-second video uploaded to YouTube. They showed the women and children seated along the perimeter of a roofed outdoor area, in the presence of an armed guard in a balaclava. Talal saw his three youngest children among them, but not his wife or eldest daughter, Lojayn. The man on the phone had lied to him. Over the next month, the same captor called Talal four times, demanding a ransom of 4 million Syrian pounds (about $35,400 at the time). Talal didn't have that kind of money. He asked about his wife. The captor said she was dead. Talal didn't believe him. "Do you think your wife is the only one who died?" the captor said. "Many women died."

. . .

TALAL'S MIDDLE DAUGHTER, Jawa, the eight-year-old, felt the responsibility of caring for her wounded older sister, Hanin, as well as her baby brother. She wondered whether she'd ever see her father again, and whether her mother and older sister really were dead, as those girls had told her. Soon after all of the kidnapped Alawite women and children were transported to a dirty two-room house, Hanin was whisked away by their rebel captors. Jawa wasn't sure where her sister was, or whether she'd return.

Jawa sat in the kitchen of that grimy house, near a basket of cucumbers, her baby brother in her lap. "It's up to me now," she told him. "I have to raise you. How am I going to raise you? It's just you and me now." A woman overheard her. She told Jawa that she was a distant relative. "Don't worry, darling," the woman said, "you're not alone. I will help you."

Hanin returned days later. She'd received medical treatment. She didn't know where she'd been taken or who had removed the bullet from her left buttock, just that the doctor and his staff had treated her kindly. Jawa was relieved to see her sister again. "She was wearing new pajamas, her hair was combed and tied, her nails were cut and painted with polish. They looked after her the way Mama might have looked after her," said Jawa. It lessened her fear a little. The male doctor and a female nurse later checked on Hanin and the other wounded captives. Jawa thought the man had a kind face. His name, she recalled, was Dr. Rami.

THE SHOUT CAME from the rubble-strewn street outside one of the two field clinics in Salma, the closest to the Latakian front line. "It's one of the Alawites! It's one of the Alawites!" a man yelled. The clinic's director, Dr. Rami Habib, forty-three, hearing the cry through the sandbagged window of his dark basement office, ran toward the nine-bed, street-level emergency room. A little girl, one of the Alawite prisoners, was carried in by her captor, a foreign fighter, and carefully set on a sapphire-blue plastic sheet covering a bed.

The child was Talal's niece, a six-year-old named Reema. "Uncle, please don't hurt me!" said the little girl as the doctor reached for her bandaged left foot. Her bloodied dressings were stained brown. She wore clean, three-quarter-length pink leggings and a pink T-shirt. Her hair was short, her brown bangs swept up into a tiny ponytail that sprouted from her head like a mushroom.

"Don't be scared. We need to change these bandages," Dr. Rami said.

"Uncle, it hurts a lot," she cried. "I'm scared."

A warplane roared overhead before the doctor could reach for a pair of scissors. Rebel antiaircraft fire thundered from several positions around the clinic. The little girl screamed. Her captor (who was unarmed except for a knife) patted her ponytail while another doctor fetched a packet of biscuits and offered her one. Reema declined the biscuit. An explosion outside. The little girl was now wailing, interspersing her screams with "Uncle! Uncle! Uncle!"

Several of her toes were dark brown. Large sections of skin on the top of her foot had sluffed off, revealing red-raw flesh that bled. Dr. Rami changed her dressing and took aside the young jihadi fighter who had brought her in. A jihadi group of foreign fighters named the Battalion of Emigrants was holding the prisoners. "Tell your emir that I say hello and that this girl needs to go to a hospital because her wounds must be cleaned under general anesthetic," the doctor said. The foreign fighter nodded, swept up the child, and left.

The one-year-old field clinic was in an otherwise-abandoned apartment building. It had four doctors and ten nurses, most of them male, who lived and slept where they worked. There was no running water or electricity in the facility, which relied on diesel-run generators to power medical equipment, including a digital X-ray machine, an ultrasound machine, and a portable ventilator. The clinic, which was funded by US- and UK-based charities, was well stocked, unlike many others that lacked even basics such as anesthesia and bandages. Water came via a pipe that dipped into a spring on higher ground three kilometers away. Months earlier, the six-story building had taken a direct hit—a barrel bomb blew out most of its windows and pancaked the two upper floors, spewing chunks of crushed concrete onto rose bushes below. The pink flowers, however, still bloomed.

Dr. Rami returned to his small office—or control room, as he called it—and sat on one of the thin mattresses around its perimeter. A 10.5mm handgun in a brown holster was tucked into the space between the mattress and the wall. A TV sat in one corner, near two walkie-talkies set up to interact with the other field clinic in Salma. "I miss normal life," said the doctor. "I miss watching a movie." He reached for a pack of Red Gauloises cigarettes. There was an explosion outside that tossed bits of rubble into the room through the glassless window. Two minutes later, another explosion shook the room.

"*As-haf!* [Emergency!]" The call came from the street above. Dr. Rami rushed to intercept the casualty, a Syrian fighter hit by a large piece of shrapnel, his legs barely attached to his torso. The fighter didn't live long.

Throughout the night, men moved in and out of the control room with requests for Dr. Rami—seeking help finding accommodations for an FSA group, stocks to replenish frontline first-aid kits, supplies for a midwife. A father, clutching his daughter's hand, wanted to have his child vaccinated, but Dr. Rami said vaccines weren't available in "liberated Syria," only in regime-held areas where the Health Ministry functioned, and from international aid organizations that only dealt with governments. In "liberated Syria," hospitals were targets for regime air strikes, not government vaccination programs. A local farmer walked in with a bag of fresh green beans he donated to the clinic. "Plane in the air!" yelled somebody from the hallway. Ten minutes later, an explosion outside. It didn't take long for the call to come again from the rubble-strewn street: "Emergency!"

Two men lay on the sapphire-blue plastic sheets covering the beds— a Syrian with shrapnel in his left foot and a Chechen with two bullets in his right leg. The Chechen had been brought in by several of his countrymen. They were all dressed the same—green skullcaps on their shaved heads, T-shirts, and loose pants so short they rode halfway up their shins. "What brought you here?" one of the Syrian nurses asked the wounded Chechen.

"We came for God's name," he replied in formal, stilted Arabic.

Both men were treated and sent to better-supplied clinics farther north, away from the front and closer to Turkey. Dr. Rami returned to his control room. He'd tended to about thirty fighters and almost as many civilians that day.

"You know what we forgot to do today?" said Dr. Rami to a colleague reclining on a thin mattress. "Send the tractor to dig more graves. We'll need about ten by tomorrow, and then another twenty or thirty."

The colleague nodded. "Yes, we forgot to do that."

The doctor lit up another cigarette. "It's a slow day today, thank God," he said. Outside, the sounds of explosions continued, near and far.

BY AUGUST 19, two weeks after the eleven Alawite villages were captured, the regime regained all of them. Two days later, Talal drove to his hometown of Blouta. He saw burned and ransacked homes (including his own) and a mass grave with human remains scooped into a yellow bulldozer. Syrian soldiers in fluorescent orange vests placed bodies in bags, including two of Talal's brothers and his father. Talal had no information about his wife and children or what had happened to them. The rebel perpetrators left behind graffiti on schools and homes. GOD IS GREAT, SUQOOR EL EZZ was spray painted on one wall. JABHAT AL-NUSRA WILL BRING VICTORY TO THE PEOPLE OF SYRIA was written elsewhere.

Syrian state media reported mass graves in two of the eleven Alawite villages but didn't specify the number of dead, beyond stating there were dozens. On October 10, Human Rights Watch put the figure at 190 killed, most on August 4, including at least fifty-seven women, eighteen children, and fourteen elderly men, in "incidents that amount to war crimes."

"I was there," an Islamist foreign fighter I have known for years told me later. "There were people there who said, 'Come and see what *Daesh* [the Arabic acronym for ISIS] has done.' I walked into a room, a small room. It was full of men they had killed. They were fighting-age men, I wasn't sad for them, it's war. But when they showed us another house, my hair—not just on the back of my neck, but on my head—stood up. I was embarrassed to consider myself a human, and [realize] that other humans could do that. They had gathered women and girls in this room, from the ages of what looked like six or seven to the elderly. It was odd. There were only very young or old, there weren't any young women. They'd killed them all, and piled them on top of each other. There is no religion, no morals, no ideology that could accept that. That's what *Daesh* did, and in the name of Islam. It made me sick."

MOHAMMAD SAID THAT Suqoor el Ezz, which headed the offensive's operations room along with ISIS, had been tasked with kidnapping the Alawite women and children. "I saw some being detained and I saw others killed," he said. He was unapologetic about the killings, describing them as "one crime against hundreds of thousands of crimes committed by the regime." The Alawites, he said, "are happy that Bashar is killing us, so they needed to feel something, to feel that their stance, if not with Bashar, but not against him, was part of the crime. They had to be made to feel that. We didn't lose anything," he said after the regime regained the villages. "We killed everything in them, took everything from them, burned everything in them. We gave them a taste of what we experience."

SULEIMAN

Suleiman had survived the worst of the many dungeons belonging to Air Force Intelligence, but he was still behind bars, in Damascus Central Prison in Adra, on the outskirts of the capital. He started a diary in the child's notebook he'd bought months earlier. He titled each entry, "Tired of the Journey," then dated and signed it. He inked his first words on June 18, 2013.

> *Tired of the Journey*
> *18-6-2013*
> Another day passes. I'm sitting on my bed now, drink-
> ing warm coffee as bitter as my days, watching a silent
> challenge, a dull challenge between two friends playing
> chess. They don't seem to tire or bore of this game. . . .
> I've spent so much time in so many military and civilian
> prisons. But hope never vanishes. I almost never feel bored
> of the hope of what is to come. . . . Without hope and
> optimism I wouldn't have survived until this moment.
> And still, the chess game continues in front of me and
> the only chess stone left is the king. Will it end soon,
> I wonder? Or will he hold the ground and stay in this
> game that I watch every day, hoping that when tomorrow
> comes, I will be out of here.

There was a second entry that day, after Suleiman met a prisoner named Ragheed al-Tutari, a fifty-eight-year-old former pilot arrested in 1981 for trying to defect. Tutari was one of Syria's longest-held prisoners of conscience. A quiet man, he had spent more than three decades behind bars, shuffled among Tadmor, Sednaya, and Adra prisons. He liked to draw portraits to pass the time. Suleiman asked him to do a drawing, but not of what he looked like now. He handed Tutari a passport photo his mother had included in a care package. When Tutari spoke, his conversation was about his plans for the future after he was released. "People died because of the psychological pressure, but this man has given me the ability to look forward for fifty years if I have to!" Suleiman wrote after meeting Tutari.

> *Tired of the Journey*
> *18-6-2013*
> Optimism is our fuel! It is life. You have to taste its
> bitter and sweet, but till when I wonder? Will I enjoy
> its sweetness before time and age betray me? Till when
> will I be chained here? Till when will our freedom be
> chained? . . . . O God, I'm so surprised that I'm still
> alive! How have I survived until now? . . . . I had so many
> moments when I felt nothing. I felt I'd reached a point
> where I became numb, senseless, to the degree of despair
> and the point of depression and not feeling that I'm alive.

Three days later, Ragheed al-Tutari gave Suleiman a black-and-white portrait of a handsome, clean-shaven man in a suit and tie, a hint of a smile on full lips, his short hair slicked back. The dedication said: "This is a drawing by Ragheed Ahmad al-Tutari, born in Anawat, Damascus in 1955, a former pilot and a prisoner since November 24, 1981 until the present day. This is dedicated to my brother, Suleiman Tlass Farzat."

AFTER TWO MORE prison visits from his mother, Suleiman asked her not to come. The road from Homs, where his parents now lived in a relative's home, was full of checkpoints. His father never saw him behind bars. The old man said he could not bear it. Suleiman's parents sent him money via couriers. Suleiman wrote poetry in his diary, quizzed himself on general knowledge, quoted famous personalities, including Gandhi, Che Guevara, Shakespeare, Plato, and Henry Kissinger. He drew pictures of the woman with whom he was on a date on March 15, 2011, in a café in Homs, the day the Syrian revolution began. She was the only other person, apart from his parents, to whom he spoke in the three-minute phone calls he was allowed every two weeks. He drew her image in color portraits that filled pages, with brown wavy hair and red lips, almond-shaped eyes staring out from the lined paper.

> *Tired of the Journey*
> *9-9-2013*
> Happiness and Hope
> Come and join me like the moon in the sky
> Come and stir my life like the moon lights the darkest nights
> Come and replenish my life that has been barren for so long
> Rain on my life, love and passing. Help me to forget the
> days of misery
> Come and embrace me like a mother welcoming her children
> Let us plant the seeds of our love to flourish into green leaves
> Let us fill our life with joy, continue a hope that never vanishes
> Fly high with me to spread our love story everywhere
> Let us draw our dream and live together with love and loyalty.

On the opposite page, with a different colored pen, several undated lines:

> Prison is the life of the dead
> The cemetery of the living
> Recognizing friends and gloating enemies

It was the last entry in the book.

DAMASCUS

The gray pebbles at the Air Force Intelligence detention center in Mezzeh squeaked under my feet. I saw their color—unlike Suleiman, who had stood there barefoot and blindfolded on August 6, 2012, waiting for a bullet that never came. It was December 2013 and Damascus temporarily suspended my three arrest warrants (including one from Air Force Intelligence), to show me what it billed as something special.

Brigadier General Abdel-Salam Fajr Mahmoud, director of the investigative branch, stepped out from behind his first-floor desk, a short, gray-haired, mustachioed man in a white shirt, navy-blue pants, and parka. On the wall behind him were large portraits of Hafez and Bashar al-Assad, separated by a fake apple tree with red and yellow plastic fruit. The brigadier general was a Sunni from Idlib Province, from a rebel-held town named Binnish, which he hadn't seen since the uprising began. "In government areas, there are people from Idlib and other rebel zones," he said, "but can a loyalist dare to live in rebel areas?"

In 2012, the European Union sanctioned the general for being a "person responsible for the violent repression against the civilian population in Syria." In late 2016, the United States would name him one of thirteen Syrian officials responsible for torture, among other things.

Over two hours and three power cuts, seated in a black leather armchair in his office, the brigadier general expounded on who was in his forty-two cells and why. The prisoners were "Free Army and jihadists, extremist Islamists," he said, "including many foreigners who don't even know the places they are fighting in," as well as "old detainees from Al-Qaeda and

its affiliates who were in Syrian jails, some of them were released in 2011."
More than ten thousand prisoners had passed through his facility since the
"*ahdass*," or events of 2011, as he called them.

"In the beginning of the events, there was action to get citizens into
the streets by devilish means," the brigadier general said, like the promise
of cash handouts. Protesters like Suleiman were duped into gathering in
front of government offices to collect money, "and next thing you knew,
banners were raised and the gathering was filmed and sent to TV channels as if it were a protest. There were people known as the *tansiqiya* who
would wait for people to leave the mosques on Fridays, then they would
appear carrying banners that they would film. This became clear during
our interrogations. It is the truth and we have evidence. Foreign supporters, financial and otherwise, pushed Syrians to do this. We know this
from confessions."

Prerevolution Syria had problems, he admitted, including political
issues, but the state responded to calls for reform within weeks. The regime
did quickly institute a host of new measures in early 2011—backpedaling
on a decision to trim state subsidies, announcing a 72 percent increase
in heating-fuel assistance for two million public-sector employees, raising
public-sector wages, and issuing small cash payments to 420,000 of Syria's
poorest families. It granted citizenship to thousands of stateless Kurds living in Syria, ended the state of emergency (replacing it with a law just as
severe), and freed some detainees.

The general insisted that the security forces were attacked by protesters, not the opposite. "The orders were that no security man could disperse
a protest with a single bullet. We used to—I swear to God—a soldier or
security man before being dispatched to a protest was checked from head
to toe, and anybody found with even a knife would be penalized, and this
is the truth, until we caught some people in these gatherings, protesters,
who were killing our people."

He gestured to a man seated near him and told him to prepare prisoners to be interviewed in a well-lit room downstairs. Five blindfolded
men were paraded individually, their hands and feet shackled, their heads

bowed. The prisoners, a mix of Iraqis and Syrians, all said they were Jabhat al-Nusra. They played their roles, meekly offered their confessions. Some glanced at the intelligence agent in the room as they answered. I'd asked the agent to leave me alone with the prisoners, a request the agent denied. One prisoner claimed to have assassinated Sheikh Mohammad Ramadan Said al-Bouti, the pro-regime cleric whose death Suleiman learned of while he was blindfolded on a bus out of here. Another cried when I asked about his family. Broken, passive men who had been "fucked for months," as the intelligence agent bluntly put it.

Lunch was served in the brigadier general's office. The intelligence agent recounted parts of the prisoners' confessions as the general and his colleagues ate store-bought chicken strips and fried potato slices from aluminum packages. "You can't believe them, they're here," the brigadier general said without irony. "Many people, after being detained for less than an hour, express regret, they cry like a baby." He pointed to the chicken strips. "A prisoner here eats the same as a Syrian soldier, unfortunately. We offer them food, drink, medical treatment." Several Alawite detainees, *shabiha*, were brought into his office during lunch, to prove, the general said, that the regime also detains Alawites from the security forces if they have done wrong. The men were handcuffed, but their feet were unshackled.

After lunch, I was permitted to see a cell. I walked down a well-lit corridor with domed security cameras embedded in its ceiling. A heavy metal door. The eye-level slit opened like fingernails on a chalkboard. Silence. I put my hand through the opening, into a space dark and quiet, thinking the cell was empty. "Hey, come here!" a guard yelled. The faces of men emerged, more than half a dozen of them, blinking in the harsh light streaming in from the corridor.

2014/2015

MOHAMMAD

The brutal February chill penetrated the concrete walls of an abandoned two-story home in northern Syria. Mohammad lit the wood-fired *sobya* in the center of the living room, unaware that the heater's chimney was blocked, before sinking back onto a thin mattress on a tiled floor so cold it felt wet. The room was nearly bare, save for a faded pistachio-green couch, a walnut-colored wood-and-glass display cabinet, and a firing squad of Kalashnikovs lined against a wall. An electricity generator purred outside, keeping the lights on.

Mohammad was now an emir, one of Jabhat al-Nusra's nine senior leaders in Idlib. The province was divided into three sectors: northeastern, southern, and western. Mohammad was based in the western sector, an area of operations that extended into adjacent parts of Latakia Province. Every sector had three emirs—military, administrative, and religious (a *Shari'iy*). Mohammad was an administrative emir, responsible for evaluating membership requests and, as he put it, "ensuring all the needs of the *mujahideen*," including food, ammunition, and money. It had been months since he'd doled out a stipend to his five to six hundred men. The payments were now irregular and diminished after Nusra lost the eastern oil fields around Raqqa to ISIS the previous year. Instead of $100, single men received 6,000 Syrian pounds—about $40 at the time—married men an extra 6,000 pounds, and those with children, another 2,000 pounds per child. Mohammad counted on "donations from Muslims around the world"—either cash physically collected and then transported via couriers through Turkey into Syria, or Western

Union payments picked up in Turkey and sent across the border. He also relied on war booty—not the military spoils like weapons and ammunition used in battle, "but cars, jewelry, cash." He didn't like that part of the job. He was a fighter, not an accountant. The money shortages hampered his ability to recruit. He'd just lost a skilled defector, a colonel specialized in logistics and military planning. "He had seven children," Mohammad said of the defector. "I couldn't offer him enough to feed his children, so he went elsewhere. Before we lost the east, we were something; after we lost the east, it is a different story," he said. "People think we are Al-Qaeda so we have money, but we don't have states supporting us." He had lost the defector to Ahrar al-Sham, a Turkish- and Qatari-backed Salafi faction.

Tear-inducing smoke filled the living room, but it was too cold to turn off the *sobya*. One of Mohammad's two younger brothers slid open a window. His sister Sara and her husband also lived in the house, which was just a short walk from Mohammad's Jabhat al-Nusra base. The men of the family were all Nusra. Sara, a twenty-nine-year-old with impeccable cheekbones, perfect teeth, and a cascade of waist-length brown hair twirled into a bun, carried a large round aluminum tray from the kitchen and placed it in the middle of the floor. The family huddled around it, digging spoons into communal bowls of lentils, and red beans and rice. A message crackled over Mohammad's walkie-talkie. A suspicious vehicle was approaching a Nusra checkpoint near Mohammad's base. "Don't let it pass," a voice relayed. "Order them out. Whoever they are, they can't pass without being searched."

Mohammad pulled away from his dinner and stared at the walkie-talkie as though it were a television screen. He was expecting ISIS suicide car bombers. He'd received a tip days earlier, he told his family, "a message on WhatsApp from a Salafi Jihadi from Latakia I know from way back. He was in an ISIS meeting and he told me what they said. The ISIS emir is planning to take us on."

Sara's face betrayed her fears. Mohammad looked at her calmly: "We are ready for them," he said.

. . .

THE DEATH OF ONE MAN in the first days of January had put rebel Syria on high alert. The man, Abu Rayyan, an Ahrar al-Sham commander and doctor, was detained by ISIS in December after he approached the group, offering to mediate a dispute. Twenty days later, he was returned a corpse. He'd been shot almost two dozen times, was missing an ear, had several broken bones, smashed teeth, and a face that looked flattened. Graphic images of Abu Rayyan's body quickly spread on Syrian social media, igniting an anger that united rebels in northern Syria against ISIS.

The fearsome group crumbled under the sustained rebel onslaught. "They were just cardboard cutouts," an FSA commander in Idlib said. Within weeks, ISIS was driven out of most of Aleppo, Idlib, and Latakia Provinces. ISIS members fled to Turkey, or eastward toward their stronghold of Raqqa, where rebels hoped to expel them across the border into Iraq. Jabhat al-Nusra leader Abu Mohammad al-Jolani warned against the special targeting of *muhajireen*, who often bore the brunt of the rebel wrath. He offered his bases as sanctuaries for the foreign fighters, even as some Nusra units fought to avenge a Nusra emir, Abu Saad al-Hadrame, killed by ISIS fighters in Raqqa. Jolani and other jihadi leaders, both inside Syria and farther afield, tried to mediate an end to the conflict, but ISIS refused arbitration, including an independent Sharia court.

Tensions were high. In early February, ISIS was still present in Mohammad's area of operations, a strip that included several smuggling routes across the Turkish border. A local unit of Ahrar al-Sham had just bungled an assassination attempt against the ISIS emir in Latakia. Revenge, indiscriminate and brutal, was expected.

Mohammad changed the locations of his eight Nusra bases. His fighters set up checkpoints and bulldozed dirt into earthen berms ahead of them. Passengers and drivers were made to walk from the artificial ridges through the checkpoints while their vehicles were examined. Mohammad waited now, his eyes fixed on the walkie-talkie while his family listened and ate in silence. A burst of static, a new message. The men in the car were identified as *muhajireen,* their noms de guerre broadcast. They were known ISIS fighters, but Mohammad's hunched shoulders relaxed. "Those Chechens are with us now," he said into the walkie-talkie. "Let them through." He returned to his dinner as Sara went into the kitchen to boil water for tea.

Days earlier, on February 3, a month after rebels turned on ISIS, Al-Qaeda's central command made it clear that it was "in no way connected" to ISIS, a group it said had formed without its permission. "[ISIS] is not a branch of Al-Qaeda and there is no organizational link connecting them, and [Al-Qaeda] is not responsible for its actions," the statement said. Mohammad felt unchained by the words. "It's a green light from Al-Qaeda's command in Afghanistan," he said when he heard the news. "Now we can respond to ISIS's provocations." He had long despised the group. As far as he was concerned, its brutal haughtiness was "ruining the good name of Al-Qaeda."

Both Al-Qaeda and ISIS shared the same transnational ideology, the same ultimate goal—an Islamic state that spread from Syria throughout the Middle East, reestablishing a caliphate that ended in 1924 after the fall of the Ottoman Empire. They differed over who should lead the effort, the tactics and timing to achieve it. Jabhat al-Nusra was playing a long game. It advocated indoctrinating Sunnis to its message through *dawa,* or proselytizing, and enmeshing itself in communities by providing social services, all with the aim of building a consensus for its future caliphate. It wanted to be wanted.

ISIS seemed to prefer being feared. Although it also provided social services and won some appreciation from Syrians in its territories for clearing out criminal gangs and rebel units engaged in banditry, it terrorized Syrians into following its rules. Disobedience was met with brute force. Nusra did not practice *hudud* (Sharia punishments, like cutting off the hands of thieves), but only because it followed the Islamic principle that such penalties were suspended during times of war and applied after the creation of an Islamic state. ISIS considered itself that state.

"All the previous jihadi experiences," Mohammad said, "from Afghanistan,

Chechnya, Somalia, to Iraq, make it clear that you will fail if you lack support from the people of those countries," he said. "Jabhat al-Nusra is the best face of Al-Qaeda, and the newest. We have learned from those experiences and overcome every mistake committed in the past, by avoiding strictness with locals, not declaring new borders or a state prematurely before we can ensure its stability, and many other issues that turned locals against *mujahideen*."

He was expecting more ISIS defections to Nusra, like the Chechens who were stopped earlier at the roadblock. Fifteen fighters had already switched sides from the dwindling ISIS force in Latakia. Mohammad sent a handful of the ISIS defectors to a Jabhat al-Nusra training camp and had the rest "reeducated" by Nusra clerics in their bases. There were more than a dozen Jabhat al-Nusra military training camps in Syria, divided into basic and advanced training, with one camp that only trained snipers.

Mohammad's cell phone bleeped with a WhatsApp video message. He was close enough to the Turkish border to pick up its cell reception, which in any case extended deeper into Syria ever since the Turks erected additional towers along the frontier in late 2012 and 2013. The message was from his daughter, a primary schooler who lived in southern Turkey with her mother and younger brother. "Baba, when will you come home?" she asked. "*Khalas*, enough. I miss you."

"I miss you, too," Mohammad replied, "but you know I'm here because I have work to do." The messages went back and forth. He asked his daughter about her grades, told her to focus on school and to obey her mother. He didn't know when he'd be back, he said, "but your mother will tell me if you or your brother misbehave."

Mohammad's battlefield was larger than Syria. Borders meant nothing to him. "You forget all other affiliations—tribal, national, family, or geographic—you just have Islam," Mohammad said, "so honestly, Syria doesn't mean anything to me. My goal isn't this country." At the height of the Afghan jihad against the Soviets, he said, there was one Al-Qaeda training base in Afghanistan called the Farouq Camp. "There are now Farouq training camps, not a camp, in Syria," he said proudly. "The one

Farouq training camp in Afghanistan, it's very famous. Its graduates include [9/11 hijacker] Mohammad Atta. If it did all of this to the world, then what do you think the many camps in Syria will do?"

Mohammad was doing his part to lay the foundations for exporting jihad, setting up a sleeper cell of Palestinians and Arab Israelis in Israel. The first node was in place, a twenty-five-year-old Arab Israeli from Jerusalem transplanted to Syria. The man had contacted Mohammad four months earlier via Facebook and then Skype, asking to undertake a suicide mission in Syria. After two months of talking, and extensive background checks—*tazkiya*—by Salafi Jihadis in Palestine and Jordan, Mohammad facilitated the Arab Israeli's travel to Syria. "I placed the condition before he came here that, as soon as he arrived, he was going on a martyrdom mission, and he was keen to do that," said Mohammad. It was a test. "If he was with [the Israeli intelligence agency] Mossad, he wouldn't have done that. He might have said he didn't want to die immediately." The Arab Israeli was an expert in hand-to-hand combat. Mohammad made him a trainer in a Jabhat al-Nusra camp near Aleppo, while he mined the young man's contacts in Israel until he had a cell of almost three dozen men. Six of the Arab Israeli's friends followed him to Syria. "You'd be surprised if you saw him," Mohammad said. "You won't think that he is a Salafi Jihadi." He scrolled through his Samsung phone, stopping at photos of a muscular, clean-shaven young man in tight, fashionable clothes—the same man whose passport and other identification papers were in a plastic pocket in the walnut-colored wood-and-glass display cabinet in the living room.

Mohammad's phone rang, the tone a snippet of an Osama bin Laden speech. The local ISIS emir, a Tunisian, was at Mohammad's Nusra base down the road and wanted to see him. Mohammad sipped his tea slowly. The Tunisian could wait. Mohammad wasn't in the mood for another confrontation. He'd already had several with the Tunisian since rebels turned against ISIS. "You have betrayed us," Mohammad remembered the Tunisian saying. "How can you call yourselves our brothers and we're fighting these apostates and you're sitting and watching us?"

"What are you talking about?" Mohammad recalled telling the Tunisian.

"As far as we're concerned, you're Muslim and they're Muslim and you're fighting each other. You have forgotten about Bashar." But that conversation was before Al-Qaeda's disavowal of ISIS. "Perhaps in our history there have never been the kinds of disputes between Salafi Jihadis like the ones we are seeing in Syria," Mohammad said.

He finished his tea and reached into his jacket for a white envelope, placing it on the lone glass-topped coffee table in the living room. "These are the passports for the Germans," he told his sister, "in case they come for them while I'm not here." The envelope contained forged Syrian passports, bought for $1,700 each, for a German ISIS fighter, his wife, several children, and two other German women whose husbands were killed in action. The foreign fighter had asked Mohammad for refuge and a way out of Syria. Although Mohammad disliked ISIS, he felt duty-bound to aid a Muslim who sought his help. He placed the Germans on the first floor of the two-story home where he was squatting. The Germans spent more than a week there, before moving onto another location. The women, Sara said, barely spoke any Arabic, although she was happy for the female company. She rose to put the envelope in the walnut-colored display cabinet, near the plastic pocket containing the Arab Israeli's passport, as her brother drew his jacket tight around him and slipped into an icy night.

MOHAMMAD'S YOUNGER BROTHER was looking rather pleased with himself. He stood among the bulging black plastic bags covering the living-room floor like a general surveying a battlefield. It had taken him days of scrounging around local stores to secure enough nonperishable food items and cleaning products to fill the fifty bags around him. He'd even conducted a minisurvey: "I asked around what people wanted before I went shopping," he said. "Detergent was the most important."

He was shorter and smaller than Mohammad in every way—twenty-five years old, with plenty he felt he needed to prove. He was a defector— he had worn the stain of a Syrian army uniform during the revolution before Mohammad helped him defect. He lacked the status of being a graduate of Sednaya or Palestine Branch or any other of Assad's prisons. He was still just a teenager when his eldest brother, Hossam, the one who was presumed dead, fought with Al-Qaeda in Iraq in the epic battle for Fallujah against the Americans. What had he done? He couldn't even defect without Mohammad's help. A good death, he figured, would make up for his unremarkable life.

He was a young man impatient to die, willing forward a Judgment Day he believed was near. Like his missing brother, Hossam, he hoped that he too would have his epic battle, perhaps the one foretold in prophecy between a Muslim army and the infidel forces of Rome—the ancient empire referred to in the old scriptures represented by the modern Christian West. "This is nothing," the young man said of the hundreds of thousands already killed in Syria. "What we're seeing now is nothing." The dead would soon litter the earth, he said, ahead of Judgment Day, leaving barely a handspan free of corpses: "Their stench will make the birds fall from the sky." He spoke of it with relish. He wanted to be in Dabiq, a sleepy farming village in the Aleppan countryside about ten kilometers from the Turkish border, the site the scriptures said was the location for the apocalyptic clash. It was close, just a drive away, but there was one problem as Mohammad's brother saw it: "Dabiq is now controlled by ISIS," he said, "but we will win it back in time. We must."

The fifty bags—each one packed with vegetable oil, rice, sugar, bulgur, tea, pasta, laundry detergent, dishwashing liquid, *miswak* sticks, and candies—were to be distributed to families living around his Nusra base. A Saudi colleague in Jabhat al-Nusra had donated $700 for the supplies. Mohammad's brother readied Nusra pamphlets about appropriate female dress and the group's message of *dawa*, to distribute alongside the small aid package.

In Mohammad's area, Nusra had much bigger relief programs, with free medical clinics and pharmacies, a system mirrored throughout northern Syria. Nusra ran its own bakery, selling twenty loaves of flat Arabic bread for 70 Syrian pounds, and posted guards outside other facilities to prevent less-disciplined rebel groups from pushing into line and demanding free bread. In certain neighborhoods of Aleppo, after regime air strikes targeted bakeries, Nusra made home deliveries of bread, a goodwill gesture that endeared it to locals, while enabling the group to collect detailed demographic information about who lived in its vicinity.

Mohammad's brother heard his name called from outside. Several of his Nusra colleagues, including the Saudi donor and two Algerians, were waiting for him. He lugged the plastic bags down to his black Kia Rio, loading up the trunk and most of the backseat of a vehicle that bore a Jabhat al-Nusra license plate (but no number), and white lettering across its hood that spelled out the same. The Algerians relayed the morning's news—three roadside bombs had detonated near a Jabhat al-Nusra car, killing two of its three passengers. "May God rest their souls, and may we follow them soon," said Mohammad's brother. He suspected ISIS. The Saudi nodded and sat in the front seat as the Algerians walked back to their base.

MOHAMMAD'S SISTER, Sara, busied herself in a living room now free of the clutter of her younger brother's black bags. She dipped a cloth into a bowl of water and wiped a fine ash powder, deposited like a thick layer of dust by the blocked *sobya* the night before, from the few items of furniture. It was a crisp, sunny Friday.

The midday call to prayer floated in through the open window. The Tunisian ISIS emir was giving the day's sermon, broadcast over loudspeakers. He began with a rant against the evils of democracy and those who advocated it, a view shared by Nusra. He had seen what he termed "the reality of these people" in Tunisia, before his pilgrimage to Syria. "They curse God and the Prophet, peace be upon him, and say it is freedom of expression. They walk around naked and say this is freedom! If you are a Muslim and express your opinion, you are a terrorist! If you call one of them an infidel, they say you are an extremist!"

He turned to the news of the day—the rebel attacks against ISIS—but did not directly address Al-Qaeda's repudiation of his group. "Look at our enemies. Who are they, what is their ideology, and who are their backers?" he asked. "Their financing is from countries that don't want an Islamic project in Syria or Iraq. Think about it! How can we accept those in Syria who sit with Turkish and Qatari intelligence?" The Tunisian led the congregation in prayers: "God keep us far from *fitna* [discord]. God help us create an Islamic state. God make us victorious over the infidels. God grant us victory over Bashar."

The men streamed out of the mosque. Sara peeked from behind a curtain, pointing out those she knew. There was a Syrian teenager, drowning in a sea-blue *shalwar kameez*, who had publicly declared his father an infidel because he opposed ISIS. A redheaded Chechen Nusra fighter passed under the window, walking alongside a Syrian colleague who lived next door to Sara. The Syrian, Sara said, "killed his own father and uncle after Nusra found them guilty of collaborating with the regime. He shot them dead. See the front porch? He killed them there." She spoke without emotion about a man who had made his mother a widow.

She had once had another life. A city girl, Sara had grown up in the capital of Latakia and worked on the assembly line of a honey factory in the southern Turkish town of Antakya while her husband was incarcerated. He was released five months ago. "I enjoyed working. I worked for three years, and I can work now if I want. People think that if we wear a *hijab*, we are from the Stone Age. We are not the same as the Qaeda of Pakistan or other places. Our society is different here," she said. "Look at Saudi Arabia, they're not Al-Qaeda, but women there have fewer rights than we have here. They can't come and go freely or drive cars. I can. Look at my brother Mohammad. Where is his wife? She's in Turkey. She's working, living in her own apartment. She doesn't wear *niqab* or anything like that, and he's a Nusra emir."

Sara took pride in her current role. "The thing that makes me happiest now is to see my brothers after they come back from an operation. I'm the first to see them, to cook for them, wash their clothes, and the same for my husband. This is enough for me now. There is no need to think about another life."

To Sara, Al-Qaeda wasn't simply a group her family was part of. While she did the housework, she listened to Osama bin Laden speeches archived on a Samsung laptop, and she read the group's manifestos.

Her husband had returned home after prayers and headed into the shower. "Hand me the nail clippers!" he yelled from the bathroom.

"Where are they?" Sara bellowed.

"Next to the grenades," he said. She reached into the walnut-colored wood-and-glass display cabinet for the nail clippers and pulled out a bottle of moisturizer she applied to her hands.

"Look at my hands!" she said. "When did my nails ever look like this? I feel like I'm on a front too. I have to do everything here, and all by hand— the laundry, the dishes. I used to use cucumber face masks, take afternoon naps, comb my hair, wear makeup. My whole life has changed."

A FEW DAYS LATER, Mohammad came to Sara with a request. The detained Alawite women and children, including Talal's family, were now under the supervision of Syrians from the Free Syrian Army (instead of the group of foreign fighters), although Nusra controlled their fate. Nusra needed women who would see to the Alawites' needs. Mohammad asked Sara whether she would volunteer. She shook her head. One of her friends was helping the captives, she said, but she wasn't interested.

"I used to have Alawite friends," she told me. "We never in our lives thought of sectarianism in our country, we never talked like this. I never thought that I would want to live far from the Alawites. Never. Now I do. I am scared of them and they are scared of us. There is blood between us, both ours and theirs. I feel bad for those women [in detention], but I feel worse for our women in Assad's jails. At least the Alawites aren't being raped. I will not help them."

Her previous life in Latakia, the one with her Alawite friends, was a distant memory. "We have nothing to do with the other parts, the regime areas, or the people in them. We are two different countries now."

BANDAR

There was no point in sleeping. The first flickers of a January sun, impatient to crack through a dark sky, would soon bring light, but no warmth. Bandar slid behind the wheel of a black Hyundai Avanti he'd borrowed. Two of his cousins, aged sixteen and seventeen, climbed into the backseat, while a friend in his midtwenties got comfortable in the front. They had a long drive ahead—from Raqqa City to a small village on the outskirts of Aleppo, where Bandar's two cousins lived. He had promised to get them home. He always preferred traveling in the darkness, when the roads and the skies were empty. Assad's pilots generally worked day shifts.

The fighter at the ISIS checkpoint just outside Raqqa City assured Bandar the road ahead was clear. The ISIS fighter even offered the men in the vehicle an early morning coffee, but they politely declined. Two hours later, a little before 6 a.m., Bandar slowed at another ISIS checkpoint, this one just ahead of the Tishreen Dam on the Euphrates River. The dam was in the northeastern Aleppan countryside, no more than twenty kilometers from his cousins' home. There was just one armed man, his face covered in a scarf, at the checkpoint. He asked Bandar where he was going and his family name. "We know you," he said.

"How do you know me?" Bandar replied. "I'm just a civilian. What's going on?"

"What's going on?" the ISIS fighter asked. "You don't know what's going on? Your Free Army is killing our brothers and raping our sisters."

"What are you talking about, and what do I have to do with any of that?" Bandar asked. It was January 4. He hadn't heard the news. He didn't know that on January 3 a rebel uprising had been unleashed against ISIS, and that it had started in the countryside around Aleppo.

The ISIS fighter radioed for backup. "Routine procedure," he said. A pickup truck of armed men arrived, their faces covered. Bandar was ordered to drive behind them to a nondescript concrete office adjacent to the dam, some five minutes away. He remembered looking at the still waters on either side of him, the way the morning sun glinted off the surface like a mirror. He felt as calm as the waters until the men rushed out of the vehicle, pulled their guns on him and his friends, and dragged them out of their car. They were marched, confused, into the office, where another man who seemed to be in charge was waiting for them. The commander's accent revealed he was from Hama.

"Your family is Free Army," he said. Several of Bandar's clansmen were indeed part of a Free Syrian Army battalion in the Aleppan countryside.

Another ISIS fighter reached toward the bulge created by a pack of cigarettes in Bandar's shirt pocket and crushed the pack under his feet. "Look at what the infidels smoke," he said, laughing.

"These men are worse than infidels," the commander said. "They are apostates. Take them to the jail."

"We won't go!" Bandar blurted out. "You're mistaken! We have nothing to do with anything!" He didn't know anyone who'd been released alive from an ISIS prison. "I'm the brother of a martyr from Baba Amr!" he said. It usually garnered him respect, but the ISIS commander just stared at him with eyes Bandar couldn't read. "Bashar al-Assad wants us and to you we are apostates? We're Muslims," said Bandar. "This is ridiculous! A mistake! We won't go! You don't know anything about us, you haven't asked us anything!"

An ISIS fighter whispered into the commander's ear. "Bring them," the commander said. Two teenagers, about the same age as Bandar's cousins, walked in. The ISIS commander told the pair to take a few steps until they were standing in the frame of the front door. They were FSA, he said. He lifted a pistol and, without another word, shot each boy in the head. Bandar feared his knees would buckle. When an ISIS fighter in the room told his new prisoners to empty their pockets, take off their belts, and follow him, Bandar and his companions did so meekly, stepping over the streaks of blood formed by the bodies being dragged away.

ABU AZZAM AND THE REMNANTS OF THE FAROUQ

Abu Azzam despised exile. He couldn't get used to it. The waiting to return, the wanting, only deepened as time fattened the space between the *then* of Syria and the *now* of Turkey. If he couldn't be home, he had to be as close as possible, in a Turkish town adjacent to a border post he once controlled. Nusra and ISIS and their death threats were on the other side. His new home was a small apartment, cramped and crowded with his mother, younger brother, his late brother's two children and widow, as well as assorted other relatives.

He missed Syrian dirt on his boots, missed commanding battles instead of reading about them. He wanted to fight—against Assad, Nusra, ISIS, and all those trying to "force Islamist beards on the revolution," as he put it. He was a pious man, that was his personal inclination, but he didn't believe in imposing his views on others.

"Exile is just a phase," he would say, repeating it like a mantra. He wondered which group he would fight with when—not if—he returned to Syria. The Farouq Battalions had collapsed, killed by internal leadership rivalries and the fickleness of international sponsors. They had tried to stay independent, to avoid relying on any one benefactor, but independence was not a virtue that donors cherished. "We were too big," Abu Azzam said of the Farouq. "If I recruit someone and turn him into a soldier and I'm not feeding him, I'm basically telling him to go and steal. For me, it would have been better to keep two hundred fighters and manage them, relying on spoils of war and donations from here and there, instead of eight hundred I could not feed."

Elements of the Farouq reorganized, led by its strongest northern branch along the Turkish border, which merged in January 2014 with twenty-one small rebel units to form the core of a new militia called the Hazm Movement. Hazm's leader was one of the Farouq's founders, the former realtor Abu Hashem, the man with the foreign connections. Abu Azzam didn't like him. He wanted to fight, but not with these former Farouq colleagues in Hazm: "They didn't come and support me during my battle against ISIS and Nusra," Abu Azzam said. "That's the reason."

He still attended meetings as a member of the FSA's thirty-man Supreme Military Council, a body with no leverage over groups on the ground, but for Abu Azzam, at the very least their peers had elected the members. That alone made it worth trying to salvage. "We need institutions, not the politics of personalities like the Assads," Abu Azzam would say. "We must build new institutions for a new Syria. Even if they are weak, it is better than if they're nonexistent."

The Supreme Military Council's chief, General Doctor Engineer Salim Idris, had fallen into the same predicament that the Joint Command and Istanbul Room had faced. He couldn't always count on weapons and ammunition from states backing the revolution. It was now early 2014. The last time he'd unpacked an ammunition shipment was August 20, 2013. Securing the arms pipeline was one issue, what happened to those guns inside Syria perhaps the bigger problem. Some rebel warlords stockpiled and sold what Idris provided. He despised some of these civilians-turned-warlords, and they in turn detested his past military service. "They are upset that Bashar is pillaging Syria only because it means they can't," Idris said of them. "They are stockpiling, thinking Bashar will soon fall, and after that, they will need to flex their power to get a piece of what Bashar lost."

In early 2014, it became worse for Idris after the FSA's emergency stockpile of weapons and ammunition—the strategic reserve he kept in a warehouse near the Bab al-Hawa border crossing—was stolen by rebels. Soon afterward, Idris was dethroned in an FSA coup within the so-called leadership body. Meanwhile, covertly, the Americans, via the Central Intelligence Agency, had, since mid-2013, been working on a new mechanism for the distribution of arms and ammunition. It was code-named Timber Sycamore.

AFTER YEARS OF being on the sidelines of the Syrian uprising, the Americans, via the CIA, moved into the lead. The program began with the delivery of nonlethal aid—including the uniforms and radios that General Salim Idris had once scorned—a means for the Americans to establish relationships and the reliability of certain rebels, and to set up supply lines. Within months, toward the end of 2013, the White House approved amending Timber Sycamore to allow lethal assistance. The northern and southern fronts of the insurgency were to be fed from across the Turkish and Jordanian borders, respectively. In Turkey, this new operations room was known as the MOM, for Müşterek Operasyon Merkezi, while its Jordanian counterpart was called the MOC, the Military Operations Command. Unlike Okab Sakr's Istanbul Room, the Joint Command, or the Supreme Military Council, this newest attempt to coordinate and supervise the flow of arms and ammunition was not staffed with Syrians. Instead, it gathered representatives of several states and their intelligence agencies, including the United States, Saudi Arabia, Qatar, Turkey, Jordan, France, and the UAE. The CIA chose, vetted, and trained select Syrian armed groups, while the MOM/MOC provided them with money and weapons, including—for the first time—US-made TOW antitank missiles from Saudi stockpiles. It was all highly secretive.

Abu Hashem's Hazm Movement, the new incarnation of Farouq—with its four thousand fighters across Idlib, Aleppo, Hama, and Homs Provinces, as well as parts of the Damascene countryside—was entrusted with the first advanced US weaponry to enter the Syrian battlefield, the TOWs. The group's commanders had presented the Turks and Americans with a blueprint for their new faction many months ahead of its formal announcement on January 25, 2014. "It was a complete program for a new future army and social movement," said one of Hazm's leading commanders. The proposal was divided into phases: the current military effort to topple the regime; then a postconflict transition in which Hazm's military units would be incorporated into a new national army, and its political component transformed into a party in a civil state. "The CIA said, 'Go ahead, we'll support you.' They gave us the green light."

The CIA vetting was done in batches of between fifty to a hundred Syrians, mainly in southern Turkish hotels and sometimes on the training bases. A few hundred of Hazm's four thousand men went through the process. Almost all passed the CIA screening. "You could count them on your fingers, the ones who were rejected from all five training rounds," Abu Hashem said. The Hazm fighters were flown to camps in Qatar and Saudi Arabia for three weeks of instruction on the types of Russian-made light weapons many had been using for years. No more than sixty members of Hazm were trained in operating TOWs. The fighters returned to Syria with new uniforms and monthly salaries of between $100 and $150 a man.

The MOM was based in Turkey, not far from Reyhanlı. Representatives from Hazm, and later other Syrian groups, were expected to present detailed battlefield strategies, including the amount and type of ammunition required. Requests were evaluated by the MOM's member states. Maps were studied, satellite imagery consulted. It was more of a war room than any of its earlier incarnations, and one that intended to enforce accountability and ensure weapons didn't end up in nonvetted hands. New TOW missiles were only provided after spent TOW casings were returned. Each launch had to be recorded, the videos of their use submitted to the MOM. Salaries were paid out in fresh $100 bills. Hazm's monthly budget averaged $500,000 and later expanded to $700,000. "We were comfortable," a former Farouq commander in Hazm said. At least initially. The MOM was soon plagued, however, by the same problems that affected earlier attempts to streamline supplies: The foreign states played favorites with groups on the ground, picking their teams. "Some states back plans to support factions that are in its interests and its worldview, not the revolution," Abu Hashem once said. "We, the Syrians, are still a playground for everyone." Bureaucracy inside the MOM delayed battles. Events on the ground could change within hours, but plans sometimes took weeks to get approval, deliveries of weapons and ammunition just as long.

With its four TOW launchers, Hazm was instrumental in helping repel both ISIS and the regime from parts of northern Syria in early 2014. "We had victories we couldn't have dreamed of," a senior Hazm official said. "The regime had two things that we previously couldn't counter— armored vehicles and aircraft. The CIA wouldn't give us antiaircraft weapons, but the TOWs forced regime tanks back once we hit a few of them. They started sending bulldozers ahead of their tanks, and we hit them, too. It helped us advance in many areas, enough to alter the balance during battles."

The TOWs weren't the first antitank weaponry on the Syrian battle-field. Rebels had captured and used regime stockpiles of the Russian-made Konkurs, Metis, and Kornet, and while Hazm's TOWs (BGM-71 missiles about two decades old) weren't the latest version, they signaled a shift in the US approach to the Syrian conflict. It was psychological assistance as much as practical. "It meant the Americans were serious," the senior Hazm official said, "and the Americans are doers."

BANDAR

The makeshift ISIS prison at the Tishreen Dam was a storage room two floors underground. Bandar knew several of the men in there, including an old university friend named Mohammad, an English major like Bandar who had studied at Aleppo University. Mohammad was detained on his wedding day, stopped at the same ISIS checkpoint near the dam before he reached his sister's home on the other side of the reservoir. He had gone to pick her up to attend his wedding. The ceremony never occurred. The ISIS fighters said he was an apostate because he'd once worked as an administrator with the Farouq Battalions in Minbej, in the Aleppan countryside. That's why he was there, with Bandar and all the other men, in a cell measuring four meters by four meters with no windows, no light. Dank and cold, empty except for thin mattresses on the floor and a few blankets. Bandar was sure he could fix his misunderstanding once he explained himself to an ISIS judge. His eyes adjusted to the dark. He kept them fixed on the green door that led upstairs to where the ISIS fighters congregated, overlooking the water.

That first night, Bandar was summoned upstairs alone, spat on by fighters—and, more distressing to him, also by children ISIS was training—as he was directed into a room to see the same ISIS commander. Bandar's laptop, camera, and mobile phone were on the mattress near the ISIS emir. They'd been in his car.

"Do you know that the Free Army has killed our brothers?" the emir asked.

Bandar shook his head.

"Your family is Free Army. What is this equipment? You are a journalist."
Bandar said he wasn't.

"You're a journalist," the emir repeated, "and journalists leave behind
electronic taggers for warplanes. You must deal with the West, too, given
your English."

Electronic taggers. Always the same excuse, Bandar thought. These
Islamists were obsessed with the idea that people were tossing electronic
taggers to guide warplanes to their locations. Why? It's not as if their bases
were secret. Everyone knew where they were, and besides, they were
rarely hit. Most of the regime air strikes in Raqqa targeted civilians.

"What West?" Bandar asked. "Who in the West? I have nothing to do
with anything you have just said except that I studied English at university."

"You and people like you have dirtied our jihad," the ISIS emir
responded. "You are from a dirty Free Army family."

"How did we dirty anything?" Bandar asked. "Were you in Homs like
my brother?"

Anger shot the words from his mouth before he could swallow them.
The emir's face was covered, but his eyes smiled. He turned another laptop toward Bandar. "Look what we do to people like you," he said. The
image on the screen was of men kneeling in a row. The executioner's knife
was busy farther up the line. Islam prohibited the slaughter of an animal
in front of another, let alone a man. Bandar's jaw muscles tightened: I'm
going to get out of here, he told himself, and I'll somehow make these sav-
ages pay. I'll find somebody, some armed group to hold them accountable.
It was a thought as fanciful as the charge of apostasy against him.

He had witnessed public executions twice in Raqqa's squares, walked
past heads placed on the spikes of the roundabout near the bakery where
he used to buy his morning pastries. "Life is black," Bandar once told me
after ISIS became a force in Raqqa. "Everything is black. They kill people
in front of children. They raid homes looking for satellite Internet. Blackness. They have killed life." He especially hated the group after it desecrated the Armenian church in the center of town. He watched them do
it. He was walking home after having breakfast with a friend at a café when

he saw the ISIS fighters approach the church. They yanked the crosses off the building and replaced them with black flags. To Bandar, that's when ISIS killed what remained of the revolution. Later that night, under cover of darkness, a small group of Syrians returned to the church, hoisted a fallen cross over their shoulders, and chanted, "One, one, one! The Syrian people are one!" It was impossibly brave. Bandar would have joined them had he known about it earlier. In the weeks and months that followed, he turned day into night, sleeping until the evening and rarely venturing outdoors. He refused to see the blackness of Raqqa except in the dark.

He hated everything about the ISIS emir sitting opposite him near the Tishreen Dam. Hated his smug entitlement to an absolute power he'd stolen from a revolution he scorned, his bastardization of a movement through barbaric force, his ignorance. Bandar was returned to the darkness of the underground cell, walking past the fighters and children who laughed and spat on him as he descended the stairs. "You smell like an infidel!" a child said. "The FSA are infidels, apostates!"

THE PRISONERS could hear the bullets, even two floors below the earth. The dam was a training ground of sorts, a camp for child recruits as well as adults. The numbers swelled behind the green door. Fifteen became thirty, and soon approached fifty. One man had been detained for selling cigarettes. He was released after a few days, or at least he didn't come back. Seven men from a Free Syrian Army unit in Deir Ezzor. A Nusra fighter from Aleppo. A civilian activist. A man caught with an illegal satellite device who developed appendicitis and was released on medical grounds. Bandar envied him. He wished he'd be stricken with some similar affliction, but then again, it was unlikely to get him out. His charge was far more serious than a satellite Internet connection. Bandar kept asking the guards for a trial, to explain himself to an ISIS *Shari'iy*. They ignored him.

The prisoners were marched up the stairs five times a day, spat on and insulted on their way to perform ablutions and obligatory prayers. Sometimes, in the evenings before the last prayers, when the ISIS recruits and trainers were done for the day, they'd fire bullets at the prisoners' feet and watch them jump, just for fun. The same guards who fed their prisoners chicken, fish, and kebabs would randomly pull men out of the cell and beat them near the door, where the other inmates could hear them. One prisoner became hysterical. He'd laugh as he was pummeled, laugh and laugh until he was tossed back inside. Bandar worried about his younger cousins, tried to keep their spirits up even as his own sagged. He'd stopped believing they'd get out. He couldn't eat. Could barely sleep. Nobody knew they were there. Why hadn't he told anyone he was traveling that morning so somebody would expect him? Why hadn't he called someone to find out about the road? Why had he taken that road when there was another? Why hadn't he just blown past that one guard at the checkpoint instead of waiting while he called for backup? Why hadn't he listened to the news the day before? So many whys. Too much time to contemplate them. Simple mistakes. Stupid decisions. Fear and regret consumed his hours. None of it helped. He was where he was.

The men in the cell learned to fear one person: Salaheddine al-Turki, a Turkish ISIS executioner based in Raqqa. "Salaheddine is here!" the child recruits would chirp upstairs. The beatings became beheadings when Salaheddine arrived. Two of Bandar's cellmates were summoned, one after the other, and didn't return. "They've been released," he told his young cousins. "They'll tell our family where we are." One night, when the men were sleeping, an ISIS guard walked into the cell and stepped over Bandar to whisper into the ear of his friend Mohammad, the man detained on his wedding day, who was lying near Bandar: "Tomorrow we will cut you," he said. "Salaheddine is coming." Mohammad didn't believe him. He hadn't done anything, and besides, in addition to English he was also a Sharia graduate. He was sure he could use the Quran to convince Salaheddine and anyone else that he'd been wronged. The next night, before evening prayers, Mohammad was called to the door. He went quietly. Soon after, Bandar was summoned. He walked up the stairs to see an ISIS guard holding Mohammad's severed head by his short hair. "This is your friend, isn't it?" the guard asked.

Bandar stared at the floor.

"Look at him!" the guard yelled. He shoved Mohammad's head in front of Bandar's face. A thin piece of bloody flesh dangled from the neck. The cut was messy. Mohammad's eyes were closed. He looked peaceful. "This is your friend," the guard said, before walking away.

Bandar was back in the cell. He prayed his face would conceal what he'd seen. He didn't want to scare his teenage cousins. Every day after that he was certain was his last. I will end here, he thought. He rewound his life, remembered it in fragments, paused at images of Homs that wouldn't leave his mind, the earliest days of the revolution. His late brother Bassem. His poems. He silently recited the lines, couldn't get past more than two without feeling that his heart would stop. Sometimes he'd forget Bassem was dead and wonder where he was, wonder whether his older brother would rescue him. He remembered how, some three months after Bassem's death, several of his friends found Bandar and gave him the 700 Syrian pounds that remained of the 10,000 Bassem had taken with him into Baba Amr. "That's how honorable those Farouq were, that's how it started. How did we go from that to rebels who started kidnapping for ransom and in the name of the revolution?"

Bassem and his friends had been just a few guys with a few guns defending a neighborhood they believed they'd freed from a tyrant. Our revolution died soon after Bassem, Bandar thought. It died there in Baba Amr. His brother had a cause, one that Bandar continued after Bassem's death. Bandar had turned to volunteer relief work. He wasn't a fighter, and at least there was honor, pure and untainted, in pulling people from rubble. Pain, too, which came to him in flashes: the child's hand, so soft and small and human, that he retrieved from the ruins of a home after an air strike. He couldn't find the rest of the body. The woman in Raqqa eating out of a dumpster who was too proud to take his money. He followed her home and left a food basket on her door that night and many nights thereafter. The boy, no more than four or five, tugging at his dead mother's leg, asking her why she was ignoring him. He dreamed of a dead aunt who had helped raise him, saw her in the few hours of sleep he stole in the ISIS cell and when he was awake, too. He was sure of it.

He remembered hiding from the regime when it still controlled Raqqa, moving among the homes of friends and family after learning that he was wanted because of his late brother. The seaside café in Latakia he loved. The nights he'd spent with friends there. The girls he'd known. He returned to the demonstrations, waving the revolutionary flag, his flag, and thought about the Islamists who took over and now wanted to kill him because of that flag. How the world changed, how we went backward, he thought. How did it happen? Where did these extremist ideas come from?

One Wednesday, an ISIS fighter, one of the less-nasty ones who took a liking to Bandar, called him out of the cell to tell him his turn had come: "They're going to cut you on Friday after prayers," he said. He was telling him as a favor: "For your sake, make peace with God."

Numbness. Bandar couldn't even cry. He looked at his two cousins. They'd die of fear if they knew. They asked him what the guard said. Bandar told them he might be transferred in a few days, maybe to Raqqa or Iraq, and that the guards would say they'd killed him. "Don't believe them," Bandar told his cousins. "They might even photoshop pictures of me, but don't believe them."

Mainly, Bandar thought of his mother. She still hadn't accepted Bassem's death. "Every time she saw a man with a gun, she'd ask him if he knew her son, if he'd heard of the Farouq." She didn't believe Bassem was dead. What would happen to her? Bandar told his mother he had photographic proof Bassem was dead. She didn't want to see it but silently donned the black of mourning, vowing never to take it off. His father cried like a child when he saw the photo. Bandar remembered several instances when ISIS sent severed heads to the victims' parents in Bandar's hometown. He worried they would do that to his family. He begged that same sympathetic ISIS guard not to send his severed head home. "I'll pass on your last requests," the guard told Bandar on Thursday. Bandar made two: Don't send my head to my mother, and kill me with a bullet, not a knife. The first was promised, the second denied. He thought about the knife. He hoped it would be sharp. He'd once seen a video of a man killed with a blunt knife. It took longer. Would he feel it all or would the nerves be cut, sparing him the pain?

Friday morning. Bandar heard his name. It was still hours before noon prayers. He reached the door, but his feet refused to further aid him toward his death. He was dragged up the stairs by his jailers. The ISIS emir was waiting for him. He handed Bandar a piece of paper. It was official ISIS stationery. "Your father brought this," the emir said, "but I think it's a forgery." He wanted to know how Bandar's father had learned that his son was at the Tishreen Dam. Several ISIS fighters ran their fingers through Bandar's hair, told him to take off all his clothes, made him open his mouth, stick out his tongue. They suspected he might be wearing a tracking device or something similar, but they found nothing.

Bandar read the note. It said three ISIS fighters vouched for his good character. They testified that Bandar had found them bleeding on a battlefield months earlier, taken them to his home, and, at his own expense, paid a doctor to treat them. Bandar felt the air rush back into his lungs, the blood to his feet, his hands, his heart, his head. He remembered helping the fighters and telling his father about it, including their names. He didn't know they were ISIS when he picked them up, they were just wounded men who needed help—a Syrian, a Jordanian, and a Saudi.

One of Bandar's former cellmates, the man who developed appendicitis and was released, had found Bandar's father and told him where his son was. It took Bandar's father five days to track down the three ISIS fighters, then a further seven days to get the ISIS *wali*, or governor, of Al-Bab in the Aleppan countryside to write the note. Bandar's father arrived at the Tishreen Dam at 10 a.m. on the Friday morning his son was due to be executed after noon prayers. Rebels had overrun a number of ISIS posts in the area. The ISIS emir suspected the stationery might be stolen, the note faked. He postponed Bandar's execution until he could speak to the ISIS *wali* in Al-Bab via Skype.

Bandar was allowed to see his father. Twenty-three days after Bandar, his two cousins, and his friend were detained, the four walked out of the

Tishreen Dam lockup. Bandar had lost thirteen kilograms. An armed convoy of cars escorted them home. There was celebratory gunfire at the entrance to his village. "It was like a wedding," Bandar remembered. His mother took off the black of mourning and wore a white headscarf the day her son came home, but only for that one day. His father danced and cried.

Bandar was free, but at night in his dreams he was still in that underground ISIS cell. In his waking hours, local ISIS fighters harassed him. "Every time something happened, ISIS suspected somebody, they'd knock on my door thinking I was involved," Bandar said. He felt trapped.

On September 1, 2014, at 10:14 a.m., I sent Bandar a WhatsApp message, asking where he was.

"Tomorrow I'm sneaking into Turkey," he said. He promised to tell me when he was safely on the other side. It wouldn't take more than a few hours, a day at most, if the routes were difficult, or a few days if he had to try several times. September 10 came and went and still no word. My messages to him were unread. On September 22, at 7:38 p.m., Bandar contacted me from a new telephone number: "Hi, how are you?" he wrote. "I just arrived in Germany."

HAZM

Rebel-held Syria had become like the Afghanistan of the 1980s: failed state territory, lawless, a magnet for foreign and local jihadis, for Al-Qaeda, ISIS, and other independent groups of *muhajireen*. Secular-leaning rebels like those in Hazm, and nationalist-inclined Islamists like Abu Azzam, watched the influx of jihadis with concern. They hadn't started a revolution so that men like that could come to power, but what could they do to stop them?

At the very least, Hazm was determined to know who these foreign fighters were and what they were doing, information it gathered and passed on to its CIA backers in the hope that the United States would help Hazm eliminate a shared enemy. Some of the group's members gathered intelligence. They were gutsy, tech-savvy, and war-hardened young men who learned on the job. They mined kinship ties, reached out to protest buddies, ideological brothers, and called in favors from those they helped with money, an RPG or two in a pinch, or cameras and communications devices. It was dangerous work, made more so by the American connection. It didn't take much to be branded a spy; the mere suspicion was enough to get a person killed.

One Hazm operative, a university graduate who knew nothing about spying beyond a few books about espionage he bought from Amazon Turkey, told me he knew the extreme danger, but his motivation was simple: "Who the fuck are these people? What are they doing in my country, and trying to control it? They are my enemies before they are the enemies of the US or anyone else."

It was old-school, on-site intelligence gathering: geolocation using mobile phones; close surveillance; photos of personnel, training camps, barracks, and checkpoints shot with Nikon DSLRs; eavesdropping devices planted near bases; and—when possible—recruitment of moles within factions or people close to them. The young Hazm operative, the former university student, had a monthly budget of $15,000, drawn from Hazm's account, from which he paid salaries to his six cells. The CIA provided neither equipment nor training and did not request specific information. It took what it was given on flash drives the Hazm operative delivered in person to Americans, including women, who identified themselves as CIA agents. The exchanges—always in five-star hotel rooms—were most often in the southern Turkish city of Adana, home to the İncirlik Air Base and its US military presence, but sometimes in Ankara or Istanbul.

Latakia, part of Nusra emir Mohammad's area of operations, with its high concentration of *muhajireen*, was a focal point. The Hazm agent communicated regularly with his sources, using the same enhanced Turkish cell-phone signal (thanks to new towers along the border) that Mohammad had relied on to send his daughter messages via WhatsApp.

In early 2014, the operative gave the CIA the GPS coordinates for the home of the Iraqi ISIS emir in Latakia, as well as the real-time movements of the Chechen Abu Omar al-Shishani, a former Georgian soldier-turned-senior-ISIS-emir responsible for all of northern Syria, who would become the ISIS overall military commander. "We had Omar al-Shishani's exact location several times, with the make and color of his vehicle, and even the Skype address of his assistant," the operative said. The information was relayed to the CIA immediately. "The Americans didn't do anything about it. It was high-value information. The only other thing we could have topped it with was [ISIS leader Abu Bakr] al-Baghdadi's location."

Detailed regional reports were updated monthly on Latakia, Raqqa, Aleppo, Deir Ezzor, Idlib, and specific towns within the provinces. They included pages of coordinates for ISIS barracks, Internet cafés, weapons warehouses and IED factories, checkpoints, training centers, and prisons—including the dungeon at the Tishreen Dam where Bandar had languished. The Hazm operative and his sources kept tabs on ISIS personnel, mapping out hierarchical command structures down to names of those who interacted with the regime's fuel traders. They also monitored all of the *muhajireen* groups in Latakia who pushed into the eleven Alawite villages in August 2013, capturing the 106 Alawite women and children and tearing Talal's family from him. They provided the CIA with details of satellite devices used by Chechen, Tunisian, and Moroccan emirs, including the serial numbers and locations of the devices. "I said, 'Let's bug the devices, sabotage them, do something to know what they're planning,'" the Hazm operative said. "The Americans said no. I could get the photos but I couldn't hack the devices. I am sure the Americans could."

Hazm surveilled the Latakian bases of several different Chechen groups. In one *muhajireen* training camp, located in a well-worn clearing near olive trees, they photographed eleven men sitting in a circle around a bearded instructor with shoulder-length brown hair, identified as Abu Osama al-Amriki ("the American").

Abu Osama was not of Arab heritage. "Abu Osama is a convert. He was a soldier, US Special Forces, and he became a Muslim in the Iraq War," one of his Syrian colleagues fighting alongside him told me in Latakia. "He's here with us and his family. He named his son Osama. He brings him to the training camp sometimes. The camp is open to *mujahideen* from other groups, too, it's not just us." Abu Osama was honored among jihadists. "His American wife doesn't know how to speak Arabic. She converted, too," said Abu Osama's Syrian colleague. "You should see how they live, so humbly among us. Some of the *shabab* at first thought he might be a spy, but he has entrusted his family to our protection, knowing we can harm him and them if we suspect him. He is a respected brother."

In April 2014, the Hazm operative and his reconnaissance teams noticed a new group of foreigners—Uighurs—moving into abandoned Alawite villages in Latakia. The four villages had been looted, the homes stripped of everything, including wooden shutters and electrical wiring. "Suddenly we noticed a few buildings had windows, newly installed. There's a washing line, so somebody is now living in it. There's a car. They weren't many at first—they came in the dozens. We thought, 'Who are these people?' They didn't have weapons or a flag, but in the next months they started carrying weapons, and more of them came," the Hazm operative said. They soon numbered about four hundred and raised a banner over their settlements—the flag of the Turkistan Islamic Party.

With growing distress, the Hazm operative relayed his reports to Syrian colleagues and American contacts. "We watched as these foreigners took entire villages and nobody did anything, not Turkey or America or anyone, and we didn't have the means to attack them, because we didn't have a presence in Latakia," he said. Hazm's thirty-eight bases were mainly in Idlib, Aleppo, and Hama. The operative was getting frustrated with the Americans. "I told them, 'We are providing you everything, exact locations of some high-value targets, but I don't see that you're doing anything with it.' Even my agents on the ground said, 'And? What now? What next? What are we doing? What's the point?' They were giving me information and I wasn't sending them a silenced pistol to kill the targets, nor a team, nor air strikes. What's the point of what we're doing? It killed motivation."

All he could do was monitor the groups, most of whom fought alongside Mohammad's Jabhat al-Nusra. Many of their leaders were Mohammad's friends. One day, the operative stumbled across a Nusra IED factory and a small training camp with a dozen tents, but, apart from noting it for future reference, he did little with that information. Nusra wasn't the focus. And besides, its main training camp was elsewhere—in Ras al-Hosn, in Idlib Province.

JABHAT AL-NUSRA

The Ras al-Hosn camp, adjacent to the village cemetery, was the site where, in 2013, Abu Bakr al-Baghdadi had summoned Nusra's emirs and slaughtered a Syrian officer midmeeting, shortly before he announced his intention to subsume the group into ISIS.

The Nusra emir in Ras al-Hosn was a local named Abu Ratib, in his early thirties and a father of three. He arrived at the Nusra checkpoint at the entrance to the town in a gray Mitsubishi Jeep with opaque windows. Abu Ratib's area of operations extended to Atmeh, the Syrian town across from Turkey that served as a major conduit for foreign fighters. He agreed to speak to me in principle but first needed the permission of the general emir for Idlib Province, who oversaw Nusra's nine other senior emirs, including Mohammad. The emir was traveling.

Abu Ratib drove to his home, nestled among olive trees with gnarled trunks contorted like dancers midpose, and scattered Byzantine ruins. I was to wait with his family in case he heard from the leader, who happened to be his brother. Abu Ratib's wife, a harried twenty-seven-year-old with deep dimples that made her look younger, led me into the women's room, where she spent most of the day with her children: two girls under three and a son born just sixty days earlier. Her mother-in-law sat on the carpeted floor, rocking her grandson from a swinging cot attached by rope to a hook in the ceiling.

Female neighbors joined them, trading news and gossip over coffee and dates. A local female doctor was killed by her husband, an Egyptian ISIS member, one woman said. He had branded her an apostate for working alongside a male colleague. "Now, who is going to treat us?" Abu Ratib's wife asked. "They say he slit her throat," a neighbor added. The emir's mother relayed a story she'd heard from her sons about a woman who marched into their Nusra base recently: "She was hysterical, crying and screaming. She took off her *hijab* and said that she no longer wanted to be a Muslim." The emir's mother lowered her voice, as if embarrassed to continue: "She was forced to be with seven ISIS fighters, they married her one after the other on the same night." It was gang rape. "This is not our religion," the old lady said. The women tut-tutted and shook their heads. "These men are not like our men," said a neighbor.

I left the next morning and returned to Syria weeks later, on April 14, with formal permission to speak to Abu Ratib. Rather than head straight to Ras al-Hosn, I detoured to Kassab, a Syrian Armenian village along the Turkish border, a summer resort town that had fallen to a handful of Islamist rebels, including Nusra, in late March. I needed to see someone there.

ABU OTHMAN, Mohammad's old cellmate in Palestine Branch, was in Kassab. He had escaped from ISIS. He sat on a plastic chair, alone on the flat rooftop of a two-story villa that Nusra had turned into a base. ISIS was easier to join than to leave. Abandoning it, as far as the organization was concerned, meant abandoning Islam—for which the penalty was death. ISIS hunted defectors.

Kassab was emptied of its people, some two thousand members of a centuries-old Armenian Christian community. A few elderly, too slow or sick or stubborn to flee, were evacuated to the borders of regime territory, or to Turkey, by the armed strangers who now occupied their homes. The town was taken without resistance. The strangers planted their black flags on balconies and lampposts, placed their improvised mortar—known as Hell Cannons, tall and black and tubular—among the shocks of yellow wildflowers and blood-red poppies carpeting the pretty hills. They shot up the crosses on the local church and turned the rectory into a *Hayaa Shar'iya,* an Islamist administrative body.

A Nusra checkpoint at the entrance to the town turned away everyone except fighters from the handful of Islamist groups that had taken Kassab. I was waved through. Abu Othman had returned to Jabhat al-Nusra. He had trimmed his once-chest-length beard, clipped his shaggy locks, discarded his nom de guerre and chosen another. He had served as a senior judge in an ISIS Sharia court in Aleppo. The group wasn't the Islamic utopia he expected. He saw his chance to escape in the rebel backlash against ISIS in early 2014. The group was in retreat, his colleagues busy trying to survive and hold ground. He figured they wouldn't notice if he slipped away, so one day, he said, "I just disappeared."

He feared revenge from his many enemies—because he had been ISIS, because he had decided the fates of men in court, because he had defected. Paranoid by nature, he now was more so. He needed to leave Aleppo, so he turned to Mohammad, his old cellmate, who had long urged him to defect back to Nusra. Mohammad dispatched his two brothers to Aleppo to facilitate Abu Othman's safe passage to Latakia. He placed his old friend in Kassab, among men who didn't know his past.

ISIS had withdrawn from Latakia Province, simply disappeared one night in early March, abandoning its bases and everything in them. It was a covert, coordinated, and hasty withdrawal, one keenly noted by the Hazm operative in his reports. Mohammad appropriated a Mercedes sedan and a pair of BMPs (armored vehicles) from an ISIS base near him. He was glad they were gone. So was Abu Othman—a once-feared man who was now afraid. He peered over the edge of the rooftop, watched fighters in the garden lining up mortar rounds in shin-high grass. "If you're going to ask me about ad-Dawla [the State] and my ties to it," he began, "I was with it for a while, but I left because the Sharia I learned told me that ad-Dawla's actions were incorrect. I cannot say more about what I think because I fear for myself." Some of his new Nusra colleagues, he said, could be ISIS spies.

The conversation shifted, and then we moved to another border town, another Nusra home, another flat rooftop, this one belonging to a Sednaya graduate with whom Abu Othman felt more comfortable. He hadn't left ISIS because of the group's barbarity, he said. Abu Othman was not squea-

NO TURNING BACK · 277

mish, he had killed men. He believed in the application of *hudud* punishments, which he viewed as a deterrent. "After one public punishment," he said, "who will then steal? Sharia doesn't mean walking around cutting off hands and crucifying people, because there's no need for that after the first example."

It wasn't the punishments per se, it was the application of them. He said the courts where he'd served were a sham. "The judiciary was politicized in the interests of *Daesh*'s politics," he said, using the Arabic acronym for the group. "In a real Islamic state, the word of the *Shari'iy*, of Sharia, is paramount. A judge's ruling is supposed to be final and obeyed, but there were other sides, the group's security agents, the *amniyeen,* who politicized the judiciary and imposed their views on it. I can't accept this and they came to know it."

If the *amniyeen* wanted a person disappeared, but with a religious cover and the suggestion of an institution at work rather than a silencer, the judges had to deliver that verdict. Religious novices and men unschooled in religion were elevated to senior positions based on their loyalty to ISIS. "They don't want old ones like me, who have been Salafi Jihadis for years, members who are aware of our ideology, who have studied its books and teachers," Abu Othman said. "They wanted people who would follow their orders and not know that they were wrong."

For Abu Othman, Al-Qaeda's disavowal of ISIS was a deep blow. He realized he was on the wrong side of a group whose ideology he had followed for more than fifteen years. "I was too afraid to speak against what they were doing," Abu Othman said of ISIS. "There is a certain politics, and anybody who doesn't follow it is killed or sidelined. They kill a lot of people," he said, "and they kill for the slightest reasons. They make you feel that at any moment, they could easily kill you. Its end will come from within. There are many assassinations within their ranks, different factions. Some are more conservative than others, and they will clash and kill each other."

Nusra, too, had problems. After its split with ISIS in 2013, it had hemorrhaged men and then relaxed its membership rules to make up for it. Even cigarette smugglers were accepted, despite the fact Nusra considered smoking a sin. Abu Othman, seated on the rooftop of the Nusra safe house along the border, grimaced at Nusra recruits who emerged from the Turkish scrub carrying empty burlap bags fashioned into long, rectangular backpacks. The bags were used to smuggle cigarettes from Syria, where a packet cost about 50 Syrian pounds, to Turkey, where they could sell it for 200.

"We'll get to you," Abu Othman told the men, shaking his head. Some of the recruits looked up, grinning, thinking the *Shari'iy* was joking about reprimanding them. Abu Othman did not smile back. "If we are to pick people the way we did before, Jabhat al-Nusra wouldn't have more than four or five hundred people in all of Syria," Abu Othman said. "These people, the new ones, they will not reach the level of decision making. They will be sent to a training camp for about a month, then into battles."

Abu Othman had changed groups, but his goal remained the same— an Islamic state in Syria—as did his enmity for all those, local and foreign, who sought to prevent it. "God willing, we will implement Sharia in Syria," he said, "and whoever stands against us we will fight, whoever it is—America or others. To America and its friends, Syria is a swamp for fighting and bloodshed, and let everyone associated with jihad come and work and die in Syria, that's how America sees it, but the future leaders will come from Syria. This war will not [just] give rise to the next Osama bin Laden," he said. "There will be Osamas."

ON APRIL 14, as Abu Othman sat on a rooftop in Latakia, four armed men—three Tunisians and a Moroccan—sneaked through the olive groves of Ras al-Hosn and knocked on Abu Ratib's door. His brother, the Nusra emir for Idlib Province, was also inside, bedridden, recuperating from a car accident. The door was opened. The *muhajireen* took a few short steps into the men's room on the right, shot and killed Abu Ratib, his brother, and another man before continuing to the women's room on the left. They sprayed it with bullets, killing Abu Ratib's wife, three-year-old daughter, and thirteen-year-old niece and injuring most of the other children. Abu Ratib's mother and baby son, hiding in another room, were unharmed.

Nusra tracked the ISIS perpetrators to a nearby home. "Two of them blew themselves up, and that led to the death of the third," Nusra said in a statement. The fourth was captured and executed. ISIS didn't comment on the murders of the two Nusra emirs in Idlib.

ISIS denied involvement in a much-higher-profile suicide bombing weeks earlier, on February 23, that killed Abu Khalid al-Suri, a man the United States considered Al-Qaeda's representative in Syria. He was a gray-bearded veteran of both Syria's Islamist insurrection against Hafez al-Assad in the 1980s and the Afghan campaign against the Soviets. Abu Khalid al-Suri was a personal friend of Osama bin Laden, and he had recently been tasked by bin Laden's successor, Zawahiri, with mediating an end to the dispute with ISIS in Syria. In the month before his death, Abu Khalid accused ISIS of "crimes and erroneous practices in the name of jihad." He was a storied jihadi, killed in Aleppo by other jihadis. Western counterterrorism officials didn't have to fire a shot.

Zawahiri eulogized his friend Abu Khalid and called for an end to the "strife of the blind" in Syria. "Everyone who has fallen into these sins must remember that they accomplish for the enemies of Islam what they could not accomplish by their own abilities," Zawahiri said in a statement. His words, as before, fell flat on a battleground from which he was too far removed. In May, Zawahiri tried again. If only ISIS emir Baghdadi had stayed in Iraq, "which needs double its efforts," the Al-Qaeda leader said, it could have avoided the "waterfall of blood" caused by the infighting in Syria. "Listen to and obey your emir once again," Zawahiri said, addressing Baghdadi. "Come back to what your sheikhs, emirs, and those who preceded you on the path of jihad have worked hard for."

In May, ISIS's fire-breathing spokesman, the Syrian Abu Mohammad al-Adnani, sealed his group's divorce from Al-Qaeda: "Apologies, emir of Al-Qaeda," Adnani said, addressing Zawahiri, "*ad-Dawla* is not a branch that is subordinate to Al-Qaeda, nor shall there be a day where it is such." If Zawahiri wanted to set foot in "the land of the Islamic State," he needed to pledge allegiance to it and be a "soldier of its emir," Baghdadi. It was Zawahiri who needed to "recognize [his] fault and correct it and change course," Adnani said, not ISIS. Syria had precipitated what one of Nusra's most senior sheikhs termed "the biggest rift in the global jihad since . . . the fall of the Caliphate" in 1924.

Saleh, the aide to Nusra leader Abu Mohammad al-Jolani, was dismayed by the jihadi infighting and Ayman al-Zawahiri's inability to stop it. "I tell you, if Sheikh Osama was still alive, the problems in Syria wouldn't have happened," Saleh said. "Sheikh Osama had a presence, his word was final. It was not like the word of Ayman al-Zawahiri." Jolani's new recruitment drive and his focus on "quantity not quality, the opposite of what we used to do," also disturbed Saleh. It was diluting the ideological rigor of the group. After Abu Khalid al-Suri's assassination, Nusra leader Jolani hid in Damascus. Saleh didn't follow him there. Instead, he went home to the east. "The number-one war in Syria is ideological," he said, "and *Daesh* is strongest ideologically. I'm not talking about whether their ideology is right or wrong, but they're convinced of it. Killing *Daesh* isn't easy." He recalled a meeting he'd attended between a Nusra emir and an ISIS emir in the eastern city of Deir Ezzor. The three Syrians were all friends and had known each other for years. The ISIS emir turned to his friend in Nusra: "If it comes to it," he told him, "I will kill you, and then I will cry for you."

ON JUNE 10, 2014, ISIS seized Mosul, Iraq's second-largest city, and barreled south toward a Baghdad it would not reach. On June 29, the first day of Ramadan, the group proclaimed a caliphate across the vast swaths of contiguous territory it controlled in Syria and Iraq. It changed its name to Islamic State (IS) and declared its leader, Abu Bakr al-Baghdadi, the caliph, saying it was incumbent upon all Muslims to pledge allegiance to him. Raqqa City was the de facto seat of this so-called caliphate, although it was never formally announced as such. The city had played that role before. In the eighth century, the Abbasid Caliph Harun al-Rashid moved his residence from Baghdad, then the cultural capital of the Islamic world, to Raqqa. The caliph's reign was a time of learning and culture, of scien-

NO TURNING BACK · *281*

tific and mathematic innovation, and irreverent court poetry about wine and forbidden love. The Abbasid Caliphate founded the House of Wisdom in Baghdad, a multicultural, multireligious intellectual powerhouse that, among other things, translated classic Greek texts and transmitted them back to a Europe emerging from the Dark Ages. Islamic State's idea of a caliphate was very different.

SULEIMAN

Suleiman had left Damascus Central Prison in Adra, with its clean, well-lit corridors, stalls, and regular access to bathrooms. He was back in the darkness of a *mukhabarat* cell. He'd been in so many cells since September 9, 2013—the day he thought he was free. He'd left Adra that morning in a windowless "meat-fridge truck" like the one that had brought him there, headed to Damascus's Counterterrorism Court to finally see a judge. He stood handcuffed in his black-and-white-striped prison uniform as the investigating magistrate read out his indictments—membership in a terrorist organization, promoting terrorist acts and financing them, and spreading *fitna* (discord) among Syrians. The financing charge alone carried between fifteen and twenty years of hard labor. It was the first time Suleiman learned of the charges against him.

Suleiman's father had hired his son a lawyer, a suited man who didn't utter a word during the short proceedings and wasn't allowed to confer with his client. The magistrate's questions to Suleiman were clear and simple: What are your ties to the *tansiqiya* in Rastan? What is your relationship to Abdel-Razzak Tlass? How many demonstrations did you participate in? Suleiman denied everything—he hadn't protested, didn't know his relative, the defector Abdel-Razzak Tlass, and wasn't part of any *tansiqiya*. On the advice of inmates in Adra, he repudiated his earlier testimony. He fingerprinted the notary's record of his answers and was ordered out of the court. It was over within minutes.

"What does it mean, *sidi?*" Suleiman asked as he was dragged away. "What happens now?" The charges, he was told, were dropped. "Based on

Air Force Intelligence investigation number 1626 . . . . and the accused's questioning on September 9, 2013 by the Counterterrorism Court's second investigating magistrate, the accused will be released," the court's paperwork read. "He is not wanted by any other branch." Suleiman didn't know that his father had bought the verdict for 500,000 Syrian pounds, about $4,000 at the time, and that the lawyer's job was to bribe the judge.

Suleiman returned to Adra physically weightless, mentally unshackled. His cousin Samer Tlass had already been transferred, but nobody knew where. Suleiman signed his release form in the prison's administration office and counted down the minutes until the next morning, when he was delivered to the Criminal Security Branch in Bab Musalla, Damascus.

The officer behind that desk told Suleiman he was not free. The judge had only dropped the charges filed by Air Force Intelligence, and despite what the court papers said, Suleiman was still wanted by other *mukhabarat* agencies, as well as the army for absconding from his compulsory military service. Since he'd graduated in 2007, he'd been paying a fee, essentially a bribe, to be exempted from wearing a uniform, but he stopped forking out the money in the revolution. The same military that killed his friends, the system that jailed and tortured him, expected him to fight for it. How short the distance between hope and hopelessness, Suleiman thought. He'd walked into the office thinking he was a free man. Now he was about to reenter the purgatory of the *mukhabarat*. He was alone with the officer. He dug his hand into his pocket and fished out all of his money, 50,000 Syrian pounds.

"*Sidi*," he whispered, "I have 50,000. If there's a possibility. . . ."

"Shut up or I'll add bribery to your file!"

Handcuffed. Back in a van, sandwiched between men in uniform. Overnighted at the Political Security branch in Al-Fayha, Damascus, then transferred to the Political Security branch in Homs. Back to the interrogations, to blindfolds, to handcuffs. The same questions, but not the beatings he braced for, just the threat of them. He'd already confessed at the Air Force Intelligence branches, he told his interrogator. "Here, everything is different," came the reply. "You have to make new confessions."

So, he was surprised when, on September 17, he was handed back his 50,000 Syrian pounds, his watch, and other personal belongings in a large brown envelope and released from Political Security's custody. He walked out of the branch unaccompanied, stood in the street, and allowed himself to hope, despite the wounds of experience, that this was real. He was in Homs, not far from where his parents were staying. What was the quickest route there? He imagined knocking on their door, pictured his father's face, his mother's reaction. He hadn't yet moved when handcuffs snapped tightly across his wrists. "Sir, why are you doing this?" He was screaming now. "Can I ask you where are you taking me, sir?" The *mukhabarat* officer didn't say a word. He just bundled Suleiman into an unmarked car that had pulled up to the curb.

Suleiman wasn't blindfolded, so when the vehicle turned into a street behind the train station, he knew that he was headed to Military Security Branch 261. That's it, I'm done, he thought. Does anyone ever enter prison in Syria and get out of it? He remembered walking into the hangar in the Air Force Intelligence branch in Mezzeh and seeing former cellmates he thought had been released. He was one of them now, a body cycled in perpetuity through a labyrinth of suffering. Once inside 261, he was stripped of his money, his watch, his belongings, his humanity, and then tossed into the filth of another black hole.

He was once again a shadow, his eyes adjusting to the other phantoms in the dark. He counted the days, marked them off on a wall with a piece of broken zipper his fingers found. After a month and a half, he begged a jailer to know why he'd been forgotten. When would they question him? The next evening, in the hours between midnight and dawn, Suleiman was summoned. He stood blindfolded in a room heavy with silence. Minutes passed, then the music of Naem al-Sheikh began to play, a Syrian singer ironically from Rastan. One song ended and another began. Suleiman felt others in the room. "Okay," somebody said after a while, "give me what you have. What are you going to tell us before going to Heaven?"

The inmates warned each other about the worst interrogators, the most wretched rooms. The upstairs room at the end of the hallway was a hell ruled by Abu Khatem, "the Father of the Ring," as he was nicknamed by the inmates, because his jewelry cut cheeks and broke teeth. Was Suleiman in the room at the end of the corridor? How long was the corridor? He had asked to be questioned, he reminded himself, thinking an interrogation might free him sooner. "I'll say whatever you want me to say," Suleiman said. "I confessed at the Air Force Intelligence and the Political Security. . . ." He was interrupted.

"No, no no. Here it's different. We are different here. Anyhow, your case is going to take a long time, we need a long session with you." The voice spoke to another in the room: "I want you to turn this guy into art. I want to see colors on his skin."

So many blunt instruments hurting him that he couldn't tell if one was a ring. When it was over, Suleiman was dragged back to the cell, only to be hauled to another interrogation hours later. A different voice. This one directed Suleiman toward a chair, told him to sit and take a rest, because he looked like a decent, educated young man. Suleiman was asked the same questions, gave the same answers. "If you don't tell me everything, I'll hang you from the corridor by your wrists, like the others," the interrogator said. "I'll say whatever you want me to say," Suleiman replied. The thick plastic cables lacerated his red-raw skin. This interrogator had phone records, as well as transcripts. He asked Suleiman about his Facebook account and other things that Air Force Intelligence and Political Security hadn't bothered with. Despite his pain, Suleiman was impressed by the man's thoroughness. Forced to sign a confession he wasn't allowed to read, he then was returned to the cell. Months passed. Wounds healed. Suleiman remembered how to fall asleep to the cries of men being savaged in other rooms. He remembered to try to position himself near the cell door, where, if he could just get his cheek to the floor, he could breathe air seeping in from the corridor that didn't smell of sweat and excrement and blood.

In December 2013, Suleiman was transferred from Military Intelligence Branch 261 in Homs to the worst place he had ever been—235 in Damascus, the notorious Palestine Branch, alma mater of the Nusra emir Mohammad and his old cellmate Abu Othman and other Islamists. Its very name evoked fear. Suleiman was in one of its larger cells, four meters by seven meters, crammed with men. He counted 131. In there, he stopped being Suleiman Tlass Farzat, at least to his tormentors. He was Number 28 in a tomb for the living dead.

A squat toilet in a corner overflowed. Lice and other insects, felt but not seen in the dark, made their homes in ears and hair and beards and wounds. Body heat, suffocating even in winter, weighted the air. Squalor. Sickness. By the end of the first month, the prisoners were naked, their clothes used to clean themselves. Time slowed. Only corpses left the cell.

After two months, the interrogations began. Number 28 was called one day, along with two other men whose names were Ayad and Omar. There were no questions. The three were ordered to lie on the floor. Thick PVC pipes were produced. The pipes were green, *akhdar* in Arabic. Both prisoners and security agents nicknamed the weapon "*al-akhdar al-Brahimi*," after Lakhdar al-Brahimi, who was the United Nations and Arab League special envoy to Syria. *Al-akhdar* did the talking—its blows so ferocious Suleiman was sure he had broken bones. Ayad lost his life that night, Omar his mind. He started hallucinating, talking to his wife and mother. Later, much later, when Omar could walk again, he spent his days searching for his son in the cell, picked fights with other prisoners he accused of hiding his boy. For weeks, Suleiman couldn't stand. A doctor entered the cell once to ask the prisoners if anyone would donate money to buy medications for the group. Suleiman volunteered. He asked for anti-inflammatory medications, antidiarrhea tablets, antibiotics. He signed a receipt for 20,000 Syrian pounds and was surprised when the doctor kept his word and delivered the goods.

By April 2014, there were sixty men in the cell. Fewer than ten walked out alive. Suleiman focused on memorizing the names of the dead. Remember details, remember dates, remember who and what you are. He thought back to his first diary entries in Adra prison—"Optimism is our fuel!" That's what he'd written. Now he had to believe it. Despair simply hastened death. He had seen it happen to others.

In early May, he was summoned again, this time alone. The same questions, the same answers, the same means of extracting them. "What did you lack, you people of Rastan?" the interrogator asked him. "Rastan was the second Qardaha. Why did you do this?"

Why? Suleiman thought. Because he was there, because he could be buried there and nobody would know, because thousands had been there before him, because the system was corrupt, a dictatorship ruled by a family business. That's what he wanted to say. Instead, he parroted something about a foreign conspiracy and being duped by Syrians in exile. He signed and fingerprinted his confession and was returned to the cell.

Days later, he was called to the administration office to sign a release form. He was being transferred back to Damascus Central Prison in Adra—without his 30,000 Syrian pounds. An officer in Palestine Branch waved the money in front of Suleiman's face and then returned it to his desk drawer.

MAY 12, 2014. Suleiman was back in Adra, in a different space—room 7, wing 8. He borrowed money to buy an exercise book and called his parents as soon as he could. His mother brought him cash that he used to rent a bed. He began unspooling all that he remembered, recording the names of the dead. His first entry:

> *Tired of the Journey*
> 12-5-2014
> They Promised:
> Today, ten months since I first entered Adra and after
> almost two years of imprisonment, I'm back again in
> Damascus Central Prison. I'm full of hope that I'll be
> released soon *inshallah*, God willing, that I'll see my
> family and especially my parents who I miss so much.
> I fear for them while I'm in prison. . . .

On May 23, the second anniversary of his arrest, Suleiman wrote that he had "no feeling of despair or remorse for anything. My hope for freedom and release is still bigger than the darkness that I'm still living in." On June 2, he called the woman he had been on a date with on March 15, 2011. It was, he wrote, "an unforgettable call from a dear person," one that left him feeling the happiest he'd been in more than two years.

A week later, on June 8, 2014, Suleiman was in the Counterterrorism Court in Damascus, in front of a different judge, one who'd also been paid 500,000 Syrian pounds to secure a favorable verdict. The investigating magistrate read out the same charges as those that were earlier dropped by the other judge. Suleiman pointed out that he'd been cleared in a previous court hearing. "If the other judge decided to release you, it doesn't mean that I will," the magistrate said. Suleiman again denied the charges, but this time, despite the bribe, he was told that, based on reports provided by Palestine Branch, the case against him would move forward. He faced at least fifteen years in jail. He returned to Adra and called his mother: "Forget me, Mama," he told her. "I'm done. I won't get out of here." In his diary entry that day, he wrote, "The biggest shock came with the total crushing of the hope that has kept me going and alive until this moment. I don't know what to say. I'm devastated."

One entry the next day contained a poem:

> *Tired of the Journey*
> 9-6-2014
> Confessions of an Outsider
> Toward the shore of the beginning
> I'll gather my things, secure my luggage
> And leave
> I'll take the fear and terror with me,
> I'll take the humiliation, torture and oppression of more
> than two years
> And I'll leave
> I have to kill myself and that newborn

The baby of misery, the son of agony
And I'll leave
I'll leave, but before that
I'll give a rose to everyone who mistreated me
I'll pardon all who hurt me.

On June 16, 2014, just before dinner, Suleiman's name was one of five called over Adra prison's loudspeaker. He was included in a presidential amnesty, a general pardon for crimes committed before June 9, 2014, outlined in Legislative Decree No. 22 for 2014. The law was issued less than a week after President Bashar al-Assad was reelected—such as elections were in Syria—to another seven-year term. A month after the decree, a rights organization named the Violations Documentation Center in Syria (VDC) found that no more than a thousand inmates were released as part of the amnesty. Nobody—except the regime—really knew how many men and women were behind bars.

TALAL

The Alawite detainees had been moved again, this time to a ground-level apartment. Their new prison had a little terrace where the children could play, and the women could hang laundry. They had been in so many different places. There was their first jail—a dirty two-room house for 106 people, with one blocked toilet that overflowed. They stayed there for a few weeks before being moved to a clean villa with a large kitchen that had electricity via a generator. The empty chicken farm had been the worst, at least to Jawa, Talal's youngest daughter, the eight-year-old. It crawled with bugs that scared her.

The doctor from the rebel field clinic in Salma, Rami Habib, and his nurses regularly checked on the women and children, supplying them with fresh vegetables, meat, rice, clothes, female sanitary products, and medical attention as required. The Alawite women were given utensils to cook for themselves and the children.

Their days melted into weeks and months in captivity, until May 7, 2014. The detainees were told that about half of them would be released as part of a broader prisoner exchange tied to a Homs ceasefire deal. There was a catch—detainees from the same family could not all be released. Somebody had to stay behind, the captors said, to pressure the family members in regime-held territories to force Assad to negotiate their release. The more families represented the better. Hanin and Jawa argued over which sister should stay, each wanted the other to leave. They didn't have much time to decide.

"You're wounded and an asthmatic," Jawa told Hanin. "You should return to Baba with our brother."

"I'm older than you," Hanin told her sister. "I'll stay, you go home. Keep your faith in God and take care of our brother."

The captors were distributing food to the women and children who were to be released, to know whom to load onto the trucks. Hanin handed her juice and biscuits to Jawa. "If I get out, I'll have access to everything, you have nothing here," Jawa told her sister. "You drink the juice."

Hanin refused, and Jawa and their baby brother, juice in hand, were ushered into waiting trucks. Hanin watched them walk away.

TALAL, LIKE THE other relatives of the detainees, learned of the prisoner release on May 7, the day it happened. A cousin working in the government hospital in Latakia called him at 1:30 p.m. and told him that the governor had asked to prepare a ward for Alawite hostages on their way who needed to be examined. "I just assumed it was another lie," Talal said. "All I heard was that some of the detainees were being released. I hoped my wife and children were among them."

Jawa and her baby brother arrived at Latakia Government Hospital that afternoon. The little girl cried at the kindness of hospital staff, who brought her and the other freed detainees biscuits, falafel, shawarma sandwiches, French fries. "They kept telling us we were free, we were safe, we would soon be home," Jawa said. "I couldn't believe it, but I worried about Hanin. I wished she had come with us."

It was too late for Talal to travel to Latakia and see his children that day. It was already 4 p.m., and the road from Damascus to Latakia was dangerous at night. He'd have to wait until the next morning. The children's aunt, their mother's sister, lived in Latakia City, not far from the hospital. The children were discharged into her care.

"My aunt's house was full of people," Jawa recalled. "Aunty couldn't keep up with serving coffee. So many people were there to check on us. My aunt was crying so much she went hoarse, she couldn't speak."

The next morning, Talal left Damascus at 5 a.m. and was in Latakia by 10 a.m. He ran into his sister-in-law's house, screaming out the names of his children. He saw two of them.

"They seemed as if they had shrunk, like they were years younger," Talal said. "Jawa was thin. She didn't know me, her words burned me."

Jawa mistook her father for her uncle. "I asked him, 'Where is my father?'" Jawa said. "He seemed very different to me, older, tired."

Talal realized that his wife and eldest daughter, Lojayn, were probably dead because they weren't among the detainees—either those released or those still held. His "heart burned" that Hanin was still in captivity. "Hanin is very special to me," he said. "She has asthma. I used to take her once or twice a month to hospital to have her lungs and sinuses cleared. I imagine her in the dust of battles, of places they are hiding them, the dirt. How is she living there with them?"

SULEIMAN

June 17, 2014. A promised freedom. Suleiman prayed it wasn't another false hope. He woke early after a night sleepless with anticipation, gave away his spare clothes and some of his money to cellmates, then signed and fingerprinted his release form in Adra's administration office. This time, there was a wire on the desk from the Criminal Security Branch in Bab Musalla, Damascus, that said there was nothing on him, not even pending military service, which surprised him. His father had paid 400,000 Syrian pounds for that paper, and hundreds of thousands more, to delay Suleiman's military service until October 23, 2014. A little after 11 a.m., Suleiman walked out of Damascus Central Prison in jeans and a navy-blue T-shirt, carrying his pajamas, two diaries, and paperwork in a plastic bag.

He felt like a newborn, unable to orientate himself, unsure where to go. To his parents in Homs? He had no idea what the road was like. To Damascus? It was closer and he had relatives there—a safer bet, he decided—but which way to the capital? He flagged down a *micro*, clambered into the seat near the driver, and asked to borrow his phone.

"Hello, Baba. I'm out of prison."

His father cried, his mother ululated. *"Mabrouk! Mabrouk!* My son! Congratulations!"

His mother took the phone and warned him not to travel to Homs and risk the checkpoints. She told him to call his aunt in Damascus. His aunt, in tears, said she was on her way to meet him. He'd wait for her near the Central Bank at the Square of the Seven Fountains.

An older woman in the *micro* tapped Suleiman on the shoulder. She handed him a passport photo of her son, she spoke his name. Did Suleiman know him? Had he seen him in prison? She'd been searching for two years, she said, two years of begging *mukhabarat* branches for information about her boy. He disappeared from their hometown of Haffeh, in Latakia. Suleiman turned to face her. She could have been his mother. He wished he knew something about her son, but he apologized—he didn't.

His aunt neared the square, her husband steering the wheel with one hand, clutching a smartphone in the other, filming the moment: "Look to the right! Do you see him? Where is he?" he said. He scanned a street busy with pedestrians.

"Where is the bank? Where is the bank? Stop! Stop! Let me out! There he is!" said his aunt.

The wheels were still turning when Suleiman's aunt jumped out and rushed to her nephew, arms outstretched. She forcefully embraced him, kissed his cheeks, his head, his eyes. Suleiman clung to her. "*Habibi*, my darling, it's over! It's finally over! You look good, *habibi*. What can I get you, *habibi*, what do you need, what do you want? Whatever you want! Just tell me! It's over! It's over!"

Relatives assembled at his aunt's house in Damascus, others began gathering in Homs. The congratulatory phone calls left Suleiman dizzy. Too much noise. Too many people. He had grown used to solitary silence. A relative snapped a photo of him—of a tired, thinner Suleiman smiling broadly, who was still all eyelashes and sweet dimpled grin. "This is a photo of me an hour after my release from a detention that lasted two years, twenty-three days, and eleven hours," Suleiman later wrote on Facebook after he reopened an account.

Arrangements were made to get him to Homs that afternoon. A cousin paid a *mukhabarat* agent he knew to escort him and Suleiman through the checkpoints to Homs so they wouldn't be harassed. At every roadblock, the agent flashed his ID card and was waved through. Suleiman's father was pacing the street outside the apartment. Finally, Suleiman glimpsed his father for the first time in more than two years. An emotional avalanche, exhilaration, relief, guilt, love, overpowering and jumbled, tears warm and uninhibited, a reunion cut short by Suleiman's mother, who hurried father and son into the house, fearing neighbors' prying eyes. The apartment was in a government-controlled area. Suleiman's mother did what Syrian mothers do—she prepared a feast of all her son's favorite foods. He had returned. He wasn't in Rastan—that house had been destroyed—but his parents were his home.

THE DECISION WAS MADE for him. Suleiman was to leave Syria. Only one of his sisters was still in the country, his only brother and other sister were already in Egypt. Suleiman's relatives warned of men they knew who were rearrested days and weeks after their release from prison. Suleiman's mother was convinced he was imperiled every time he left the house. His father feared he could not indefinitely delay his son's conscription. The old man made all the arrangements, paid 200,000 Syrian pounds for a new passport, and decided on the destination—Turkey. Suleiman agreed, but he still had one more thing to do in Damascus—there was someone he had to see.

He saw her on his third day of freedom, the woman he'd called from Adra, the one he'd drawn in his diaries, his date at that café in Homs on March 15, 2011, the start of the Syrian uprising. She'd sent him close to six hundred messages via Facebook during his incarceration. She took the day off work to see him. They met in a park. His future was uncertain. He would be leaving and didn't know when or whether he could return. Her life was in Damascus, so he released her from his heart. It hurt to let her go. Would he have married her had he not been detained? He didn't know. The only thing he was certain of was that he loved her, that the hope of seeing her had sustained him in the darkness, and that she deserved better than an unstable life in an uncertain exile. He didn't tell her he was leaving, couldn't bring himself to, but she sensed it. "I feel this is the last day I'm going to see you," she told him. She was right.

. . .

On June 27, ten days after his release, Suleiman and his parents took a taxi from Homs to Tripoli, in northern Lebanon, escorted to the Syrian border by a paid member of the *mukhabarat*. From there, they boarded an overnight ferry to Taşucu, about a hundred kilometers south of Mersin, in southern Turkey. Suleiman posed for photos on the deck like a carefree tourist: clean-shaven and smiling, in a powder-blue Lacoste polo shirt and faded jeans, beads of summer sweat on his forehead, arms around his parents, calm blue waters behind him.

A cousin met them at the harbor in Turkey. Days later, he drove Suleiman and his parents on a fifteen-hour trip to Istanbul to seek the counsel of Suleiman's eldest uncle, the one who owned shares in the bank in Aleppo, who had interceded on his nephew's behalf with the mufti's son at Aleppo's Air Force Intelligence branch.

Suleiman felt unanchored in his freedom and adrift in exile. He'd never wanted to leave Syria. He met up with old friends living in Turkey and working for various Syrian political opposition bodies. They'd changed in ways that disgusted him. "Almost all of them were looking for material benefits, and if there were no such benefits, they wouldn't do a thing," Suleiman said. He understood the need to make a living, but this was something else: "There was no revolution—only business, personal benefits, personal cliques, and corruption. Very few of them had a conscience." He thought of his friends in Rastan's original *tansiqiya*, killed in that dawn raid on their hideout near the dam in late 2011. "Those who worked from their hearts for nothing," Suleiman said, "were either arrested, killed, or quit."

He declined a high-paying job arranged by his uncle in the opposition's interim Ministry of Finance. Like many Syrians inside Syria, Suleiman also despised these exiles. They were little more than a toothless club of well-paid big talkers who represented only themselves and their foreign backers. "If there was a one percent chance to do something honorable for the revolution, I would have stayed," Suleiman said, "but it had taken a different direction." His parents returned to Syria. Suleiman stayed with his cousin in Mersin. He looked for work but found none. He explored educational opportunities, but little suited him.

He thought about applying for UN asylum to be relocated, or registering at a European university and hoping for a student visa. It would take many months at least—if he was lucky—and he knew of friends who had tried both and been rejected. I've already wasted a lot of my life, he thought. I've gone backward, lost everything. Egypt wasn't an option. Local authorities were intimidating Syrians to the degree that Suleiman's siblings were looking to flee. Lebanon was no better. He had a good friend from Rastan, a university colleague he'd known since primary school, who'd migrated to Germany before the revolution and advised him to try to join him there. In Mersin, Suleiman heard the talk of smugglers and people risking the sea to Europe. He wanted a life. Perhaps he'd find one in Germany. He told his father and uncle. Both men opposed the idea at first, but eventually they relented and between them handed Suleiman $6,000. That was the smuggler's fee.

SULEIMAN NEVER MET the smuggler he entrusted with his life and $6,000. He found him the way many Syrians did back then—somebody knew somebody who knew somebody who had heard of him. It was the summer before hundreds of thousands would attempt similar journeys seeking sanctuary in Europe, aided by public Facebook pages advertising routes and brokers. The smuggler, a Kurdish man, was based in Istanbul. He provided instructions over the phone—Suleiman was to pay upfront in an insurance office in Reyhanlı, a four-hour bus ride from Mersin. No receipt, no guarantee. The destination was southern Italy. There were other, cheaper options, such as Greece, but that was farther from Germany. It meant more overland borders to sneak across. Suleiman returned to Mersin and waited for the designated departure date.

The smuggler kept his word and his appointment. On July 24, 2014, Suleiman milled outside the Mersin Arena, a 25,500-seat stadium, where he and others had been instructed by phone to wait. Suleiman was surprised to see one of his relatives—a doctor and his wife and three young daughters. They, too, were about to brave the sea. It was just after dusk in the last days of Ramadan. Suleiman and his soon-to-be fellow travelers broke their fast together, murmured prayers for God's protection. The darkness deepened. After several hours, a bus arrived to transport them to an isolated stretch of the Turkish Mediterranean about sixty kilometers away.

Suleiman's possessions fit into a rucksack. A few changes of clothes, pitted dates and biscuits for the journey, money and paperwork, including his prison diaries, wrapped in cling film and placed in ziplock bags, and a life jacket. He didn't pack water, which he was told would be provided on the boat. He had nothing from home except memories.

They disembarked from the bus. No cigarettes, no lighters, no illumination from mobile phones, the driver warned, nothing that might compromise their location. Thick foliage hiding their approach to the water's edge. Inky darkness, not even a streetlight. Life jackets strapped on. Parents hushed children. The sound of lapping waves and whispered prayers.

In the grainy moonlight, Suleiman made out a hulk of metal floating offshore. About a hundred refugees, from two buses, were herded in shifts onto a skiff that carried them to the waiting fishing trawler. It was approaching midnight. The captain, a fisherman from Latakia, and his crew of four Syrians, directed women and children to the upper decks, men to the lower. The Mediterranean was calm as the boat headed across the sea toward Cyprus, where they would wait just outside Egyptian waters to pick up another two hundred refugees, according to the captain's announcement. There was no sign of the other desperate souls. People on the trawler grew antsy. Was this a trap? How long could the boat wait before being noticed? They'd been told there'd be no stops, and that they'd be in Italy in six days. A few men begged the captain to push forward without the Egyptian contingent. Others made a suggestion to sweeten the deal—that everyone on board pay an extra $100 to the captain, $50 for children, to forget the Egyptians. They'd been waiting four hours already. The captain agreed, the passengers paid, and the trawler moved on.

Suleiman was seasick for most of the journey. He mainly slept and tried to combat the nausea but also documented the trip for his family. He posed for photos, leaning against the knee-high railing wrapped around the bow. There was plenty of space on the boat, thanks to the Egyptian no-shows. After the first night, people felt relaxed enough to take off their life jackets. Every now and again, the captain told them where they were, but Suleiman relied on his phone's GPS to capture his coordinates, and Google maps of his journey he'd downloaded to figure out where he was. In addition to his relatives, there were about ten other young men from Rastan aboard. How random, Suleiman thought, to meet them years later on a sky-blue trawler with rusty patches on its hull, trying to sneak into Europe.

Some of the men fished, using rods on board, sharing their catch with passengers. A group of teenagers and children sat on the deck, providing entertainment. They used an empty watercooler bottle as a drum. Men and women clapped and sang along. The sea was flat, the sky a brilliant blue. A pod of dolphins escorted the travelers one day, graceful and free, gliding just below a surface that shimmered in the sun. Children and adults alike were giddy at the sight. Suleiman considered it a good omen. Despite his seasickness, the trip felt like a holiday. For the first time in years, he marked Eid al-Fitr, the end of Ramadan, in natural light, not in the darkness of a cell. The passengers on the boat exchanged Eid greetings, but otherwise it was a regular day. Some of them fretted constantly about being caught. Suleiman didn't care. What are they going to do? he thought. I survived Bashar al-Assad's prisons. Nothing could be worse except death.

On the ninth day—three longer than passengers had expected—the faint outline of Sicily appeared in the far distance. To Suleiman, those hazy hills meant hope, freedom, a new start. The captain sent a distress signal via radio, stated his coordinates, and then dumped overboard the radio, a Thuraya satellite phone, and other navigational devices. "I'm not a smuggler,

I was just paid for this trip," he told the stunned faces around him. "Now, I'm one of you." He and his crew said they wanted to get to Sweden.

Before long, a plane swooped over the boat. The refugees waved and whooped and yelled. A white speedboat cut the waves toward them, the passengers on deck applauding the approach of the *Guardia costiera*, the Italian Coast Guard. Two men on the Italian craft, in identical white polo shirts and black caps, tossed bottles of water onto the trawler. "Thank you! Thank you!" the Syrians shouted in English.

The passengers were transferred to another larger vessel, which docked in Sicily. That same day, Suleiman and another refugee from the boat boarded a bus for a twenty-six-hour journey to Milan, where they parted ways. The other young man headed toward Sweden. Suleiman spent the night of August 4 in Milan, before continuing to Munich by bus, a twelve-hour ride. Suleiman's old primary-school friend from Rastan had helped map out his journey. It was another three-hour train ride from Munich to his friend's home in Mannheim. On August 12, 2014, Suleiman registered as a refugee in Germany. That same day, he sent me a message on Facebook: "Hello, Rania. Do you remember me?"

SULEIMAN WAS WAITING for me at the bus stop in a navy-blue tracksuit his mother had mailed him from Syria. It was 10:15 p.m. on November 14, 2014. The bus stop was just steps from his temporary home, a single-story hostel he shared with ten other Syrian asylum seekers, all men. The town of Güglingen in Heilbronn, southern Germany, seemed transplanted from a fairy tale, with its half-timbered buildings and steep sloping roofs, pretty fountains, ponds tucked around corners like hidden treasures, and a population of only six thousand.

Suleiman shared a room with a blond, curly-haired man in his twenties from Daraa, who had worked in a medical field clinic there, and a shy, soft-spoken, forty-something father from Latakia.

"Look at us," Suleiman said to his roommates after they introduced themselves. "We've become like the Palestinians, we're displaced everywhere."

"No, the Palestinians are better," replied the man from Latakia. "They kept their keys when they fled. We didn't bother because we no longer had doors or homes to return to."

They were three men from across Syria united in exile, strangers who had become brothers, all yearning for the war's end so they could go home. They shared the hostel with a group of Assad supporters, a tense arrangement that almost brought the men to blows several times. The two groups, pro- and anti-Assad, tried to avoid each other, especially in the shared kitchen. They were all waiting for permanent resettlement after being granted temporary residency.

Suleiman's physical scars were fading, his back still occasionally pained him, but the gashes across it were becoming paler, the white lines that looked like cuts crisscrossing his legs and ankles less prominent.

"The stories he's told us," said his roommate from Daraa. "I was detained too, but I didn't go through what he did. He still has the scars of his torture, even now."

"Everything disappears with time," Suleiman said, "except the memories. We must keep the memories."

EXILE IS ABOUT more than displacement. It is the physical rupture of community, the erasure of memory and identity, an untethering from those who know your family and history. It means having to explain who you are. In Germany, Suleiman was just another foreigner, another refugee, another Syrian, another Arab Muslim, another number. "You are the stranger, you will always feel that humiliation, that pang of indignity," he said. "Nobody comes here to be nothing. In Syria, I was somebody."

He was building a new life in a new tongue, teaching himself German while he waited to be enrolled in a government-sponsored language program. He switched his phone from Arabic to immerse himself in the letters and sounds of this new place. He could already make himself understood to bus drivers and waiters and store clerks, stumbling over certain words but pushing through his embarrassment. He gave himself a year to learn the language well enough to apply for a master's degree program and get a job. But what he really wanted to do was return to Syria.

He was homesick for a country he struggled to recognize. How much had changed during his incarceration. He couldn't fathom how there were now media activists covering battalions instead of protests. "All of those military factions," he said one day, "there are thousands of them. And this ISIS, I can't understand what it is. Where did it come from? Where is the revolutionary spirit that was there in the beginning, when we said we want to go out and peacefully raise our voices? I've never held a weapon and never want to."

"We were naive," said Suleiman. "From the first day in the revolution, we went out thinking the president would be toppled the next week. The week after that, we said it's going to happen the next week, and so on, but it turned out to be bigger than that, bigger than all of us. It's an ugly global game, and everybody seems happy to let it continue."

He found comfort in small things that made his exile easier, like cooking Syrian dishes with his roommates, or the day the trio found a Lebanese shopkeeper who stocked cans of *hummus* and *ful*, as well as Cafe Najjar coffee, then stumbling upon another store that sold Turkish coffeepots. He didn't feel as guilty as he used to about being safe, now that his family was reconstituting in Germany. His younger brother had smuggled himself there from Egypt for $5,000, but his asylum application was being processed in a different part of the country. One sister and her family paid smugglers $17,000 to escape Syria. His other sister's husband had also made a perilous journey by sea from Egypt. He'd done so alone, hoping his wife and children could join him (via plane) through a family-reunification program. Only Suleiman's parents remained in Syria.

Suleiman was relieved to learn that his cousin Samer Tlass had been freed in a prisoner exchange months earlier, on September 11, 2014. Samer had been sentenced to death on seven counts. He fled to Turkey and began campaigning to remember those still languishing in the darkness. Samer set up a Turkey-based NGO and a countrywide network inside

Syria to find released detainees and record their testimony, to learn who was incarcerated with them in order to inform their families. "We must save the rest," Samer once said from southern Turkey. "I refused to be broken by them inside. They'd say, 'You want a revolution?' as they hit me, and I'd say, 'Yes, we want a revolution.' What more could they do except kill me? I am determined to continue this. I remind myself of our goals, of our cause."

Suleiman emerged from his ordeal without bitterness, without regret, and free of hate. He chose to let go of a heavy emotional burden that would only harm him. It was perhaps his greatest act of freedom—to choose how to respond to those who had taken most of his other freedoms. He did not forgive them, but he refused to continue being their victim.

He had made mistakes, he knew that, and he sometimes thought of them, but not often. He should have been more careful on the phone, with his electronic communications, shouldn't have assumed he could lead a double life for long, but they were mistakes, not regrets. The woman he'd let go had moved on and was already engaged to be married. "Because I love her, I'm happy for her," Suleiman said. "May God keep her and make her path easy. Life is like this. I had to go away. The truth is," he said, "even when I was in prison and now, I don't regret anything that I did in my life or in the revolution. I am proud of what I did in the revolution. I believed in a cause."

His phone beeped one day as we were talking on a park bench. It was his mother wishing him a happy birthday. Suleiman had forgotten the date. "June 17 is my birthday now," he said. "The day I left prison." We stopped at a bakery to buy a cake to share with his roommates. "Thank God, I always remembered, I didn't go mad in there," Suleiman said as we walked back. "I remembered it all but I don't live in that darkness. I don't go back there in my mind."

Instead, when he closes his eyes, his dreams transport him to Rastan. It is Ramadan 2011. A balmy summer night. He's standing on the balcony of the State Security building, opposite Al-Kabir Mosque, filming a sea of faces turned upward, hands clapping in tune to the chants. Mohammad

Darwish, the student who first shouted "Freedom!" is leading the chants, as he always did. In Suleiman's dreams, the protest singer is still alive. Merhi and all of his friends in the *tansiqiya* are still alive. Suleiman's house, the stone villa on an incline with a view of the Rastan Dam, has not been destroyed. It is still standing, the trees in its garden heavy with fruit, and his parents are inside, waiting for their son to return home.

RUHA

Ruha's little sister Tala, whose illness was the reason the family fled to Turkey, couldn't remember Syria. She'd forgotten the warplanes and barrel bombs and mortars that had scared her sick, couldn't recall details of her home or the harrowing trip across the border. Perhaps that's why she seemed to her mother the best adjusted of the children. It was late 2014, and they'd been refugees for two years—a long time in the life of a five-year-old. Tala had reverted, physically and emotionally, to being a normal little girl again, one unburdened by memory. Ruha envied her that. Some days Ruha wanted to forget too, other days she clung to the memories, the good ones, wrapped herself in them like a life jacket. "I can't forget Syria," she said, "but I want to forget what I saw in Syria, because it's ugly. I want to forget especially when Baba was shot. I try very hard, but I can't."

She had a new baby brother, Ibrahim, born that summer, who drew his mother out of her grief. Ruha was twelve now, and, like many girls entering puberty, had taken to wearing a *hijab*. It was her choice to do so. It made her feel grown-up. She was still attending the Syrian school in Antakya with her sister Alaa. Her brother Mohammad had transferred to an all-boys' Turkish school nearby. His classmates called him Mehmet, the Turkish form of his name, which his sisters teased him about, but he didn't mind. He'd laugh along with them. The children were learning Turkish at school, and they took pride in the new words they'd share with me. We'd stand back-to-back to see how much they'd grown, go on walks, and play in parks. Ruha had started contemplating her future. "I'm thinking I want to be a doctor, a pediatrician to help other children. What subjects do I have to take to be a doctor?" she asked. "I want to return to Syria. I want to rebuild my country, take our rights. I think of Syria every day, but it's getting less. I don't think about my house as much anymore. I wonder sometimes and I feel guilty that my house is still standing and others aren't." Saraqeb, she said, was her life, "my other life, the real one."

Her father, Maysaara, didn't tell her that the house in Saraqeb was so damaged it was unlivable. The family members in Syria had moved permanently to the farmhouse. Friends and relatives who had land did the same. Ruha's Aunt Mariam still visited the old neighborhood from time to time. She didn't like going there but felt drawn to it. "I go, cry, and come back," Mariam said. "There's so much rubble, so many destroyed homes." Mariam still taught at a local primary school. The schools in Saraqeb also ran in two shifts, because buildings were either destroyed by war or were bases for armed groups, including Nusra. "Four or five schools have started using one school building now," Mariam said. With planes in the air, the teachers reduced the curriculum and eliminated sports, music, and art classes to minimize the time spent in schools. One day, there were two air strikes while Mariam was teaching. "The children were scared. I told them not to be, that it was a friendly plane and it wouldn't hit us." The older children, she said, were the ones who cried and screamed, not the younger ones, "maybe because the [younger ones] were born into this environment, they don't know anything else."

Mariam was teaching, running a household, and taking care of the business of the farm. Her brother, Ruha's Uncle Mohammad, was ill; in June 2015, he succumbed to stomach cancer. Mariam rented portions of the family's vast land holdings to people who could farm them. She scoffed at the idea of leaving Syria, even temporarily. "Leave?" she said, "And go where? I won't go anywhere! I will die on our land. There is no place that I'd even think of going. Not one!"

That summer, Maysaara, like tens of thousands of Syrians, contemplated risking Turkish waters to reach Europe and a new life. He traveled to Mersin, as Suleiman had, and looked out onto a calm sea, the serenity of the water belying its bloodlust. Its dangers had been demonstrated in refugee boats that capsized, drowning dreams and belching corpses. Smugglers now openly did business in cafés in Turkish coastal cities. Store mannequins displayed bright orange life vests. Refugees mapped out their trips through Facebook pages and WhatsApp groups, slept in cheap hotels or on the streets, waiting their turn to leave. Maysaara watched a family, not unlike his, haggling with a smuggler. The smuggler insisted he wasn't like others who overfilled their rubber dinghies, that he had a conscience. The parents listened and walked away. They couldn't afford the premium for a conscience. Maysaara called me very late one night from Mersin. He was outside a smuggler's office. He'd been in Syria twenty days earlier for about a week and said it was worse than ever. His words tumbled out, as if he needed to hear them, a soliloquy to convince himself.

"There's no more hope," he said. "Now it's clear this isn't going to end anytime soon. Everybody's trying to figure out what to do, how to live, where to live, how to survive. It's gone on for too long. There aren't many of us left, the ones who started it, who aren't dead or detained. These new commanders, these new defectors, are something different. They want to tell you about our history! Where were they during that period? There are a million things in my head and I don't know what to do, which path to take. All the *shabab* are saying that, at the end of the day, we should leave the country. How can we leave? Leave our homes? Leave our lands? Leave it to whom? I'm in Turkey, but I still feel like I'm close to Syria, that I can get to it when I need to. Europe is a different kind of exile. If I lose Syria, I lose everything. If you leave it, you don't deserve to return. People died for it. We paid in blood. What am I if I leave? What will I become?"

Maysaara didn't get on a boat. His memories, heavy and rich and painful and proud, weighed him down. He returned to Antakya, bade farewell to his wife and children, and crossed into Syria alone. He sold a piece of land for enough money to live comfortably in any of Syria's neighboring states, but that wasn't his plan. On September 19, 2015, he sent me a photo of a pile of metal he'd just bought, and room-size holes dug into cinnamon-colored earth that would soon be filled with concrete. He planned to build a factory to process the land's bounty in Saraqeb, to provide employment for his community. "This is our land and our country," he said. "Our land is our honor, it is our past and, God willing, our future."

ALTHOUGH MAYSAARA DID NOT head to Europe, Saleh did, the Nusra insider and Jolani confidant. He was sick of the infighting between Jabhat al-Nusra and Islamic State. "I have a passport," he told me one day that summer. "I want to leave everything behind." He landed somewhere in Europe, where he wouldn't say. "I don't have any ties to my previous life," he said. "I hope you understand me." I asked if he'd left with the approval of his big brother—our code name for Jolani—or if he'd escaped: "Yes, everything is fine," he replied. "One day, I will see you and explain."

ABU AZZAM

Abu Azzam had married, a union arranged by his formidable mother, his "chief of staff," as he still called her. His bride, Alaa, was from his hometown of Tabqa, the daughter of family friends, although the couple didn't know each other before they married. That wasn't unusual in parts of Syria. Alaa was nineteen, petite, with fair skin and fine, mousy-blonde hair that cascaded past her slender waist. She hadn't planned to marry early, at least not before her twenty-fifth birthday, when she imagined she'd have a university degree and some independence.

If a heart attack hadn't killed her father, she figured she'd still be living at home in Tabqa, in the villa she shared with her parents, an older brother, and two younger sisters. But Baba was gone and Mama had to contend with the Islamic State suitors from the base next door asking for her hand. Her mother was running out of excuses for turning them away.

As occurred elsewhere in the north, Islamic State wrested Tabqa and other territory from the Free Syrian Army and other groups that had won it from the regime. It imposed its female dress code and threatened to punish men whose mothers, sisters, wives, and daughters didn't follow the rules. Alaa couldn't stand wearing the face veil—or, more precisely, couldn't stand being forced to wear it. If she was going to don the *niqab*, it had to be her choice. She'd already had several run-ins with the *hisbee*, or morality police, roving the streets. "Look at you, are these clothes? You're in a bellydancing outfit," a Syrian member of the *hisbee* once told her. Only her face was showing. The Syrian said he'd detain Alaa's father or husband because of her transgression. She told him she had neither. He called her a loose woman, then called for backup. A group of IS *muhajireen*, mainly Saudis, arrived. They were kinder to Alaa than the Syrian had been. They apologized for his offensive language and let her go. "I was never insulted by a *muhajir*, only by the Syrians of *ad-Dawla*," said Alaa. "The Syrians were hypocrites. Did they think we didn't know their women, how they used to dress and act before, and now, suddenly these same men were enforcers of dress codes and virtue? The *muhajireen* were more honorable."

Alaa befriended a French Moroccan *muhajira* who had moved to Tabqa with her French Moroccan husband after Islamic State evacuated from Latakia. She introduced Alaa to other women in Islamic State who cemented her view that the foreigners in the group were better than the Syrians. But that didn't mean she wanted to marry one. Her mother feared her daughter's feistiness would land her only son in Islamic State detention. Alaa felt the pressure on her mother. "I wanted to get out of the environment I was in, and Mama couldn't keep saying no to Islamic State proposals, so I agreed to marry Abu Azzam." He was Syrian and a local. She knew his family. They were good people.

The groom could not travel to Syria, so the bride went to him. She'd never crossed the Turkish border before. They wedded in September 2014. Ironically, the union landed Alaa's brother in an Islamic State prison anyway. Alaa had married a former commander in the Farouq, a man Islamic State decreed an apostate. "My brother came here to Turkey after I married to check on me; on his way back, he was imprisoned because *ad-Dawla* suspected he was collaborating with my husband." She learned that her brother would be released if she divorced, returned to IS-held territory, and married an Islamic State fighter. "I can't accept that he's suffering because of me," Alaa said. "I feel like I've fallen between two fires, my husband and my brother."

Abu Azzam felt as guilty as his wife for his brother-in-law's troubles, and he knew she was homesick. At mealtimes, he fed her by hand before he ate. He joked that she was his interior minister, usually the most powerful cabinet position in any Arab government. He kept his problems from her to avoid putting any further burden on her. He was still shuffling between one feckless military council in exile to another, hoping to rekindle a revolution he said was now "coals under the ashes."

The newlyweds couldn't afford a place of their own. They shared an apartment with Abu Azzam's former commander in the Farouq Battalions, the lawyer Abu Sayyeh, one of the Farouq's original leaders. It was January 2015, and they lived in Reyhanlı, near the Bab al-Hawa border crossing Abu Azzam once controlled.

One night, Abu Azzam walked to the store in a light rain that intensified, refusing my outstretched umbrella. He turned his face toward a dark sky. "Rain cleanses the soul before the body," he said. He let it soak him, stream down his face. "The revolution must go back to square one," he said. "We need a second revolution, but this time it will be organized. We were simple, naive when we started. It was spontaneous. We were focused on the military side and forgot about the civilian one—services. If God grants me the chance to work again, I won't make that mistake again. I will not expand into territory [for which] I cannot provide anything. I've realized that people turned away from the Free Army and looked at Nusra or *Daesh* as their salvation for one reason—because the Free Army was disorganized factions. In the liberated areas, there was no law. I've been thinking about it a lot. I will work again, if God grants me days to do so."

He just needed to find a way back into rebel Syria. It was a time of *tasfiyat*, assassinations, across the border. Feuds old and new were settled with IEDs, ambushes, and silencers. It was difficult to tell friend from foe, even within the same faction, difficult to trust anyone. Like Abu Azzam, thousands of fighters escaped into exile—fearing men on their own side.

Abu Azzam walked home, took off his boots at the front door, grabbed a towel, and sat with his phone, watching cartoons. It relaxed him. "That's how he spends his evenings," his wife said. "He just wants to forget about other things." Abu Azzam now smoked heavily. He hadn't been able to write a poem since leaving Baba Amr, an activity that used to soothe him. "I can't write anything because this life of garbage we're living is uninspiring. It's painful. There's no peace of mind or physical rest. We can't rest until we end it."

What upset him most was seeing the regime's narrative playing out—that its opponents were all extremists, terrorists, and Assad was the bulwark against them. "Our regime is focused on eliminating us, the moderate opposition, and it is in the regime's interests to surrender areas like Raqqa and Tabqa to tell the whole world, 'Look at who is ruling it.' In the eyes of the West, a dictator is a lesser evil than an extremist."

He still believed in a Syrianness that transcended frontlines and sect and geography. He didn't demonize the entire regime, or every Syrian on the other side as a regime supporter. Assad and his political, military, and security leaders had to go, he said, "but I believe there are some in the regime who refuse to kill their own people. People who are with it ideologically but who refuse to kill. These are men I can respect and could meet. We may have to do this to fight these groups we both consider terrorists. We must remove this sectarianism. We will. Syria will be different. We will forgive each other."

HAZM

On September 23, 2014, after years of watching the ascendancy of Jabhat al-Nusra and Islamic State, America's military directly intervened in Syria's war, striking Islamic State positions and lobbing missiles toward eight locations in Idlib and Aleppo held by the Nusra-affiliated Khorasan Group. The United States had launched its war on ISIS in Iraq on August 8, and expanded it into Syria the following month. Many Syrians wondered why the United States waited until Islamic State was at the height of its power to attack it.

Hazm's leader, Abu Hashem, learned of the US air strikes from a television news report. The Hazm intelligence operative, like others in the group, was furious: "We told the MOM [the international operations room in Turkey] and the CIA, 'How could you strike them from the air without at least telling us? You are hitting Nusra positions in *our* territories, and we are known as being American supported, so what are we supposed to do?'"

Hazm and other US-backed factions in the MOM feared the US strikes would backfire on them. Hazm promptly issued a statement denouncing the American action. "We weren't collaborators," the intelligence operative said. "We didn't have problems with Nusra, but from that moment, we feared that the Americans may have brought *Daesh* and Nusra and all the Islamists closer together with these strikes."

In early November, Nusra fighters easily routed Hazm from its main stronghold in Idlib Province, seizing Hazm's cache of US-supplied weapons, including TOW antitank missiles. The base fell without a fight, and

314 · RANIA ABOUZEID

the hundreds of Hazm fighters either escaped to Aleppo, defected to Nusra, or were detained. "We were prepared to fight Islamic State because of its ideology, but not yet ready to fight Nusra," said a Hazm commander in Idlib. "Honestly, most of Jabhat al-Nusra, with the exception of the foreign commanders, are of us. They are our people. They are our cousins, our friends."

Hazm leader Abu Hashem consolidated his forces in and around Aleppo. His men held fire, he said, because Nusra "succeeded in presenting an image of itself as fighting the regime . . . that they were Islamists defending the people, and there was no conviction among our fighters to shed their blood."

MOHAMMAD

Mohammad, the Nusra emir, eyed Hazm warily. He detested its CIA backers, its talk of a secular state. He suspected it of deeper dealings with foreign intelligence agencies beyond the Americans, including the French and the Germans. He didn't like reports from Nusra colleagues in the Aleppan countryside that Hazm was detaining Nusra members at its checkpoints. The two groups had briefly clashed since Hazm lost its Idlib headquarters.

It wasn't simply Hazm's dealings with the Americans per se that concerned Mohammad, it was the nature of those interactions. "If a group meets with the Americans," he said, "and tries to get help to fight Bashar al-Assad, so what? But if it's meeting with the Americans to be its representative or one of its wings in Syria to fight Qaeda and Islamists and jihadis? That's another story. There's a huge difference."

Mohammad was in a Nusra safe house, just inside the Turkish border, with an Egyptian colleague waiting to cross into Syria. The Egyptian *muhajir* had been in Syria since August 2013. Their wives were in the kitchen preparing dinner. The once-porous frontier had tightened since mid-2014, when Turkey, under international pressure to trap jihadists in Syria's killing fields, began erecting a concrete barrier of blast walls topped with coiled razor wire, placing it well inside Syrian territory. Some stretches of the border were monitored with thermal cameras that Mohammad and his colleagues learned didn't work so well at dusk and dawn, or when it was raining and foggy. The Turks were shooting dead anyone trying to get through—fighters and refugee families alike—although they sometimes held fire and instead detained and deported those they caught. It wasn't as hard to get into Syria as it was to get out. Smugglers were arrested, intimidated, and killed, but the jihadists still had several dedicated smuggling routes.

Mohammad's wife knocked on the door, indicating dinner was ready. The men ate separately from their wives. Mohammad carried in a tray of lentil soup, salad, and chicken in tomato salsa. They discussed spies among the *muhajireen*. Most Jordanian would-be recruits were rejected outright, immediately suspected of working for Jordan's powerful intelligence agency. "I tell you, brother, I sent a Spaniard home last week," Mohammad said. "He had *tazkiya*, but when we were talking about the jihad, it was clear he viewed *ad-Dawla* and Nusra as the same. I didn't trust him—he might be a *Dawla* spy or an intelligence agent."

"Brother," the Egyptian said, "there was an Egyptian in my unit, a first-line fighter, at the front of the frontline, unafraid of death, always keen." The man was caught with tracking equipment and executed.

Mohammad said there was a double agent working with the US-led coalition tasked with mapping Nusra targets using a device Mohammad described as "part GPS that also detects and locks cell-phone signals." The agent informed Mohammad about his missions. "Recently, he was asked to walk past three Nusra outposts. Our men all cleared out of the buildings, turned off their phones and other electronics, and the guy completed his task and sent along the information."

Both men paused eating to laugh heartily at my question about whether the US-led strikes against Islamic State were significantly harming the group. "Please, if the West really wanted to hit Islamic State, they'd wipe them out," the Egyptian said. "Their convoys move very comfortably between Iraq and Syria. And their bases are known, they're painted black and fly their flag. They are not hiding."

"These strikes are a good thing for us," the Egyptian continued, "because our security is tighter now. We're more aware of threats around us, but, based on my limited reading of history, wars aren't won from the air. The Americans won't fight on the ground, so they will do so through partners, men they support, like Hazm. That's their only hope against us, but they will fail."

ABU AZZAM

Abu Azzam was clashing with his wife, Alaa—not over the running of the household or other marital issues, but Islamic State. More and more, Alaa was coming to identify with IS. Her French Moroccan friend in Tabqa sent her messages on WhatsApp. Her brother was released from IS detention, but rather than resent the group, he joined it. Her brother then made friends with a French Moroccan engineer who asked to marry Alaa's younger sister. The rest of the family was pleased. The *muhajir* treated his new wife and his in-laws well. "He isn't in Syria for a $100 salary," Alaa said, "he's very wealthy." It was February 2015. She was pregnant by an FSA "apostate," while her sister was pregnant by an IS foreign fighter. The two husbands didn't talk to each other. Alaa, under the influence of her family and IS friends, wanted to return to Syria. "If only people under-stood the Islamic State, they would want to live under it," she said. It was the kind of talk that enraged Abu Azzam: "You're a half-*Daeshy*!" he would tell his wife. But one short trip into Syria would change his mind.

Meanwhile, men from Hazm—Abu Azzam's former Farouq colleagues—killed his relative Abu Issa al-Tabqa, a man Abu Azzam called "uncle." Abu Issa had been a Nusra emir in Tabqa. Abu Azzam mourned his relative but held no grudge against his killers: "I loved my uncle and he loved me. He was one of the dearest people in my heart, but I don't blame those who killed him," he said. "This is the nature of our war. If my brother is in Nusra and I am fighting Nusra, I will fight him. He is an enemy."

Hazm braced itself for reprisals. Abu Issa had been killed along with several other Nusra captives. "From the beginning, we insisted to the Americans that the bigger threat was Jabhat al-Nusra more than *Daesh*, because they were among us," said Hazm leader Abu Hashem. "*Daesh* had been removed from the area." He said that although Nusra was a wing of Al-Qaeda, that was no longer secret, "the Americans didn't see any threat that wasn't *Daesh*. I don't know why."

Nusra stormed Hazm's bases in and around Aleppo, overrunning its last positions. No one came to Hazm's aid—neither its American backers nor other Syrian groups in the MOM. On March 1, Hazm announced its dissolution. Nusra continued to hunt the group's members, snatching them from their homes and hideouts and "reeducating" them in its prisons. Hazm didn't even know how many of its men were detained. Its leadership, and those who could, fled to Turkey. Mohammad put the number at four hundred prisoners, but he said most were released. He advocated their "reeducation," but not the way it was being done. "What is happening in Nusra's prisons is beatings and torture, just like in the regime's prisons," he said. "If the American collaborators weren't entirely convinced about fighting you, after you've tortured them, they will be. You're creating a fiercer enemy, and it's the same thing with a *Daeshy*. The aim isn't to hit him and beat him and then release him, it's to show him why he's wrong."

Hazm drew lessons from its defeat. "What we learned," a Hazm official said, "was that you can't count on America. I don't trust them now, none of us do. We are not the children of America for them to care for us, but we had shared interests."

Abu Hashem, Hazm's leader, gambled on US support after his experience as the Farouq's foreign liaison, dealing with Turkey and the Gulf states. "Did the US abandon us? Clearly," he said. "Let Nusra say whatever it wants to say, it used our American support as a pretext to attack us, but . . . I don't care what it says. . . . We were here first. They have no place in Syria." Abu Hashem was speaking from exile in Turkey.

In Washington, rebel advocates in close contact with US policymakers were dismayed by the reaction to Hazm's routing. "We got the sense the failure of the flagship moderate brigade was a relief to the administration, like they were happy Hazm was eliminated," one advocate said. "Now they could say, 'There's nobody in Syria to support.'"

Hazm collapsed that spring as the Pentagon embarked on a new $500 million program to "train and equip" rebels to counter Islamic State (but not the regime). It intended to ready a force of some three thousand by year's end and graduate another five thousand every year thereafter. But despite spending $384 million, it managed to recruit only 180 fighters before the program was suspended in October 2015. Rebels weren't keen just to fight Islamic State and to forget the regime. The first fifty-four graduates of the Pentagon program were ambushed by Jabhat al-Nusra on July 31, within hours of crossing the Turkish border into Syria. The second group surrendered its weapons, ammunition, and trucks to Nusra in exchange for safe passage. In September, the Pentagon admitted that only "four or five" of its trainees were still fighting in Syria. By 2016, militias in northern Syria funded by the Pentagon would be fighting those armed by the CIA. In July 2017, the Trump administration ended the CIA program. It had reportedly cost more than $1 billion and was riddled with problems, not least the open secret that Nusra extracted a "tax" from some CIA-vetted groups—a cut of their supplies.

"The United States had people, it had partners in us," said the Hazm intelligence operative, "but I don't think the Americans are real allies. I'm not anti-American—on the contrary, I very much wanted the new Syria to view the West as real partners in everything—but today I am convinced that Russia is more honorable and trustworthy than the United States, because at least it is really standing alongside its ally. But America? It doesn't even know who its friends are or what it is doing."

2016

RUHA

March 2016. Maysaara hadn't seen his wife and children for more than seven months. He was in Syria and they were in southern Turkey—the days of moving easily between the two countries as distant as the idea of peace. Sneaking into Turkey was no longer simply a tough hike with the fear of a Turkish jail or deportation to Syria. Turkey's concrete blast walls and its shoot-to-kill policy along the border meant risking death.

Maysaara wanted his family with him. His youngest, Ibrahim, had forgotten him. He called every male relative Baba. Manal feared returning to a Syria that was no better than the one she'd fled, but she didn't want her children growing up without their father. They were going back that summer. Manal walked around her living room one day in March, wondering how to pack up her "half-life" and what dangers were awaiting her and her family. Two families she knew of, sixteen people, were recently obliterated in a farmhouse. "There is no safe place in Syria, even our farmhouse is not safe," Manal said. "What can I do except try to calm the children and tell them not to be afraid? This is the Syrian woman's burden—caught between worrying about our men and [worrying about] our children."

Her eldest, Ruha, who had pined for Syria, was now a teenager who suddenly didn't want to return. "We are children of now, not children of before," she said one day. Friends and rap music and hairstyles and fashion were displacing thoughts of Saraqeb. She dearly missed her father, but beyond that, she was accustomed to freedoms in Turkey she didn't think she could carry across the border. Her classes that year were during the school's morning shift. Her afternoons, when she didn't have homework and it wasn't raining, were spent in a park with an eclectic group of girls: the Chechen born in Turkey whose father was fighting in Syria, a Turk whose mother owned a stationery store across from the park, and a Syrian who always arrived after 4:30 p.m., the end of her day at a sewing factory. Her family needed her wages more than her education. The girls didn't share a language—just a few Turkish words here, Arabic there, lots of sign language and laughter.

Ruha sat on a bench with her sister Alaa one day, waiting for her friends to arrive. She discreetly pointed to a Syrian woman, in a long, belted over-coat and a face veil, pushing a child on a swing. "Look at my clothes and look at the Syrians here, look how they're dressed," she said. Ruha was in skinny jeans, a long sweater, and a *hijab*, common attire for a Muslim Syrian girl, but she expected to have to dress like the woman in the park if she went back to Saraqeb. She had heard her relatives talking about how it was more conservative now. "I have a lot of freedom here," she said. "If I go to Syria, that freedom will be imprisoned. I'll have to wear a coat down to my ankles like that woman. I can't do that."

She was growing up. She didn't want to burden her parents with her concerns. "The family used to sit together at mealtime, talk about our day, but now I feel like everybody is in a different universe," she said. "Now, whatever happens to me, I don't have the courage to tell Baba, to ask him anything. I know he has other things to worry about. I don't tell Mama, either. I prefer to speak to others my age. That's why I come here. We haven't seen Baba in more than seven months. That's wrong. When we were in Syria, in the war, Baba wasn't with us much, but we used to see him occasionally. Even if I saw him for an hour, I felt like that hour was worth the entire world and everything in it. Now . . ." She couldn't finish her sentence.

MAY 2016. THE SUN was low in the sky, its golden light soft and warm and diffused. It cast long shadows on the handful of construction workers ending their day. Maysaara watched them climb down from a two-story wooden scaffolding hugging the building's rectangular shell. His factory was coming together. It had four walls and no roof, its exterior built in the traditional manner, with great blocks of locally sourced white stone, not the cheaper concrete. Saraqeb's silhouette rose five kilometers in the distance, on the other side of green carpets of shin-high lentil crops and young stalks of wheat. Sprinklers pulsed rhythmically. Deep-orange pomegranate flowers were in bloom. Birds chirped in the quietness when the warplanes weren't overhead.

Maysaara walked through his empty factory, proud and excited, explaining where the equipment would go. The machinery would come either from regime-held Hama (through the forty-nine government checkpoints along the route, each one demanding a bribe) or from Turkey, with its raft of paperwork and tight restrictions at the border. It depended on the roads, the planes, and the required bribes, but he wasn't overly worried about it.

The construction site was a short drive from the farmhouse, on land the family had owned for generations. Maysaara surveyed its sweep, pointing to the plot in the far distance where a hundred fig trees would soon be rooted, near the olive groves his late father had planted decades earlier. He had bought half a dozen sheep and a puppy his daughter Tala named Molly, after one of her favorite cartoon characters. He had plans to restart the family's cucumber pickling business, to give young men an alternative to emigrating or joining a battalion to earn $50 a month. And he wanted to buy a horse, recounting a Hadith about how those who treat a horse well are blessed against poverty. He scooped up a handful of earth, let it fall through his fingers. "This," he said, "is everything. I swear a person doesn't find himself or feel dignity except in his own land. I lived in Turkey for three years. I lived well, was treated well, but I am still a foreigner there. I mean, the Japanese were hit with nuclear bombs and they stayed in their country and didn't give up on it! How can we? Look," he stretched out his arms, "here there is life." His Syria had shrunk, he knew that. Regime territory and Islamic State were other countries, but his space was enough for him. "Before the revolution, I wasn't somebody who spent a lot of time on Latakia's coasts. I will sacrifice seeing the sea. This is my land. This is my area. This is my country." Wasn't he afraid to bring his family back? "Life and death are in God's hands," he said. "Some people survive being in a building hit by a barrel bomb that others die in. It's not their time. Nobody knows when their time is up."

It was getting dark. The workers had long left. Maysaara drove back to the farmhouse in his red Toyota HiLux pickup truck, the same vehicle in which he'd been shot back in January 2012. It had been idle for years while he decided what to do with it. He patched its forty-eight bullet holes and cleared its bloodstains. He refused to sell it. It was a reminder of what he'd survived and what others, like his friend Abu Rabieh, who had died in the front seat, had lost.

RUHA'S AUNT MARIAM was up early the next morning, and so were the planes. It was not yet 8 a.m. when the first one roared overhead. Mariam walked into the living room carrying a tray of Turkish coffee. "Good morning," she said. The bombs tumbled to earth somewhere far enough away not to worry about them. "Who wants coffee?"

A walkie-talkie set near the window screeched out an alert about another warplane: "Sukhoi 27 is coordinating with Homs, be careful." Saraqeb, like every town in the rebel-held north, had developed an early warning system to identify threats in the air. Men known as *marasid*, observers, were tasked with intercepting regime communications between pilots and airbases and relaying that information via walkie-talkies. They latched onto regime frequencies that constantly changed and tried to break the coded language sometimes used to identify targets. More often, the targets were simply stated. The planes had few real predators. If the threat to Saraqeb was direct, and there was time, the alert would boom from the minarets of mosques. The town had five *marasid*, their task made harder since September 2015, when Russian warplanes joined their Syrian allies in the skies, turning the conflict decisively in Assad's favor. There were Western planes in the air, too, the rebel backers bombing Islamic State positions in other parts of Syria and the occasional Nusra post, but the Western planes didn't target the regime. Mariam laughed when I asked how people without transmitters coped. "Even beggars have walkie-talkies these days," she said.

The farmhouse was self-sufficient, with twenty-four-hour electricity courtesy of solar panels, two generators as backup, satellite Internet, and two water wells. Residents who couldn't afford their own generators or solar panels subscribed to private neighborhood generators that distributed amperes for a monthly fee. Cell-phone reception was still dead. The landlines worked, but only for local calls within a province.

Mariam didn't have classes that day. She got behind the wheel of her gray Kia Picanto, said a prayer under her breath, and drove to the market inside Saraqeb. Along the way, she recounted how a member of Jabhat al-Nusra had recently stormed into the school, demanding that religious instruction be expanded and social studies be struck from the curriculum. "We all debated him," Mariam said, until a compromise was reached: Religious instruction would remain unchanged, social studies would be taught, but all references to the Baath Party, democracy, and socialism would be removed. "We slammed him into the wall with our words until he came out the other end!" Mariam laughed. "We will not be silent to them or anyone anymore."

She had never acquiesced to the growing Islamization of her town. She always drove herself, was politely waved through Nusra and Islamic State checkpoints, and never covered her face with a *niqab*, although many more women in Saraqeb now did. Ruha was right about that.

The graffitied walls displaying revolutionary slogans around Saraqeb's cultural center had faded. Shelling had amputated letters and images from the artwork, the missing pieces filled in with bare cinderblocks. A canvas of resistance damaged, repaired, resilient—a reminder of the time of colors before Saraqeb and most of Idlib Province was draped in Islamist black. The most recent revolutionary graffiti was dated 2013.

Other slogans had come to predominate in Idlib, displayed on billboards that once bore quotidian advertisements for things like restaurants and cooking oil. The billboards were painted black. In handwritten white lettering, they proclaimed that democracy was the religion of the West. Secularism was blasphemy. Democracy led to *zinna* (unlawful sex), and Shiites were the enemies of Islam. The black billboards were simply signed YOUR BROTHERS THE *MUJAHIDEEN*, with no group affiliation. They emerged shortly after March 2015, when the provincial capital, Idlib City, fell to an Islamist coalition anchored by Ahrar al-Sham and Jabhat al-Nusra. Idlib City was only the second of Syria's fourteen provincial capitals not under regime control, and, like the other—Raqqa City—Islamists also ruled it, although with a lighter hand. The coalition in Idlib, which called itself the Army of Conquest, imposed new conservative social measures in the city, including a female dress code enforced by roving patrols of the *hisbee*—the morality police who traveled in minivans with black-tinted windows, accosting people who failed to conform to the new standards. The Army of Conquest decreed that belted overcoats were insufficiently conservative and insisted that women (and even prepubescent girls) wear loose black *abayas*. It banned brightly colored headscarves; only black, brown, and navy blue were permitted. Men were required to wear beards. But the measures applied only to Idlib City, and by the end of the year, they were watered down due to their unpopularity.

Mariam stopped at a makeshift stall selling gasoline out of large plastic barrels. The fuel sellers usually offered a choice between *nizam* or *dawla* (regime or state)—the gas coming from either Assad-controlled areas or from Islamic State's oil wells in the east. Regime fuel was cleaner and generally more expensive than Islamic State's, which tended to be crudely refined in makeshift facilities, although both price and quality fluctuated, depending on availability. In any case, the fuel seller was out of both that morning. Mariam continued her chores. "Before, in the beginning, I used to think we have to be frugal, not use too much cooking gas, too much diesel, too much fuel. Now I don't think like that," Mariam said. "Now, I don't care if all of my paycheck is spent. We are in a state of war, who cares about money? Why die with money in your pocket? Why not live as comfortably as we can while we can?"

In the beginning, as Mariam put it, there was one martyrs' cemetery in Saraqeb for those killed in the conflict. Five years later, there were three. On another day, at one of the newer cemeteries, the gravedigger was busy shoveling red earth out of a deep hole. He always prepared ahead. The graves were arranged into sixteen rows, each extending at least a hundred meters, each column broken by plain white headstones like rungs on a ladder. Daisies sprouted from the graves. At least twenty belonged to unidentified victims, some placed in the earth just months earlier. The gravedigger explained what happened: "A plane struck, two fuel sellers were hit. Their supplies exploded, killing them and killing people in a Kia Rio that was passing by," he said. "The bodies were charcoal, there was nothing left for us to identify them. Nobody knows who they were or where they were from or going. We put notices on Facebook, but nobody has asked about them." Even the cemeteries weren't safe from the planes, the gravedigger said. Another one in town had been shelled. "The living were martyred and the dead were martyred twice," he said. "Life is the cheapest thing in Syria now."

MARIAM'S ELDEST SISTER needed cooking pots. Hers were riddled with shrapnel. Mariam offered to take her first to the family complex in the center of Saraqeb to see if there were any left behind before she bought new ones. The sisters drove around piles of rubble and twisted metal, Mariam cataloguing the lives lost at each gray mound. Four. Fourteen. Twenty-two. Six. "This was a little store," she said, pointing to a concrete skeleton, the missile's entry point clear. On a surviving column was a message spray-painted in red: HERE THERE WAS LIFE. Two men died there.

Mariam turned into their old street. Her sister waited in the car: "I don't want to see it," she said. "It hurts my heart." Mariam fumbled with the keys to the heavy metal door, its yellow fiberglass paneling long since blown out. It was the same door a once-nine-year-old Ruha opened to security forces back in 2011, the first time they invaded to look for her father.

Mariam's footsteps echoed in the emptiness. The windows, all glassless, were filled in with cinderblocks. Doors blown off hinges, window frames, too. The wind whistled through holes in several walls. A warplane overhead. Washed dishes gathered dust in the kitchen rack. A bottle of olive oil and spice jars on the bench. The inner courtyard, where Ruha and her siblings once played, where Mariam and her sisters would gather in the evenings, was strewn with rubble. In a coral-pink bedroom, dolls and teddy bears waited for two little girls who'd outgrown them. A fourth-grade social studies textbook lay on a bed. Colorful socks in a drawer. Mariam didn't find any pots. "I feel numb when I come here. I say to myself, 'Don't get upset, the whole country has been destroyed.' At least we're all okay, but I always feel tired after coming here, physically worn out."

The old family complex empty. Life had relocated. Ruha's extended family now gathered at the farmhouse every week, turning every Friday into Mother's Day. The matriarch, Ruha's grandmother, Zahida, was frailer, her body confined to a wheelchair but her mind still formidable, the anchor of the family. She expected updates on the crops, the price of lentils, the currency fluctuations, how her thirty-five grandchildren were faring, and what was happening in town. She sat on a couch one Friday afternoon—a new couch, not the faded blue one that had molded to her shape. Mariam was in the kitchen preparing lunch with a few of her sisters. The smell of fried onions and bay leaves and spices. She made *kibbe*, a labor-intensive dish of finely ground meat and bulgur, cinnamon and allspice, fashioned into palm-size, football-shaped croquettes, each one stuffed with minced meat, onions, garlic, and spices. It was a festive food, served in times of celebration. She hadn't made it in five years. "Why should you die wishing you'd eaten something?" Mariam said. That was reason enough to prepare it.

A male relative walked into the kitchen and joked that Jabhat al-Nusra wouldn't approve of the gender mixing. They laughed and mocked the black billboards and their Islamist messages. "They just make people hate them more," a sister said. "Did you all hear about what Abu Stayf did?" Maysaara asked. The lines outside bakeries were gender-segregated, with armed Nusra guards supervising the distribution. The bakeries were also targets for Assad's warplanes, so women tended to stay away. The men's line was always longer. Abu Stayf, a local man, had wrapped his face in a scarf and stood near a female friend in the shorter line. The Nusra fighter on duty, a foreigner, approached the woman suspiciously, asked her who was standing next to her but wouldn't look directly at her. "This is my sister, but she's hairy," the woman said, referring to Abu Stayf. The Nusra fighter took her word for it and simply asked, "How many loaves?" when the pair got to the front of the line. Abu Stayf walked away, bread in hand, to applause and chants of Abu Stayf! Abu Stayf! "He turned around and made a V-for-victory sign!" Maysaara said, chuckling.

One of Ruha's aunts talked about her detained son. A former prisoner from Saraqeb had been released recently and was expected home soon. Ruha's aunt wondered whether he'd seen her boy behind bars. She was dealing with a middleman who claimed he could release her son, but he demanded tens of thousands of dollars in advance without providing proof of life. "If he'd only give us something to believe Abdullah was alive, we'd sell land to raise the money," Ruha's aunt said. Abdullah had been detained on April 21, 2012. His mother, aunts, cousins, and grandmother remembered him fondly that afternoon, recalled his laugh, argued about whether he had one dimple or two. "You wonder what they are doing to him, what they've done. God help him," Mariam whispered. "The mothers of the detained have it much harder than the mothers of the martyrs. My friends, mothers of martyrs, at least they know what happened to their children."

In early July 2016, Ruha and her family returned home. Her father met them on the Syrian side of the border and escorted them to a farmhouse full of relatives waiting for them. Despite her earlier misgivings, Ruha was glad to be back, glad to be reunited with family, and pleased to know she didn't have to dress as conservatively as she had feared. She started school, made new friends. She was a ninth-grader now. "Everything has changed," she said of her hometown, "or maybe I'd forgotten the details. It's like I am seeing it for the first time. I wasn't expecting this destruction." She was upset that her home in the grand old family complex was too damaged and dangerous to live in. She also was surprised by how much she'd acclimatized to Turkey, how easily she'd forgotten the fear of life in wartime. "If I want to go to the *souq*, I have to think about whether it's worth it, think about the planes, and make it a quick trip. Even in school, when I'm in school and a plane passes, I'm terrified. Everybody is. The teachers freak out."

In Turkey, she said, "I felt the exile, the distance, but I also felt safe. I'm happy here with my family, but I got used to safety. *Inshallah* the future is better. *Inshallah* we stay united and the fear disappears, because I don't want to have to feel like I need to choose between living with family and being safe. Why can't we have both in Syria? Nobody wants to have to leave their country just to feel secure."

In July 2017, Saraqeb's sons and daughters, including Ruha's family, protested against the armed Islamists with the black flags in their hometown, peacefully driving them out of Saraqeb, although few expected them to stay away. The revolutionary flag fluttered from vacated Islamist outposts, and for the first time in years, a new revolutionary slogan appeared on Saraqeb's walls near other, earlier faded hopes: SAY TO THOSE WHO TRY TO DESTROY US THAT THE BEAUTY OF OUR SOULS CANNOT BE DEFEATED—SARAQEB 2017.

MOHAMMAD

April 2016. Mohammad was no longer a Nusra emir. He resigned his duties in Idlib and focused on what had become a harder task—bringing in *muhajireen,* a job he did halfheartedly. When he wasn't in a safe house on either side of the border, he spent time with his wife and children in southern Turkey, focusing on what his wife called "jihad of the family." He hadn't lived with them for years. Mohammad was disillusioned and disappointed with Jabhat al-Nusra. It was a failure, he said, that was losing men and influence to Islamic State. *Ad-Dawla* had better recruitment and stronger media outreach, more money. Like many Nusra members, Mohammad considered reconciliation with Islamic State an impossibility—a truce was the best scenario short of defeating the group. Their dispute wasn't just about personalities or pledges of loyalty. It was ideological, even though they both shared the same goal and referenced the same teachings. "We are as far apart as the Muslim Brotherhood and Al-Qaeda," Mohammad said, "even though the origin is the same—[the writings of] Sayyid Qutb. We want an Islamic state too, but only after we've liberated Syria and start liberating Lebanon, Palestine, and Jordan can we establish a caliphate. How can you declare a caliphate when you're still just basically in Raqqa and have one city out of fourteen [provincial capitals] in Syria? We must move in stages. You can't climb a staircase in a single step."

He was rejecting *muhajireen* who exhibited what he called "*Daeshy* tendencies" and ignoring most requests. He had pulled away. "Look," he said, holding out his phone, "today more than ten contacted me, they want to come in. I haven't responded to them yet." He scrolled through dozens of

WhatsApp messages. A Saudi living in Idlib City wanted his two brothers in the kingdom to join him. He'd used Mohammad before. An Algerian provided *tazkiya* for a countryman waiting at the Turkish border. "Blessings be upon you, brother. Abu Saad sent me to you," another message read. It was a Syrian sheikh who wanted five of his students to join him. Mohammad put away his phone. "The good ones aren't coming to Nusra," he said. "*Daesh* now dominates the Salafi Jihadi movement because Nusra and other jihadi groups are failures—administrative and financial failures with a weak leadership circle."

His experience with Nusra, said Mohammad, was like "when a person sees an island from afar, you imagine it's an island of your dreams, but when you get to it, you see that it's all mud, and it has many ugly things. You try to improve it, but when you reach the point where you feel it cannot be reformed, you move away from it. That's what happened."

Al-Qaeda's most evolved franchise was in deep turmoil and had been for years. Its leader, Abu Mohammad al-Jolani, once publicly acknowledged that if it weren't for the Syrian uprising, "Syria would not have been ready for us." The revolution, he said, "removed many of the obstacles and paved the way for us to enter this blessed land." That Jabhat al-Nusra managed to establish a foothold in a country where even the Muslim Brotherhood had been extinguished was no easy feat. The group's success rejuvenated its parent organization in Iraq, enabling it to march into Mosul and declare a caliphate. But Nusra 2016 was not Nusra 2012. Some of its senior members advocated cutting ties to Al-Qaeda, while others considered the affiliation their identity. Nusra was a US- and UN-sanctioned terrorist group in need of money. Losing the Al-Qaeda label, if only publicly, could boost funding by removing legal obstacles to supporting it, as well as unifying the Syrian jihad by enabling groups who recoiled from the Al-Qaeda brand to merge with it. Nusra had turned to kidnapping foreigners, aid workers, and journalists, to raise money. Abu Othman, Mohammad's onetime cellmate, was involved in the case of two young female Italian aid workers seized near Aleppo in the summer of 2014. Nusra demanded $20 million for their release. It got $12 million.

The women were freed in January 2015. Nusra also had a Japanese man in its custody, captured in mid-2015. Abu Othman, like other Nusra members, was scouting for foreigners—they were walking ATMs. He asked me once if I wouldn't mind being Nusra's "guest" until an embassy paid my ransom. "We won't harm you, there won't be any violence," he said. I convinced him it wasn't a good idea and that nobody would pay for me. "We must kidnap journalists. We need money," he said.

"You are part of a global organization, doesn't it finance you?" I asked.

"We have moved from an organization to a mindset, and we need money," he replied.

Mohammad thought kidnapping for ransom was a mistake, one of many Nusra was making. "You're losing your reputation, even if you can justify it on religious grounds," he said. "Al-Qaeda's leadership has said before that its strikes and attacks against civilians lose it popular support, so why make a citizen pay like this, and in so doing, lose popular support again? It's a mistake. We're repeating the same mistakes of the old Al-Qaeda. We've gone backward."

Abu Othman didn't share Mohammad's qualms about Nusra's trajectory. He remained on the Syrian battlefield, fighting with Nusra in his home base of Aleppo.

In late July, Jabhat al-Nusra severed its ties to Al-Qaeda and rebranded itself under a new name, Jabhat Fatih al-Sham. The change was cosmetic. Only its name and flag differed. Mohammad didn't care what it was called, or whether it was formally affiliated with Al-Qaeda. "Al-Qaeda is not an organization, it's bigger than that, it's an idea," he said, "and the goal is the key, not what you call yourself to get there."

By August, Mohammad had returned to living in Idlib and ferrying *muhajireen* into Syria in greater numbers than earlier in the year. Most of the new recruits he brought in were from Central Asia, from places like Kazakhstan and Uzbekistan. He remained a loyal but disappointed Al-Qaeda soldier. He considered himself part of the global movement, even if its local branch was in shambles. He wasn't fighting for Syria. He didn't believe in it.

"I am proud of the work I've done," he said. Mohammad, who as a young boy in Jisr al-Shughour watched the *mukhabarat* humiliate his neighbor Abu Ammar and others in the late 1970s and '80s, had become a man who did the same thing—and worse—to other children's fathers, to sons and brothers and husbands. What of the Syria in which he grew up, the mixed Alawite–Christian neighborhood in Latakia? What would he tell his son about the Syria he was trying to destroy? "The Alawites tied their fate to Bashar's, so there is no retreat—no turning back—for them or for us," he said. "It's impossible. I'm not saying we won't kill Sunnis as well—we will and do kill Sunnis who are with them. I will tell my son, beware the Alawites, the Shiites, the Christians, regardless of how well they treat you or speak to you, in his heart he hates you. I cannot convince my son that there should be coexistence, I don't believe it."

And what of the hate he was sowing in the hearts of those he'd harmed? Did he wonder whether a little boy today viewed him the way he once feared the *mukhabarat* as a little boy? He didn't need to think about the answer: "I know that they have suffered, but they are the oppressors. This bill is going to be paid by both sides. The high death toll on our side is the price for forty years of silence against their oppression, and the high death toll on their side is the price of killing and humiliating us for forty years. One of us has to be broken by the other, one of us has to submit. There is no other way."

TALAL

The ambulance was smeared with mud to make it harder for warplanes to see. It bounced along potholed Idlib roads rendered almost impassable by shelling. Dr. Rami Habib was in the front seat, scanning the skies through a bullet-fractured windshield. His field clinic in Salma, Latakia Province, had been destroyed in Russian air strikes that had helped the regime win back most of the province. Entire villages in Latakia were displaced and reconstituted in clusters near the Turkish border. The temporary towns were a patchwork of thousands of tents, some canvas, others simply sheets of plastic or burlap bags sewn together, their occupants hoping the air strikes that drove them from home wouldn't hunt them so close to Turkey's blast walls. Dr. Rami had evacuated as much medical equipment as he could carry. He was personally financing the building of two hangars to serve as a new hospital as well as a hundred adjacent greenhouse-shaped homes, each seven meters by four meters, to shelter some of the displaced. Until the hospital was functional, his team of fifteen (down from twenty-six) spent their days moving from camp to camp in the three ambulances they still had, treating patients as best they could. Dr. Rami's new hospital, however, would never open. On November 8, 2016, when it was almost ready, its two operating rooms fully tiled, a regime air strike destroyed it all, including the homes he was building. Cockpit-view footage of the strike was broadcast on Syrian state television, lauding the destruction of "a terrorist military camp belonging to the Turkistan Islamic Party."

But on April 25, 2016, as the mud-caked ambulance climbed higher into Idlib's green hills, that was yet to pass. Dull thuds, several per minute, rumbled like distant thunder. The sound of shelling elsewhere. The ambulance turned into the narrow streets of the once-majority-Christian village of Ghassaniyeh, an area draped in the black flags of the Turkistan Islamic Party. Non-Arabic-speaking Uighurs manned checkpoints, aimlessly waving people through. The destination was a village church, its crosses removed by the foreign Islamists. The building now served as a prison for the fifty-four remaining Alawite detainees, including Talal's daughter Hanin, almost three years into their ordeal.

Dr. Rami periodically checked on the women and children. He was embarrassed by their continued detention. "This is a nightmare. I have nightmares about this," he said. "It's a stain on the revolution, a catastrophe. This crisis is a deep wound, but what I know is that even deep wounds heal."

A Western-vetted unit of the Free Syrian Army called the First Coastal Division, a recipient of TOW missiles, guarded the hostages. The group was not involved in their kidnapping, which had been the work of Mohammad's *muhajireen* friends and other conservative Islamist battalions.

A pair of armed guards sat in the church's courtyard, drinking yerba mate from a blackened teapot. They worked twenty-four-hour shifts and were frustrated with their "babysitting" duty. Jabhat al-Nusra and its allies were the decision makers. "Their expenses, their security, nobody is helping us," one of the guards said. "Our job isn't to stand here over hostages. We are supposed to be on a front line fighting the enemy, not having guys occupied with this." His partner complained that the captives didn't seem to be as valuable as had been hoped. "They're not asking about them," he said, referring to the regime. "They won't negotiate for them. We are surprised."

The women and children had been moved at least six times to escape shelling and other rebel militias trying to steal them. "There are hundreds who want to harm them, but we won't let them," one of the guards said. "We will be judged by the Almighty for how we treat them. This duty was imposed on us, but we must protect them. They must stay in our hands. We can't just release them without anything in return. There are thousands of our women in Assad's prisons, and I assure you they are not treated the way these women are. Nobody has touched the Alawites, we don't even look at them. Our women are raped in prison. We want an exchange, women for women, that's it."

The heavy, black-metal gate at the entrance to the church hall was newly installed—the detainees had been there less than a week. The padlock clicked open. The men stayed outside. The captives sat silently on thin mattresses around the perimeter of the room, twenty women and thirty-four children. They were dressed not in the casual skin-baring fashion of Alawites but in conservative Muslim garb—long robes, headscarves, and *niqabs*. They hadn't been permitted calls to their families since September 19, seven months earlier. Their captors no longer saw the usefulness of communications meant to pressure the regime to seek their release. "We are of no value, it seems," said a detainee named Shaza al-Hatab, who served as the group's spokeswoman. "That was the last we heard, that nobody is responding because we are dogs to the regime." Behind the padlocked door, the women and children were free to move around in a number of rooms, to cook and use the bathrooms at will. They spent their days sewing, teaching the children, and reading the Quran in a bid to impress their captors.

Hanin was wearing a pink dress and gray *hijab*. She was now twelve and a half, almost the same age as Ruha. She sat near her thirteen-year-old cousin Sally—quiet, scared, fidgeting, staring at her hands but wanting to talk. She recounted the night three years earlier when she woke to gunfire and strangers in her home in Blouta, the moment a bullet burned her left buttock while she hid under her parents' bed. The wound had left a puckered scar. She remembered what the strangers said when they made her mother and eldest sister Lojayn stay behind: "They said our army massacred people in Baniyas and that this was in response to that."

She had heard from those two girls, fellow detainees, who went back into the house that her mother and sister were dead, but Hanin wasn't sure. In every one of the five calls she'd been allowed to make in almost three years, she asked Baba where her mother was. "He kept telling me she was with him," she said. Hanin was relieved that her two siblings were free, and she wondered when she'd join them. She wasn't the only child hostage alone without immediate family. There were eleven others, all adopted by women who vowed to care for them until their fate was decided, one way or the other.

"I think about my house, my school, about my siblings," Hanin said. "I think about my future, which has been completely destroyed. I wanted to be a doctor, but it's impossible now that I'll be a doctor."

"Nothing is impossible," one of the women told her.

Hanin had a message for her father, Talal, one she struggled to articulate through tears, pausing often: "Baba, I miss you and my siblings. When are we going to be released? Baba, I miss my school. I miss my freedom." Her voice broke in her throat. "I can't speak. I'm not able to speak."

HANIN'S FATHER, Talal, lived in Mezzeh 86, an overcrowded Alawite slum on a hill in southwest Damascus not far from the presidential palace. Its dilapidated, thin-walled cinderblock towers searched for sunlight, buildings so cramped their outer walls kissed. Posters of Assad adorned every surface, alongside images of the regime's martyrs, the men frozen in youth. The noise of too many people, too many cars, in too small a space. Checkpoints at the foot of the hill, checkpoints within it, armed men and soldiers roaming two-way streets barely wide enough for traffic in one direction. Overhead, a spiderweb of tangled electricity cables stretched between the warrens. It was considered a regime stronghold. I entered unnoticed, just another woman in a taxi. I had slipped away from a government-sponsored conference in Damascus that I was permitted to attend despite the arrest warrants against me.

Talal locked his tiny perfume store, as he did every afternoon for a few hours, crossed the street, and walked up a darkened stairwell to his first-floor apartment. There was no electricity, as usual. He tried to be home before his daughter Jawa and his son arrived from school, but they were already inside when he turned the key. Jawa sat on a mattress in the small lounge, one of four rooms in the house, trying to do her English homework by the dim light of an overcast November day.

Talal hadn't heard Hanin's voice in more than a year. He wept as he listened to his daughter's brief taped message. Jawa, dry-eyed and steely, handed her father a tissue. He had knocked on so many doors, he said, heard so many promises from officials who "all sold us pretty words" but seemed to do nothing to free the detainees. Back in 2013, a senior presidential adviser had even publicly claimed that the captured Alawites were all dead, the real victims of an August 21, 2013, chemical attack against the rebel town of Ghouta, an attack the adviser insisted was perpetrated by rebels, not the regime. Talal had followed the news of Christian nuns held hostage by Nusra and exchanged for Nusra prisoners, of Russians and Iranians swapped for hundreds of opposition fighters. "What about our children from the Latakian countryside?" he said. "Why is it just our case that is in the shadows, that nobody wants to talk about?" Some of the Alawite families had discussed kidnapping Sunni women and children from Salma and Doreen to force a swap. Talal rejected the idea. "I won't make another family cry," he said, "and I won't seek revenge for my murdered wife and daughter."

If only the men holding his daughter wanted money, he said, he'd try to raise it, but they were asking for something he couldn't do. "Why should our women and children pay the price for their victims? We are not responsible for whatever happened to them. We are victims, too. We're not living in paradise over here because we're Alawites," he said. "Our villages are poor. I was in eighth grade before my village got electricity. Municipal water came only in 2010. I'm not saying things were great before, I am neither with the regime nor the opposition, but there had to be a thousand solutions instead of arms, to kill a fellow human just because he's with the regime or opposition."

If he could sell his house in his hometown of Blouta, he would, he said. He hated going to the village, seeing where his wife and eldest daughter were killed. He felt helpless. A widower struggling with the loss of his wife and daughter while trying to raise traumatized children who woke at night screaming. He kept Hanin's clothes in her closet, her school report cards within easy reach. Hanin's purple slippers were by the door with everyone else's. "Sometimes he just sits and stares at Hanin's slippers for hours," Jawa whispered to me. She had turned back to her English homework. The assignment was to recall a special day. She wondered what to write about, then decided on a family trip to the Latakian coast in 2009. A picnic lunch, shells from the shore, sand in her shoes, games in the water. "We were all together. My parents, siblings, cousins. That's what made it a special day."

"We need to forgive each other," Talal said. "That's the only solution to end this. I forgive because nothing will bring back my wife and my daughter Lojayn. Let them know I forgive them, maybe it will help the killers and criminals remember their humanity. Are they able to wash the hate that they have for me out of their hearts? We were neighbors. I used to go to Doreen and Salma whenever I wanted. I have friends from there. How did they suddenly become killers and kidnappers?"

ON FEBRUARY 8, 2017, Hanin was freed. The fifty-four Alawite detainees were exchanged for fifty-five Sunni women held by the regime. The next day, Hanin and the other women and children met President Assad and his wife, Asma. For the first time in years, Talal's daughter allowed her brown hair to flow to her waist. She listened, dressed in gray pants and a sky-blue sweatshirt, as Assad welcomed them home, kissed and greeted every person. "There wasn't a day that passed when people weren't looking for you," he told them. Assad said he knew what the women and children had suffered in captivity: "You lived in a warped society, without any humanity whatsoever. For three years you lived with people who know nothing of decency, of education, of civilization."

Days later, Talal posted photos on Facebook of Hanin playing with her siblings in a park, and penned these words:

Good morning
You have returned Hanin and language betrays me
The letters celebrate a wild ibex accosting its hunter
I cannot write anything except I am born again seeing you
Good morning to friends and enemies, you are my brothers
Good morning, Hanin
There was no morning before you or after you.

ABU AZZAM

Spring 2016. Abu Azzam had become a father. He doted on his baby son, wanted to capture and share every moment of his first six months. He would wake him to play. He and his wife, Alaa, were expecting another baby in the summer. The young family still lived in a Turkish border town but changed streets and apartments often, downsizing for financial reasons as much as for security. Reyhanlı, near Bab al-Hawa, was a dangerous place, a back office for rebels, gunrunners, smugglers, and, increasingly, assassins. Personal wars crossed the border, grievances settled with sticky bombs and silenced pistols in Turkey (as well as in Syria). Several of Abu Azzam's friends, former Farouq men, had been targeted. One survived a shot in the back of the neck in broad daylight outside a busy chicken restaurant on Reyhanlı's main street. The culprit was never identified.

Abu Azzam had left the FSA's military councils and regretted ever having been part of them, of command bodies that were façades, hostage to foreign powers. He paid the rent through a few hours of Arabic-language instruction at a local school for Syrian refugee children. Months earlier, in the winter before his teaching job, he and his family had smuggled themselves back across the border into the Aleppan countryside. He was ashamed that he had let death threats cement him in Turkey. His life and death, after all, were in God's hands. Why, he wondered, had the university student who entered Baba Amr without a gun, at a time when doing so meant "walking in dead," become a commander-in-exile afraid of dying? He returned to Syria to see what he could do, because, he said, "I don't want to stand before God one day and say I didn't search for that opportunity."

He entered Syria to fight Islamic State but returned to Turkey a week later, convinced that IS was "the most honorable" group on the ground. He went to Azaz, a town in the Aleppan countryside. At the time, it was a front line against Islamic State. The many factions aligned against *ad-Dawla,* he said, were "thieves in every sense of the word. Frankly, they were worse than the regime. I looked around me and thought, Islamic State is cleaner than them, a thousand times cleaner, even though you know how much I dislike them and the bad blood between us." Yes, he admitted, some of his Farouq fighters "dipped their hand into the money at the border crossing, and some took from people and I looked the other way because I didn't have the money to feed them," but what he saw in Azaz and across northern Syria was something else. "Banditry! Banditry! Banditry!" he said. "My worst men, if you compared them to the best emirs of the groups in Azaz, would seem like companions of the Prophet."

One of the measures of a man, he said, was "to speak the truth and what is right even if it contradicts himself." The truth, he'd come to believe, was that life in Islamic State's caliphate was better than in FSA- or Nusra-controlled zones. "At the very least, civilians in *ad-Dawla* areas deal with one faction, not the chaos of elsewhere. There's no looting or stealing, civilians are safe except from Russian and American and regime planes." That's what his wife's family in IS-controlled Tabqa told him, as did his many other friends and relatives living in the east.

Islamic State's errors, Abu Azzam said, were the errors of individual commanders, not policy. "I suffered a lot because of this faction. They declare people like me apostates for no reason, but I won't taint them all. When I see that *ad-Dawla* is removing the oppressors within its ranks and putting better people in place, I am prepared to join it. I was taught to hate the mistake, not the wrongdoer, especially if the wrongdoer fixes his errors."

He insisted that he hadn't fundamentally changed. "Did I say before that I didn't want Islam and now I do?" he asked. "What has changed is that I'm seeing a difference in the running of areas based on the emir in charge. Some are better than others. *Ad-Dawla* made many mistakes and I am not hiding their faults, but, all in all, they are the most honorable faction fighting on the ground."

In August, a daughter joined Abu Azzam's family. Over the summer before her birth, he'd become more convinced of Islamic State's path. US and Russian air strikes that killed civilians in his hometown and other parts of the east angered him. Only IS stood against the foreign aggressors, he said, even though IS's presence had drawn the air strikes.

He didn't agree with everything Islamic State did—not its sexual enslavement of Yazidi women, nor its imposition of a female dress code, although he advocated conservative dress, but not forcing it. He still believed in choice. He had a ready answer for some of the group's other actions, like beheadings, which, he said, were "more merciful" than other ways to die because nerves were quickly cut, dulling pain. The aim of the punishments was also to "plant terror in the hearts of their enemies the same way their enemies are doing it with their planes and rockets and drones." Even the *muhajireen* he once despised weren't that bad, he said. "They shouldn't have been allowed to take control of areas and battalions instead of the sons of the country. Many mistakes were made because many of them didn't understand Arabic. But, in the end, all those who have come to defend us, we cannot but thank them. We should have restricted their entry, but it wasn't in our hands, it was international policy. Why did the Turks let them cross?"

His wife was pleased with his views. She wanted to go home. "If my husband could return, I'd return tomorrow," Alaa said, "and if he can't come with me, I'll leave him and go alone, but I fear for my husband. He needs to resolve his situation." Islamic State still considered him an apostate. He petitioned its members, via WhatsApp, to clear his name.

"Many won't understand my words for sure, because they don't understand our religion. I want my religion to rule me," said Abu Azzam. "I've told you many times that I won't force anybody to live a certain way. Why do those who disagree with me want to force me to live like them? My conviction is that there is no solution except Sharia, and I've been honest about that and I'm not embarrassed to say that because Islam doesn't oppress anyone. If there are mistakes, it is in the application and interpretation," he said. "If I will be considered an extremist because I follow my religion, then fine, I'm an extremist and I'm proud of it. At the end of the day, we will all die and meet our maker. God Almighty will judge, no one else."

In November 2016, Abu Azzam, his wife, and their two children crossed into Syria. He intended to fight to the death but was unsure of which group to join. "If I see that *ad-Dawla* or Nusra or Ahrar [al-Sham] or the Free Army or whatever group you want to talk about returns to working the way we were before, any faction, I will join it," he said.

"If I live long enough, one day I will tell my son what happened, the same way I have told you," Abu Azzam said before he left Turkey. "By the grace of God, I will die a martyr because I came out for a cause. My cause was to remove the injustice from the people. I don't want to die anywhere except Syria, and God will know that I did not pick up arms to glorify myself. On the contrary."

SALEH

Saleh, the former member of Jabhat al-Nusra's inner circle, was in a
European city where he didn't live, a neutral location where we'd agreed
to meet. Wearing rust-colored skinny pants and a gray polo shirt, he
looked like a hipster, not a one-time confidant of Syria's Al-Qaeda leader,
Abu Mohammad al-Jolani.

He'd defected from Nusra with Jolani's tacit blessing, claiming to
have left his old life behind. In the year since he'd fled, he'd added two
European languages to his English and Arabic, busying himself, he said,
"with learning something, anything, to quiet the thoughts in my head."
He reflected on Nusra's mistakes, on his path to militant Islamism, and a
Syria he'd worked to cloak in black. "Now I can see the whole chessboard;
before, I was a piece," he said. "I wasn't a regular soldier, I was with the
command. I saw things," he said, pausing for a long while. "There are
many people we oppressed."

With distance, he saw that members of the Free Syrian Army weren't
the *kuffar*, infidels, he'd been conditioned to despise, the men Nusra
planned to destroy after the fall of the regime. Nusra was just as unscrupu-
lous as the groups he'd self-righteously berated, and could be as ruthless as
Islamic State. It killed Muslims and non-Muslims alike, it stole from civilians and institutions. It had commanders hungry for power and money,
driven by ego and fame, men who Saleh said "wanted to be the next Osama
bin Laden," who could kill a friend as easily as drink a sip of water. The
infighting with Islamic State proved that. That was Saleh's breaking point:

"We were brothers and days later we were killing each other," he said. "I started wondering, what are people like this made of?"

He sneaked into a Europe that feared men like him, a Europe that, after absorbing millions of refugees, was shifting right, under pressure to close its doors after terror attacks in France and Belgium to keep men like him from slipping in. Saleh had been an aide to Syria's Al-Qaeda leader. He claimed he'd discarded his ideology, along with his nom de guerre, that Europe had taught him to live and let live, that he wasn't a threat. "I have no problem now with all of these people walking in the street. Before, when I first became a Salafi Jihadi, I had a problem with everyone who wasn't like me. It was planted in me—why is this woman not in a *hijab*? Why is this woman in heavy makeup? But I am not a God to hold people accountable. If I consider things wrong, I learned that I should not do them, but others can do as they please. Neither I, nor Jolani, nor Osama bin Laden could change anything, and when they controlled things, they became *Daesh*, killing Muslims before non-Muslims. What I've seen here in Europe, of the *kuffar*, as we used to call them, I've met people who are so much better than the people I met in jihad. They mind their own business and are respectful of others." But did he mean it? Could a man like that really change?

He had entered the world of Salafi Jihadism in his late teens, exposed to the banned writings of Islamist leaders before he was detained, just shy of his nineteenth birthday. "I was a kid," he said, jailed with Al-Qaeda members. "Sednaya [Prison] made me what I became." A six-year sleep ended when the regime opened his cell door in 2011. With Syria in the throes of revolution, he formally joined his freed cellmates in Al-Qaeda. "Ten years of my life like this," he said, "I haven't lived a normal day. You know what I do now? I work in a restaurant. I clean tables after customers. I wipe them down. That's my job and I'm happy doing it. When I wipe a table, I feel normal, like this is what a normal person might do." It was also one of the only jobs he could get. "What was I going to put on my CV, that I'd graduated from a sniper training course?"

He had European friends who surprised him with the kindness they showed a Syrian refugee. His former Nusra colleagues didn't know where he was. He avoided Syrians and other Arabs, lest they learn his background. Only his family knew his whereabouts. He had once been a Jabhat al-Nusra *amni*, a security agent, tasked with finding and surveilling Al-Qaeda's enemies and defectors in Turkey—men like him. He knew what might happen if an *amni* found him. He didn't dwell on it, although he had trouble sleeping, sometimes for days. A European friend introduced him to a psychiatrist, thinking he was traumatized from witnessing war, not knowing he had been a senior member of Al-Qaeda. Saleh attended a few sessions and then stopped. "What was the point?" he said. "I was lying to the doctor and to myself. I couldn't tell him who I really was." He had killed men in battle but said he never executed anyone. He had watched others do it, though, "many, many times."

"Humanity died in Syria," Saleh said. "I was dealing with monsters." He wondered whether he was right to leave his country. He'd abandoned its children to Assad's warplanes, he said, or to brainwashing by his former colleagues and Islamic State, or to drowning in the Mediterranean while trying to flee both. He still believed in a conservative Islam, in a future Syria that was "not like the Europeans and not like *Daesh*, something in between." He was torn and confused. "I can't speak to anyone except my family. You've known me for years now," he said. "Be honest with me, do you think I made the right decisions?"

SULEIMAN

August 2016. Suleiman waited on the pavement outside his apartment, a one-bedroom, third-floor walkup in Heilbronn, Germany. He had moved out of the hostel and was once again a working man with a skilled job—a project manager at a logistics company. He was proud to earn money and pay taxes, to have German residency, to understand and be understood in a tongue that was not his. "I didn't come here for handouts," he said. "I just needed help for a few months, I wanted to work." He had augmented a government-sponsored language course with his own studies in the public library, quickly gaining a fluency that enabled him to pass an advanced language class. He now taught Arabic at an institute in the evenings after work. Bandar, Abu Azzam's friend, who lived in another part of Germany, was also teaching at an institute, helping new Syrian refugees learn German.

Suleiman paced the sidewalk, the summer sun raining heat on his head. It was a Saturday. Two of his German friends, a retired couple named Werner and Agnes, pulled up to the curb in a black BMW. Suleiman, clad in a crisp pink polo shirt and beige shorts, got into the backseat. They had met each other more than a year before, in March 2015, through a local initiative called the Contact Café, a place where refugees and their neighbors became friends. The café operated for just a few hours every Thursday afternoon, enough time for Suleiman to feel less isolated. He immediately bonded with Werner, an engineer, and Agnes, a teacher.

The German couple had sought out the Contact Café after seeing news reports about refugees in their country. "I thought we have to do

352 · RANIA ABOUZEID

something, we should help them," Agnes said. For Werner, it started with small things—helping refugees fill out government forms and spruce up CVs, but it quickly developed into something deeper, especially with Suleiman, whom they started seeing regularly outside the café. "We really became friends not just to help him," Werner said as he drove. "We talk about everything and we joke a lot, but not every day is he in the mood to laugh, but we try and keep him laughing. We learn from him, we learn about different cultures."

Suleiman introduced them to Syrian dishes, shared photos of his family and of his new fiancée. He had become engaged to a Syrian refugee in Lebanon named Aime. She was a pharmacist, an old family friend who had escaped Syria three years earlier. Suleiman traveled to Lebanon in late 2015 to formalize the union. The engagement was a small affair—just his parents, her mother, and several aunts. The bride-to-be wore a tailored pink jacket over a black knee-length dress. Suleiman adorned her with gold bracelets and rings his mother had brought with her from Syria. His parents danced around him, his mother ululated and wished blessings upon the couple. Aime could not travel to Germany with Suleiman. She was stuck in Lebanon, waiting for a visa to Germany that was proving difficult to secure.

Werner drove past rows of vineyards on gently sloping hills, fields of rustling corn taller than a man. They were headed to Eppingen, another fairy-tale town some twenty-five kilometers away, to attend its eighteenth annual potato festival. The event opened with odes to the potato and the ceremonial tapping of a wooden beer keg, using a mallet. A Heilbronn MP made a speech and then joined his friends Werner and Agnes at their table. The MP sympathized with Suleiman's plight. He too was a refugee, he said, a Croatian who fled the Balkans war with his family. But in the same breath, the MP linked refugees with Islamic extremism. Suleiman shifted uncomfortably. He despised the extremists who tainted his faith and was tired of constantly feeling that he had to prove he wasn't like them. His phone's ringtone used to be the Muslim call to prayer, and he didn't think anything of it, but he changed it after noticing it made some people around him uncomfortable.

Werner sensed Suleiman's unease. "Some people in Germany want to close borders, to live behind a wall," he told the MP, "but we remember the Iron Curtain. It's crazy to close ourselves off. What we have learned most about Syrians is their hospitality."

"And their respect for elders," his wife added.

The couple had made dinner reservations at a local landmark, Castle Ravensburg, ten minutes away in Sulzfeld. An inflamed sun was painting the sky pomegranate pink as Werner drove into the castle grounds. Suleiman walked ahead, toward the great stone walls of the medieval fortress, pausing at the entrance to watch a bride and groom exchange vows in the grounds near a vineyard.

"You know," Agnes said, "I often think how difficult it is, how patient he is. Sometimes I think he's okay, but most of the time he's sad."

"I often ask my German friends, 'What would you do if you were Suleiman?'" Werner said. "A man with everything, who had a good job, he was a manager, his family around him, his community, and then he became a refugee. We cannot imagine."

The bride and groom kissed to applause as their guests released heart-shaped balloons into the sky. Werner hugged Suleiman. "Don't worry," he told him. "Aime will soon be here, and when she arrives we will return to this place and celebrate." Suleiman smiled and nodded. He stared at the ground. "*Inshallah*," he whispered.

On October 19, Aime received her visa.

It was February 23, 2011. Arab uprisings had claimed the Egyptian and Tunisian presidents and Libya's leader was teetering. I was in Damascus that day to see how one of the Arab world's most policed states was reacting to the changes around it. Bashar al-Assad had told the *Wall Street Journal* that Syria was stable. "Why?" he said, in an interview published on January 31, 2011. "Because you have to be very closely linked to the beliefs of the people. This is the core issue." He was talking about his foreign policy.

I had entered Syria days earlier, legally but clandestinely (not via the Information Ministry, to avoid being saddled with government minders), and found a vantage point—a fast-food restaurant opposite the Libyan Embassy—that allowed me to loiter without suspicion while security forces assembled across the street. I was the only customer. I interviewed three of the fourteen men detained and released after that night's protest, as well as others present.

I knew Syria before 2011, before the period Syrians now refer to by many names: the revolution, the war, the foreign conspiracy, the crisis, the *ahdass* (events). I knew it as a reporter for Western media and as a traveler to the cobbled streets of old Damascus, just an hour-and-a-half drive from my home base of Beirut. After the start of the uprising, I entered Syria clandestinely so many times I lost count. For years, I was either inside Syria or on its periphery, interviewing Syrians before reentering their country, spending no more than a week to ten days a month at home in Lebanon. This book is the product of that intensive on-the-ground reporting. It is born of events I witnessed, some of which I chronicled for news outlets, including *Time, Foreign Policy, Foreign Affairs, Politico,* Al Jazeera America, and *The New Yorker*, and others based on extensive interviews and watching many hours of amateur video, both published and unpublished. I visited most of the locations described in this book to verify information, as well as other towns, villages, and cities across the country I didn't have space to include. I spoke to many more people than I could possibly reference without crowding the narrative, but every minute of those experiences informs these pages. I make no claim to presenting a comprehensive story of Syria, or even of rebel-held Syria or my reporting within it. In fact, most of my published Syria work, more than 150,000 words of it, is not in this book. This account is but a fraction of the story. After this book was written, I cut a book out of it—about sixty thousand words.

One of my biggest challenges in writing this account was deciding whose stories to tell. Over the years, I'd come to know many Syrians well enough to profile them intimately, but the handful I chose were selected because some played a pivotal role in the revolution's trajectory, were in important places at key times, had proven themselves exceptionally reliable sources, and/or their paths intersected with others in the book, whether they knew it or not. I interviewed and reinterviewed the main characters over years, as well as people close to them, including their families, members of their communities, their colleagues, friends, and enemies. I am certain some must have thought me dimwitted by the end of it, given my tendency to push repeatedly for details and to return to certain events over and over again. I am grateful for their patience. Where I describe somebody's thoughts, the person to whom I ascribe the thoughts relayed those sentiments to me.

Some readers may object to my presenting the stories of men like Mohammad, Abu Othman, and Saleh the same way I tell the tale of other characters, such as Ruha and her family. My goal is not to judge, and not to turn characters into caricatures, but to present information about an individual's motivations, worldview, and actions to help readers understand him or her and arrive at their own conclusions.

Readers may naturally question how I know what I know. The simple answer is, I was there. I speak Arabic and can physically blend in; there was no filter, no buffer, no translation problem—linguistic or cultural—

between my sources and me. I spent so much time in northern Syria that fighters who moved from battle to battle often recognized me on various fronts, a fact that helped me gain the access—and trust—of a number of armed groups. Witnessing, however, is one thing—trusting a person's testimony is another. I believe nothing until I have what I deem a critical mass of information to consider something true. It's an unemotional skepticism that is central to my work.

Regarding the details of Suleiman's story, I met Suleiman and his family in Rastan in the summer of 2011 and stayed in contact with him until early 2012, before he disappeared. I spoke to dozens of people in his hometown and in the diaspora who were at the same protests he attended and to others who stayed off the streets, as well as protesters from Talbiseh. I watched countless hours of video (Suleiman's and others') from those demonstrations, the taped speeches of mourners after the violence at the Military Security branch, as well as the Orient TV footage from March 15, 2011, that Suleiman viewed in that café in Homs. I met the parents of Hajar al-Khatib, the little girl described by the opposition as the first female child martyr, at their home in Rastan soon after their daughter was killed on her eleventh birthday. The figure for gun ownership in Syria comes from a 2007 study by the Geneva-based Small Arms Survey, and that for broadband Internet subscribers from the International Telecommunication Union, referenced in a 2012 Freedom House fact sheet, *Freedom on the Net*.

I spent time with all of the members of Rastan's early *tansiqiya*. I was on one of those three motorbikes as they swerved through Rastan's alleyways toward the safe house hiding the defectors, including First Lieutenant Abdel-Razzak Tlass. I stayed in contact with some of the defectors for years afterward. I knew the young protest singer Mohammad Darwish, stood beside him on the balcony of the State Security building as he led chants. I attended Fady Kism's funeral and visited his mother. The account of Merhi Merhi's death comes from Suleiman and survivors I interviewed, including Maamoun, as well as the published work of the Violations Documentation Center in Syria (VDC), which noted the killings.

The saga of Suleiman's arrest and his cycling through the various detention centers is based on his testimony, his prison diaries, and court documents, which he generously shared with me, plus interviews with former detainees (including his cousin, the lawyer Samer Tlass) who were held in the same facilities and/or nabbed by the same intelligence agencies in different parts of the country. That is to say, I spoke to men detained by Air Force Intelligence in Aleppo as well as others captured by Air Force Intelligence in Idlib and Latakia, places Suleiman was not held. Their accounts were remarkably similar across geography and were also consistent with testimony provided to rights groups and documented in reports, including Amnesty International's *Deadly Reprisals* (June 14, 2012), Human Rights Watch's *Torture Archipelago* (July 3, 2012), and *If the Dead Could Speak* (December 16, 2015), to name a few. I independently tracked down some of the men Suleiman said were in prison with him, or their families if they were still detained, to corroborate parts of his account. I chose Suleiman in large part because he was a meticulous details man with a knack for remembering dates. I had copies of his prison IDs, his aunt's video footage of his first moments of freedom, as well as the photos and private video clips he made for his family, detailing his escape to Germany.

Ruha and her extended family generously opened their homes and their hearts to me, allowing me to witness their highs and lows over six tumultuous years. I wasn't with them during those first raids when Ruha opened the door to security forces, accounts re-created by interviewing every member of her family who was in the house on those two days, but I was present or in direct contact with them for just about every other event thereafter. The figures for homes burned and destroyed during the army's March 2012 incursion come from a May 2, 2012, Human Rights Watch report called *They Burned My Heart*. The account of the unexploded canister and the chemical attack on Saraqeb was based on interviews with local activists (including unpublished footage privately shared with me showing one activist hiding the canister) and a December 13, 2013, report by the Organisation for the Prohibition of Chemical Weapons (OPCW) entitled

United Nations Mission to Investigate Allegations of the Use of Chemical Weapons in the Syrian Arab Republic.

The stories of Abu Azzam, Bandar, and the Free Syrian Army stream of this book are based on extensive time inside Syria, from Homs to Bab al-Hawa, Tal Abyad, Idlib, Aleppo, and Raqqa, plus Turkey, and (in Bandar's case) Germany. Abu Azzam has been described in previous media interviews as older than is stated in this book, because he was using a fake ID at the time. I have corrected his age in these pages.

I was briefly in Baba Amr in the summer of 2011 but did not meet Abu Azzam until 2012, after he'd become a senior commander in the Farouq Battalions. Over the years, I tracked down dozens of members of the Farouq who were in Baba Amr in those early days (and also spoke to Abdel-Razzak Tlass about that period). I interviewed Abu Azzam's family members, including his mother, wife, siblings, aunts, and uncles in their homes in eastern Syria, and later in the diaspora, after many of them fled, as well as Bandar and his family in Raqqa and its surroundings. I saw footage of Bandar's brother Bassem in Baba Amr, listened to Bassem's taped recitations of his poetry, spoke to civilians in Baba Amr who knew the pair of poets and others who didn't, watched many videos from the neighborhood, including images of the visiting Arab League delegation and the women who approached them. I interviewed two of the Farouq's three founding leaders—Abu Sayyeh and Abu Hashem—as well as a number of their aides. The third founder—the Sheikh Amjad Bitar—declined an interview request.

Saad Hariri's Future Movement has repeatedly denied Okab Sakr's role in arming the uprising through the so-called Istanbul Room, claiming Sakr spent 2012 on leave from the political party in Belgium. Back in 2012, I was the first journalist to detail the Istanbul Room's workings, and frankly could have written an entire book solely about the arming of the uprising (and another about its Islamization). At different times over the past six years, I interviewed three of the four distributors inside the room (the fourth—the SNN cofounder Abulhassan Abazeed—was detained by Syrian security forces in 2012, and his fate is unknown), as well as many of the lower-level middlemen who cycled in and out of the program from different parts of Syria, and several who attended Sakr's meetings in Turkish hotels whose accounts all matched.

The temperament and plans of the Islamist Firas al-Absi, the man who was ISIS before ISIS, are based on video footage of Absi at Bab al-Hawa, as well as men who knew him, including Abu Azzam, Mohammad, and Saleh, and another Free Syrian Army commander stationed near Bab al-Hawa who also tried to convince Absi to take down the black flag. I visited Abu Azzam in Tal Abyad several times and was with him the day Jabhat al-Nusra tried to assassinate him, as well as in the hotel during that first meeting between the Saudis and the FSA's Supreme Military Council in May 2013.

I knew the heads of many of the Free Syrian Army's military councils in northern Syria, as well as senior defectors and civilian revolutionary leaders operating in the area. I am one of the few journalists to have sneaked into the officers' camp housing the defectors in Apaydın, Turkey, in February 2012. I visited the Joint Command's General Mithqal Ibtaysh in his headquarters less than a week after the body's formation, and I spoke to him several times after its disintegration. I had a number of meetings between 2012 and 2016, both in Syria and in Turkey, with the FSA's General Salim Idris. I interacted with weapons smugglers in various parts of northern Syria, visited IED factories, sat in on meetings with Libyans who traveled to Turkey seeking to arm their Syrian brothers, watched weapons deals being negotiated, battles planned—all of which I'd published in various news outlets but didn't have space to recount in this book. It all informed my understanding of the arming of the uprising and the challenges faced by the FSA.

Regarding Hazm, I interviewed its leader, Abu Hashem, and a number of its fighters, as well as men from other factions inside the MOM, and mined Hazm's statements. Although in the book I detail the account of one Hazm intelligence operative, I interviewed two. The Hazm operative I referenced shared copies of his reports with me, information I carefully independently cross-referenced with jihadi contacts on the ground during trips to Syria, without either group's knowing how I got the information.

Mohammad's storyline, detailing the role of Jabhat al-Nusra and Islamic

State, was, to put it mildly, difficult to report. The account of Mohammad's early life, including his incarcerations, was based on his testimony as well as that of his parents, siblings, wife, and in-laws. I visited the village outside Jisr al-Shughour where a young Mohammad watched Abu Ammar being beaten by the *mukhabarat*. Abu Ammar still lives there. (I also interviewed Abu Ammar's brother, Abu Hassan, in Antakya, southern Turkey.)

For information about the Islamist-versus-Baath altercations in the late 1970s and early 1980s, I'm indebted to a number of books, principally Raphaël Lefèvre's *Ashes of Hama: The Muslim Brotherhood in Syria* (Oxford University Press, 2013) and Lina Khatib's *Islamic Revivalism in Syria: The Rise and Fall of Ba'thist Secularism* (Routledge, 2011). I also sneaked into Hama in mid-2011, interviewed survivors from that period, and was taken to the locations of the alleged decades-old mass graves.

In 2014, I met one of the Salafis from Latakia who served as a facilitator to funnel *mujahideen* into post-2003 Iraq. He was a friend and contemporary of Mohammad's mentor, Abu Barra al-Haddad. When I saw the facilitator, he was still fighting in the Latakian countryside. Regarding Sednaya Prison, in addition to the testimonies of Abu Othman and Saleh detailed in this book, I also spoke to other Islamists who had been behind the prison's "black door" who verified the accounts of the other two men. The various presidential amnesties were posted on the Syrian Arab News Agency's website. The young man from Daraa accused of writing graffiti on a school wall who walked into Abu Othman's cell in Palestine Branch now lives in a Gulf state with his family.

The truth about Jisr al-Shughour and the *moqadam* Hussein Harmoush's role was revealed to me many years after my reporting of the event. I spoke to Basil al-Masry's brother back in 2011. Later I hunted—and that's what it felt like—men who were in the public garden that day to tell me what really happened. I noted Fouad's account in these pages, but others also admitted the same to me. Some showed me private videos and photos of Syrian government forces killed that day. In 2016, I sneaked into Jisr al-Shughour to see where it all unfolded.

Saleh was one of several of my high-placed contacts within Jabhat al-Nusra, including members of the group's small governing (or Shura) council who verified some of Saleh's account. "How on earth did you get that information?" a Shura council member once asked me when I sought him out to confirm a detail. "People are going to start thinking you work for the CIA." It was a common accusation, sometimes accompanied by (nonviolent) rebel interrogations inside Syria.

I focused on Saleh not only because he was in the inner circle but also because he was fastidious about details. He'd admit what he didn't know, and his information always panned out. I'd often ask him in real time about news burning up the Twittersphere, such as reports of Jolani's assassination. Saleh would insist the news was false, and he was always proven correct. Some of his information also jibed with an anonymous Twitter account in Arabic called @wikibaghdady, which purported to reveal some of the Islamic State's inner workings.

I knew what Camp Bucca looked like because I walked through it in March 2009 and saw where the US military told me it detained "the worst of the worst." Osama bin Laden's views about Al-Qaeda's mistakes and the group's troubled relationship with its Iraqi affiliate were detailed in the so-called *Abbottabad Papers*, hundreds of pages of letters recovered from bin Laden's Abbottabad hideaway in Pakistan after his killing in 2011, and published online in Arabic and English by West Point's Combating Terrorism Center.

I was the first journalist to interview both a foot soldier in Jabhat al-Nusra (in July 2012) and later an official (in December 2012), and I had vast dealings with many of the group's members, as well as Islamic State fighters, all of which infused my account of Nusra's role in the uprising, even if those meetings were not individually recounted here.

I met Talal, the Alawite man whose family was kidnapped from their home in the Latakian countryside, in Beirut, weeks after they were taken. I remained in contact with him as well as with others whose families were in rebel captivity. Their plight was also detailed in an October 10, 2013, Human Rights Watch report titled *You Can Still See Their Blood*. I knew the Nusra emirs in charge of the detainees' fate, the FSA unit babysitting them, and I spoke to some of the women and children in detention as well as those who were freed earlier than others. Assad's comments in 2017 were filmed and uploaded to the Internet. I knew some of the many changing interlocutors on both sides of an issue I had followed closely since the raid in August 2013. Like most things in this book, my access came from being there, and sticking with the story.

It is a privilege and a responsibility to be entrusted with another person's testimony and to verify its truth. The Syrian war, like every war, is about many things, but at its core, it's about people. The terrible things they see and do or have done to them, bonds forged and broken, the attempts to cling to the normalcy of their old lives and what they think about their new ones. It is dehumanizing, but it is still about three-dimensional human beings. If nothing else, I hope that, in telling these stories, I have at least conveyed that.

ACKNOWLEDGMENTS

I am deeply indebted to the people whose stories I tell in these pages, as well as the hundreds of other Syrians who shared with me their time, testimony, and experiences, often during some of the worst moments of their lives. I never for a second took any of that for granted. I am forever humbled by the generosity of Syrians who hosted me in their homes, their tents, and their military bases with a hospitality that is as boundless as it is typically Syrian.

How to thank the Syrians who warned me of kidnapping threats? The ones who kept me safe? The many, some now dead, who helped me navigate borders and understand the social, military, and political terrain I entered? I wish I could publicly name and thank you all, but it's still not safe to do so without endangering some of you. *Shukran jazilan*, and *inshallah* your worst days, and Syria's, are behind you.

I could not have written this book without the generous support of the New America Fellows Program, particularly Director Peter Bergen, and Board Member William Gerrity. The wonderful people at the Carey Institute in upstate New York offered me a residency in a setting so serene and beautiful it mitigated the pain of reopening my notebooks and reliving the story, as I first attempted to write it. Elaina Richardson kindly invited me to the heaven of Yaddo, gifting me a writer's residency in Truman Capote's majestic former workspace in the Tower. My friend and agent at Sterling Lord Literistic, Robert Guinsler, believed I had a Syria book in me before I did, and had my back at every crisis. Editor Tom Mayer at Norton is a writer's dream. He understood and respected my vision for this book and helped make it better. Thank you Tom, Sarah Bolling, Emma Hitchcock, and all the behind-the-scenes staff at Norton, including sharp-eyed copyeditor Kathleen Brandes.

Thank you to everyone at my UK publisher, Oneworld, and editor Shadi Doostdar, who having once lived in Syria, recognized in a personal way the loss, life, and resilience conveyed in these pages. She knew the importance of these stories, and helped bring them to a wider audience.

Freelance journalism is a tough, lonely hustle. Good publishing opportunies are like unicorns. I'm grateful to the many editors who published my Syria work over the years at *Time* (thanks Howard Chua-Eoan!), *Politico*, *Foreign Policy*, *Foreign Affairs*, Al-Jazeera America, and *The New Yorker*, particularly Amy Davidson Sorkin and David Remnick, who have always been very generous to me.

I am strengthened by the many circles of sisterhood that envelop me, starting with my own sisters: Marian, Reema, Mirna, and Leanne—only borders separate us. My darling nieces and nephew. The formidable ladies of Beirut's *Jabhat al-Niswan*: Leena Saidi, Suzan Haidamous, Dalia Khamissy, Mariam Karouny, Nour Samaha, and my guardian angel, Hwaida Saad. My cybersisters in ink: Vivian Salama, Hannah Allam, Alia Malek, Maria Abi Habib, Leila Fadel, Rym Momtaz, and Anne Barnard. Thank you, Nazha Merabi and Connie Zandi, for your constant encouragement over the years. The brothers who are honorary sisters, some of whom I inflicted my manuscript on: Matthias Bruggmann, Ghaith Abdul-Ahad, Nir Rosen, Martin Chulov, and Mohammed Aly Sergie. The Deca writers' collective, of which I'm honored to be a part, helped brainstorm the subtitle (especially Delphine!).

Shukran Abu Jacky for translating most of the poems.

Finally, thank you to my selfless, hard-working mum and dad for raising daughters to know we could do and be anything. You taught us that our greatest assets in life were each other, and blessings such as a solid education, the things you carry within you not with you when one of those "single abrupt events that can upend everything" happens. You knew from experience.

INDEX

Maliki, Nouri al-, 27
Mamlouk, Ali, 28
Manal (Ruha's mother):
  and civil uprising, 38, 84, 85
  and civil war escalation, 137, 152
  and escape to Turkey, 157–60
  refugee life, 177, 178, 179, 180, 220–21
Mariam (Ruha's aunt):
  background of, 42
  and Battle of Saraqeb (Mar. 2012), 133
  and civil uprising, 83–85
  and civil war (2016), 326–31
  and civil war escalation, 136, 142–43, 153,
    180–81, 218, 219
  and Kaban Checkpoint attack, 141
Masry, Basil al-, 56
Mattar, Osama, 165, 184
Maysaara (Ruha's father):
  and civil uprising, 82–83, 84, 86
  and civil war escalation (2012–2013), 132,
    134, 136
  and criminal exploitation of early insur-
    gency, 154
  and escape to Turkey, 157–60
  and governance, 155
  medical supply smuggling, 152, 178–79
  memories of, 326
  refugee life, 178–80, 220–21, 306–7
  return to Saraqeb, 307–8, 323, 324–26
  shooting of, 87–88
  and suppression of civil uprising, 39–41,
    42–43
medical care, 156–57
Merhi Merhi, 89–90, 91–92, 93–94
military defectors:
  and civil uprising, 54
  and Damascus bombing (2012), 137
  detainment of, 184
  and early insurgency, 65, 67–71, 107
  and Farouq Battalions, 100
  Free Officers' Movement, 60, 68–69
  and Free Syrian Army, 105, 168, 227
  misinformation about, 59–61
  underground network for, 86
  and weapons acquisition, 107
Minbar Suria al-Islami, 27–28
MIT (Turkish National Intelligence Agency),
  107–8, 149
Mohammad (member of Jabhat al-Nusra):
  Assad regime detainment of, 14–17

  and Assad regime suppression of Islamists,
    21–24, 25
  background of, 18
  and beginning of civil uprising, 30–31
  and Firas al-Absi, 144
  on Free Syrian Army, 226–27
  and governance, 226, 243
  and international nature of Al-Qaeda,
    247–48
  and ISIS formation, 207
  and Israeli Jabhat al-Nusra cells, 248
  and Jabhat al-Nusra-Hazm conflict, 315,
    316, 318
  and Jabhat al-Nusra struggles (2016), 335
  and Jihadi passage to Iraq, 27, 28, 29
  and Jisr al-Shughour conflict (June 2011),
    56, 57, 59
  and Latakia Alawite detainees, 222, 253
  and muhajireen smuggling, 120–23, 127,
    333–34, 335
  radicalization of, 24–25, 26
  and rebel-ISIS conflict, 244–47, 248–49, 251
  and weapons acquisition, 55
Mohammad (Ruha's brother), 42, 84, 305
Mohammad (Ruha's uncle):
  and civil uprising, 41, 84
  and civil war escalation, 154, 215, 217, 218
  death of, 306
  detainment of, 85–86
  and governance, 155–56
MOM (Müşterek Operasyon Merkezi),
  259–61
muhajireen:
  Hazm Movement intelligence gathering,
    270–73
  and ISIS governance, 310
  and Jabhat al-Nusra, 120–23, 126–28, 204,
    205, 333–34, 335
  and Latakia offensive (2013), 222
  marriages with, 181–82, 203
  and rebel-ISIS conflict, 245–46, 333–34
  smuggling operations, 120–23, 127–28,
    333–34, 335
  see also Al-Qaeda; Jabhat al-Nusra
mujahideen, 191
  see also Al-Qaeda; Islamic state as goal;
    Islamist rebel groups; Jihadi passage to Iraq
mukhabarat:
  and Assad regime suppression of Islamists,
    21–23